Maritime Order and the Law in East Asia

Many of the maritime disputes today represent a competing interest of two groups: coastal states and user states. This edited volume evaluates the role of the United Nations Convention on the Law of the Sea (UNCLOS) in managing maritime order in East Asia after its ratification in 1994, while reflecting upon various interpretations of UNCLOS. Providing an overview of the key maritime disputes occurring in the Asia Pacific, it examines case studies from a selection of representative countries to consider how these conflicts of interest reflect their respective national interests, and the wider issues that these interpretations have created in relation to navigation regimes, maritime entitlement, boundary delimitation and dispute settlement.

Gordon Houlden is the Director of the China Institute, Professor of Political Science and Adjunct Professor of the Alberta School of Business at the University of Alberta.

Nong Hong heads the Institute for China-America Studies (ICAS). She is a research fellow with China Institute, University of Alberta, the National Institute for South China Sea Studies and the China Center for Collaborated Studies on the South China Sea, Nanjing University.

Maritime Order and the Law in East Asia

Edited by
Gordon Houlden and Nong Hong

Routledge
Taylor & Francis Group
LONDON AND NEW YORK

First published 2018
by Routledge
2 Park Square, Milton Park, Abingdon, Oxon OX14 4RN

and by Routledge
711 Third Avenue, New York, NY 10017

Routledge is an imprint of the Taylor & Francis Group, an informa business

British Library Cataloguing in Publication Data
A catalogue record for this book is available from the British Library

Library of Congress Cataloging in Publication Data
Names: Houlden, Gordon, author. | Hong, Nong, author.
Title: Maritime order and the law in East Asia /
Gordon Houlden and Nong Hong.
Description: Abingdon, Oxon [UK] ; New York, NY : Routledge, 2018.
Identifiers: LCCN 2017055442 | ISBN 9781138561656 (hbk) |
ISBN 9780203710555 (ebk)
Subjects: LCSH: Maritime boundaries–East Asia. | Territorial waters–East Asia. | Maritime law–East Asia. | Maritime boundaries–Southeast Asia. | United Nations Convention on the Law of the Sea (1982 December 10) | South China Sea–International status. | East China Sea–International status.
Classification: LCC KZA1686 .H68 2018 | DDC 341.4/4091642–dc23
LC record available at https://lccn.loc.gov/2017055442

ISBN: 978-1-138-56165-6 (hbk)
ISBN: 978-0-203-71055-5 (ebk)

Typeset in Galliard
by Out of House Publishing

Contents

Editor and contributor biographies

Editors

Gordon Houlden is the Director of the China Institute, Professor of Political Science and Adjunct Professor of the Alberta School of Business at the University of Alberta. He is a former Canadian career diplomat specialized in East Asia affairs. He has lectured at international conferences in Canada, the United States (including the US State Department) and China (including the National Defence University PLA China). He has been interviewed by many Canadian, Chinese and other international media on Asian economic, trade, and investment issues.

Nong Hong heads the Institute for China-America Studies (ICAS), an independent, non-profit academic institution based in Washington D.C. She also holds a joint position of research fellow with China Institute, University of Alberta (CIUA), National Institute for South China Sea Studies (NISCSS), and the China Center for Collaborated Studies on the South China Sea, Nanjing University. Dr. Hong received her PhD of interdisciplinary study of international law and international relations from the University of Alberta, Canada and held a Postdoctoral Fellowship in the University's China Institute. She was ITLOS-Nippon Fellow for International Dispute Settlement, and Visiting Fellow at the Center of Oceans Law and Policy, University of Virginia and at the Max Planck Institute for Comparative Public Law and International Law.

Contributors

Sourabh Gupta is a resident senior fellow at the Institute for China-America Studies (ICAS) in Washington, D.C. and a specialist in international relations of the Asia-Pacific. His areas of expertise include: analysis of key major power relationships in the Asia-Pacific region (China–U.S, China–Japan, China–India, US–Japan, US–India, Japan–India relations); political, security, and economic risk evaluation of key states in the Asia-Pacific region; and, territorial disputes and maritime law-related developments in the Asia-Pacific region. His most recent study is an analysis of China's U-shaped line titled *The Nine Dash*

Line as a Possible 'Historic Rights' Line and its Basis in International Law. He is a member of the United States Council for Security Cooperation in the Asia-Pacific (USCSCAP). He holds master's degrees from Georgetown University and Syracuse University.

Reinhard Drifte is Emeritus Professor of Newcastle University (UK). Since his retirement he has been visiting professor at various Japanese and French universities and was Visiting Fellow in 2014 at the Chinese National Institute for South China Sea Studies in Haikou. His subject area is Japanese foreign policy, focusing currently on various aspects of Japan-China relations, including the disputes in the East China Sea and the South China Sea. Book publications include *Japan's Security Relations with China since 1989*, (Routledge 2002), *Japan's Quest for a Permanent Security Council Seat: A matter of pride or justice?* (Macmillan 1999), and *Japan's Foreign Policy in the 1990s: From economic superpower to what power?* (Macmillan 1996).

Jay L. Batongbacal is an Associate Professor at the University of the Philippines College of Law, and Director of the Institute for Maritime Affairs & Law of the Sea of the U.P. Law Center. He holds the degrees of Master of Marine Management, and Doctor in the Science of Law, both from Dalhousie University in Canada. Since 1997, he has done diverse work in maritime affairs, including community based fisheries management, coastal resource management, marine environment protection, maritime boundaries, high seas fishing, offshore energy, seafaring, and shipping. He was legal advisor to the Philippine delegation that from 2009–2012 successfully laid claim to a continental shelf beyond 200 nautical miles in the Benham Rise Region before the Commission on the Limits of the Continental Shelf. He is also among the List of Experts on Marine Scientific Research for purposes of Special Arbitration under Annex VIII of the UNCLOS.

Etty R. Agoes is a professor of International Law (Ret.), Universitas Padjadjaran, Bandung, Indonesia, and a member of the Indonesia National Maritime Council. He also serves as advisor to the national negotiating team for boundary delimitation, and was formerly Director (now Advisor) to the Indonesian Center for the Law of the Sea.

Hao Duy Phan is a Senior Research Fellow at the Centre for International Law (CIL), a university-wide research centre at the National University of Singapore (NUS). He is the author of many articles on various issues of international law. Prior to joining CIL, he worked as a legal expert at the Department of International Law and Treaties, Ministry of Foreign Affairs of Vietnam, and a visiting research fellow at the East-West Center in Washington D.C. and the Institute of Southeast Asian Studies in Singapore. Hao Duy Phan received a B.A. from the Institute for International Relations of Vietnam, an LL.M. from the University of Notre Dame Law School (*summa cum laude*), and an S.J.D. from the American University Washington College of Law.

Anastasia Telesetsky is a Professor at University of Idaho College of Law and member of the Natural Resource and Environmental Law faculty. A graduate of UC Berkeley Boalt Hall School of Law, she is currently the co-chair for the ABA Section of International Law International Environmental Law Committee, a member of the World Commission on Environment Law for the International Union for the Conservation of Nature, and an editorial board member of the Asia-Pacific Journal for Ocean Law and Policy. In 2016, she became the Ian Axford Public Policy Fellow at the New Zealand Ministry of Primary Industries focusing on fisheries sustainability issues.

Mira Rapp-Hooper is a Senior Research Scholar in Law at Yale Law School, as well as a Senior Fellow at Yale's Paul Tsai China Center. She studies and writes on US-China relations and national security issues in Asia and is currently completing a book on the role of alliances in American strategy. Dr. Rapp-Hooper was formerly a Senior Fellow with the Asia-Pacific Security Program at the Center for a New American Security (CNAS), a Fellow with the CSIS Asia Program, and the Director of the CSIS Asia Maritime Transparency Initiative. She was also a Stanton Nuclear Security Fellow at the Council on Foreign Relations. Dr. Rapp-Hooper's academic writings have appeared in *Political Science Quarterly*, *Security Studies*, and *Survival*. Her policy writings have appeared in *The National Interest*, *Foreign Affairs*, and *The Washington Quarterly*, and her analysis has been featured in *The New York Times*, *The Washington Post*, and on NPR, MSNBC, and the BBC.

Ying Yang is an Associate Research Fellow at Law School and the Strategic Research Institute of the South China Sea, Sun Yat-Sen University, China. She received her PhD of international law from Wuhan University, China (2015). Her researching field is international law with a focus on the law of the sea, especially on the military activities at the sea. She participated in the Summer Courses of the Hague Academy of International Law in July 2012 and studied as a visiting scholar at the Center of Oceans Law and Policy, University of Virginia, US. (2013–2014). She has already published papers in the *Social Science Journal*, *Journal of Theory monthly*, *Journal of Presentday Law Science*, *Journal of Chinese People's Public Security University*, *Journal of Xi'an Politics Institute of PLA*, *Xinhua Digest*, and more.

Yan Yan is a research fellow at the National Institute for South China Sea Studies (NISCSS) and currently a Ph.D candidate at the Faculty of Law of the University of Hong Kong. Prior to joining the NISCSS, she had been an interpreter in the Foreign Affairs Office in Hainan Province. She graduated from London School of Economics and Political Science (LSE) in 2005. Her research has focused on the legal regime on peacetime military activities at sea. Her research themes include the right of innocent passage of warships in the territorial sea; intelligence gathering activities and marine scientific research; the establishment of security zones and military exercises and weapon test in the high seas etc.

Michael Sheng-ti Gau has degrees of LL.B. (National Taiwan University), LL.M. (Cambridge), LL.M. (London), and Ph.D. (Leiden), all focusing on public international law. He is now teaching at Law School of Hainan University. He is also the director of the newly established Research Institute for International Justice and Arbitration at Hainan University. For the past seven years, he has been focusing on outer continental shelf, CLCS and the South China Sea legal issues, with publications at *Ocean Yearbook*, *Ocean Development and International Law*, *Chinese Journal of International Law*, *Journal of East Asia and International Law*, etc.

Sophia Kopela is a lecturer in law at Lancaster University Law School. Sophia holds an LLB from the University of Athens (Greece), an LLM in Public International Law from the University of Nottingham (UK), and a PhD in International Law of the Sea from Bristol University (UK). Her specialisation lies in international law of the sea, international environmental law and public international law. She has contributed articles and papers in international journals and conferences. Her article '2007 Archipelagic Legislation of the Dominican Republic: An Assessment' was awarded the first Gerard Mangone Prize for the best article in the *International Journal of Marine and Coastal Law* for 2009. She is the author of a monograph titled *Dependent archipelagos in the law of the sea* published by Martinus Nijhoff/ BRILL in 2013.

Yinan Bao is a Research Associate with School of International Law, East China University of Political Science and Law. He did his PhD studies in diplomatic law at University of Sussex from 2010 to 2014 with a thesis entitled *When Old Principles Face New Challenges: A Critical Analysis of the Principle of Diplomatic Inviolability*. He had previously studied LLM in Public International Law at the University of Leicester from 2009 to 2010. Dr Bao's major research interest is in public international law, especially in diplomatic law, territorial disputes and the law of the sea. His major academic work includes 'The US Theory of "Excessive Maritime Claims" and Its Practice: A Critical Analysis' in *Chinese International Studies* (Chinese version is in Issue 5, September 2017), 'On the Historical Evolution of the Principle of Diplomatic Inviolability' (*Chinese International Law Review*, Beijing: Social Sciences Academic Press, 2012) and 'International Law Issues Concerning the Referendum of Crimea: A Preliminary Analysis' (*Chinese Yearbook of International Law 2014*, Beijing: Law Press, 2015).

Natalie Klein is a Professor at UNSW Faculty of Law, Sydney, Australia. She was previously at Macquarie University where she served as Dean of Macquarie Law School between 2011 and 2017, as well as Acting Head of the Department for Policing, Intelligence and Counter-Terrorism at Macquarie in 2013–2014. Professor Klein teaches and researches in different areas of international law, with a focus on law of the sea and international dispute settlement. Professor Klein is the author of *Dispute Settlement and the UN Convention on the Law* *of the Sea* (Cambridge University Press, 2005) and *Maritime Security and the Law of the Sea* (Oxford University Press, 2011). She provides advice, undertakes consultancies and interacts with the media on law of the sea issues. Prior to joining Macquarie, Professor Klein worked in the international litigation and arbitration practice of Debevoise & Plimpton LLP, served as counsel to the Government of Eritrea (1998–2002) and was a consultant in the Office of Legal Affairs at the United Nations. Her masters and doctorate in law were earned at Yale Law School and she is a Fellow of the Australian Academy of Law.

Introduction

Gordon Houlden and Nong Hong

This edited volume explores the legal challenges associated with the role of United Nations Convention on the Law of the Sea (UNCLOS) in managing maritime order in East Asia. Many of the maritime disputes today represent competing interest between two groups, coastal states whose interests stem from extended national jurisdiction arising from the new regime of UNCLOS, e.g. Exclusive Economize Zone (EEZ) and the Continental Shelf, and user states who seek the continuation of freedom of navigation and other rights. Among coastal states, there are divergent interpretations of UNCLOS clauses, for instance, the interpretation of Article 121 (3) on defining the legal status of insular features, Article 74 and 83 on maritime delimitation etc.

East Asia encompasses two important maritime regions characterized by long-standing territorial and maritime disputes, the settlement of which has been pending for decades. Despite great effort at conflict management, the settlement of the decades-old maritime disputes in this region seem to be politically deadlocked. The status quo in East Asia maritime domain is attributed to, in addition to geopolitical factors and competition for resources, the interpretive ambiguities embedded in UNCLOS provisions about the rights and obligation of user states and coastal states respectively, and about competing claims over national jurisdiction among coastal states based on UNCLOS.

This edited volume is composed of four parts. Part I lays out an overview of the maritime disputes occurring in East Asia that currently garner much attention. Both of the two chapters on the East China Sea and the South China Sea respectively provide an overview of the various issues as far as they are relevant to UNCLOS, and investigates to what extent the UNCLOS regime has been adhered to by the coastal states, and has been helpful or not in guiding the concerned states to deal with their different interests.

In Chapter 1, Sourabh Gupta provides an overview of the political state of affairs in the South China Sea, especially in the context of China–ASEAN relations. China and ASEAN are apparently entering a period of calm in their South China Sea-related bilateral relations, following the issuance of the South China Sea Arbitration Award on July 12, 2016. While the underlying sovereignty claims to land features in this body of water will not be resolved anytime soon, China and some South China Sea claimant states enjoy a unique opportunity to creatively address a number of their competing sovereign rights claims under the framework of Beijing's "dual track" approach.

Reinhard Drifte, in Chapter 2, analyzes to what extent UNCLOS has contributed to the management of the disputes in the East China Sea which revolve around the territorial dispute over the sovereignty of the Diaoyu/Senkaku Islands and the pending delimitation of maritime borders between China, Japan and South Korea. At the center of this enquiry is how far has the UNCLOS regime been adhered to by the littoral states, and has been helpful or not in guiding the concerned states to deal with their differences.

Part II is composed of five chapters from the respective country's perspective, the composition of which represents different types of countries, including China as a growing maritime power and key coastal state in East Asia, key claimant states of the South China Sea – the Philippines and Vietnam, and a key Archipelago state, Indonesia, and the United States as a non-claimant state in this region that has strategic interests there. The fact that the United States, despite its non-ratification of the Convention, developed its Freedom of Navigation Program alongside UNCLOS and remains the only country to support such a program, suggests that its investment in this principle is not strictly derivative of UNCLOS. The inclusion of the chapter on the United States in this Part also reflects common or similar interests and stands of other external powers and user states such as Japan, Australia, and India.

In Chapter 3, Nong Hong elaborates China's historic claim in the South China Sea and points to the conflicts among the claimants in the South China Sea due to the competition between historic concepts and the new maritime regime. The Tribunal of the South China Sea Arbitration has set a precedent related to this question by analyzing the relations between UNCLOS and historic rights. However, the arguments provided in the Award are problematic and warrant further academic scrutiny.

Jay L. Batongbacal, in Chapter 4, considers in greater detail the contours and interfaces of the navigational rights, freedoms, and interests asserted by all coastal and user states currently embroiled in the South China Sea disputes. Applying the practice of the Philippines, he argues that the South China Sea Arbitration has laid one option, that of allocating maritime jurisdictions in a more conservative manner in line with the existing practice of the smaller Southeast Asian States, that provides an opening for engaging the multiple duties to cooperate in ocean management enshrined in UNCLOS and encourages multi-lateral cooperation and management of the disputes that may hold promise of future resolution.

In Chapter 5, Etty R. Agoes analyzes Indonesia's view which sees maritime diplomacy as a means for establishing cooperative regional relationships, thereby ensuring its security and demonstrating its leadership credentials to mediate interstate boundary disputes in the region. Indonesia's successful management of its border disputes is an example of its implementation of preventive diplomacy in the management of regional issues that involve or threaten military conflict.

Hao Duy Phan, in Chapter 6, examines Vietnam's positions on major contested issues regarding the rights of coastal states versus the rights of user states as provided in UNCLOS. He concludes that Vietnam has increasingly relied on UNCLOS as a guide and instrument to balance its rights as a coastal state and the rights of user states in its maritime zones. As UNCLOS assumes increasing importance for Vietnam, it also plays the key role in Vietnam's perception of the legal order of the oceans.

Anastasia Telesetsky, in Chapter 7, argues that while there are palpable tensions between coastal states and user states over core rights such as navigational rights, these tensions are not the current basis for the US not acceding to the treaty. She explains how US ocean policy conforms with UNCLOS obligations as a coastal state and as a user of global ocean resources. The US benefits from the UNCLOS regime but will not become a member to the Treaty until there is internal reconciliation within US domestic politics and a return to genuine bipartisanship.

Part III discusses classic contesting issues on navigation regimes and the interpretation of UNCLOS. The conclusion of the text of UNCLOS after the lengthy negotiation process reflects a compromising package which accommodates the interest of both coastal states and user states. The rationale of focusing on "navigation regime" in this Part is based on the editors' observation that it reflects very precisely the competing interests of user states and coastal states. In explaining why the navigation and overflight regime in East Asia is increasingly challenged, in addition to the competition between the littoral states trying to either expand their maritime claims or to consolidate and protect their existing jurisdictions, the differences between the littoral states and external powers is a significant contributing factor. Coastal states may be expected to guard their exclusive jurisdictions just as zealously as user states could be expected to protect their navigation and overflight rights and freedoms.

In Chapter 8, Mira Rapp-Hooper writes about freedom of navigation which she sees now the primary declared US national interest in the South China Sea, and one with which Chinese leaders insist they have never interfered and seek to uphold. She argues that the language of these debates is rooted in and closely linked to competing interpretations of UNCLOS, but these are fundamentally geopolitical disagreements, and the contours of these contentions will continue to evolve as China's ascent proceeds and regional competition accelerates.

Ying Yang, in the following Chapter 9, explores the question of whether the warship of the foreign States should provide prior notification to the coastal states before entering its EEZ. She sees this problem as a dispute between the sea powers represented by the US and coastal countries represented by China. She argues that the formation of a customary law might address this issue.

In Chapter 10, Yan Yan attempts to answer how to reduce the risks of miscalculations of close encounter between naval vessels and aircrafts between China and the United States in the South China Sea. She examines the development of the legal regime of encounter and collision, as well as the confidence-building measures between the US and the USSR navies. This chapter concludes that while the MOUs signed by China and the United State play a positive role in reducing the risk of maritime crisis, they will not eliminate the fundamental divergence between them.

Part IV focuses on contesting issues with regard to maritime entitlement, boundary delimitation and dispute settlement arising from the interpretation of UNCLOS. This part serves to highlight the close connection of maritime order in East Asia and UNCLOS related legal debate among coastal states. While we see from navigation regime the difference between user states and coastal states, these issues discussed in Part IV represent the divergence of views among claimant states. The chapter on the comprehensive overview of the SCS Arbitration leads to the following two chapters in this Part on the topic of archipelagic regime and low-tide elevation, which are key concepts discussed in the Arbitral Award. The last chapter provides an analysis on the legal framework of resolving disputes under UNCLOS when the coastal and user states are disputed.

Chapter 11 by Michael Gau, provides an overview on the South China Sea Arbitration, explains why the Merits Award of the South China Sea Arbitration (SCS) is non-implementable. He asserts that the U-Shaped Line (USL) representing China's territorial claims cannot be erased since the Tribunal cannot settle territorial disputes. Representing China's provisional maritime claims, the USL cannot be over-ruled as the Tribunal may not settle the disputes concerning the application of Articles 74 and 83 on maritime delimitation. Philippine claims against China's historic rights within USL suffer from mootness. Philippine selective claims concerning legal status of some maritime features is pointless, as China never uses individual features to claim EEZ and continental shelf there. Philippine traditional fishing rights in Scarborough Shoal are unreal, whereas the territorial disputes underlying Submission 13 concerning near-collision incidents surrounding Scarborough Shoal renders the Award unenforceable.

In Chapter 12, Sophia Kopela assesses the application of Part IV of UNCLOS and the practice of archipelagic states with respect to the drawing of archipelagic baselines and the status of archipelagic waters. She further examines the practice of non-archipelagic states in their outlying archipelagos in order to identify potential developments with respect to the endorsement of the archipelagic concept in the law of the sea. She tries to answer the question whether UNCLOS has been able to effectively balance and accommodate the interests of archipelagos vis-à-vis those of third states.

Yinan Bao, in Chapter 13, provides a brief analysis of the legal status of low-tide elevations and argues that there is no uniform standard on the determination of the status of low-tide elevations and the status of low-tide elevations should be exclusively determined by international arbitral or judicial bodies when a relevant dispute arises. In addition, low-tide elevations should not be considered as state territory and they cannot be appropriated by states. He also argues that the expected global sea level rise may greatly affect the status of low-tide elevations.

In Chapter 14, Natalie Klein discusses the legality of construction activities on and around a disputed island. She concludes that the prospects for UNCLOS dispute settlement remain notable, even if territorial sovereignty disputes remain outside the scope of this dispute settlement regime. Most particularly, the opportunity for state parties to UNCLOS to resort to compulsory arbitration or adjudication may help with the peaceful resolution of international disputes and limit unilateral actions at sea.

To summarize, this book brings together in one volume a basket of views on the application of the law of the sea to the thorny mix of rival claims in the South China Sea. The significance of the issues is underscored not only by the large scope of the claims, but also by the divergent views of the contending parties. It is to be hoped that a careful assessment of applicable international law and thoughtful review by all parties of the benefits of reduced tension in the South China Sea will facilitate the peaceful resolution of the globe's most complex maritime dispute.

Part I

Regional maritime order overview

1 China–ASEAN relations in the South China Sea

Persistent features and obstacles to cooperation

Sourabh Gupta

On July 12, 2016, in a courtroom in The Hague, an arbitral tribunal constituted under the United Nations Convention on the Law of the Sea (UNCLOS) issued a highly awaited award which ruled that many of China's maritime claims – and actions in defense of those claims – in the South China Sea were contrary to UNCLOS and had thereby violated the Philippines' sovereign maritime rights and freedoms. The tribunal made four sweeping observations.

First, it ruled that no land feature in the northern sector or the southern sector of the South China Sea that was the subject of the dispute was capable of sustaining human habitation or economic life of its own. As such, none of the features met the definition of an "island" – or as the Tribunal called it "a fully entitled feature" – within the meaning of Article 121 of the Law of the Sea Convention (LOSC). As such, none of the features was entitled to a 200-nautical mile exclusive economic zone (EEZ).[1] Second, the tribunal judged that China's nine-dash line claims to "historic rights" was in fact an exclusive claim of sovereign rights and jurisdiction within the exclusive economic zone of the Philippines.[2] This, it ruled, was contrary to the Law of the Sea Convention and without lawful effect because it exceeded the geographic and substantive limits of China's maritime entitlements under the Convention.[3]

Third, the tribunal found that China's law enforcement vessels had failed to observe – and in fact had repeatedly violated – many international navigation-related regulations, notably the Convention on the International Regulations for Preventing Collisions at Sea (COLREGS) during the course of its enforcement operations in the vicinity of Scarborough Shoal.[4] In the course of doing so, these law enforcement vessels had also violated the Philippines' sovereign rights in this northern sector of the South China Sea. Finally, the tribunal ruled that Chinese fishermen and Chinese flagged vessels had engaged in destructive activities that had harmed the marine environment and that Chinese authorities were in a position to prevent such activities but failed to exercise their due responsibility.[5] Further, that China's land reclamation activities had caused harm to the coral reef ecosystem and, in violation of its international treaty obligations, had thereby damaged the marine environment. Along the way, the tribunal pointed out that China's denial of Filipino artisanal fishermen to engage in traditional fishing within the territorial sea of the Scarborough Shoal was contrary to its international law obligations.[6]

China–ASEAN relations in the wake of the arbitration award

The extent of the one-sidedness of the award took observers by surprise. More surprising however was what followed thereafter. Most countries held their tongue and, by-and-large, remaining silent or neutral on the issue of demanding that China comply with the award. Only seven countries explicitly called on China to comply.[7] Two weeks after the award, at their forty-ninth Ministerial Meeting, the ten ASEAN foreign ministers meeting in Vientiane, Laos signed four documents, none of which censured China or even referenced the award. In their all-important Joint Communique, the ASEAN foreign ministers only called for the non-militarization of the South China Sea land features and urged parties to exercise self-restraint by "refraining from … inhabiting the presently uninhabited islands, reefs, shoals, cays and other features."[8] On August 5, 2017, at their fiftieth Ministerial Meeting in Manila, the same pattern ensued. Far from referencing the July 2016 award – let alone criticize China, the ten ASEAN foreign ministers "warmly welcomed" the improving cooperation between ASEAN and China.[9] Their communiqué did take note though of some countries' concerns regarding land reclamations and re-emphasized the importance of non-militarization and self-restraint in the conduct of activities in the South China Sea. The same pattern repeated itself at the thirty-first ASEAN Leaders Summit in November 2017. If the purpose of third party arbitration is to entrench respect for the body of international law within state practice, the judges in *Philippines v. China* have been less-than-successful, to say the least, so far, especially in Southeast Asia.

For ASEAN and China, the issuance of the award on July 12, 2016 constituted the closing of a tense chapter in their recent interactions and the opportunity to turn a new page of cooperation.[10] That post-July 2016 cooperation has been manifested in a *Joint Statement on the Application of the Code for Unplanned Encounters at Sea (CUES) in the South China Sea*, the drawing up of a *Framework of the Code of Conduct in the South China Sea* and the successful operationalization of the *Guidelines for Hotline Communications among Senior Officials of the Ministries of Foreign Affairs of ASEAN Member States and China in Response to Maritime Emergencies in the Implementation of the Declaration on the Conduct of Parties in the South China Sea*.

This turning of the wheel in favor of stability and cooperation in China–ASEAN relations with regard to the South China Sea is a welcome relief from the elevated level of tension that had appeared to descend over this contested waterway during the first half of this decade. There were apprehensions that the disputes in this body of water were evolving from claims related to sovereign rights and maritime jurisdiction pertaining to the islets and reefs in the water to fiercer forms of geopolitical contestation and waterway control involving China and major external stakeholders, notably the US.[11] The turning of the wheel in favor of stability and cooperation is also consistent with a discernible pattern of easing and deterioration in China–ASEAN relations with regard to the South China Sea over the past quarter-century. There have been four such cycles: two deteriorating cycles between 1992 and 1999 and 2009 and 2016, and two easing cycles between 2002 and 2008 and the current cycle that began in July 2016. Although no two easing or deteriorating cycles are identical, this chapter will argue that there have been three identifiable features.

First, in one form or the other, a Law of the Sea Convention (LOSC)-linked timeline or deadline has been a visible or invisible presence in the background throughout this period. Second, cycles of deterioration have typically been led by China slapping down a controversial maritime rights claim, which has been accompanied by subsequent actions that have visibly disturbed the status quo. In 1992, China promulgated its Law on the Territorial Sea and the Contiguous Zone and followed up by constructing structures on the Philippines' continental shelf at Mischief Reef in 1995. In 2009, China officially appended a map of the nine-dash line and followed it up with a series of large-scale land reclamations from mid-2013 onwards in response to Manila filing the arbitration case. Third, the Philippines has felt the most violated among the claimant states by China's actions, yet has been the most capricious in its policy responses. There have been stark pro-and anti-China pendulum swings, coinciding with the elevation of new presidents dating back to 2001 which have amplified these cycles. This has also hurt ASEAN's ability to speak with one voice.

Looking ahead, the chapter will conclude by arguing that easing cycles have lent themselves to imaginative approaches by China and ASEAN and by China and claimant states in the South China Sea to address and manage their common challenges. The 2005 Joint Marine Seismic Undertaking (JMSU) involving the national oil companies of the Philippines, China and Vietnam was one such example. So also now, with Filipino President Rodrigo Duterte's readiness to forego near-term implementation of the arbitration award and his insistence on scaling back naval cooperation with the US in the South China Sea, an important opportunity has been unlocked for Beijing and Manila and for China and ASEAN as a whole to move beyond managing their differences to resolving some of them in this vital body of water. Some creative approaches will be briefly outlined within the context of China's "dual track" policy which would, both, enable China to imperceptibly bring its practices into compliance with aspects of the arbitration award as well as enable China and ASEAN to manage the differences responsibly.

But, first, before delving into the cycles of easing and deterioration in China–ASEAN relations over the past quarter-century, this chapter will at some length touch upon the underlying sovereignty quarrels and sovereign rights and jurisdiction quarrels among the claimant states which has made management and resolution of disputes in the South China Sea so intractable. In particular, this chapter will argue that the Law of the Sea Convention (LOSC), in its application in the South China Sea, has hitherto sown more confusion than clarity and has confounded the search for cooperative solutions to their common challenges in this body of water. It will lay out four means by which LOSC has done so.

Competing sovereignty claims in the South China Sea

The Asia-Pacific presents a veritable paradox. There are numerous sources of inter-state tensions in the Asia-Pacific, yet there has been no outbreak of major conflict since the late-1970s. This is particularly remarkable given that there are major powers transitions taking shape in the region. Typically, rapid shifts in inter-country power differentials has been a key marker of inter-state conflict in other regions.[12] The Asia-Pacific region also hosts a number of contested maritime boundaries that provide intermittent political fodder for populist politicians and nationalist audiences on all sides, yet there has been minimal to no loss of life during military tensions or standoffs related to these contested boundaries. Most notably, the Asia-Pacific region exhibits what has been described as "Asia Paradox" – the disconnect between the region's growing economic interdependence on the one hand, and the relative lack of political-security cooperation on the other. There is an "Economic Asia," a dynamic Asia crisscrossed by dynamic and integrated production sharing networks, and then there is a "Security Asia," a region of "mistrustful powers, prone to nationalism and irredentism, escalating their territorial disputes over tiny rocks and shoals, and arming for conflict."[13] To a significant degree, the South China Sea too is an illustrative example of these various paradoxes at play in the Asia-Pacific region.

The tensions in the South China Sea stem, first and foremost, from the underlying – and unresolved – sovereignty disputes among the claimant states surrounding this body of water. The numerous land features in the South China Sea are occupied and administered by a number of claimants. Although the Paracels group of islands, which are claimed by China and Vietnam, is wholly under Beijing's control, the occupation of the Spratly group of islands is spread across four claimant states – China presently occupies seven features, Vietnam twenty-one, the Philippines nine, and Malaysia six. Additionally, the largest island in the Spratlys group, Itu Aba or Taiping Island, is occupied and administered by the Republic of China (Taiwan). Given that the claimant states have displayed effective control over the land features for a couple of decades now and these features have become part-and-parcel of their publics' territorial consciousness, it will be very difficult to resolve the competing bilateral claims politically. Third party resolution by way of judicial opinion or international arbitration is also unforeseeable given that countries in the region either view third part mechanisms to resolve sovereignty questions dimly or have explicitly excluded themselves from the compulsory jurisdiction of the International Court of Justice (ICJ) or the optional jurisdiction of a court that is constitute-able under Chapter XV of the United Nations Convention on the Law of the Sea (UNCLOS).[14]

The poisoned chalice of San Francisco

The sovereignty disputes in the South China Sea have their modern-day provenance in the unfulfilled territorial provisions of the post-war San Francisco Treaty and the Republic of China–Japan Treaty of Taipei. On September 8, 1951, at the United States and United Kingdom stage-managed San Francisco Peace Conference to sign a peace treaty with Japan, Tokyo renounced all rights, titles and claims to a number of territories "which she ha[d] seized or occupied … [or] stolen … [or was to] be expelled from [because they were] taken by violence and greed."[15] Article 2(f) of the San Francisco Treaty reads:[16] "Japan renounces all right, title and claim to the Spratly Islands and to the Paracel Islands. "

The Spratly Islands and the Paracel Islands were one among a number of territories that were renounced by Japan in San Francisco. These also included the Korean Peninsula, Taiwan, Penghu (the Pescadores), the Kuril Islands, South Sakhalin and the Pacific Islands. Crucially, the sovereign to whom each of these territories would devolve to was not named in the treaty.

Nevertheless, on April 28, 1952, hours *before* this renunciation was to come into force, the Yoshida government in Tokyo renounced Taiwan, Penghu and the Spratly and Paracel Islands to the Chiang Kai-shek led the nationalist Republic of China government in Taipei.[17] As per Article 2 of the Treaty of Peace between the Republic of China and Japan, also known as the Taipei Treaty, Tokyo resolved to recognize:[18]

> that under Article 2 of the Treaty of Peace which Japan signed at the city of San Francisco on 8 September 1951 (hereinafter referred to as the San Francisco Treaty), Japan has renounced all right, title, and claim to Taiwan (Formosa) and Penghu (the Pescadores) as well as the Spratley Islands and the Paracel Islands.

Legions of commentators have since observed that because no recipient of the territorial renunciations, including the Spratly and Paracel Island, was stipulated by Japan in the San Francisco Treaty, their final sovereign status remains as yet undetermined. The implication further is that the territorial provisions in the San Francisco Treaty have no bearing on who, in the instance of the Spratly and Paracel Islands, should be considered its rightful owner. San Francisco supposedly was agnostic on this question all along.

This is not an accurate characterization. To the contrary, it was the considered judgment of the signatories at San Francisco and in Taipei that the Spratly and Paracel Islands should revert to their most superior claimant – China. Indeed, this was not even a point of contention among the US, its allies, and Japan. The point of contention, rather, was over the contingent form of sovereignty being exercised by Chiang Kai-shek's nationalist government in Taipei that Washington and Tokyo were prepared to recognize.[19] Only nationals and juridical persons who resided in or were registered on territories under Chiang's current or future sway were to be recognized as falling under the Republic of China's sovereignty.[20] This was done so that if Nationalist forces were ever ousted from the territories they currently held, there could be no legal basis for Mainland China to be able to claim sovereignty over the territories – Taiwan, Penghu, and the Spratly and Paracel Islands – that were due to formally revert to Chiang's Republic of China government in Taipei.[21]

This conditioning in the treaty text was, in turn, imposed by the US, the architect of both the San Francisco and the Taipei treaties, for purely geo-strategic considerations. With the outbreak of the Korean War in June 1950, the island of Taiwan had assumed critical defense policy ramifications for the US and its allies' position in the Western Pacific. Leaving these territories final disposition suitably vague in the treaties signed in San Francisco and in Taipei would ensure that these territories – the island of Taiwan in particular – could not legally devolve under any circumstances to "a hostile regime (i.e. the communist government in Beijing) ... that could enable [it] to endanger the [US Seventh Fleet's] defensive position which is so vital in keeping the Pacific a friendly body of water."[22]

The Treaty of Peace between the Republic of China and Japan, being a bilateral treaty, does not bind the other South China Sea claimant states – Malaysia, Vietnam, Brunei or the Philippines – who were non-signatories. For its part, Beijing – excluded from the San Francisco Conference – traces its claim to the Paracel and Spratly islands to the war-time Cairo and Potsdam Declarations, which was confirmed in Article 3 of its September 1972 normalization agreement with Tokyo.[23] This having been said, no other regional claimant can produce a Spratly and Paracel renunciation or reversion clause in its own post-war normalization agreement with Tokyo.

This short historical background notwithstanding, the territorial disputes involving the land features in the South China Sea are not about to be sorted out anytime soon. As previously noted, the claimant states refuse as a matter of principle, formality or political convenience to have their claims resolved bilaterally or tested and awarded under third-party arbitration. This contest of sovereignties in the South China Sea is fated to last well into the future. They will not be reconciled anytime soon.

The Law of the Sea Convention: sowing more confusion than clarity so far

Compounding the sovereignty challenges in the South China Sea has been the introduction, role and development of international maritime law, notably the law of the sea as developed at successive international conferences during the second half of the twentieth century. The most notable of these conferences was the Third United Nations Conference on the Law of the Sea which over a nine-year period crafted what became the United Nations Convention on the Law of the Sea (UNCLOS) in 1982.[24] UNCLOS provides a comprehensive legal framework governing all uses of the ocean and its resources and has been described as a "constitution for the oceans." In its application in the South China Sea, it has hitherto also sown more confusion than clarity and has complicated the management of security and politics in this body of water. The LOS Convention has confounded the search for cooperative solutions to the common challenges in the South China Sea in four ways.[25]

First, the Law of the Sea Convention (LOSC) has created a sense of resource consciousness – and fairly so – among states and their publics within the international system, including in Southeast Asia. The Convention confers a 200-nautical mile exclusive economic zone (EEZ) where the coastal state can explore, exploit, conserve and manage the natural resources, whether living or non-living, of the sea. Certain exclusive continental shelf rights extend beyond 200 nautical miles too if particular geological and geomorphological criteria are satisfied. Resource consciousness can easily drift, and has easily drifted, into resource nationalism however, and a scramble to corner the resources of the sea. Periods of friction in the South China Sea have uniquely coincided in one form or other with a Law of the Sea-related trigger – be it in the 1970s, 1990s or the 2010s. The most notable of these triggers pertained to the scramble by the South China Sea littoral states to occupy many of the land features in this body of water through the 1970s.[26] The scramble was prompted by a finding in a U.N. Economics Commission for Asia and the Far East report of 1969 which confirmed via geological survey that "substantial energy deposits" existed in both the East China Sea and the South China Sea.[27] The value of these hydrocarbon deposits was magnified, in turn, by the then-on-going discussions at the Third United Nations Conference on the Law of the Sea (1973–1982), where the new legal regime of a 200-nautical mile EEZ and continental shelf regime – the key innovation of the Third Conference – was developed and instituted. Because maritime entitlements are generated on the basis of the "land dominates the sea" principle, states felt the need to race each other in occupying as many of the land features of the South China Sea as possible. To this day, this scramble for territory has severely complicated the outlook for resolving the sovereign rights and jurisdiction claims as well as the underlying sovereignty claims in these waters.[28]

Second, the Law of the Sea Convention's (LOSC) founding agnosticism to determining competing claims over land territory while at the same time basing permissible maritime claims on the "land dominates the sea" principle has, both, exacerbated the sovereignty and sovereign rights and jurisdiction disputes in the South China Sea and made them harder to resolve. It has elevated a legal-technical approach to dispute management and resolution in this body of water above the imperative for political compromise – in turn, going against the grain of tried-and-tested models of successful territory-related dispute resolution in Asia. Sovereignty over land territory can be acquired by a state by being the first to establish effective control. That mechanism does not apply to the sea. UNCLOS in fact operates on the premise that sovereignty over territory has already been established.[29] That premise does not hold either in the South China Sea. Because the premise does not hold, the sovereign rights and jurisdiction that originate from these features is also in dispute. Yet too often the sovereign right to explore, exploit, conserve and manage the living and non-living resources of the sea in the exclusive economic zone (EEZ) is conflated by aroused nationalistic publics as an attribute equivalent of that associated with territorial sovereignty – which it is not.[30] From a political standpoint, this resource nationalism-based fusing of sovereign rights-based claims with sovereignty claims has made the search for political compromise and the need to share these living and non-living resources in overlapping and disputed maritime zones that much harder to achieve.

Had it nevertheless been left solely to the leaders of the coastal states of South China Sea to marshal the support of their citizens and arrive at political compromises to resolve their contested resource sovereignty-driven quarrels, this might have been possible. Asia – and China in particular – enjoys a rich tradition of successful resolution of contested (land) boundaries on the basis of win–win compromises. Fully, 14 of 16 of China's disputed Asian frontiers, including with Southeast Asian countries (Myanmar in 1960; Vietnam from 1999 to 2008) were resolved in this manner.[31] Two salient characteristics have underlain these successful settlements. First, a *political imperative* of boundary settlement has vastly overshadowed any territorial imperative – indeed stabilization of the heartland and periphery have held considerably greater importance than incremental territory that might be gained or lost during the course of a boundary negotiation.[32] Second, the *act of framing political principles guiding settlemen*t and thereafter enshrined in a bilateral or plurilateral agreement *has always preceded the legal-technical effort of marking a delimited boundary* on the ground.

Neither of these power and politics-based principles and characteristics hold or can be easily brought to bear to facilitate the resolution of overlapping and disputed maritime rights claim. To the contrary, the resolution of these overlapping sovereign rights and jurisdiction claims are governed by a set of rules that are set forth in the LOSC. These rules have the effect of inverting the sequence between framing broad political principles for settlement of an overlapping sovereign rights claim and thereafter sharing or dividing the resources at sea on a win–win basis. In doing so, the LOSC rules also negate the space and scope for political agency and, in privileging a legal-technical approach to overlapping claims redressal, go against the grain of the win–win political approaches that has characterized China and Southeast Asian countries' earlier successful approaches to sovereignty-related dispute resolution.

The low procedural bar of Article 281(1)

Third, and on a related note, the wide latitude accorded by the Law of the Sea Convention (LOSC) to convention-constituted tribunals to arbitrarily frame the parameters of their jurisdiction while hearing cases has gravely encroached upon and short-circuited the role of political compromise to resolve disputes in the South China Sea and beyond. Article 281(1), paired with Article 288(4) in particular of Part XV of the Convention, which pertains to dispute settlement, bears the lion's share of the responsibility in this regard. Article 281(1) of Part XV of the LOSC states:[33]

> If the States Parties which are parties to a dispute concerning the interpretation or application of this Convention have agreed to seek settlement of the dispute by a peaceful means of their own choice, the procedures provided for in this Part apply only where no settlement has been reached by recourse to such means and the agreement between the parties does not exclude any further procedure.

The purpose and object of this provision was to ensure that the automatic and compulsory jurisdiction envisaged in Section 2 of Part XV (Articles 286–96) to frame an award on the merits of a maritime dispute would only kick-in once the mutual political consultations had failed or local remedies were exhausted. LOSC-constituted courts however have failed to heed this injunction in its totality.[34] Rather, they have tended to place an absurdly low threshold for an aggrieved party to satisfy the requirement that prior political efforts to "seek settlement of the dispute by a peaceful means of their own choice" has been exhausted.[35] This has had the unfortunate effect of circumventing the political process of arriving at hard-fought compromises among disputant states and has instead incentivized parties to make a dash to the court-house for redress – even in instances when an active consensus to resolve the differences through mutual consultations with the other party has utterly *not* been exhausted. LOSC-constituted courts have thereafter gladly taken recourse to Article 288(4)[36] of Part XV to self-indulgently find competence to proceed to the merits stage of the case at hand.[37]

In the *South China Sea Arbitration (Philippines v. China) case*, the tribunal set aside the injunction to exhaust all local remedies and assigned unto itself the jurisdiction to proceed to the merits stage, even though China and ASEAN have been actively involved – and continue to remain in active discussions – towards framing a Code of Conduct to manage and resolve their differences in the South China Sea for the past two decades.[38] In defeating the original purpose Article 281(1) and incentivizing this rush to litigate, the tribunal has also called into question in the South China Sea and beyond the value of political undertakings, such as the proposed Code of Conduct, that are solemnly arrived at and seek to resolve differences by mutual consensus.

The *South China Sea Arbitration (Philippines v. China) case* is not the most egregious instance of interpretive abuse of Article 281(1). That would be the *Democratic Republic of Timor-Leste v. Commonwealth of Australia* case which is currently nearing completion under an Annex V (of LOSC) conciliation process.[39] In Article 4 of their then-extant 2006 Treaty on Certain Maritime Arrangements in the Timor Sea (CMATS),[40] Australia and Timor-Leste were legally bound to "neither assert, pursue or further by any means its … claims to sovereign rights and jurisdiction and maritime boundaries" (Article 4.1)[41] nor "commence or pursue any proceedings against the other party before any court, tribunal or other dispute settlement mechanism that would raise … issues or findings of relevance to maritime boundaries or delimitation in the Timor Sea" (Article 4.4).[42] Any court, tribunal or other dispute settlement body too was under binding treaty instructions to "not consider, comment on nor make findings … on issues or findings of relevance to maritime boundaries or delimitation in the Timor Sea" (Article 4.5).[43] Clearly, there should be no basis for a third party arbitrator to be seized of a Dili-Canberra maritime delimitation matter in the Timor Sea.

At the pleading of Timor-Leste during the jurisdiction stage, the conciliation commission however blithely tossed this treaty language aside without so much as a basic explanation why its interpretation of Article 281(1) and ruling on jurisdiction should supersede that of a solemn treaty. In its reasoning, it first noted what

CMATS was about. It stated that "CMATS [was] an agreement *not* to seek settlement of the parties' dispute over maritime boundaries." Next it observed what Article 281(1) of the LOSC convention was supposed to be about. It observed that the article was about "seek[ing] settlement of disputes by a peaceful means of the Parties' own choice."[44] Juxtaposing these two points, it thereafter observed that because CMATS was not an agreement to seek settlement of the disputes by a peaceful means of the Parties' own choice (because it did not provide for such a mechanism), the commission was at liberty to conclude that CMATS was "not an agreement pursuant to Article 281 that would preclude recourse to compulsory conciliation."[45] With this legal sleight of hand, it proceeded to find competence to take the case onward to compulsory conciliation and is preparing to publicly deliver its award shortly on the merits.

If even cast-iron treaty language that is consensually arrived-at by the parties won't stop enterprising judges to self-servingly lower the already-low Article 281(1) bar and inject themselves into the political mix, then nothing else will! It begs the fundamental question what the object and purpose of a treaty is in the first place. This extraordinary intrusion into the realm of political compromise cannot but diminish the standing of the LOSC, and international law more broadly, down-the-line in the eyes of its primary users – the Member States of the United Nations, both in Asia and beyond.

Instability of jurisprudence on LOS textual provisions

Finally, the interpretive ambiguities embedded in the Law of the Sea Convention's provisions with regard to resource entitlements in overlapping and disputed maritime zones has incentivized the smaller claimant states of the South China Sea to advocate for exclusivist solutions to these overlapping sovereign rights and jurisdiction challenges. This has led to unpredictability and tensions in their bilateral and multi-sided interactions with fellow claimants. The Law of the Sea Convention's (LOSC), as a relatively young body of international law, is understandably prone to violent fluctuations in the course of its interpretive development. The Convention's text, after all, was a package of political compromises reached by representatives of more than 160 sovereign states. Political compromises left interpretive gaps, willy-nilly, which subsequent LOSC-constituted dispute settlement panels have not always handled wisely.[46] Of recent note of interest in this regard, insofar as the South China Sea is concerned, is the jurisprudence on small insular formations in the sea and the suite of maritime zones that they are capable of generating.[47]

The ambiguity of Article 121(3), namely, the ability of a small islet "to sustain human habitation or economic life of [its] own" and thereby qualify as an "island" and generate a vast exclusive economic zone (EEZ) and continental shelf has long vexed legal specialists and lay persons alike. The wording that became the agreed text in April 1975 was the product of an informal consultative process, which left few records of its work due to the deep divisions among the state parties. Unable to form a consensus on this "island/rock" distinction, the Meetings of the State Parties of the Law of the Sea Convention (SPLOS) have periodically stayed the hand of statutory international expert bodies from weighing-in till the divergence of views is resolved politically. Taking the cue, international courts too had tended to find artful ways to navigate around this contested definition in the course of maritime delimitation cases.

The recent International Court of Justice (ICJ) award in the *Nicaragua v. Colombia* case and the Annex VII tribunal award in the *Philippines v. China* case have veritably upset this applecart. In its judgment in *Nicaragua v. Colombia*, the ICJ drew an unusually literalist construction of what constitutes an "island."[48] With reference to "Quitasueno 32," a rock among various others features in the Quitasueno area, the court ruled that:[49]

> even using Nicaragua's preferred tidal model, QS 32 is above water at high tide by some 0.7 metres. The Court recalls that in the case concerning Maritime Delimitation and Territorial Questions between Qatar and Bahrain (Qatar v. Bahrain) (Merits Judgment, I.C.J. 2001, p. 99, para. 197), it found that Qit'at Jaradah was an island, notwithstanding that it was only 0.4 metres above water at high tide. The fact that QS 32 is very small does not make any difference, since international law does not prescribe any minimum size which a feature must possess in order to be considered an island.

The classification of "Quitasueno 32" has been described as an "extreme example" of what passes as an "island" as per Article 121(3).[50] In *Philippines v. China*, the tribunal took a diametrically opposite tack and proceeded to strip a land feature (Itu Aba or Taiping Island) in the South China Sea – which by all reasonable accounts can, has, and does sustain human habitation and economic life of its own – of its entitlement to generate a maritime zone beyond its 12-nautical mile territorial sea. The tribunal did so in two stages. First, it separated the definition of an "island" from a "rock" based on whether the feature has sustained human habitation in the past or not.[51] Effectively, henceforth, features "which *haven't* sustained human habitation or economic life of its own" are to be categorized as "rocks." Next, it pronounced that the "human habitation" referenced in Article 121(3) was to "be [now] understood to involve the inhabitation of the feature by a stable community of people for whom the feature constitutes a home and on which they can remain."[52] In doing so, the tribunal substantially expanded and transformed the literal definition of a "rock" from one which "cannot sustain human habitation or economic life of their own" to one which "*hasn't [historically] sustained a settled community of inhabitants* or economic life of their own."[53] This expansive and substantial transformation of the vexed interpretation of Article 121(3) is unlikely to pass muster when the next UNCLOS-constituted tribunal is seized of this same definitional question. In all likelihood, the interpretation will be pulled back towards a point somewhere between *Nicaragua v. Colombia* and *Philippines v. China*.

The fundamental underlying criticism being made nevertheless bears reiterating. UNCLOS is a young body of law which is still at an early stage of its interpretive development, and hence prone to volatility. This flux in the interpretation of the law is not conducive to stable inter-state interactions among coastal states in the South China Sea. Indeed, to the contrary, this volatility of the law has incentivized the smaller claimant states in this body of water to advocate for exclusivist solutions to their overlapping sovereign rights and jurisdiction challenges, present *fait accompli's* to their regional rivals by positioning themselves at the forefront to unilaterally exploit the resources of the sea, and tempted their dash to the court-house which has by-passed the more arduous but necessary political compromise and consensus-building process in the South China Sea.

China–ASEAN relations in the South China Sea and persistent features

Ever since a map displaying the nine-dash line[54] was appended to a *Note Verbale* communicated by the People's Republic of China to the United Nations Secretary General in May 2009[55] to object to a joint and an individual South China Sea-related submission by Vietnam and Malaysia[56] and by Vietnam,[57] respectively, an elevated level of tension appeared to descend over the contested waterway. In the notes appended to the map, China claimed indisputable sovereignty over the islands in the South China Sea and their adjacent waters as well as sovereign rights and jurisdiction over the relevant waters as well as the seabed and subsoil thereof. A year later, in mid-2010, newly elected Filipino president Benigno Aquino III raised Beijing's ire by granting an oil service contract to a London-based oil and gas company, Forum Energy, in what had hitherto been a disputed section of the South China Sea (the Reed Bank area). The strained environment was exacerbated during the summer of 2012 when the Chinese government displaced the Philippine navy and took physical administrative control over the Scarborough Shoal. President Aquino raised the tensions a notch higher in January 2013 when his administration launched arbitral proceedings against China at a LOSC-constituted Annex VII tribunal, asserting that many of Beijing's maritime claims – and actions in defense of those claims – in the South China Sea were contrary to UNCLOS and had thereby violated the Philippines' sovereign maritime rights and freedoms. In December 2014, the US too – though neither a party to the arbitration nor to the Law of the Sea Convention – waded into the fray by releasing a study of the nine-dash line that purported to buttress an important aspect of Manila's case.[58] The round of tensions only abated following the election and swearing-in of Rodrigo Duterte on June 30, 2016 as the sixteenth president of The Philippines and the issuance of the arbitral award twelve days later.

Four important observations can be formed from the chain of events described above. First, the Law of the Sea Convention (LOSC) was never far from the surface during this period of strain. The infringing maritime rights claim issued by China was precipitated, in part, by a LOSC-linked deadline – in this case, the deadline being May 13, 2009 for Malaysia and Vietnam to submit national claims over the extended continental shelf to the Commission on the Limits of the Continental Shelf (CLCS).[59] Once Manila filed its memorial and instituted Annex VII arbitral proceedings against China in January 2013, the tensions seemed indissoluble. Second, China was the first to stir unease in these waters by unilaterally issuing what was widely deemed to be a non-conforming South China Sea-related maritime rights claim. China's *Note Verbale* and nine-dash line map was slapped down on May 7, 2009, a day after Malaysia and Vietnam issued their joint submission to the CLCS. Three years later, it took physical actions that disturbed the status quo on the ground – in this case, the exclusive physical occupation of Scarborough Shoal which was subsequently closed-off to traditional Filipino fishermen. Land reclamations followed a year later. Third, a newly elected Filipino leader broke with his predecessor's conciliatory policies toward Beijing and stirred the pot by attempting to unilaterally exploit hydrocarbon resources in a hitherto-disputed area which had once been subject to a far-sighted joint exploration agreement with China – in this case, the Joint Marine Seismic Undertaking (JMSU) initialed during the term of his predecessor, Gloria Arroyo. President Aquino was not shy to leverage the US's strategic presence thereafter in his quarrels with Beijing, severely complicating the security dynamics of the South China Sea. Finally, the US was determined not to let the cycle of tension – and opportunities for geopolitical gain therein – to pass, and dived-in with both feet into these roiled waters.[60] Loudly advertised Freedom of Navigation operations (FONOPS) were publicly conducted and a legal analysis of the nine-dash line, as part of its *Limits in the Seas* series, was issued.[61]

Cycles of strain and progress in relations

These observations are not unique to the strains that appeared to set in post-2009. There have in fact been four cycles of easing and deterioration in the politics and security of the South China Sea region. Two easing cycles can be dated to 2002–2008 and the current cycle starting in July 2016; and two deteriorating cycles, too, dated to 1992–1999 and 2009–2016.

The cycle of deterioration that started in 1992 was sparked when China promulgated its *Law on the Territorial Sea and the Contiguous Zone*, which declared that the Paracel and the Spratly islands, among others, were part of the land territory of the People's Republic. It was followed with the signing of a contract between a Chinese national oil company (China National Offshore Oil Corporation) and a US private firm (Crestone Energy Corporation) in an area near Vanguard Bank which overlapped with an existing Vietnamese-granted oil block in the southern sector of the South China Sea. Kuala Lumpur immediately sought formal clarifications regarding the territorial sea law, Manila and Jakarta lodged diplomatic protests and Hanoi sent across a secret protest note to challenge the claims.[62] At regional level, the six ASEAN foreign ministers adopted the *Manila Declaration* at their meeting on July 22, 1992, calling on all parties to exercise restraint and resolve the sovereignty and jurisdictional disputes peacefully. ASEAN's common stance in the South China Sea stems, to this day, from the *Manila Declaration* – the first such declaration at the region-wide level that sought to launch a code of conduct in the South China Sea.

Two-and-half-years later, in February 1995, the Philippines discovered Chinese-built structures on a rocky outcrop, Mischief Reef, 130-odd nautical miles west of the island of Palawan. It was the first instance when Beijing had physically occupied a feature in dispute against an ASEAN member state.[63] For fear of break-out of military confrontation, Filipino president Fidel Ramos made no effort to evict the Chinese presence from Mischief Reef. To the contrary, Manila stayed calm and engaged Beijing diplomatically, while also working regionally and extra-regionally to de-escalate the situation. The China–Philippines eight-point code of conduct of August 1995, as well as the formal idea of a region-wide Code of Conduct, which was endorsed at the ASEAN Ministerial Meeting in 1996, dates to this period of strain. ASEAN unity, however, gradually began to peter away in the subsequent years as differences in various parties' conception of what the Code of Conduct should cover came to the fore. In part, this dis-unity on the code was triggered by Malaysia's own pre-emptive occupation of Investigator Shoal and its two-storey building and helipad construction on another Manila-contested land feature, Erica Shoal, in mid-1999. This was the first time that an ASEAN member state had physically moved against the claims of a fellow compatriot in the South China Sea.[64] The Code of Conduct-related discussion within ASEAN and between ASEAN and China was finally papered over at the eighth ASEAN–China summit in Phnom Penh in November 2002 by calling the proposed instrument a "declaration" rather than a "code." Malaysia, which along with Vietnam had concerns about the geographic coverage of the instrument, took the lead in devising this compromise.

For its part, the US during this period of strain issued its first comprehensive statement on the insular land formations in this semi-enclosed sea. On May 10, 1995, in the wake of the Mischief Reef occupation, it issued a statement on the Spratly Islands and the South China Sea, which stated that Washington would view with serious concern any claim or restriction on maritime activity that was inconsistent with international law, including UNCLOS.[65] A year later, it privately warned Beijing that it would not respect China's May 1996 formal announcement of its territorial sea baseline adjacent to the Paracel Islands[66] and, not-so-privately, conducted freedom of navigation assertions in these waters in 1997. These actions at the table and at sea foreshadowed those of US Secretary of State, Hillary Clinton, at the ASEAN Regional Forum meeting in Hanoi in July 2010 and the FONOPS conducted by the Obama administration during the October 2015 to January 2017 period.

Easing cycles on the other hand have been conducive to making political progress on China–ASEAN relations as well as China's bilateral relations with individual Southeast Asian countries, most notably the Philippines. The workmanlike improvement in China–ASEAN relations at the turn of the millennium facilitated the signing of the *Declaration on the Conduct of Parties in the South China Sea* in November 2002. A year later, on October 8, 2003, China and ASEAN signed the *Joint Declaration of the Heads of State/Government on Strategic Partnership for Peace and Prosperity* and Beijing became the first non-ASEAN country to officially accede to the *Treaty of Amity and Cooperation in Southeast Asia (TAC).*

The China–ASEAN Senior Officials Meeting (SOM) format, whose institutionalization continues to this day, was regularized during this phase of easing. The first SOM was held in Kuala Lumpur in December 2004 and led to the establishment of a Joint Working Group (JWG) to suggest confidence-building activities in the South China Sea. China's bilateral relations with ASEAN countries also reached important highs during this period, leading to what came to be termed, then, as Beijing's "charm offensive" towards Southeast Asia.[67]

China–Philippines relations too moved beyond their South China Sea spats and was qualitatively transformed under the presidency of Gloria Arroyo. Like Rodrigo Duterte a decade-and-half hence, she looked to China as a key economic engine that could rejuvenate the Philippines economy and bring development to its non-metropolitan regions. By 2005, the two countries were hailing their ties as having entered a "golden age" and the first annual China–Philippines defense talks were held later that year. An imaginative joint resource exploration project in what was hitherto a disputed section of the southern sector of the South China Sea – the Joint Marine Seismic Undertaking (JMSU), was the cherry on top. Signed as a tripartite commercial agreement between the national oil companies of China, Vietnam and the Philippines, it neither formally touched upon the sovereignty claims of the participating countries nor did it involve actual drilling for resources in the designated area. The Undertaking was nevertheless a "historic … breakthrough in implementing the provisions of the code of conduct … and turn[ing] the South China Sea into an area of cooperation rather than an area of conflict."[68] It was also an important first step towards realizing Deng Xiaoping's far-sighted entreaty to President Corazon Aquino in 1988 to "set aside disputes and pursue joint development."[69] The failure to renew the JMSU at the end of its three-year term in July 2008 in the face of charges of corruption, and even treason, was a damaging initial step towards the closing of the window of opportunity that the *Declaration of Conduct of Parties* and the *Joint Declaration on Strategic Partnership* had opened earlier in the decade. The conversion of this geophysical survey into an oil service contract and its award to London-based Forum Energy under the Philippines' exclusive jurisdiction in mid-2010 added to the aggravated spiral in tensions thereafter.

A couple of key takeaways

Three persistent features can be identified from the ebb and flow of these South China Sea-related events over the past twenty-five years. First, in one form or the other, a Law of the Sea Convention-linked timeline, deadline or event, has been a visible or invisible presence in the backdrop, all along. Be it in 1992 (and China's territorial sea law), 2002 (and the Declaration on Conduct of Parties), 2009 (and the CLCS deadline and China's nine dash line) or 2016 (and the arbitral award), UNCLOS has left an indelible mark. Second, cycles of deterioration have typically been led by China slapping down a controversial maritime rights claim, which has been accompanied by subsequent actions that visibly disturbed the status quo. In 1992, China promulgated its Territorial Sea Law and followed up by constructing structures on the Philippines' continental shelf at Mischief Reef in 1995. In 2009, China officially appended a map of the nine-dash line and followed it by taking administrative control over the Scarborough Shoal in 2012 and conducting a series of large-scale land reclamations from mid-2013 onwards in response to Manila filing the arbitration case.

On a related note, the US has been consigned to a secondary role, by-and-large, in the affairs of the South China Sea, *except during the deteriorating cycles.* Before Hillary Clinton's forceful intervention at the ARF meeting in Hanoi in 2010, the most comprehensive earlier statement on the Spratlys and the South China Sea had occurred in May 1995 following Beijing's occupation of Mischief Reef. The highly self-publicized freedom of navigation operations, too, have been conducted during this down cycle. The received view, currently, that the South China Sea disputes have migrated from competing sovereign rights and maritime jurisdiction claims to fiercer forms of geopolitical contests and waterway control involving the established power (the US) and the rising power (China), and that this "new normal" is here to stay, is a misreading of the dynamics at play. The current easing cycle, rather, will lend itself to a period of strategic calm in this critically important waterway. Without an agitated local claimant on whose behalf it can claim to be intervening to uphold the stability of the South China Sea, the US has few other tools at its disposal to assert its relevance and authority in this body of water other than to endlessly navigate its length and breadth.

Finally, the Philippines (and to a lesser extent Vietnam) has felt the most violated among the claimant states by China's actions, yet has been the most capricious in its policy responses. There have been stark pro-and anti-China pendulum swings, coinciding with the elevation of new presidents dating back to 2001 which have amplified these cycles. Easing cycles have also lent themselves to creative joint approaches to cooperatively develop energy resources in the South China Sea. President Rodrigo Duterte's revival of the possibility of joint development in early 2017 – albeit as a non-state-to-state project under the Philippines' sovereign rights and jurisdiction, suggests that this potential for imaginative and cooperative resource exploitation during easing cycles remains alive and well.

Concluding remarks and looking ahead

The South China Sea region is an illustrative example of "Asia Paradox" – the disconnect between the region's growing economic interdependence on the one hand, and the relative lack of political-security cooperation on the other. The sovereignty disputes in the South China Sea have their modern-day provenance in the unfulfilled territorial provisions of the post-war San Francisco Treaty and the Republic of China–Japan Treaty of Taipei. In four ways, the United Nations Convention on the Law of the Sea (UNCLOS), in its application to the South China Sea, has sown more confusion than clarity and has complicated the search for cooperative solutions to the sovereign rights and jurisdiction challenges in this semi-enclosed sea.

First, it has triggered a scramble for territory – and, thereby, lay a superior claim to the resources of the sea – among the claimant states, which has severely complicated the outlook for resolving the sovereign rights and jurisdiction claims as well as the underlying sovereignty claims in this body of water. Next, in privileging a legal-technical approach to overlapping claims redressal, it has gone against the grain of win–win political approaches that has characterized China and Southeast Asian countries' earlier successful approaches to sovereignty-related dispute resolution. Third, the wide latitude accorded by the Law of the Sea Convention (LOSC) to convention-constituted tribunals to arbitrarily frame the parameters of their jurisdiction while hearing cases has gravely encroached upon and short-circuited the role of political compromise to resolve the sovereign rights and jurisdiction disputes in this semi-enclosed sea. Finally, the interpretive ambiguities embedded in the Convention's provisions, particularly the instability of recent jurisprudence on small insular formations in the sea and the suite of maritime zones that they can generate, has incentivized the smaller claimant states in this body of water to advocate for exclusivist solutions to their overlapping sovereign rights and jurisdiction challenges. These states have also been hesitant to reach out creatively to their counterparts for fear that such outreach might jeopardize their legal position – should the overlapping sovereign rights claim become the subject matter of a dispute in a Convention-constituted tribunal.

These sovereign rights and jurisdiction quarrels have tended to metastasize during deteriorating cycles in the South China Sea, of which there have been two over the past twenty-five years: from 1992–1999 and from 2009–2016. The slapping down of a controversial maritime rights claim by China, accompanied down-the-line by subsequent actions that have visibly disturbed the status quo, has been a common feature during this down cycle. Easing cycles on the other hand, of which there too have been two (from 2002–2008 and from July 2016 onwards), have lent themselves to imaginative approaches by China and ASEAN and by China and claimant states in the South China Sea to address and manage their common challenges. A notable expression in this regard was the Joint Marine Seismic Undertaking (JMSU) of the mid-2000s involving the national oil companies of China, Vietnam and the Philippines.

Going forward, President Rodrigo Duterte's cancellation of major joint military exercises with the US, his barring of American naval vessels from using Philippine bases for freedom of navigation exercises, his cessation of plans for joint patrols in the South China Sea, and his blocking of US requests to upgrade and utilize an airbase that lies close to the China–Philippines area of dispute,[70] has once again opened up political space to conduct imaginative joint and cooperative hydrocarbon development activities on the Philippines' continental shelf. Unlike the case of the earlier tripartite agreement, however, China–Philippines cooperation this time around will have to be structured as a non-state-to-state agreement conducted under Philippines sovereign law. Examples of similarly structured joint development projects abound, including at the *Chunxiao* oil block along the hypothetical median line in the East China Sea that, in principle, is to be developed by China and Japan.[71]

Within the context of its "dual track" policy, China should also imperceptibly aim to bring its sovereign rights and jurisdictional practices in the South China Sea into compliance with aspects of the arbitration award.[72] There are creative means to do so. Building on its readiness to allow the return of traditional Filipino fishermen to the Scarborough Shoal, China should cease enforcing its summertime fishing moratorium in the northern sector in areas beyond its territorial sea limits. China should also withdraw its paramilitary presence from the vicinity of the Second Thomas Shoal, which is a low-tide elevation on the Philippines' continental shelf. Over time, if joint oil and gas development is successfully realized, Beijing and the Duterte government should devise a condominium arrangement to govern the administration of Mischief Reef – yet another low-tide elevation on the Philippines' continental shelf. A common property regime on Mischief Reef that includes clear rules of management, principled bases for those rules, and mechanisms for enforcement of those rules can be devised.[73] Beijing should also clarify that the "historic rights" it pursues within the nine-dash line in this semi-enclosed sea is limited solely to a non-exclusively exercised right to living resources for its artisanal fishermen. And on this basis, it should cease interference with all oil and gas development-related activity beyond the 200-nautical mile radius of Woody Island, the largest island in the Paracel group that it has continuously administered since the mid-1950s.

In parallel, China and ASEAN should devise a forward-looking and multi-layered Code of Conduct for the South China Sea that covers the claimant and non-claimant states of the region alike, is comprehensive in scope, subjects its signatories to some form of binding regional dispute settlement, and encourages extra-regional partners to adhere and accede to its purposes.[74] China and ASEAN enjoy an important opportunity to move beyond managing their differences to resolving some of them during this easing cycle. They should rise to the occasion and safeguard peace, prosperity and cooperation in the South China Sea.

Notes

1 *The South China Sea Arbitration (The Republic of Philippines v. The People's Republic of China) case*, Award of the Arbitral Tribunal, July 12, 2016, pp. 259–60, paras. 643–48, available at: www.pcacases.com/web/sendAttach/2086
2 See *Philippines v. China*, p. 102, para. 243.
3 Further, the arbitral tribunal declared that following the coming-into-force of the Convention in 1994, any "historic rights" that might have existed had been superseded. See *Philippines v. China*, p. 111, para. 261
4 See *Philippines v. China*, pp. 434–35, paras. 1105–8.
5 See *Philippines v. China*, pp. 378–84, paras. 950–66.
6 See *Philippines v. China*, pp. 315–18, paras. 805–14.
7 Center for Strategic and International Studies (CSIS). *Who Is Taking Sides After the South China Sea Ruling?* CSIS, August 15, 2016, https://amti.csis.org/sides-in-south-china-sea/
8 Association of Southeast Asian Nations (ASEAN), 49th Foreign Ministers' Meeting, *Turning Vision into Reality for a Dynamic ASEAN Community*, available at http://asean.org/storage/2016/07/Joint-Communique-of-the-49th-AMM-ADOPTED.pdf

9 Association of Southeast Asian Nations, 50th Foreign Ministers' Meeting, *Partnering for Change, Engaging the World*, available at http://asean.org/storage/2017/08/Joint-Communique-of-the-50th-AMM_FINAL.pdf

10 Of equally great importance was the election and swearing-in of Rodrigo Duterte twelve days earlier as the sixteenth president of the Republic of Philippines. Mr. Duterte had made it abundantly clear that he was in no hurry to collect on the Award and that he would rather seek consensus and cooperation with China in terms of the Award's implementation.

11 As per this reading of the emerging security dilemma, the South China Sea is a natural line of defense for China's national security and an indispensable strategic bastion for its Hainan-based assured second strike nuclear retaliatory force as well as a future home-ported aircraft carrier. For the US, meantime, control of this waterway linking the Indian and Pacific Oceans is indispensable to its strategic primacy in the broader Indo-Pacific region. As such, the dominant Great Power and the rising Great Power are locked in a structural and strategic contest which is fated to be irreconcilable.

12 John Ravenhill, *Responding to Security Challenges in East Asia: Three Perspectives*, CIGI Papers, No. 99 (April 2016) at p. 1, www.cigionline.org/sites/default/files/cigi_paper_no.99web.pdf

13 Evan A. Feigenbaum and Robert A. Manning, *A Tale of Two Asia's*, Foreign Policy, October 31, 2012, http://foreignpolicy.com/2012/10/31/a-tale-of-two-asias/

14 UNCLOS, 1833 U.N.T.S. 397, adopted in Montego Bay, Jamaica, on December 10, 1982, entered into force on November 16, 1994.

15 *The Cairo Declaration*, 26 November 1943, History and Public Policy Program Digital Archive, Foreign Relations of the United States, Diplomatic Papers, The Conferences at Cairo and Tehran, 1943 (Washington, DC: United States Government Printing Office, 1961), pp. 448–49. https://digitalarchive.wilsoncenter.org/document/122101

16 *Treaty of Peace with Japan (with Two Declarations)*, Signed at San Francisco, September 8, 1951, Entered into force, April 28, 1952, available at: www.taiwandocuments.org/sanfrancisco01.htm

17 The timing of the Taipei Treaty was not a coincidence. The architect of the treaty (and future US Secretary of State) John Foster Dulles had resolved prior to the San Francisco Conference to restore to Japan – after it signed the San Francisco Treaty but before it came into force – all the freedoms envisioned in the treaty except military sovereignty. Japan thus enjoyed the authority to transfer Taiwan, Penghu and the Spratly and the Paracel Islands to the Republic of China, as per the San Francisco Treaty.

18 *Treaty of Peace between the Republic of China and Japan (Treaty of Taipei)*, Signed at Taipei, April 28, 1952, Entered into force, August 5, 1952, available from http://china.usc.edu/treaty-peace-between-republic-china-and-japan-treaty-taipei-1952

19 Dean Acheson, *Telegram from Secretary of State to the Embassy in the Republic of China*, Foreign Relations of the United States, Vol. XIV, Part 2, China and Japan, 1952–54 (Washington, DC: United States Government Printing Office), Document 502.

20 At the time, there were no Republic of China nationals or juridical persons residing or registered in the Paracel and Spratlys.

21 John Foster Dulles was unambiguously clear on this point. In a memorandum to the US Secretary of Defense that was written barely 75 days before the San Francisco Conference, Dulles instructed that: "It should be made certain that there be no basis, either stated or implied, written into the [San Francisco] Treaty which might provide for the possible legal claim of Communist China to sovereignty over Formosa, the Pescadores, Paracel, and Spratly Islands and to property in the other islands referred to in Article 3 … It would appear that in [the draft treaty's] present form the second sentence of Article 4(a) might afford Communist China a valid claim over that territory were it to sign and ratify this Treaty." Dulles, *Memorandum for the Secretary of Defense*, Japanese Peace Treaty, Foreign Relations of the United States, Asia and the

Pacific, Vol.VI, 1951 (Washington, DC: United States Government Printing Office), p. 1157.

22 See John J. Tkacik, Jr., *Taiwan's "Unsettled" International Status: Preserving U.S. Options in the Pacific*, Heritage Backgrounder, No. 2146 (June 19, 2008) at p. 6, www.heritage.org/asia/report/taiwans-unsettled-international-status-preserving-us-options-the-pacific. To this day, the US does not accept or reject the claim that Taiwan is a part of China, as part of its "One China" policy, and, under this pretext, claims its intrusion into cross-straits affairs is technically not an interference in the internal affairs of China.

23 *Treaty of Peace and Friendship between Japan and the People's Republic of China*, August 12, 1978, available at: www.mofa.go.jp/region/asia-paci/china/treaty78.html

24 *The United Nations Convention on the Law of the Sea (A Historical Perspective)*, Originally prepared for the International Year of the Ocean, 1998, available at: www.un.org/depts/los/convention_agreements/convention_historical_perspective.htm

25 This is not to argue that the LOSC has been uniformly negative. Far from it indeed. In a number of areas, LOS-constituted courts ranging from the rights and obligations of states in areas of overlapping claims (provisional measures) to necessary law enforcement requirements for fulfillment in the case of hot pursuits in exclusive maritime zones to the three-stage process for delimitation of maritime boundaries, LOSC and LOS-constituted courts have provided predictability and certainty to maritime interactions among member states. These are worthy achievements.

26 Between 1970 and 1980, the Philippines occupied Nanshan Island, Flat Island, Thitu Island, Loaita Island, Northeast Cay, West York Island, Panata, and Commodore Reef. Between 1973 and 1978, Vietnam occupied Nam Yit Island, Southwest Cay, Sandy Cay, Spratly Island, Sin Cowe Island, Amboyna Cay, Grierson Reef (a sand bank sometimes called East Sin Cowe Island), Central Reef, and Pearson Reef. Malaysia occupied Swallow Reef and Ardasier Reef in 1977 and Mariveles Reef in 1979.

27 *Economics Survey of Asia and the Far East.* Publication. 4th edn. Vol. XIX. Bangkok: United Nations, 1969. Print.

28 For a concurring view, see Yann-huei Song and Stein Tonnesson, "The Impact of the Law of the Sea Convention on Conflict and Conflict Management in the South China Sea," 44 *Ocean Development and International Law* (2013) at p. 239.

29 David Anderson and Youri van Logchem, "Rights and Obligations in Areas of Overlapping Maritime Claims," in *The South China Sea Disputes and Law of the Sea*, edited by S. Jayakumar, Tommy Koh and Robert Beckman, Cheltenham: Edward Elgar Publishing (2014) at p. 222.

30 An EEZ is a *sui generis* maritime zone in which certain exclusive coastal state rights co-habit with user states' high seas rights. There is no specific order of priority with respect to these coastal and user states' rights in the EEZ nor can residual rights, i.e. those not specifically attributed to the coastal or user state, be appropriated by any one side. On this point, see Erik Franckx, "American and Chinese Views on Navigational Rights of Warships," 10 *Chinese Journal of International Law* (2011) at pp. 200–1.

31 See Maung Maung, "The Burma-China Boundary Settlement," *Asian Survey* 1 (1961), p. 39. See also Daphne Whittam, "The Sino-Burmese Boundary Treaty," *Pacific Affairs* 34 (Summer 1961), p. 175.

32 On this point, see M. Taylor Fravel, *Strong Borders, Secure Nation: Cooperation and Conflict in China's Territorial Disputes* (Princeton University Press, Princeton, NJ, 2008).

33 See Article 281 (1) of UNCLOS. UNCLOS, 1833 U.N.T.S. 397, adopted in Montego Bay, Jamaica, on December 10, 1982, entered into force on November 16, 1994.

34 Other instances of previous cases where Article 281 has been considered include: *Barbados v. Trinidad and Tobago, Land Reclamation in and around the Straits of Johor* and the *Southern Bluefin Tuna Arbitration.*

35 See Article 281 (1) of UNCLOS.

36 The text of Article 288 (4) reads as: *In the event of a dispute as to whether a court or tribunal has jurisdiction, the matter shall be settled by decision of that court or tribunal.* UNCLOS, 1833 U.N.T.S. 397, adopted in Montego Bay, Jamaica, on December 10, 1982, entered into force on November 16, 1994.

37 At first blush, Article 288(4) would appear to be a common norm in international courts. Article 36(6) of the International Court of Justice also employs almost-identical language empowering the court to determine its own jurisdiction – a common concept in private international law known as *competence-competence*. The relative youth of LOSC-constituted Annex VII courts however has ensured that Article 288(4) of part XV, paired with Article 281(1), has incentivized enterprising judges to lower the bar to find jurisdictional competence, and thereby self-indulgently stretch the perimeter of law into what should wholly have been the realm of power, politics and political compromise.

38 See Seokwoo Lee and Nong Hong, *Chinese Perspectives on the Philippines-China Arbitration Case in the South China Sea*, Vol. 20, No. 2 (2013) at p. 178, http://chinaus-icas.org/wp-content/uploads/2016/03/LeeHong-Chinese-Perspectives-on-the-Philippines-China-Arbitration-Case-in-the-South-China-Sea.pdf

39 *Democratic Republic of Timor-Leste v. Australia*, Decision on Australia's Objections to Competence, September 19, 2016, available at: https://pcacases.com/web/sendAttach/1921

40 *Treaty on Certain Maritime Arrangements in the Timor Sea (CMATS)*, Australian Treaty Series, Canberra (2006). Available at: www.austlii.edu.au/au/other/dfat/treaties/2007/12.html. The treaty was terminated earlier this year.

41 *Democratic Republic of Timor-Leste v. Australia*, p. 14, para. 59.

42 *Democratic Republic of Timor-Leste v. Australia*, p. 14, para. 59.

43 *Democratic Republic of Timor-Leste v. Australia*, p. 15, para. 59.

44 *Democratic Republic of Timor-Leste v. Australia*, p. 15, para. 62.

45 *Democratic Republic of Timor-Leste v. Australia*, p. 16, para. 64.

46 Again, this is not to argue that wise judgements have not been rendered. See endnote 25.

47 For a comprehensive summary of the academic literature on the island/rock Article 121(3) debate, see Clive R. Symmons, "Maritime Zones from islands and rocks," in *The South China Sea Disputes and Law of the Sea*, edited by S. Jayakumar, Tommy Koh and Robert Beckman, Cheltenham: Edward Elgar Publishing (2014) pp. 55–120.

48 *Nicaragua v Colombia*, Award of the International Court of Justice, November 19, 2012, available at: www.icj-cij.org/files/case-related/124/124-20121119-JUD-01-00-EN.pdf

49 See *Nicaragua v Colombia*, p. 645, para. 37.

50 On this point, see Tullio Treves, "Maritime delimitation and offshore features" in *The South China Sea Disputes and Law of the Sea*, edited by S. Jayakumar, Tommy Koh and Robert Beckman, Cheltenham: Edward Elgar Publishing (2014) at p. 134.

51 See *Philippines v. China*, p. 207 and 230, paras. 487 and 549 in particular.

52 See *Philippines v. China*, p. 227, para. 542.

53 The Tribunal's interpretation bears utterly little resemblance to the letter or spirit of Article 121 and situates at the outer end of the academic literature on the subject. The provision lays down no requirement – implicit or other – that the "human" presence referenced be an exclusively civilian one; that the "habitation" on the feature be a "non-transient one who have chosen to stay and reside"; that the feature must furnish an abstract "proper standard" of lifestyle; or that the feature's entitlement was exclusively intended for a beneficial indigenous population. And while the object and purpose of Article 121 was indeed intended to not enable a tiny feature to generate a disproportionately large entitlement to maritime space, there is nothing in the official record of the Law of the Sea negotiations to suggest that a "stable group or

community" standard was envisioned to qualify a feature as a full-entitled island that can "sustain human habitation." The Tribunal's interpretation is also at variance with discernable state practice, as others have observed.

54 There is a formidable literature associated with the nine dash line. See amongst others Li Jinming and Li Dexia, "The Dotted Line on the Chinese Map of the South China Sea: A Note," 34 *Ocean Development and International Law*, pp. 287–95 (2003); Gao Zhiguo and Jia Bing Bing, "The Nine-Dash Line in the South China Sea: History, Status, and Implications," 107 *The American Journal of International Law*, pp. 98–124 (2013); and Robert Beckman, "The U.N. Convention on the Law of the Sea and the Maritime Disputes in the South China Sea," 107 *The American Journal of International Law*, pp. 142–63 (2013).

55 People's Republic of China, "*Note Verbale to the Secretary-General of the United Nations – CML/17/2009*," (May 7, 2009), available at: www.un.org/Depts/los/clcs_new/submissions_files/mysvnm33_09/chn_2009re_mys_vnm_e.pdf

56 Malaysia-Socialist Republic of Vietnam, "*Joint Submission to the Commission on the Limits of the Continental Shelf Pursuant to Article 76, paragraph 8 of the United Nations Convention on the Law of the Sea 1982 in Respect of the Southern Part of the South China Sea, Executive Summary*" (May 2009), available at: www.un.org/Depts/los/clcs_new/submissions_files/mysvnm33_09/mys_vnm2009excutivesummary.pdf

57 Socialist Republic of Vietnam, "*Submission to the Commission on the Limits of the Continental Shelf Pursuant to Article 76, paragraph 8 of the United Nations Convention on the Law of the Sea 1982, Partial Submission in Respect of Vietnam's Extended Continental Shelf: North Area (VNM-N), Executive Summary*" (April 2009), available at: www.un.org/Depts/los/clcs_new/submissions_files/vnm37_09/vnm2009n_executivesummary.pdf

58 Manila had pleaded in its memorial to the court that "China's maritime claims in the South China Sea based on its so-called 'nine dash' line are contrary to UNCLOS and invalid."

59 The Commission on the Limits of the Continental Shelf (CLCS) is a LOSC-linked scientific and technical body of experts, which is tasked to inspect and make recommendations on the submitted national claims over their respective extended continental shelf limits.

60 US Secretary of State Hillary Clinton had in fact led this charge as early as July 2010 when she, along with five ASEAN foreign ministers, rose to voice her country's concerns against China's assertiveness in the South China Sea at the 17th ASEAN Regional Forum (ARF) meeting in Hanoi. Ms. Clinton declared that the US had a "national interest" in freedom of navigation, and respect for international law in the South China Sea – the first time that a US Secretary of State had delivered a statement on the U.S. position at an official regional foreign ministers gathering. The ARF meeting in Hanoi was widely recorded as one of the rarer instances where the US, with its favored ASEAN partners, had cornered China at a regional summit meeting.

61 US State Department, "China: Maritime Claims in the South China Sea," *Limits in the Seas No. 143* (December 5, 2014), online: www.state.gov/documents/organization/234936.pdf

62 Tran Truong Thuy, "The Declaration on the Conduct of Parties in the South China Sea and Developing Maritime Energy Resources," in *Maritime Energy Resources in Asia: Energy and Geopolitics*, edited by Clive Schofield, NBR Special Report #55 (December 2011) at p. 176.

63 Vietnam, Laos, Cambodia and Myanmar had not yet been admitted to ASEAN at the time.

64 Christopher Chung, "Southeast Asia and the South China Sea dispute," in *Security and International Politics in the South China Sea: Towards a cooperative management regime*, edited by Sam Bateman and Ralf Emmers, London: Routledge (2008) at p. 100.

65 On this point, see Yann-huei Song and Stein Tonnesson, "The Impact of the Law of the Sea Convention on Conflict and Conflict Management in the South China Sea," 44 *Ocean Development and International Law* (2013) at p. 247.
66 Song and Tonnesson, "The Impact of the Law of the Sea Convention …" p. 248.
67 This is not to argue that easing cycles have all been smooth sailing or even that the 2002–8 cycle did not witness its fair share of frictions. For a Vietnamese view of China's unilateral acts during this period, see Nguyen Hong Thao, "The Declaration on the Conduct of Parties in the South China Sea: A Vietnamese perspective, 2002–2007," in *Security and International Politics in the South China Sea: Towards a cooperative management regime*, edited by Sam Bateman and Ralf Emmers, London: Routledge (2008) pp. 207–21.
68 Tran Truong Thuy, "The Declaration on the Conduct of Parties in the South China Sea …" pp. 192–94.
69 *Set Aside Dispute and Pursue Joint Development*, Ministry of Foreign Affairs of the People's Republic of China, available at: www.fmprc.gov.cn/mfa_eng/ziliao_665539/3602_665543/3604_665547/t18023.shtml
70 See Richard Javad Heydarian, "Duterte's Populist Project Grinds on," in *East Asia Forum* (May 10, 2017) available at: www.eastasiaforum.org/2017/05/10/dutertes-populist-project-grinds-on/
71 *Japan-China Joint Press Statement – Cooperation between Japan and China in the East China Sea*, Japan Ministry of Foreign Affairs, available at: www.mofa.go.jp/files/000091726.pdf
72 As per the "dual track" policy, China and the claimant states should handle disputes bilaterally through negotiations and China and ASEAN as a whole should safeguard and maintain peace and stability in the South China Sea. Nothing in the "dual track" policy precludes China from creatively bringing its maritime rights-related practices in the South China Sea into compliance with aspects of the arbitration award during the course of bilateral negotiations with the Duterte government
73 Joel H. Samuels, "*Condominium Arrangements in International Practice: Reviving an Abandoned Concept of Boundary Dispute Resolution*," 29 *Mich. J. Int'l L.* 727 (2008). Available at: http://repository.law.umich.edu/mjil/vol29/iss4/3
74 Mark Valencia, "Policy Forum 11–41: A Code of Conduct for the South China Sea: What Should It Contain?", *NAPSNet Policy Forum* (December 8, 2011) available at: https://nautilus.org/napsnet/napsnet-policy-forum/a-code-of-conduct-for-the-south-china-sea-what-should-it-contain/

2 The East China Sea

Sea of regional and global confrontation

Reinhard Drifte

Introduction

All three states bordering the East China Sea (ECS) – the People's Republic of China (PRC), Japan, and the Republic of Korea (ROK) – ratified United Nations Convention on the Law of the Sea (UNCLOS) in 1996, yet no maritime border has been delimited among any of the three states despite the obligation under the Convention.[1] This failure is at the bottom of many problems in the ECS with regard to political, economic, environmental, and security issues which partly fall within the jurisdiction of UNCLOS. Since the geography of the ECS does not allow any of the littoral states to claim a 200 nautical miles (nm) Exclusive Economic Zone (EEZ), there are conflicting proposals of applying either the median line or the continental shelf principle. In the northern sector of the ECS, the EEZ claims of all three states overlap in a tri-junction and would require a trilateral negotiation process. An agreement between China and the ROK is notably difficult because of conflicting positions on whose continental shelf lies a submerged feature (Ieodo for Korea, Suyan Rock for China) which has a considerable impact on where to delimit the maritime border. In addition, Japan and China are disputing sovereignty over the Senkaku/Diaoyu Islands which is an additional obstacle for an agreement about the Japan–China maritime border in the southern sector.[2] Despite these unresolved maritime borders, all three states have concluded fisheries agreements among each other which rely on interim delimitations without prejudice to any final border agreement. However, this has not prevented frequent confrontations of Japanese and ROK coast guards with Chinese fishermen. Casualties occurred in clashes between the ROK coast guards and Chinese fishermen in the adjacent Yellow Sea. Interests in the hydrocarbon and seabed resources of the ECS are further current or future sources of conflict. The territorial dispute over the Senkaku/Diaoyu Islands is not only the most serious flash point, particularly since the incidents in 2010 and 2012, but it also draws attention to the role of the United States in the region. The United States (US) is a security partner of Japan and the ROK and it has a considerable military, notably maritime presence in this region. The issues of maritime border delimitation, freedom of navigation, and the UNCLOS objective of a stable ocean regime have therefore also to be seen against the background of the increasing regional as well as global US–China rivalry. Finally, the management of disputes in the ECS has already now an impact on the perception and handling of disputes in the South China Sea (SCS). As a result of this complex situation, the security environment of the East China Sea has become rather tense and volatile, with the coastal states' coast guards confronting each other, while their naval and air forces are hovering in the background.

This chapter gives an overview of the various issues as far as they are relevant to UNCLOS, and investigates to what extent the UNCLOS regime has been adhered to by the coastal states, and has been helpful or not to guide the concerned states to deal with their different interests. While UNCLOS defines the rights and responsibilities of states with regard to the world's oceans and their use, providing also a dispute settlement mechanism, it is not concerned with sovereignty issues. The latter has to be addressed through agreement between the concerned parties or submitted to international arbitration, notably the International Court of Justice (ICJ). The territorial dispute over the Senkaku/Diaoyu Islands will therefore only be touched to the extent that it affects UNCLOS issues. The Convention has created a clear nomenclature which should help to define issues and conclude agreements within its wide-ranging scope. In this way UNCLOS provides an example of an internationally agreed framework for how to delimit maritime borders but it still leaves considerable leeway for interpretation by the concerned parties. Of particular relevance is the stipulation that, pending an agreement on the delimitation of the EEZ (Article 74,3) or Continental Shelf (Article 83,3), nothing should be done by any party that might jeopardize a final delimitation while provisional arrangements of a practical nature are encouraged – as long as they are made without prejudice to the final delimitation. As we will see, various provisional agreements have been concluded between all three coastal states in the ECS. However, extensive rights and vagueness regarding certain issues in the Convention have whetted the appetite for maximum demands and made agreements in certain cases more difficult. In the end, this article has to conclude that resolving the various problems threatening the maritime order of the ECS depends on the political will of the three states. Failure will not only endanger regional and global peace and stability, and weaken UNCLOS, but will also deprive all concerned parties benefiting from the resources of the ECS.

Border delimitation

The maritime border delimitation in the ECS requires the resolution of various differences among the three littoral states. As we will see, UNCLOS does not provide sufficient guidance to come easily to a resolution and sometimes even adds to the complexity of the involved issues.

The most difficult delimitation is between Japan and China. Here is a summary of the various necessary steps towards a resolution: Initially, there would have to be an agreement on the method of determining basepoints and baselines from the coasts of each state as the starting point for delimiting the Territorial

Waters (TW), the EEZ, and the continental shelf (CS). However, all three states have been rather liberal in interpreting the relevant international regulations on the method to do so and there are some disputes. Notably, the US government considers some of the baselines against the regulations in UNCLOS.[3] Only after a Japan–China agreement on the sovereignty over the Senkaku/Diaoyu Islands is achieved can the foundation be laid for a delimitation of the EEZ border in the southern sector of the ECS. Japan and China will then have to agree on which principle to apply for drawing the EEZ and CS border: Japan demands the application of the principle of the median or equidistance line which would provide equity in the sense that no state can achieve a 200 nm EEZ area since the ECS's width is less than 400 nm. China, however, wants to apply the natural prolongation of the CS principle on the basis of having the longer continuous coast (whereas on the Japanese side there is only a chain of islands), a greater population, and a topography which can be interpreted as favourable to China (the latter refers to the so-called Okinawa Trough). Both interpretations refer to different historical precedents although in various judicial precedents, the principle of the equidistance or median line seems to be given nowadays more weight even if qualified with some adaptations to specific circumstances.[4] If China's choice would carry the day, the Senkaku/Diaoyu Islands would be on China's CS and strengthen China's sovereignty claim, but in case of adopting the median line principle (and assuming Japan's sovereignty claim would be accepted by China), both countries would have to agree on how to draw the baselines around the islands. In the northern sector, all three coastal states would have to agree on which principle to apply.[5]

Today, we are far from an agreement on these various issues and there are uncertainties even deriving from UNCLOS, e.g. how to define the CS based on Article 76 of UNCLOS.[6] While no agreement has been reached on the maritime border, Japan is not only demanding the median line as the maritime border, but since 2004 insists as a basis for negotiations on a zone of up to 200 nm according to Article 76 until a final agreement has been reached.[7] China is demanding not only a 200 nm EEZ, but a zone up to the Okinawa Trough, based on the principle of the extended CS, but without having provided so far any coordinates. Although pending an agreement on the delimitation of the EEZ (Article 74,3) or Continental Shelf (Article 83,3), nothing should be done to impede a future agreement on the maritime border. China has, since the 1990s, proceeded with the exploration and now exploitation of oil and gas reserves on China's side of the Japan-proposed median line. Beijing argues that this area is clearly within its EEZ despite the lack of an agreement with either Japan or the ROK. However, Japan seemed to have initially at least tacitly agreed with China's stance, even providing loans through the Asian Development Bank (ADB) and directly through its *Export-Import Bank* for two oil and gas pipelines linking these fields to China's coast.[8] On the other hand, Japan complied with the requirement of UNCLOS and did not allow any company to explore for hydrocarbons on its side of the median line. However, with the increase of China's exploration activities getting as close as 5 kilometres (km) to the median line (and Japan's concerns that China may actually tap oil and gas fields straddling this line), Tokyo started to protest China's activities (see below for the 2000 Prior Notification Agreement) and in 2004 conducted its own one-off survey on the Japanese side of the median line which, for security reasons, was not followed up by extraction activities. China immediately reacted after the announcement of the survey and warned the Japanese to 'act with caution' in what it considered to be China's EEZ. It was even reported that a Chinese surveillance vessel, and later two warships, tried to chase away the survey ship commissioned by Japan.[9]

China–ROK negotiations over the EEZ border have so far failed to narrow the gap between the two sides, notably regarding the submerged feature of what is called Ieodo by the Korean side and Suyan Rock by the Chinese side. Whereas Korea bases its proposal for the delimitation on the median line principle, and argues that the rock is on its CS, China holds the opposing view of locating the rock on the natural prolongation of its CS. In the meantime, both sides claim EEZ jurisdiction over the rock and are deploying their coast guard vessels to the area.[10]

During the post-1996 renegotiation process of a new Japan–ROK fisheries agreement (see below), the latter tried to use these negotiations as a lever to come to an agreement on the maritime border. However, this attempt failed since Korea wanted an agreement covering the borders in the Sea of Japan as well as in the ECS. Since no agreement could be reached on the disputed Dokdo/Takeshima Islands in the Sea of Japan, the negotiations were aborted. In short, an agreement on the Japan–ROK ECS border is *de facto* hostage to the Japan–ROK territorial dispute in the Sea of Japan.

The most serious roadblock for the delimitation of the maritime boundary in the southern sector of the ECS is the territorial dispute over the Senkaku/Diaoyu Islands. Japan and China both claim the islands, and Japan requests an EEZ for them which would bring the maritime border even closer to the Chinese coast.[11] Moreover, Taiwan's interests would also have to be accommodated in the southern sector and Japan would probably be more inclined to take these interests into consideration than the PRC.

UNCLOS only provides (Article 83,1) on the delimitation of the CS between states with opposite or adjacent coast, that the delimitation should be effected by 'agreement based on international law… in order to achieve an equitable solution'. The following guidance (Article 83,2) about dispute settlement in case of failing to agree is not applicable to China and South Korea because these two states opted out of the UNCLOS dispute settlement system.

The Committee on the Limit of the Continental Shelf (CLCS) was established by UNCLOS to provide technical advice considering the calculation of the CS. In accordance with UNCLOS (Article 76,8) China and Korea submitted claims for their extended CS in the ECS to the CLCS. Since China's and the ROK's submissions in 2009 and 2012 both extended the CS claims into Japan's EEZ, Japan protested these submissions and demanded a delimitation according to Article 83. In its 2012 submission, China had advanced its claim even further into the 200 nm zone of the ROK, and extended its claim also up to the Okinawa

Trough.[12] Japan and the ROK both protested against the Chinese claims, and Japan even excluded the possibility of the CLCS's recommendation being given in case all disputants agree on the Commission to act as is allowed under its regulations. But in any case, the CLCS cannot make any recommendation in case there is a maritime border or territorial dispute among the concerned states which throws the whole issue back to the three coastal states.[13]

Article 17 of UNCLOS states that ships of all states 'enjoy the right of innocent passage through the territorial sea' of other states, subject to certain conditions and definitions as specified in subsequent articles. Under Article 32, warships and other government ships operating for non-commercial purposes enjoy immunities in the TW of other countries and can therefore not be forcibly removed by the coastal state but only be asked to leave immediately if they do not comply with the laws and regulations of the coastal state (Article 30). In addition, although Article 19 defines innocent passage ('Passage is innocent so long as it is not prejudicial to the peace, good order or security of the coastal state'), it is often difficult to know whether a ship is carrying out a survey, collecting intelligence, or engaging in any kind of military operation rather than just passing. The higher the mutual distrust, the more the coastal state will assume a contravention of innocent passage.

This issue is particularly troublesome in the case of Chinese Coast Guard ships which are now regularly cruising in the TW of the Senkaku/Diaoyu Islands to reinforce the PRC's sovereignty claim.[14] As Miyoshi Masahiro has pointed out, from a Japanese perspective, the passage of Chinese government vessels as it is now occurs in the TW of the disputed islands is not 'innocent' since they exercise an official duty and their passage is not 'continuous and expeditious' as Article 18 (2) defines innocent passage. However, Japanese law and regulations do not specify countermeasures, whereas Chinese domestic law gives authorities the right to order a foreign ship to leave the territorial sea immediately when deemed in violation of Chinese regulations 'rather than when its passage is deemed not innocent'.[15] In practice both sides have so far shown self-restraint, with the Japanese Coast Guard merely asking the Chinese Coast Guard vessels to leave the TW and the Chinese side refuting this demand by claiming that they are in Chinese TW. Japan's self-restraint is also demonstrated by the fact that its Coast Guard never used water cannons against a Chinese government vessel. However, they did use water cannons in September 2012 against Taiwanese patrol boats which were trying to protect a Taiwanese fleet of 70 fishing boats outside the TW of the disputed islands.[16] Japan's reaction against foreign fishing vessels in the TW of the islands is different: The September 2010 incident occurred when the Japanese Coast Guard apprehended the crew of a Chinese fishing vessel 27 km from Kubajima because it had been operating within 12 km of Kubajima. When chased by the Japanese Coast Guard, the Chinese fishing vessel rammed two of its ships when trying to flee.[17]

There is also a contrast between China's interpretation of Article 58 which does not allow foreign military activities in its EEZ and that of the US which does – giving rise to tensions in the ECS. The US is also contesting China demanding permission even for passage through its territorial waters which the US considers contrary to the principle of 'innocent passage'. The Chinese interpretations are in a minority and led to incidents between US naval vessels and PRC vessels in the ECS in March 2001, September 2002, March 2009, and May 2009, as well as two others incidents in the SCS.[18] In order to make its point of 'innocent passage' and 'military activities in the EEZ', the US navy conducts so-called Freedom of Navigation Operations (FONOPs), including in the ECS.[19] Korea also demands prior notification for foreign military or government vessels to enter its TW which are similarly contested by the US through FONOPS, as it contests Korea's straight baselines.[20]

Submarines are required (Article 20 of UNCLOS) to navigate through the TW on the surface and show their flags. Chinese submarines regularly pass through the Japanese island chain into the Pacific Ocean which is legal if done according to this article, although not welcome by Japan. However, there was at least one reported incident between China and Japan when in November 2004, a submerged Chinese nuclear submarine went through Japan's territorial waters in the Sakishima Gunto. In response to Japan's protest, the Chinese side explained that the submarine had entered Japanese territorial waters by 'mistake' and 'regretted' this incident.[21] This incident occurred against the background of rising bilateral tensions in the ECS as a result of China's oil and gas exploitation.

In this context one has to mention the issue of the Air Defence Identification Zone (ADIZ). Like the system of Flight Information Zones, ADIZ is outside of the UNCLOS framework, and ADIZ is not even subject of an international convention but simply historical practice. According to UNCLOS Article 58, all states enjoy freedom of navigation as well as freedom of overflight within EEZs.[22] Moreover, the establishment of an ADIZ has no legal implication for territorial and maritime borders. However, when the Chinese government decreed on 23 November 2013 an ADIZ in the ECS, the Senkaku/Diaoyu Islands were inside the zone but marked with a red circle, they were assumed to be Chinese territory. Moreover, the zone overlaps with the Japanese ADIZ.[23] The Korean side was also upset because the zone included the air space around the Ieodo/Suyan feature. The Chinese ADIZ was widely interpreted as a desire to reinforce China's claim to the disputed islands and to the sea around the Ieodo/Suyan rock. Also, unusual for an ADIZ is the Chinese stipulation that it includes all aircraft (even those which are only transiting through the ADIZ) whereas normally it applies only to aircraft heading for the state that has proclaimed the ADIZ. The threat of military countermeasures in the text of the decree ('China's armed forces will adopt defensive emergency measures to respond to aircraft that do not cooperate in the identification or refuse to follow the instructions') has further heightened the possibility of a military clash.[24] China has, of course, a right to establish an ADIZ, as had been done by the ROK and Japan in the 1950s. But the above peculiarities, the timing and the lack of proper prior bilateral consultation were not seen as conducive to establishing order in the ECS. Moreover, it started an unhelpful speculation about China's future intentions regarding an

ADIZ in the SCS. According to a Japanese newspaper report based on a leaked document, there was apparently a meeting of Japanese and Chinese officials in 2010 discussing China's intention but there was no proper follow-up.[25]

Practical arrangements in the absence of agreed EEZ borders

As mentioned above, UNCLOS recommends in Article 74,3 (EEZ) and Article 83,3 (CS) that in the absence of agreed maritime borders, arrangements of a provisional nature without prejudice to any final delimitation should be made. There are examples where such practical arrangements have been made by the littoral states in order to benefit from the riches of the ECS. Such provisional arrangements have so far been limited to fisheries and hydrocarbon resources, but ad hoc agreements to deal with incidents shall also be included in this context. The following provides an overview of these arrangements between the three states to illustrate the difficulties involved and their impact on the clause of 'without prejudice to any final delimitation'.

The oldest such arrangement is an agreement between Japan and the ROK relating to the joint development of hydrocarbon resources. However, when both countries had drafted in 1974 the *Agreement between Japan and the Republic of Korea Concerning the Establishment of Boundary in the Northern Part of the Continental Shelf Adjacent to the Two Countries* and the *Agreement between Japan and the Republic of Korea concerning the Joint Development of the Southern Part. of the Continental Shelf Adjacent to the Two Countries*, China objected vigorously to the latter which refers to the ECS, and insisted on consultation without referring to any particular claim of its own.[26] As a result Japan deferred ratification of the agreements until June 1978 when it ratified the agreements without regard to China's continued opposition. Japan and South Korea conducted seven explorations on three sites between 1980 and 1986. No economically viable fields were discovered and they abandoned the search.[27] It is obvious that such a provisional agreement which ignored the protest of China could not be concluded or implemented today when China is much more assertive. The early ending of the operational implications saved all states from a larger confrontation, while also showing that unclear claims and the insistence on bilateral negotiations for border delimitations in cases concerning more than two states simply results in stalemate. The agreement for the Southern Part is valid until 2028 and it will be interesting to see whether the two parties will revise it. It can be argued whether the agreement is actually still valid as it was concluded prior to UNCLOS which was finalised in 1982.

The agreement demonstrates that compromises in the stance of Japan and Korea can help to achieve a provisional agreement. While Korea insisted on the natural prolongation of the continental shelf, Japan wanted to apply the equidistance principle. In order to overcome the deadlock, Korea disclaimed in the agreement the rights that it would have under unilateral development of the area stretching down to the Okinawa Trough, while Japan disclaimed half the right to develop the area up to the median line. As explained by Kanehara Atsuko, the 'concept principle of natural prolongation as the basis for entitlement to a continental shelf had a predominant effect on the location of the joint development zone'.[28] Of course, the agreement was only provisional and contains a provision (Article 28) denying any prejudice of the agreement to the ultimate sovereign rights of any part of the Joint Development Zone. This partial breach by both countries in their stance could be constructively applied to a future border agreement between Japan and Korea as well as between Japan and China.

Fisheries agreements under the UNCLOS regime

The ratification by all three states of UNCLOS in 1996 necessitated the revision of the bilateral fisheries agreement between them. There had been none between China and the ROK. Under Article 123 (a) of UNCLOS, states bordering an enclosed or semi-enclosed sea, should 'coordinate the management, conservation, exploration and exploitation of the living resources of the sea'. Concluding such agreements without having agreed maritime borders was one major obstacle, and the creation of complex fishery zones became necessary. All agreements contain a clause that they are provisional and have no legal implications for a later delimitation of maritime borders.

The new Japan–ROK fisheries agreement entered into effect in 1999. The two sides agreed to use the 1974 Northern Continental Shelf Boundary Agreement as a fisheries boundary. For the ECS waters not covered by that agreement, they set up a joint fishing zone. The two sides could not agree on the name of this joint fishing zone (nor for the joint fishing zone established in the Sea of Japan). Nor could the two parties agree on the specific coordinates of the southern limits of this joint fishing zone because Japan had already concluded a fisheries agreement with China (see below) which partially extended into the area demanded by Korea. Despite the Japan–Korea agreement to disagree on the coordinates for this area, China expressed the position that it did not recognise this joint Japan–ROK fishing zone which partly reached into the China–Japan fisheries area. The complexities of the Japan–Korea fisheries agreement also had negative implications for the management and conservation of fishing resources.[29] The fisheries agreement was furthermore made very difficult because it also covered fisheries in the Sea of Japan where the two parties have a territorial dispute as mentioned above.

China and the ROK concluded a fisheries agreement in 2001 which is even more complex with the creation of several different categories of fishing zones. At China's insistence it has no dispute settlement mechanism. The major part covers the Yellow Sea, but it reaches into the northern part of the ECS as well. However, this China–ROK agreement has not prevented serious incidents in the adjacent Yellow Sea as there is a dispute about the exact provisional delimitation.[30] Initially, the two states wanted to delimit the EEZ as well, but in 1997 they had reached a deadlock and had to abandon this intention.[31] Another difficulty was disagreement over the baselines.

The bilateral Japan–China fisheries Agreement was a major achievement but many difficulties had to be overcome. Although signed in 1997, it took until

2000 to enact it after several issues for fishing operations had been resolved. The Japanese government was even criticised by some domestic constituencies for having used in the Agreement, the Chinese name *Dong Hai* (East Sea) for the ECS, rather than the Japanese name *Higashi Shinakai* (East China Sea).[32] Initially, China wanted to discuss the EEZ delimitation but relented when the talks reached a deadlock and both agreed to only negotiate a fisheries agreement. The territorial dispute is excluded by the stipulation that in the waters around the Senkaku/Diaoyu Islands south of the 27th parallel, neither state will interfere in the other's fishing activities, thus creating a free fishing zone. To overcome the lack of agreed maritime borders north of the 27th parallel, the waters were designated as the Japan–China Provisional Measures Zone (PMZ) where each side can only control the fishing activities of its own state. A joint fishery committee defines permitted operations.[33]

While the 2000 Japan–China Fisheries Agreement has circumvented the territorial dispute as well as the absence of an agreed maritime border, its implementation still raises various issues. First, the Agreement and the exchange of a Note Verbale did not prevent a dispute of jurisdiction in the TW of the Senkaku/Diaoyu Islands. Although there was a political understanding that Chinese fishermen should not enter the TW of the islands, both sides took steps over the following years to assert their jurisdiction in the TW.[34] In December 2008 two vessels of the China Marine Surveillance (CMS, now the Chinese Coast Guard, CCG) entered the territorial waters around the Senkaku/Diaoyu Islands for the first time in an apparent move to strengthen China's claim to the islands, and twice in 2011.[35] The CMS had started in 1983 with patrols for environmental protection. When it became an agency within the State Ocean Administration (SOA) in 1998, it became responsible for the protection of China's maritime rights and interests. The start of entering the TW around the Senkaku/Diaoyu Islands in 2008 is probably linked to a new provision in the same year which obliged the CMS with regular patrols in areas claimed under Chinese jurisdiction.[36] More Chinese incursions into the islands' TW occurred after the 2010 incident when the Japanese Coast Guard (JCG) apprehended a Chinese fishing boat in the TW. Since the Japanese state acquired the islands from a private Japanese owner in 2012, the CCG has been regularly patrolling the TW and EEZ around the disputed islands. Second, it has been argued that the Joint Fisheries Committee does not work to maintain a sustainable development of fishery stocks, and this applies also to the other two fisheries agreement.[37] Third, Korea protested the Japan–China Agreement when it turned out that there was an overlap with its claimed fishing zone as mentioned above. Finally, the Agreement may arguably have an impact on the future EEZ delimitation. Although Article 12 of the Agreement contains a clause which emphasizes that nothing in the Agreement will prejudice either party's claims to the EEZ or the CS, Manicom argues that the PMZ has implications for a future boundary delimitation. The PMZ was delimited by a distance from each party's baseline of 52 nm, thus indicating two areas of the ECS that – according to Manicom – are not in dispute, that is, the area between each party's coastal baselines and the nearest boundary of the PMZ.

He argues this could mean that China has recognised Japan's EEZ claim to a distance of 52 nm offshore, in contrast to its official demand to the outer limits of the continental shelf.[38]

The 2008 Japan–China understanding on hydrocarbon exploitation

Since 2004, negotiations took place between China and Japan which aimed at making some headway on the delimitation of the EEZ maritime border as well as dealing with China's advances in extracting hydrocarbon resources to the west of the median line which China does not officially recognise.[39] During the negotiations, China tried to promote its EEZ border claim by proposing joint exploration between Japan's proposed median line and the Okinawa Trough, and its territorial claim by proposing joint exploration around the disputed islands. Japan was keen to keep the disputed islands out of the negotiations and to gain somehow Chinese recognition of its proposed median line by suggesting joint development in an area evenly divided by the median line and by including the various oil and gas fields being developed by China in an agreement. The outcome on the 18 June 2008 was an understanding (*ryokai* in Japanese; *gongshi* in Chinese) to cooperate in the ECS in order to turn it into a 'Sea of Peace, Cooperation and Friendship'. This cooperation – in the absence of an agreed-upon maritime border – was to be without prejudice to the legal position of either party. Without going into further details, the understanding did not lead to the desired aims of either party although a clearly defined sea area in the northern sector of the ECS for joint development partially straddles the median line. Due to the deteriorating political relationship and the contestation of the understanding by most Chinese specialists, the two sides did not only fail to come closer to the delimitation of their maritime border, but also failed to conclude a 'provisional arrangement of a practical nature' on some kind of cooperation on hydrocarbon exploitation.[40] Frustration on both sides has been growing since then: China is continuing with the exploration and extraction of an increasing number of oil/gas fields, and the Japanese ruling party is demanding that the prime minister speed up talks on concluding a treaty to realise the goals of the June 2008 understanding, and if the other side is unwilling will ask for international arbitration.[41]

Preventing and dealing with incidents

Incidents can lead to practical considerations overriding or softening of legal positions. One famous example between Japan and China was the sinking of a North Korean spy boat in December 2001 by Japan. After a fire exchange, the boat sank on the Chinese side of the Japan-claimed median line after having been discovered in Japan's EEZ and then been giving chase by the JCG. The boat was initially identified as a Chinese fishing vessel and since the JCG had the suspicion of illegal fishing, it was allowed under the Japanese Law of Fishery in the EEZ to inspect the vessel. The Japanese government recognised later in Diet interpellations the western side of the median line as the *de facto* Chinese EEZ (Kanehara uses the abbreviation of EZ) and as a result an agreement was reached with China for the Japanese authorities to lift the boat from the sea floor.[42] For the Japanese side, it was welcome that the Chinese government seemed to have implicitly recognised during the negotiations the existence of Japan's proposed median line.[43] It is unclear to this author what the legal implication of these *ad hoc* Japanese and Chinese positions are for the future of the delimitation of the EEZ border.

The 2001 Japan–China Agreement on Prior Notification was an attempt of avoiding incidents arising from Chinese survey ships in ECS waters near Japan while at the same time overcoming the lack of an agreed maritime border. In some respect it is a predecessor to the 2008 understanding which tried to deal more positively (i.e. through joint development) with issues arising from resource development rather than just preventing incidents. With the ongoing Chinese development of hydrocarbon resources in the 1990s in the ECS, an increasing number of so-called Chinese research vessels entered the Japanese side of the median line. While UNCLOS makes a difference between marine scientific surveys and resource surveys, this distinction was not clear with China using military and civilian vessels for multiple types of research on a single voyage and further complicated by the absence of agreed maritime borders.[44] These surveys occurred without prior consent by Japan as would be required under UNCLOS if the area had been part of Japan's EEZ. When challenged by the JCG, the Chinese side responded either that they were operating in the open sea, or conducting legitimate research in China's EEZ, or they simply ignored Japanese warnings. Since 1996, Chinese research vessels increasingly also entered the waters of the disputed islands. To reach a solution, six official rounds of talks were held from September 2000 to January 2001 and based on a verbal note (kojosho), a system of prior notification for ships of both countries engaging in scientific research took effect on 24 February 2001. The text of both sides refers to 'marine scientific research before the delimitation of the border is achieved'. In order to define the sea area despite the absence of agreed borders and China's non-recognition of the median line, the text refers to 'In maritime areas of interest to the Japanese side [and outside of the territorial waters]' (Nihon gawa ga kanshin wo yu suru suiiki de aru Nihonkoku no kinkai [ryokai wo nozoku]).[45] This geographic 'definition' obviously relies more on trust than on precision. But even despite this vagueness, both sides made clear that the agreement did not affect their respective position concerning the delineation of the maritime border. The agreement has not been very effective because it was voluntary and the implementation mechanism was weak. Moreover Japanese domestic laws were insufficient to police Chinese behaviour.[46] A further weak point is related to the vagueness of UNCLOS: the agreement speaks of oceanic scientific research but does not clarify whether this also applies to natural resources research, which was the main problem for Japan. Of course, it is often difficult to differentiate between marine scientific research, natural resources research, and military-related research as mentioned above. UNCLOS differentiates between marine and natural resources research: according to Article 56 paragraph 1, the coastal state has sovereign rights over exploring and exploiting the natural resources in its EEZ, but only jurisdiction (i.e. to regulate, authorise, and conduct marine research) over marine scientific research. In the end, this agreement did not effectively prevent Chinese research vessels from entering maritime areas of 'interest to the Japanese side' and thus reduce incidents, nor did it bring both sides closer to an agreement on their maritime border. There were also several occasions where Korean research vessels operating on the Japanese side of the Japan-proposed median line which were asked by the Japanese authorities to leave.[47] However, no equivalent Japan–ROK Prior Notification Agreement was ever negotiated.

In view of rising tensions in the ECS, Japan and China have started to negotiate a bilateral maritime and air communication mechanism.[48] While the agreement is likely to achieve only marginal success in avoiding incidents, its conclusion is at this moment still unknown because the two countries cannot agree on the area of application due to the lack of an agreed maritime border. Another attempt to manage incidents at sea at a regional level is the agreement in April 2014 by 21 Pacific-region navies, including Japan, China, and the US, for a Code for Unplanned Encounters at Sea (CUES). However, the agreement is non-binding, only regulates communication in 'unplanned encounters' – not behaviour, is not applicable to territorial waters, and does not cover fishing and government vessels.[49] Yet it is particularly the latter category of vessels which have been involved in confrontations in the ECS.

Conclusions

This chapter has focused on the delimitation of the maritime borders in the ECS because the failure to resolve this issue is at the bottom of many obstacles to achieve a regional order which has also global implications. China, Japan, and the ROK are still far apart from agreeing on their maritime borders, which raises or aggravates many political, economic, environmental, and security issues. As we have seen, this is due to their differences regarding the principle of equidistance or median line versus the CS where UNCLOS is not very clear, but also due to the existence of territorial disputes in the ECS (Senkaku/Diaoyu Islands) as well as outside of it (Dokto/Takeshima). Moreover, there is concern among the three states that any resolution method for any one of their existing territorial conflicts might set an unfavourable precedence (e.g. Japan's concern about any negative precedence value for the Southern Kuriles/Northern Territories dispute with Russia). Although Japan and Korea have come very close to a final delimitation in the northern sector of the ECS, a final resolution is held hostage by the demand to include the resolution of the Sea of Japan border as well. The method of drawing baselines by all three states is contested among the three as well as by some outside countries for not being consistent with UNCLOS.

Attempts to overcome the absence of agreed borders through provisional agreements of a practical nature as recommended by UNCLOS have been somewhat more successful in the case of fisheries agreements but not regarding the joint development and exploitation of hydrocarbon resources or the prevention of incidents accruing from Chinese and Korean research vessels in what Japan considers its EEZ. In the case of the China–Korea fisheries agreement, different interpretations of the geographic area and assertive Chinese fishing activities have led to serious incidents and casualties on both sides. These agreements with their complex provisional zones have also not led to a rapprochement of the positions regarding the various differences on how to delimit the maritime border. The three fisheries agreements do not adequately fulfil the obligation under UNCLOS Article 123 (a) to conserve the ECS's living resources. This could only be done by coordinating among all coastal states. The building of a weather station by South Korea on the submerged Ieodo/Suyan feature, and Chinese oil and gas production near the Japan's proposed median line are arguably not consistent with Article 83,3 which advises not 'to jeopardize or hamper the reaching of the final agreement' of EEZ borders.

To top it all, China and South Korea have opted out of Part XV of UNCLOS regarding dispute settlement: Korea made a statement on 18 April 2006, and China on 25 August 2006 that – in accordance with Article 298 of UNCLOS Part XV – they would not accept compulsory dispute settlement for the delimitation of sea borders.[50] Japan was considering in the past to invoke Part XV in its border dispute with China, but in the face of China's opposition renounced to do so.[51] The Chinese position regarding the Philippine's submission of its dispute with China in the SCS to an arbitral tribunal set up in accordance to annex 7 of UNCLOS does not give rise to optimism for international arbitration in the ECS. At such a junction, the final relevant obligation under the Convention is Article 283 which is, however, held hostage to rigid positions held by all three coastal states:

1. When a dispute arises between States Parties concerning the interpretation or application of this Convention, the parties to the dispute shall proceed expeditiously to an exchange of views regarding its settlement by negotiation or other peaceful means.
2. The parties shall also proceed expeditiously to an exchange of views where a procedure for the settlement of such a dispute has been terminated without a settlement or where a settlement has been reached and the circumstances require consultation regarding the manner of implementing the settlement.

It seems inevitable to conclude that the maritime borders in the ECS can only be delimited through direct negotiations. In principle, all three states are willing to do so. According to China's 1998 Act of the Exclusive Economic Zone and Continental Shelf, Article 2,3 reads: 'Conflicting claims regarding the EEZ and the Continental Shelf by the PRC and States with opposite or adjacent coasts shall be settled, on the basis of international law and in accordance with the principle of equity, by an agreement delimiting the area so claimed.' Japan's Law on the EEZ and Continental Shelf stipulates in Article 2 that the median line should apply 'or the line which may be agreed upon by Japan and foreign country as a substitute'. This gives both governments legal room to diverge from their current rigid positions.[52] Korea's Act on the EEZ provides that 'the EEZ boundary shall be established by agreement with the relevant States on the basis of international law'.[53] After an unsuccessful negotiation round from 1996 to 2008, South Korea and China began in December 2015 a new round to delimit their maritime border and they upgraded the level of the round from bureau chiefs to vice ministers. While South Korea proposes the principle of the median line for the partial overlap of their EEZs, China demands a wider maritime area considering its larger population, longer coastline, and continental area. The news reporting does not seem to cover the problem of the overlap with Japan's share of the northern sector of the ECS.[54]

In the end, it all boils down to political will and how the three countries evaluate the often invoked 'broader picture' of their relationship with their neighbours. The current stalemate has negative economic, environmental, political, and security implications. The ambiguous geographical partition of the ECS in the various fisheries agreements is not preventing incidents and risks also the harming of fishing stocks and the maritime environment in general. Sooner or later all three countries will clash over access to seabed resources if there are no agreed maritime borders.[55] The political relations between the three countries, notably between China and Japan, are constantly at risk of maritime incidents. The greatest dangers arise from the growing stand-off between coast guard vessels and naval forces hovering beyond them. The confrontation between the Chinese and Japanese coast guards and the deployment of air and maritime forces has created the most serious situation, particularly in the absence of established crisis control and crisis management mechanisms.[56] Chinese coast guard ships are patrolling the waters around the Ieodo/Suyan rock, and the South Korean government does as well. The divergent interpretations of relevant UNCLOS articles regarding the sovereign rights of the states in the TW and the EEZ can easily lead to serious incidents. The considerable US military presence in the area of the ECS and around it as well as the US security guarantee to Japan, which includes the disputed Senkaku/Diaoyu Islands, indicates that the unresolved border delimitation issue is also part of the regional and global power rivalry between the US and China.

If the ECS coastal states can come to agreed maritime borders, it would not only eliminate or at least considerably reduce the above economic, environmental, political, and security problems, but it could also strengthen UNCLOS as an appropriate tool for border delimitation worldwide and send a positive rather than – as it seems now the case – negative precursory signal to the coastal states of the SCS. It might also create a more appropriate environment for adapting the UNCLOS regime to better meet some of the new challenges to the ocean regime, such as climate change (rising sea levels will require the revision of baselines!). Other desirable improvements would be greater clarity of certain articles, informed by past arbitral and judicial precedents. This might provide better guidance for achieving an equitable solution for the delimitation of EEZs and CSs which would be somewhere between the concept of the equidistance line and that of the continental shelf.[57] In light of the mixed experience of the three ECS littoral states and the clear stipulation in UNCLOS, provisional agreements of a practical nature should indeed be understood as only provisional!

Notes

1 The Republic of Taiwan (Taiwan) is not specifically referred to in this chapter because of its very similar position to the PRC.

2 Tim F. Liao, Kimie Hara and Krista Wiegand, eds., *The China-Japan Border Dispute. Islands of Contention in Multidisciplinary Perspective* (Farnham: Ashgate, 2015). Reinhard Drifte, 'The Senkaku/Diaoyu Islands Territorial Dispute between Japan and China. Between the Materialization of the "China Threat" and "Reversing the Outcome of World War II"?,' *UNISCI Discussion Papers*, no. 32 May 2013: 9–62, accessed 21 March 2016, https://revistas.ucm.es/index.php/UNIS/article/download/44789/42208.

3 Nong Hong, *UNCLOS and Ocean Dispute Settlement* (London: Routledge, 2012), 127. For a US government critique of the baselines of all three countries see relevant publications at www.state.gov/e/oes/ocns/opa/c16065.htm. For a Korean critique of Japan's and China's base lines see Kim Sun Pyo, *Maritime Delimitation and Interim Arrangements in North East Asia* (The Hague: Martinus Nijhoff Publishers, 2004), pp.179, 184 and 217. Interview with members of the Treaty Bureau of the Korean Ministry of Foreign and Trade Affairs, 11 May 2009.

4 Atsuko Kanehara, 'Provisional Arrangements as Equitable Legal Management of Maritime Delimitation Disputes in the East China Sea', *NBR Special Report* no. 35 (December 2011): 133–35, accessed 21 March 2016, http://nbr.org/publications/specialreport/pdf/Preview/SR35_MERA-EnergyandGeopolitics_preview.pdf.

5 Kim Sun Pyo, op. cit., pp. 215–16.

6 For details see I Made Andi Arsana and Clive Schofield, 'Adding further Complexity? Extended Continental Shelf Submissions in East and Southeast Asia', NBR Special Report #37 (February 2012): 35–59, accessed 15 February 2012, http://nbr.org/publications/issue.aspx?id=254.

7 'Japan's legal position on the development of natural resources in the East China Sea', Ministry of Foreign Affairs, last modified 6 August 2015, accessed 21 March 2016, www.mofa.go.jp/a_o/c_m1/page3e_000358.html.

8 'Project Completion Report on the Ping Hu Oil and Gas Development Project (Loan 1419-PRC) in the PRC, May 2004', Asian Development Bank, accessed 21 March 2016, www.adb.org/sites/default/files/project-document/70039/pcr-prc-26201.pdf.

9 Reinhard Drifte, 'Japanese – Chinese Territorial Disputes in the East China Sea – between Military Confrontation and Economic Cooperation', *LSE Asia Research Centre Working Paper* no. 24 (April 2008): 18–19, accessed 21 March 2016, http://tinyurl.com/a8q7gvr.

10 Kim Young-jin, 'Why Ieodo Matters', *Korea Times*, 18 September 2012, accessed 21 March 2016, www.koreatimes.co.kr/www/news/nation/2012/09/117_120266.html, and "S. Korea to Deploy 5,000-ton Vessel to Ieodo," *Yonhap*, 26 January 2016, accessed 28 February 2016, http://english.yonhapnews.co.kr/national/2016/01/26/0301000000AEN20160126008300315.html.

11 For an official Japanese map of the country's territorial sea and EEZ see www1.kaiho.mlit.go.jp/JODC/ryokai/ryokai_setsuzoku.html, accessed 21 March 2016.

12 'Submission by the People's Republic of China Concerning the Outer Limits of the Continental Shelf Beyond 200 Nautical Miles in parts of the East China Sea', 14 December 2012, accessed 21 March 2016, www.un.org/Depts/los/clcs_new/submissions_files/chn63_12/executive%20summary_EN.pdf. For a Chinese

discussion of the Okinawa Trough see Gao Jianjun, 'The Okinawa Trough Issue in the Continental Shelf Delimitation Disputes within the East China Sea', *Chinese Journal of International Law* (2010) 9 (1): 143–77. 'Partial Submission to the Commission on the Limits of the Continental Shelf Pursuant to Article 76 Paragraph 8 of the United Nations Convention of the Law of the Sea. Executive Summary' by the Republic of Korea, December 2012, accessed 21 March 2016, www.un.org/depts/los/clcs_new/submissions_files/kor65_12/executive_summary.pdf.

13 For details see Volterra Fietta E-Newsletter, 'China and the Republic of Korea Make Overlapping Submissions to the Commission on the Limits of the Continental Shelf Regarding the East China Sea,' undated, accessed 21 March 2016, www.volterrafietta.com/china-and-the-republic-of-korea-make-overlapping-submissions-to-the-commission-on-the-limits-of-the-continental-shelf-regarding-the-east-china-sea/.

14 For information of these ship movements see www.kaiho.mlit.go.jp/mission/senkaku/ and www.diaoyudao.org.cn/node_7217868.htm.

15 Miyoshi Masahiro, 'Exercising Enforcement Jurisdiction Around the Senkaku Islands', *Review of Island Studies* (March 2015):107.

16 Hiroki Sugita, 'Taiwan seeks to fish off Senkakus, not pick sides', 3 April 2013, accessed 21 March 2016, www.japantimes.co.jp/news/2013/04/03/national/taiwan-seeks-to-fish-off-senkakus-not-pick-sides/#.UVtjuTcUPoc.

17 Hiroshi Hajime, 'Japan's Effective Control of the Senkaku Islands. The Senkaku Islands as Seen in Government White Papers and Other Documents Since the Reversion of Okinawa to Japanese Control', *Review of Island Studies* (March 2015): 122–26.

18 For a discussion of this issue see Jing Geng, 'The Legality of Foreign Military Activities in the Exclusive Economic Zone under UNCLOS', *Merkourios* vol. 28 no.74: 22–30, accessed 21 March 2016, www.google.co.uk/?gfe_rd=cr&ei=l-XvVvmJCNTW8gf84Im4CQ&gws_rd=ssl#q=Jing+Geng%2C+%E2%80%9CThe+Legality+of+Foreign+Military+Activities+in+the+Exclusive+Economic+Zone+under+UNCLOS%E2%80%9D%2C+Merkourios+. For an American perspective see Ronald O'Rourke, 'Maritime Territorial and Exclusive Economic Zone (EEZ) Disputes Involving China: Issues for Congress', Congressional Research Service, Washington D.C., 22 December 2015, accessed 21 March 2016, www.fas.org/sgp/crs/row/R42784.pdf.

19 For the US position see Jonathan G. Odon, 'FONOPs to Preserve the Right of Innocent Passage?' *The Diplomat*, 25 February 2016, accessed 25 February 2016, http://thediplomat.com/2016/02/fonops-to-preserve-the-right-of-innocent-passage/.

20 For Article 4 of the ROK's Territorial Sea and Contiguous Zone Act see www.un.org/depts/los/LEGISLATIONANDTREATIES/PDFFILES/KOR_2002_Decree.pdf. For US FONOPs regarding Korea see US Department of Defense, Freedom of Navigation Report for Fiscal Year 2014, accessed 21 March 2016, http://policy.defense.gov/Portals/11/Documents/gsa/cwmd/20150323%202015%20DoD%20Annual%20FON%20Report.pdf. All Accessed 21 March 2016.

21 Yukiya Hamamoto, 'The Incident of a Chinese Submarine Navigating Underwater in Japan's Territorial Sea', *The Japanese Annual of International Law*, no 48 (2005): 123–29.

22 For a general discussion of ADIZ see Peter A. Dutton, 'Caelum Liberam: Air Defense Identification Zones Outside Sovereign Airspace', *The American Journal of International Law*, vol 103 2009, accessed 21 March 2016, www.usnwc.edu/Research---Gaming/China-Maritime-Studies-Institute/Publications/documents/Dutton-NC-1st-proofs-%289-29-09%29-%283%291.pdf.

23 For the official Chinese map with coordinates of the ADIZ see http://news.xinhuanet.com/mil/2013-11/23/c_118262792.htm. For the English language version see http://news.xinhuanet.com/english/china/2013-11/23/c_132911635.htm. Both accessed 21 March 2016.

24 Reinhard Drifte, 'The Japan-China Confrontation Over the Senkaku/Diaoyu Islands – Between "Shelving" and "Dispute Escalation.' *The Asia-Pacific Journal*, vol. 12, Issue 30, no. 3, 28 July 2014, accessed 21 March 2016, http://apjjf.org/2014/12/30/Reinhard-Drifte/4154/article.html.

25 'Chinese Officers Told Japan About Expanded Air Defense Zone in 2010', *Mainichi Shimbun*, 1 January 2014, accessed 2 January 2014, http://mainichi.jp/english/english/newsselect/news/20140101p2a00m0na013000c.html.

26 Kim Sun Pyo, op. cit., p. 284. Text of the two agreements at www.un.org/depts/los/LEGISLATIONANDTREATIES/PDFFILES/TREATIES/jap-kor1974north.pdf and www.un.org/depts/los/LEGISLATIONANDTREATIES/PDFFILES/TREATIES/jap-kor1974south.pdf, accessed 21 March 2016.

27 Drifte, 2008, op. cit., p. 10.

28 Kanehara, Atsuko, op. cit., p. 133.

29 For a Chinese criticism of insufficient stock preservation see Xue Guifang (Julia). 'Bilateral Fisheries Agreements for the Cooperative Management of the Shared Resources of the China Seas: A Note,' *Ocean Development and International Law* 36, no. 4 (2005): 370.

30 Suk Kyoon Kim, 'Illegal Chinese fishing in the Yellow Sea: A Korean Officers Perspective', *Journal of East Asia & International Law*, vol. 5 issue 2 (Autumn 2012): 455–77.

31 Chi Young Pak, 'Resettlement of the Fisheries Order in Northeast Asia Resulting From the New Fisheries Agreements among Korea, Japan and China', *Korea Observer*, vol. 30 no. 4 (Winter 1999): 604.

32 *Yomiuri Shimbun* (online) 23 August 2002 (archived by this author).

33 Kanehara Atsuko, op. cit, p. 142. For a detailed account of the agreement see James Manicom, *China, Japan, and Maritime Order in the East China Sea. Bridging troubled Waters* (Washington D.C.: Georgetown University Press, 2014), 78–82.

34 For an excellent analysis see Sourabh Gupta, 'China-Japan trawler incident: Reviewing the dispute over Senkaku/Daioyu waters', *East Asia Forum*, 6 December 2010, accessed 28 March 2016, www.eastasiaforum.org/2010/12/06/china-japan-trawler-incident-review-of-legalities-understandings-and-practices-in-disputed-senkakudaioyu-waters/, See also Chisako T. Masuo, 'Governing a Troubled Relationship: Can the Field of Fisheries breed Sino-Japanese Cooperation?' *Japanese Journal of Political Science*, 14 (1), pp. 62–64.

35 Drifte 2013, op. cit, p. 26. 'Japan Tightens Security for Senkaku Islands', 9 September 2014, www3.nhk.or.jp/nhkworld/english/news/20140910_08.html. (accessed 9 September 2014 and archived by author).

36 Takeda Junichi, 'China's Rise as a Maritime Power: Ocean Policy from Mao Zedong to Xi Jingping', *Review of Island Studies*, ORF, March 2015, p. 334.

37 Masuo Chisako T, op. cit., pp. 51–72.

38 James Manicom, op. cit., p. 85. For a discussion of the PMZ see Yabunaka Misoji, *Kokka no unmei (The Fate of the State)* (Tokyo: Shinchosha 2010), 142–46. In a personal email of 7 March 2016, the author confirmed that the distance is in fact 52 nm, not 48 nm as he wrote on p. 146.

39 Reinhard Drifte, 'From "Sea of Confrontation" to "Sea of Peace, Cooperation and Friendship"? – Japan facing China in the East China Sea', *Japan Aktuell*, 3 (2008): 38–45, accessed 28 March 2016, http://eprint.ncl.ac.uk/file_store/production/214918/0CEFEA9C-6404-4C31-9B33-FF29A4F34DA2.pdf.

40 Zhang Xinjun: 'Why the 2008 Sino-Japanese Consensus on the East China Sea Has Stalled: Good Faith and Reciprocity Considerations in Interim Measures Pending a Maritime Boundary Delimitation', *Ocean Development & International Law*, vol. 42, no. 1 (2010): 61.

41 'Japan ruling party considers international arbitration over China dispute', 16 March 2016, accessed 28 March 2016, www.reuters.com/article/us-japan-china-idUSKCN0WI0LF.

42 Atsuko Kanehara, 'The Incident of an Unidentified Vessel in Japan's Exclusive Economic Zone', *The Japanese Journal of International Law*, no. 45 (2002): 117.
43 Asada Masahiko, 'The "Unidentified vessel" Incident in the East China Sea and the International Law of Exclusive Economic Zone', *The 2nd Japan-China Workshop on the International Law of the Sea*, 28 October 2007: 32–36.
44 For a detailed discussion see James Manicom, op. cit., chapter 4.
45 Reinhard Drifte, 'Japanese – Chinese territorial disputes in the East China Sea' 2008, op. cit., 17–20.
46 Manicom, op. cit.: 109.
47 Kim Sun Pyo, op. cit.: 221.
48 For a critical review of the planned agreement see Marta McLellan Ross, 'The Japan-China Maritime and Air Communication Mechanism: Operational and Strategic Considerations', Japan Institute for International Affairs, 30 June 2015, accessed 28 March 2016, www.google.co.uk/?gws_rd=ssl#q=Marta+McLellan+Ross+The+Japan-China+Maritime+and+Air+Communication+Mechanism:+Operational+and+Strategic +Considerations.
49 Ronald O'Rourke, op. cit.: 18.
50 Accessed 28 March 2016, www.un.org/Depts/los/settlement_of_disputes/choice_procedure.htm.
51 Interview of the author with Yachi Shotaro, former Vice Foreign Minister of Japan, 14 November 2011.
52 Reinhard Drifte, 'Japanese – Chinese territorial disputes in the East China Sea' 2008: 9.
53 Kim Pyo Sun, op. cit.: 204.
54 'Korea, China Discuss Exclusive Economic Zone at Sea', *Chosun Ilbo*, accessed 28 March 2016, http://english.chosun.com/site/data/html_dir/2015/12/23/2015122301280.html.
55 For Japan's exploration of seabed resources in the ECS see 'Govt aims to commercialize Seafloor Mining in 2020s', *The Yomiuri Shimbun*, 22 February 2015, accessed 22 February 2016, http://the-japan-news.com/news/article/0001953808.
56 Richard C. Bush, *The Perils of Proximity. China-Japan Security Relations* (Washington, D.C.: Brookings Institution Press, 2010).
57 For a good discussion of the latter two issues see Kanehara, Atsuko, 'Provisional arrangements': 135.

Part II

National perspective

3 Historic concepts vs. contemporary maritime regimes in UNCLOS

China's claims in the South China Sea

Nong Hong

China's historical claim in the South China Sea (SCS) based on the "U-shaped line" overlaps with the claims to EEZ and continental shelf areas of other claimant states. In China's view, a claim derived from historic origins may seem more forceful and valid in law than claims simply based upon the EEZ concept. While Chinese scholars tend to believe that the historic concept is still relevant in international law and much research has been conducted on "historic rights," Western scholars do not seem to be on the same page. Since there are no definitive rules in international law, which govern the status of maritime historic rights, China's claim is not a violation of international law. Similarly, since there are no such rules, it is doubtful whether China's claim could be established in international law. This remains a critical research question for scholars.

Historic concepts could refer to historic water, historic right, historic title etc. The doctrine of historic waters as such has not received much academic attention in the past, claimed by Clive R. Symmons in his new book.[1] There are publications dealing with historic bays,[2] historic titles,[3] historic rights, or historic waters.[4] However, the lack of clearance of the definitions of these concepts with historic nature brings confusion to students of historic doctrine. Historic concept plays an important role in the SCS disputes; hence it is necessary to distinguish the difference of these terms as reflected in the first section of this article. The article moves on to discuss the relationship between historic concept and maritime delimitation and historic concepts related dispute settlement under UNCLOS. The article elaborates China's historic claim in the SCS and points to the conflicts among the claimants in the SCS due to the competition between historic concepts and new maritime regime. The SCS Arbitration Case does have an implication on the question whether historic doctrine is still relevant in contemporary international law.

Definition

Historic water

There are many definitions of "historic waters." As Symmons points out, among the best definitions of the concept of "historic waters" is that of Bouchez. He defines them as: "waters over which the coastal state, contrary to the generally applicable rules of international law, clearly, effectively, continuously, and over a substantial period of time, exercises sovereign rights with the acquiescence of the community of States."[5] Gidel's (translated) definition – albeit essentially in the context of the narrower concept of "historic bays" – is more concise: namely, "those areas of water the legal status of which differs – with the consent of other States – from what it ought to have been according to the generally recognized rules."[6] It is noteworthy that both statements refer to the generally recognized/ applicable rules of international law.

Historic right

There also exists the separable term of "historic rights" – normally in high seas areas, but without any connotations as to sovereignty in the locale, such as historic fishing rights.[7] The 2006 Barbados/Trinidad and Tobago Arbitration case entails the argument of historic rights of fishing.[8] The term "historic rights" is broader than that of "historic waters." In its widest sense, it implies that a State claiming to exercise certain jurisdictional rights in what usually basically satisfy the same, or at least similar, supposed requirements for establishing "historic waters" claims *per se*, particularly those of continuous and long usage with the acquiescence of relevant other States.[9] For example, in the Tunisian pleadings in Tunisia/Libya, it was, in effect, argued that historic rights were claimable on a similar basis to that relation to historic waters, namely that they were established by exercise of peaceable and continued sovereignty, with prolonged toleration on the part of other States.[10]

Despite the close connection of rules, such claims of historic rights differ substantively from claims to historic waters.[11] Firstly, "these claimed rights only apply on a *quoad hunc* basis, not *erga omnes* as do, arguably at least, claims to historic waters; and they may not even have the word 'historic' attached to them."[12] Secondly, historic rights differ from "historic waters" inasmuch as they do not, as stated above, amount to zonal claims of jurisdiction or sovereignty. As Judge De Castro said in the Fisheries Jurisdiction cases,[13] historic rights of States concerned with "high seas fishing" do not give them "acquisition over the sea by prescription": merely "respected" rights by "long usage." Similarly, for example, in Qatar/Bahrain, the ICJ held, in relation to Bahrain's alleged historic rights over pearling banks in an area of seabed in dispute, that these had never led to the recognition of a quasi-territorial right to the fishing grounds or the superjacent waters.[14] A third possible difference between the twin concepts of historic "waters" and historic "rights" is that claimed historic waters must necessarily be adjacent to the claimant State. Bouchez, for example, has maintained that it is "impossible for a non-coastal state to be entitled over a [historic] sea areas situated near the coast of other States."[15] The adjacency requirement follows the general international legal requirement of States being allowed only to claim territorial waters immediately off and adjacent to their coastlines.[16] It appears that past confusion over the more limited notion of "historic rights" has had a "knock-on" effect which has led some States to claim sovereignty over historic bays on this basis alone – e.g., resulting from sedentary fishery rights outside territorial limits. Thus, for example, Australia seemingly recognized the historic bay concept "without sufficiently distinguishing it from the more limited 'historic right to sedentary fishing.' "[17]

Historic title

UNCLOS III did not discuss the issue of historic rights or historic waters.[18] However, historic title is recognized in various contexts in UNCLOS – in relation to maritime delimitation, the status of bays as well as the rights of States in respect of archipelagic waters and limitations and exceptions in the settlement of disputes. Article 10 (6) provides that "the foregoing provisions [on bays] do not apply to so-called 'historic' bays." Article 15 does not allow the median line to apply to special circumstances such as "by reason of historic title" for the delimitation of the territorial seas of the two states. The last provision in UNCLOS which mentions the historic bays or title is Article 298, which permits the contracting states to exclude the compulsory procedure provided for in UNCLOS from applying to the disputes "involving historic bays or titles." It is obvious that UNCLOS deliberately avoids the issue of historic rights or historic waters, leaving it to be governed by customary international law as reaffirmed in its preamble.[19] On the other hand, UNCLOS does have some bearing on the concept of historic waters in territorial seas or internal waters since it appears only in the sections on territorial sea regime and the settlement of disputes.[20]

UNCLOS further envisages claims of historic title being asserted with respect to bays. Article 10, paragraph 6 provides that the rules for drawing closing lines across the mouths of bays do not apply for "so-called 'historic' bays." At the First Conference, a proposal was submitted for a request to the General Assembly to study the regime of historic bays.[21] Although a study was prepared on the juridical regime of historic waters, including historic bays,[22] the issue was not addressed at any length at the Third Conference and Article 10 replicates the relevant provision of the Territorial Sea Convention. The classification of certain areas as historic bays has been controversial because of the potential to close off bodies of water and thereby push EEZs further into high seas areas. A notable example of this situation has been the United States' military challenges to Libya's assertion that the Gulf of Sidra constitutes a historic bay and should be closed off as internal waters.[23]

Historic concepts and maritime delimitation

The presence of historic concepts may affect the drawing of a maritime boundary.[24] The delimitation of the territorial sea specifically requires an adjustment of the median line where it is necessary to take account of "historic title or other special circumstances."[25] Historic rights were recognized in the determination of maritime boundaries by third parties in *Grisbadarna and Anglo-Norwegian Fisheries*.[26]

In the delimitation between Sweden and Norway, the Permanent Court of Arbitration decided that the Grisbadarna area should be assigned to Sweden. One of the reasons for this delimitation was the "circumstance that lobster fishing in the shoals of Grisbadarna has been carried on for a much longer time, to a much larger extent, and by much larger number of fishers by the subjects of Sweden than by the subjects of Norway."[27] The Court was willing to take this factor into account on the basis that, "it is a settled principle of the law of nations that a state of things which actually exists and has existed for a long time should be changed as little as possible."[28]

Both Article 12 of the TSC (1958) and Article 15 of UNCLOS make reference to "historic title" as a reason for departing from the general rule for delimitation of a territorial sea between States, namely, failing agreement, a median line; but no mention is made of such a proviso in respects of either delimitation of overlapping EEZs or continental shelves. The matter, however, has, received some discussion in the latter contexts from the ICJ. For example, in Tunisia/Libya case, Tunisia pleaded it had historic rights from past sedentary fishing activities. The ICJ while referring to the fact that the matter of Tunisia's historic rights might "be relevant for the decision" in a "number of ways,"[29] found it not necessary in its judgment to take the issue into account. However, in his separate Opinion on the case, Judge Arechaga opined that, by implication, the "historic factor could be relevant to continental shelf delimitation as a 'special circumstance'."[30]

The relevance of claimed historic rights to maritime delimitation of the expanded maritime zones such as EEZ and the continental shelf remains somewhat unclear in the light of the discussed cases, though State practice in recent times suggests that historic rights, even if considered irrelevant to delimitation issues, may still be independently taken into account by special agreement as to access.[31] In the Barbados/Trinidad & Tobago Arbitration, the Tribunal has decided that the pattern of fishing activity in the waters off Trinidad and Tobago was not of such a nature as to warrant the adjustment of the maritime boundary. This does not, however, mean that the argument based upon fishing activities is either without factual foundation or without legal consequences.[32] The Tribunal accordingly considers that it does not have jurisdiction to make an award establishing a right of access for Barbadian fishermen to flying fish within the EEZ of Trinidad and Tobago, because that award is outside its jurisdiction by virtue of the limitation set out in UNCLOS Article 297(3)(a).[33] Both Barbados and Trinidad and Tobago emphasized before the Tribunal their willingness to find a reasonable solution to the dispute over access to flying fish stocks.[34] Undoubtedly, some past continental shelf delimitations have taken into account historic claims in negotiating a maritime boundary. For example, in the 1974 India/Sri Lanka continental shelf delimitation treaty, the preamble referred to "historical evidence" having been taken into account, but with no mention of sedentary fisheries or any suggestion they affected a modified equidistance boundary.[35] Nonetheless, claimed Ceylonese pearl and chank fisheries in the Gulf of Manaar and Palk Bay – the latter being regarded by the UK as an area of historic waters – may have been taken into account in this delimitation treaty to recognize the traditional fishing rights.[36]

Historic concepts related dispute settlement under UNCLOS

Compulsory dispute settlement under Section 2 in Part XV of UNCLOS is available for States for disputes relating to the delimitation of the territorial sea, EEZ, continental shelf, and to historic title unless States have opted to exclude these disputes by virtue of Article 298 (1) (a). Declarations permitted under Article 298 relate first, to maritime delimitation disputes in relation to the territorial sea, EEZ or continental shelf of States with opposite or adjacent coasts, as well as disputes involving historic bays or title.

Further impetus to resort to adjudication or arbitration for determination of maritime boundaries may be derived from the highly flexible legal formulae prescribed under UNCLOS. UNCLOS provides no clear rule for States to apply in maritime delimitation of the EEZ and continental shelf beyond the exhortation that any agreement be based on international law. Similarly, no criteria are stated for establishing historic title in relation to territorial sea delimitation, bays, and fishing in archipelagic waters. The indeterminate nature of the substantive principles set out with respect to delimitation of the continental shelf and the EEZ, as well as the large degree of discretion accorded to States in asserting historic title, meant that mandatory jurisdiction would provide States with a procedure to facilitate agreement. Certainly, western States strongly favored the inclusion of a procedure entailing binding jurisdiction if the substantive rules were insufficiently determinative.[37] Moreover, the delimitation of maritime zones has been subject to third-party dispute settlement in the past despite the highly discretionary nature of the applicable legal principles.[38] It is nonetheless noticeable that the arbitral and adjudicative procedures that have been undertaken for the determination of maritime boundaries have lacked the zero sum result that is characteristic of litigated dispute resolution. The typical tactic is for States to submit maximize claims to courts and tribunals and these bodies are left the task of devising a compromise position between these claims to achieve an "equitable result." This history could indicate that the subject of the dispute would be conducive to settlement under the compulsory procedures in Part XV of UNCLOS. It may be another contributory factor as to why governments negotiating at the Third Conference did not insist on the complete exclusion of maritime delimitation and historic title disputes from the compulsory dispute settlement regime.[39]

China's historic claim in the SCS

The most important and interesting area where China could claim historic concepts is in the SCS.[40] The prevailing basis for China's historic claims to the SCS is the U-shaped line officially drawn on the Chinese map in 1947 by the then-Chinese Nationalist Government.[41] The "U-shaped line" issued by Chiang Kai-shek's government in 1947 refers to the line with nine segments off the Chinese coast on the SCS, as displayed in the Chinese map. According to China, the line has been called a "traditional maritime boundary line."[42] The dotted line encloses the main island features of the SCS: the Pratas Islands, the Paracel Islands, the Macclesfield Bank, and the Spratly Islands. The dotted line also captures James Shoal which is as far south as 4 degrees' north latitude. China seems to claim all the islands, atolls within this line, but seems to be quiet on the legal status of the waters so enclosed.

The Taiwan authorities gave the status of historic water to the water areas within the U-shaped line in 1993 when it issued the SCS Policy Guidelines, which stated that "the SCS area within the historic water limit is the maritime area under the jurisdiction of the Republic of China, in which the Republic of China possesses all rights and interests."[43] This can be regarded as Taiwan's official position on the concept of historic waters, though this claim has not acquired unanimous support among Taiwanese scholars.

In the SCS, the line provides a basis for a claim of historic water. However, the exercise of authority in the area by either mainland China or Taiwan has been infrequent since the promulgation of the line. Even these occasional exercises focused on the islands within the line rather than on the water areas.[44] The freedom of navigation and freedom of fishery seem to be unaffected by these exercises. Thus, "the question of whether there is effective control over the area within the line so as to establish it as historic waters arises."[45] It may be argued that the relative frequency of the exercise of authority should be considered *vis à vis* other claimant countries. Yet, there are still doubts on how China could establish its claim of historic waters in the SCS.

On the other hand, as Zou argued, "the nonexistence of historic waters in its traditional sense in the SCS does not necessarily mean that there exist no historic rights of any kind."[46] It is clear from China's stance that it seeks to enjoy historic privileges of some kind in the SCS. The most convincing rights that China could enjoy are fishing rights, since Chinese fishermen have been fishing in the SCS from ancient times. As for other rights, it is up to China to make clearer statements to the public.[47]

Zou argued that the provision of China's EEZ law on historical rights can be understood in a number of different ways. First, it can be interpreted to mean that the sea area in question should have the same legal status as areas under UNCLOS III (EEZ and continental shelf) regimes. Second, it can be interpreted to mean that certain sea areas to which China's historical rights are claimed go beyond the 200 nautical mile limit. Third, it can be interpreted to mean that the sea areas to which China's historical rights apply fall within the 200 nautical mile limit but will come under an alternative national management regime different from the EEZ regime. In this third view, the claimed areas of historical rights can be treated as quasi-territorial sea, or as historical waters with some modifications, or as "tempered historic waters."[48] On the other hand, it may be questioned whether China's claimed historic rights could extend to cover the continental shelf area in the SCS, since the right to the latter is *ab initio and ipso facto*, as provided in UNCLOS, and "the rights of the coastal state over the continental shelf do not depend on occupation, effective or notional, or on any express proclamation,"[49] in spite of the fact that the historic rights are included in China's EEZ/continental shelf law. The continental shelf doctrine of "inherency" should be viewed as deliberately aimed against the operation of any historic rights previously acquired.[50] The opposite view is that "a new legal concept, consisting in the notion introduced in 1958 that continental shelf rights are inherent or *'ab initio'*, cannot by itself have the effect of abolishing or denying acquired and existing rights."[51] China has to prove that its historic rights existed prior to the establishment of the customary rules on the continental shelf. Otherwise, China's claim is only relevant to the EEZ non-continental shelf area.

The provision on historic rights in China's 1998 EEZ law has been queried. A Vietnamese scholar has asked whether "this article tacitly refers to other interests that China has claimed, such as the traditional right of fishing in maritime zones of other countries and the nine broken lines claiming over 80 per cent of area of the East Sea."[52] He further stated that "[a] long time ago, regional countries pursued their normal activities in the East Sea without encountering any Chinese impediment and they have never recognized historical rights of China there."[53] Vietnam officially lodged a protest against China's historic rights in the SCS emphasizing that Vietnam will "not recognize any so-called 'historical interests' which are not consistent with international law and violate the sovereignty and sovereign rights of Vietnam and Vietnam's legitimate interests in its maritime zones and continental shelf in the East Sea."[54] It may be difficult for China to assert that there is a general acquiescence on the part of third states to its historic rights claim in the SCS given Vietnam's opposition. However, the proclamation in China's Law "may well serve to substantially stake out the declarant's legal position, expressing the State's belief that usage of waters has been sufficiently lengthy, continuous, and notorious to constitute a Choate title."[55]

Historical demands and possessions can be questioned by international law, but the Chinese see the area as a natural part of China and are of the belief that they should not have to demand something that has been, under *de facto* and *de jura* Chinese rule since 1300.[56] According to Chinese sources, Spratleys and Paracels were discovered by the Chinese, and there are Chinese texts that describe the area as Chinese since 300 AC. Harder to prove is that the area has been under *de facto* Chinese rule. However, it is apparent that China sees itself as a victim of the aggression of the imperialists/superpowers/regional states and will probably continue to see itself in this way until all Chinese territory is once more under Chinese rule.[57]

Historic concepts vs. new maritime regimes in the SCS

China's historical claim in the SCS based on the "U-shaped line" overlaps with the claims to EEZ and continental shelf areas of Vietnam, Indonesia, Malaysia, Brunei and the Philippines.[58] The perceived excessive claims put forward by other SCS countries, such as the Philippines and Malaysia, who have claimed some islands in the SCS based upon the 200-nautical mile EEZ rights of UNCLOS, may have encouraged China to insist that its SCS claim is based upon the U-shaped line. In China's view, a claim derived from historic rights may seem more forceful and valid in law than claims simply based upon the EEZ concept. While Chinese scholars tend to believe that the historic concept is still relevant in international law and much research has been conducted on "historic waters,"[59] Western scholars do not seem to be on the same page. Moore, a well-known American scholar on the law of the sea, when asked whether historic water is still relevant, noted that only the bays listed in UN 1957 Study on Historic Bays are regarded as legitimate.[60] Judges David Anderson and Gudmundur Eiriksson of ITLOS were reluctant to comment on the relevance of historic waters.[61]

Zou argued that since there are no definitive rules in international law which govern the status of maritime historic rights, China's claim is not a violation of international law. Similarly, since there are no such rules, it is doubtful whether China's claim could be established in international law.[62] What is more problematic is China's implementation of what it has claimed in the SCS or elsewhere where China may assert historic rights and interests. As the ICJ once stated, general international law does not provide for a single "regime" of historic waters or historic bays, but only for a particular regime for each of several specific, generally recognized cases of historic waters or historic bays.[63] From this point of view, China's claim can be regarded as one of these particular cases, which may stand up in international law as doctrine evolved over time.

Implication from the South China Sea arbitration case

The SCS Arbitration between the Philippines and China raised important issues regarding the relevance and validity of historic claims, and the relationship between UNCLOS and historic claims. This is the first time that a tribunal has contributed with such clarity to the issue of historic rights. However, as Kopela argues, the reasoning and conclusions reached by the Tribunal are problematic.[64]

In its notification and statement of claim, the Philippines asked the Tribunal to declare that the parties' respective rights and obligations with regard to the waters, seabed and maritime features of the SCS are governed by UNCLOS and that China's claims based on its "nine dash line" are inconsistent with the Convention and therefore invalid.[65] In its memorial, the Philippines clarified further its request in its first two submission points.

1. *China's maritime entitlements in the South China Sea, like those of the Philippines, may not extend beyond those permitted by the United Nations Convention on the Law of the Sea ("UNCLOS" or the "Convention").*
2. *China's claims to sovereign rights and jurisdictions and to historic rights with respect to the maritime areas of the South China Sea encompassed by the so-called nine-dash line are contrary to the Convention and without lawful effect to the extent that they exceed the geographic and substantive limits of China's maritime entitlements under UNCLOS.*[66]

The first question which the tribunal had to address was whether it had jurisdiction on these two submission points. This was in the light of China's argument in its Position Paper in December 2014 more generally that the "essence of the subject-matter" did not concern such UNCLOS-cased factors.[67] The Tribunal determined that contrary to what China more generally had claimed in its Position Paper, the question of historic claims did involve a dispute relating to the interpretation or application of UNCLOS because of its interaction with UNCLOS.

In the light of its finding on the meaning of "title" in Art. 298, the Tribunal found that China did not make such a claim in the SCS, as the Tribunal did not consider China's claim there within the U-shaped Line to be "equivalent to its territorial sea or internal waters."[68] Having determined what China meant by historic rights, the Tribunal proceeded to indicate that what was being claimed was different than historic title as used in Article 298(1)(a)(i) and, therefore, the Tribunal had jurisdiction to look at the merits of the claim made by the Philippines.

The Tribunal reached the above conclusion based on its presumption on China's claims associated with the U-shaped Line. There are different categories of historic rights, namely, historic titles entailing sovereignty, historic rights short of sovereignty, historic rights short of sovereignty that a quasi-territorial or zonal impact beyond the territorial sea, nonexclusive historic rights and traditional fishing rights. Nevertheless, the Tribunal considers China's historic claims within this line are all identical, without providing a clear differentiation based on facts. China's evidence of having historic title over Reed Bank proves that China's historic claims in the SCS include "historic title" and Article (1)(a)(i) exceptional provision applies.

The Tribunal then proceeded to discuss the relationship between UNCLOS and historic rights, which is essentially a question on the relationship between treaties and customary international law. The Tribunal relied on Article 311 on UNCLOS's relation to other conventions and international agreements[69] and 293(1)[70] to demonstrate that only those preexisting rights that are either expressly "permitted or preserved such as in Articles 10 and 15" or compatible with the UNCLOS would be preserved.[71] The Tribunal noted that "where independent rights and obligations have arisen prior to the entry into force of the Convention and are incompatible with its provisions, the principles set out in article 30(3) of the Vienna Convention and article 293 of the Convention provide that the Convention will prevail over the earlier, incompatible rights or obligations."[72] In other words, focusing on historic rights for fishing and continental shelf resources, the Tribunal concluded that UNCLOS precludes China's such claims within the 200 nm EEZ and continental shelf of another State.

It is obvious that the scope and contemporary relevance of historic claims was significantly restricted by the Tribunal which found that UNCLOS supersedes any previous historic titles/rights apart from those explicitly recognized in Articles 10 and 15 of UNCLOS relating to historic bays and historic titles in the territorial sea/internal waters. The challenge of the Tribunal's argument rests on, first, the lack of explanation on the reasoning of the Tribunal to explain why Article 311 on the relationship between the UNCLOS and conventions and international agreements could be analogically applied to the relationship between the UNCLOS and historic rights as rules of customary international law. Similarly, as Kopela pointed out, Article 293 concerns dispute settlement and the applicable law, rather than the relationship between the UNCLOS and other rules of international law, including historic rights.[73] The regulation of their relationship, as a complex one, has been avoided in international instruments and it is regulated by customary international law and general interpretative principles.[74] The only relevant provision that the UNCLOS entails with respect to customary international law, and unfortunately, which was not made reference to in the Award, is written in the Preamble of UNCLOS: "affirming that matters not regulated by this Convention continue to be governed by the rules and principles of general international law." UNCLOS does not contain any provisions prohibiting the preservation of rights preexisting UNCLOS or nullifying them. Potential existence of historic rights is not precluded as long as the requirements for their establishment have been met. Historic rights, relating to a particularized regime, reflects a continuous, long-established, and undisturbed situation. They should be assessed on a case-by-case basis according to the historical particularities and realities of the claim.[75]

The Tribunal also stressed the comprehensiveness of the regulatory regime of the UNCLOS and the intention of the drafters to settle all issues related to the law of the sea and to provide stability and order.[76] However, "the Tribunal failed to consider the nature and rationale of historic rights that are linked to the non-disturbance and preservation of a continuous, long-established, and accepted situation with the view to providing stability."[77] International jurisprudence implies that international courts and tribunals have accepted the preservation of historic rights in parallel to the jurisdictional regime established by the UNCLOS.[78] The nature and rationale of historic rights is to preserve stability and order based on the acceptance of a certain regime for a long period of time.

Historic doctrine: still relevant in contemporary international law

The rationale for recognizing historic doctrines is clearly grounded in notions of stability. One commentator has stated that: "Longstanding practice evidenced by a strong historic presence should not be disturbed. Judicial bodies are ill-advised to disregard a situation that has been peacefully accepted over a long period of time. To justify a division based on historic presence over the area, coupled with affirmative action toward that end, should be apparent."[79] One of the important reasons for asserting historic rights was to protect long-held economic interests in particular areas in the face of the *res communis* philosophy.[80] As such, it is arguable that historic rights should be admitted in a more restricted fashion now that coastal states have much broader entitlements to maritime jurisdiction.[81] States might be inclined to challenge declarations of historic title in certain areas if such a declaration impinges on inclusive uses of that region. Alternatively, a challenge may arise in a bilateral delimitation where the historic claim has the effect of enlarging the entitlement of States with an adjacent or opposite coast. Competing claims over the existence and opposability of historic title cannot easily be resolved under the terms of UNCLOS in light of the scant elaboration of principles on this matter. Specificity on the standard to be applied in determining claims to historic title was avoided in UNCLOS for similar reasons as maritime delimitation: the circumstance of individual cases varied too extensively to permit the formulation of a uniform standard.

The doctrine of historic concepts today may justifiably be seen as a temporary legitimizing mechanism[82] in an inter-temporal process taking in a broad range of situations. According to Symmons, it includes, at one extreme, "blatantly illegal original claims which would still be otherwise illegal today";[83] e.g., historic bay claims to areas with mouths well in excess of the present 24-mile rule distance or absurdly distant areas of the high sea (as in the short-lived Russian ukase featuring in *Alaska v. US 92005*).[84] At the other extreme, it also includes those claims which would now be valid in contemporary law.[85]

What, then, is the best way to view past claims? We have to realize that the formulation of the historic concept requires an adjustment of the generally accepted law of the sea regimes. Because of the peculiar circumstances of some maritime areas which fall within the national jurisdiction of coastal states, these areas are allowed to be part of the jurisdictional waters as an exception to the general rule. "It is predicted that the concept of historic rights will survive and be used by states as a means of claiming and expanding jurisdictional areas not only in the maritime sector, but also in the land sector."[86] As early as 1984 the question was asked whether the doctrine of historic bays and historic waters had become obsolete with the development of new, alternative concepts of national maritime expansion such as the EEZ and the continental shelf.[87] Judged by recent State practice, the answer to this question is no. Rather, there is a trend toward the application and assertion of historic claims whether to bays, waters or rights in spite of the establishment of new legal concepts such as the EEZ and continental shelf in the law of the sea.[88] Such a trend may eventually help to codify the rules of historic rights and/or historic waters in general international law.

Conclusion

This paper addresses a critical conflicting point of the SCS dispute – the historic concepts applied by China mainland and Taiwan, by Vietnam to a certain extent contradicts with the new regimes set by UNCLOS, e.g. EEZ regime on which the Philippines, Malaysia, and Brunei base their claim. Since there are no definitive rules in international law, which govern the status of maritime historic rights, China's claim is not a violation of international law. Similarly, since there are no such rules, it is doubtful whether China's claim could be established in international law. This remains a critical research question for scholars. The possibility for the third-party forum to be engaged in this scenario seems pale. Article 298

1 (a) (i) excludes historic bays or titles from compulsory procedures. The U-shaped Line map issued by China is a strong evidence for China; however, China needs to address its formal position and clarification of this map. The Tribunal of the SCS Arbitration has set a precedent to touch this question by analyzing the relations between UNCLOS and historic rights. However, the arguments it provided in the Award are problematic and are to be under academic scrutiny.

Notes

1 Clive R. Symmons, *Historic Waters in the Law of the Sea: a Modern Re-appraisal* (Leiden/Boston: Martinus Nijhoff Publishers, 2008)
2 Stroh, The International Law of Bays (1963), Leo J. Bouchez, *The Regime of Bays in International Law* (A. W. Sythoff, 1964).
3 Yehuda Z. Blum, *Historic Titles in International Law* (1965).
4 *Juridical Regime of Historic Waters, including Historic Bays* (A study prepared by UN Secretariat, March 9, 1962).
5 L.J. Bouchez, The *Regime of Bays in International Law* (Sythoff, Leyden, 1964), p. 281, see also on Symmons 2008, p. 1
6 G. Gidel, *Le droit international public de la mer* (Paris, 1932–4), v. III, p. 623.
7 Respectively (1973) *ICJ Reports* 3; and (1982) *ICJ Reports* 18, at pp. 32, 63, and 71 (para. 97) referring to the Tunisian claim that it possessed well-established historic rights, including "fixed and sedentary fisheries" in certain sea areas (historic rights from "long-established fishing activities"). The courts concluded (at p. 74, para. 100) that such rights continued to be "governed by general international law." Bouchez (at p. 248) appropriately labels these rights as "non-exclusive historic rights" in the high seas. See also Symmons, 2008, p.4.
8 See the Award at www.pca-cpa.org/showpage.asp?pag_id=1152
9 Y. Blum, "Historic Rights" in *Encyclopedias of Public International Law*, vol. 2 (Amsterdam, Elsevier), pp. 710–15, See also Symmons, 2008 p. 4.
10 See J.M. Spinnato, "Historic and Vital Bays: An Analysis of Libya's Claim to the Gulf of Sidra," 1983–84 13 *O.D.I.L.* 65, p. 72. See also Symmons, 2008, p. 4.
11 Symmons, 2008, p. 5.
12 Ibid.
13 [1974] *ICJ Rep.*3, at p. 99; Symmons, 2008, p. 5.
14 [2001] *ICJ Rep.*2001, at p. 112, para. 235, Simmons, 2008, p. 6.
15 Bouchez, p. 238; Symmons, 2008, p. 6.
16 See Tunisia/Libya, *Reply* of Lybya, *Pleadings*, vol.4 at p.114, para. 31, (areas "adjacent to the coastal States"); Symmons, 2008, p.6.
17 D.W. Nixon, "A Comparative Analysis of Historic Bay Claim", attached as a Technical Annex (II-3) to the *Reply* of Libya, *Pleadings*, vol. IV, at pp. 321, 322; See also Symmons, 2008, p. 6.
18 During the conference, the proposal advanced in 1976 by Colombia regarding the standards of claiming historic waters was discarded. See UNCLOS III, *Official Records*, (1977), Vol. 5, at p. 202. See also Zou Keyuan, "Historic Rights in International Law and in China's Practice," *Ocean Development & International Law*, 32:149–68, 2001, p. 152.
19 The preamble of UNCLOS affirms that "matters not regulated by this Convention continue to be governed by the rules and principles of general international law." See also Zou Keyuan, 2001, p. 152.
20 Zou Keyuan, "Historic Rights in International Law and in China's Practice," *Ocean Development & International Law*, 32: 149–68, 2001, p. 152.

21 India and Panama submitted this proposal, which was adopted as Resolution VII, at the First Conference. See Resolutions Adopted by the Conference, UN Doc.A/CONF.13/L.56(1958), reprinted in *First Conference, Plenary Meetings*, at p. 145. The General Assembly referred this request to the International Law Commission. The UN Secretariat undertook the study instead. See Klein, 2005, p. 251.
22 Juridical Regime of Historic Waters, including Historic Bays, *UN Doc. A/CN.4/143*, reprinted in [1962] 2 *Y.B. Int'l L.* Comm'n 1, UN Doc.A/1962/Add.1, Un Sales No. 62.V.5 (1962); see also Klein, 2005, p. 251.
23 Libya's position has been strongly criticized by commentators. See, e.g., John M. Spinnato, "Historic and Vital Bays: An Analysis of Libya's Claim to the Gulf of Sidra," 13 *Ocean Development and International Law* 65 (1983); Roger Cooling Haerr, "The Guld of Sidra," 24 *San Diego L., Rev.* 751 (1987); Yehuda Z. Blum, "The Gulf of Sidra Incident," 80 *American Journal of International Law*, p. 668 (1986). See also Natalie Klein, *Dispute settlement in the UN Convention on the Law of the Sea* (Cambridge: Cambridge University Press, 2005), p. 252).
24 Natalie Klein, *Dispute settlement in the UN Convention on the Law of the Sea* (Cambridge: Cambridge University Press, 2005), p. 250.
25 UNCLOS, Article 15.
26 See D. H. N. Johnson, "The Anglo-Norwegian Fisheries Case," in *International and Comparative Law Quarterly*, Vol.1, Part 2, April, 1952, pp. 146–80.
27 Grisbadarna, p. 233, see Klein, 2005, p. 250
28 Ibid.
29 See Y. Tanaka, *Predictability and Flexibility in the Law of Maritime Delimitation* (Hart Publishing, Oxford and Portland, Oregon, 2006), p. 299, see Symmons 2008, p. 45.
30 [1982] *ICJ Reports* 18, at p. 75, para. 102, see Symmons, 2008, p. 45
31 See Y. Tanaka, *Predictability and Flexibility in the Law of Maritime Delimitation* (Hart Publishing, Oxford and Portland, Oregon, 2006) at p. 306 for examples. See also Symmons, 2008, p. 47.
32 Award of Barbados / Trinidad & Tobago Arbitration, page 84, para. 272, at www.pca-cpa.org/upload/files/Final%20Award.pdf
33 Award of Barbados / Trinidad & Tobago Arbitration, p.87, para. 283 at www.pca-cpa.org/upload/files/Final%20Award.pdf
34 Award of Barbados / Trinidad & Tobago Arbitration, p.88, Para. 287, at www.pca-cpa.org/upload/files/Final%20Award.pdf
35 Referred to by Dupuy in oral pleading for Tunisia (*Pleadings*, vol. 4 at p. 476) who pointed out that the "modified" equidistance line there was so used to recognize the traditional fishing rights. See also Symmons, 2008, p. 47.
36 See *Pleadings*, vol. 4 at p. 211, Para. 160. Other delimitation agreements mentioned, such as the Indonesia/Australia delimitation agreement make no mention of sedentary fisheries (e.g., Queensland pearl fisheries; and the 1978 Australia/PNG delimitation agreement, which, even though setting up a special zone, allegedly makes no mention of "historic rights" as such; see Symmons, 2008, p. 47.
37 Dero J. Manner, "Settlement of Sea-Boundary Delimitation Disputes According to the Provisions of the 1982 Law of the Sea Convention," in *Essays in International Law in Honor of Judge Manfred Lachs* (Jerzy Makarczyk ed., 1984), p. 625, at pp. 636–37. See also E.D. Brown, "Dispute Settlement and the Law of the Sea: the UN Convention Regime," 21 *Marine Policy* 17 (1997), at p. 24; See also Klein, 2005 p. 254.
38 "In spite of this indeterminacy, if not because of it, coastal states have found that third-party disputes settlement procedures can effectively resolve maritime boundary delimitation disputes," Charney, "Progress in International Maritime Boundary Delimitation Law," *88 American Journal of International Law* (1994) p. 227; see also Klein, 2005, p. 254.
39 Klein, 2005, p. 254.

40 Keyuan Zou, 2001, p. 160.

41 At the beginning of the 1930s, most Chinese maps were reproductions or based upon older maps. New fieldwork had not been undertaken for many years. These maps contained errors and some, without analysis, were copies of foreign-produced maps. As a result, Chinese ocean and land boundaries were not consistently shown on the various maps. This was obviously problematic for China as regards its sovereignty in the SCS. To respond to this, in January 1930 the Chinese government promulgated Consultation between the Ministry of Internal Affairs, the Foreign Ministry, the Marine Ministry, the Ministry of Education, and the Committee of Mongolia and Tibet led to an extension and revision of the above regulations in September 1931 with *The Revised Inspection Regulations of Land and Water Maps* (*Xiuzheng shuilu ditu shencha tiaoli*). Following further consultations, a Land and Water Maps Inspection Committee, whose members were representatives sent by the relevant institutions and departments, was formed and started work on June 7, 1933. The Land and Water Maps Inspection Committee made significant contributions to the defense of China's sovereignty in the SCS. At the 25th meeting held on December 21, 1934, the Committee examined and approved both Chinese and English names for all of the Chinese islands and reefs in the SCS. In the first issue of the Committee's journal published in January 1935, they listed the names of 132 islands, reefs, and low-tide elevations in the SCS, of which 28 were in the Paracel Islands archipelago and 96 in the Spratly Islands archipelago. At the 29th meeting held on March 12, 1935, based on the various questions raised by the Ya Xin Di Xueshe, the Committee stipulated that "except on the large-scale national administrative maps of China that should delineate the Pratas Islands, the Paracel Islands, the Macclesfield Bank and the Spratly Islands, other maps need not mark or note these islands if the locations of the islands were beyond the extent of the maps."

42 For details on the line and its legal implications, see Zou Keyuan, "The Chinese Traditional Maritime Boundary Line in the SCS and Its Legal Consequences for the Resolution of the Dispute over the Spratly Islands," *International Journal of Marine and Coastal Law*, Vol. 14 (1), 1999, 27–55; see also Zou Keyuan, 2001, p. 160.

43 See Kuan-Ming Sun, "Policy of the Republic of China towards the SCS," *Marine Policy*, Vol. 19, 1995, at 408; see also Zou Keyuan, "Historic Rights in International Law and in China's Practice," p. 160.

44 Zou Keyuan, 2001, p. 162.

45 Ibid.

46 Ibid, p. 163.

47 Chinese literature mentions significant historical evidence of China's exploration of the SCS. See, for instance, Li Jinming, "Evidences of Exploration and Management of the Paracel and Spratly Islands by the Chinese People," *Southeast Asian Affairs: A Quarterly Journal* (in Chinese), No. 2, 1996, 82–89 and Teh-Kuang Chang, "China's Claim of Sovereignty over Spratly and Paracel Islands: A Historical and Legal Perspective," *Case W. Res. J. Int'L L.*, Vol. 23, 1991, 399–420. A Taiwanese scholar has taken the view that since ancient times China has sent naval forces to patrol the SCS, arrested pirates, assisted in salvage, operated fishing activities such that China enjoys historic interests within the U-shaped line in regard to economic resources, navigational management, and security of national defence. See remarks of Fu Kuen-Chen at the Workshop on "Legal Regime of China's Historic Waters in the SCS," *Issues and Studies* (Chinese edition), Vol. 32, No. 8, 1993, 1–12. See discussion of Zou Keyuan, 2001, p. 162.

48 Zou Keyuan, 2001, p. 162.

49 UNCLOS, Article 77 (3).

50 Zou Keyuan, 2001, p. 162. See also D. P. O'Connell, *The International Law of the Sea*, Vol. 2 (Oxford: Clarendon Press, 1982), at p. 713.

51 See Separate Opinion of Judge ad hoc Jimenez de Arechage, *Continental Shelf (Tunisia v. Libya*, 1982 ICJ Reports, at pp. 123–24.
52 Nguyen Hong Thao, "China's maritime moves raise neighbors' hackles," *Vietnam Law & Legal Forum*, July 1998, at p. 21.
53 Ibid. at pp. 21–22.
54 See Zou Keyuan, 2001, p. 162; See also "Vietnam: Dispute regarding the Law on the Exclusive Economic Zone and the Continental Shelf of the People's Republic of China which Was Passed on 26 June 1998," *Law of the Sea Bulletin*, No. 38, 1998, at 55.
55 See Zou Keyuan, 2001, p. 163, see also Merrill Wesley Clark, Jr., *Historic Bays and Waters: A Regime of Recent Beginnings and Continued Usage* (New York: Oceana Publications, Inc., 1994), at p. 168.
56 Nayan Chanda, "The New Nationalism," *Far Eastern Economic Review*, November 9 1995, p. 22.
57 Interviews and informal discussions with Chinese Scholars and diplomats from 2004–2011. See also Zou Keyuan, 2001, p. 165.
58 Timo Kivimäki (ed.) *War or peace in the SCS?* (Copenhagen, Denmark: NIAS Press, 2002) p. 35.
59 The National Institute for the South China Sea Studies, for example, published in 2006 a book titled as "Historic Waters."
60 The author interviewed Professor John Moore in Virginia in February 2009.
61 The author interview these former judges of ITLOS in September 2008 in Hamburg.
62 Zou Keyuan, 2001, p. 167.
63 Continental Shelf (Tunisia/Libya), *1982 ICJ Reports*, at p.74, quoted again in "Land, Island and Maritime Frontier Dispute," 1992, *ICJ Reports*, at p. 589.
64 Sophia Kopela (2017), "Historic Titles and Historic Rights in the Law of the Sea in the Light of the South China Sea Arbitration," *Ocean Development & International Law*, 48:2, pp. 181–207.
65 The Republic of the Philippines v the People's Republic of China, PCA Case N 2013–19 in the matter of the South China Arbitration, Award of 12 July 2016 (Merits), available on the Permanent Court of Arbitration website at www.pca-cpa.org, p. 28.
66 The Republic of the Philippines v the People's Republic of China, PCA Case No. 2013–19 in the matter of the South China Arbitration, Award on Jurisdiction and Admissibility of 29 October 2015, available on the PCA website, www.pca-cpa.org, para. 101.
67 Position Paper of the Government of the People's Republic of China on the Matter of Jurisdiction in the South China Sea Arbitration Initiated by the Republic of the Philippines, 2014/12/07, www.fmprc.gov.cn/mfa_eng/zxxx_662805/t1217147.shtml
68 The Republic of the Philippines v the People's Republic of China, PCA Case N 2013–19 in the matter of the South China Arbitration, Award of 12 July 2016 (Merits), available on the Permanent Court of Arbitration website at www.pca-cpa.org. Para. 213.
69 Article 311 (1)of UNCLOS: This Convention shall prevail, as between States Parties, over the Geneva Conventions on the Law of the Sea of 29 April 1958.
70 Article 293 (1) says "A court or tribunal having jurisdiction under this section shall apply this Convention and other rules of international law not incompatible with this Convention."
71 Award of 12 July 2016 (Merits), para. 238(a).
72 Ibid. para. 238(d).
73 Sophia Kopela (2017), "Historic Titles and Historic Rights in the Law of the Sea in the Light of the South China Sea Arbitration," *Ocean Development & International Law*, 48:2, pp. 181–207, at p. 184.
74 H. Thirway, "The Sources of International Law," in M. D. Evans (ed.), *International Law* (4th edn, Oxford University Press, 2014), p. 109.

75 Sophia Kopela (2017), "Historic Titles and Historic Rights in the Law of the Sea in the Light of the South China Sea Arbitration," *Ocean Development & International Law*, 48:2, pp. 181–207 at p. 199.
76 South China Sea Arbitration Award (Merits), 245.
77 Kopela, 2017, p. 185.
78 See Case Concerning the Continental Shelf (Tunisia/Libyan Arab Jamahiriya), [1982] I.C.J. Reports, para. 100. "ICJ) stated that "historic titles must enjoy respect and be reserved as they have always been by long usage". See also Case Concerning Land, Island and Maritime Frontier Dispute (El Salvador/Honduras: Nicaragua Intervening), [1992] I.C.J. Reports, p. 589, para. 384.
79 Marvin A. Fentress, "Maritime Boundary Dispute Settlement: The Nonemergence of Guiding Principles," 15 Ga. *J. Int'l & Comp. L.* (1985), pp. 592, 622–23. See also Klein, 2005, p. 249.
80 J. Ashley Roach, "Dispute Settlement in Specific Situations," 7 Geo. *International Environmental Law Review* (1995), p. 777; also Klein, 2005, p. 252.
81 Ibid. See also Klein, 2005, p. 253.
82 See e.g., Y. Blum, "The Gulf of Sidra Incident" (1986) 80 *American Journal of International Law*, p. 668; see discussion of Symmons, 2008, p. 298).
83 See Symmons, 2008, p. 298.
84 Here, obviously, continue reliance on historic title will be necessary to maintain an internal waters claim: see e.g., W. Edeson, "The Validity of Australia's Possible Maritime Historic Claims in International Law" (1974) 48 *Australian Law Journal*, 295, p. 297; see also Symmons, 2008, p. 298.
85 Symmons, 2008, p. 298.
86 Zou Keyuan, 2001, p. 167.
87 L.F.E. Goldie, "Historic Bays in International Law – an Impressionistic Overview," *Syr. J. Int'l L. & Com.*, Vol. 11, 1984, at 271–72.
88 As has been observed: "The number and frequency of coastal states' claims in this regard shows that the old concept of an historic bay is currently evolving into a more flexible notion whose crucial elements are the *bona fide* assertion of State interests and the recognition of and acquiescence of third states, rather that immemorial usage and the long passage of time." See also, Francesco Francioni, "The Status of the Gulf of Sirte in International Law," *Syr. J. Int'l L. & Com.*, Vol. 11, 1984, at p. 325.

4 Navigational rights, freedoms, and interests in the South China Sea

The Philippines' perspective

Jay L. Batongbacal

Introduction

Samuel P. Huntington's *Clash of Civilizations* posits that cultural identities will become the principal sources of conflict in the post-Cold War world.[1] While this hypothesis has lately been more associated with the sharpening frictions between Western Christian and Muslim States and ethnic groups at various geographic scales and arenas, Huntington did also touch on Chinese civilization as among the key competitors of Western power and influence in the aftermath of the Cold War. Thirty years later, China's rapidly expanding geopolitical influence internationally, coupled with internal demands for steady progress toward its centenary goals,[2] appear to be indeed creating numerous frictions with the United States (as the leading Western power) in various areas of interests, including that which has historically been the most important ingredient for America's global prominence: maritime mobility as a fundamental element of seapower.[3]

The South China Sea (SCS) has opened as the primary arena of Sino-US geo-political competition in the twenty-first century, arising with the marked resurgence in tensions over territorial and jurisdictional disputes since 2009. Navigation-related incidents in the SCS disputes have seen the most intense and sustained flare-ups, compared to the relative calm after the signing of the 2002 Declaration of Conduct.[4] Numerous incidents involving encounters between ships (and more recently, aircraft) have taken place within a very short period as a result of the unprecedented mobilization and deployment of maritime military and law enforcement assets by littoral states and external powers as a means to assert and protect individual claims and interests. The most significant change in the *status quo* occurred in 2014 with China's creation of massive artificial islands that dwarf all the other pre-existing natural islands and facilities after the Philippines launched a legal challenge against China's claims through arbitration under UNCLOS Annex VII; the proceedings concluded in July 2016. Aside from further complicating the disputes, new challenges to maritime mobility emerged as China sought to ward off other States' surveillance efforts by establishing military alert zones around the new artificial islands.

The issue of maritime mobility through the SCS has effectively evolved into a trans-regional international dispute involving a much wider array of interested parties than ever before. Interests and perspectives converge and contrast regarding navigation and overflight rights and freedoms in the SCS, since the SCS is a wide sea area used historically as an international maritime passage route. It is dotted by numerous islands and rocks that could be the basis for establishing maritime zones, and subject to competing claims to territorial sovereignty and maritime jurisdiction. It is also accessible through straits of varied width and density of use.

Navigation and overflight in UNCLOS

The navigational rights, freedoms and interests of all States beyond their own national territories encompass both maritime and aerial domains. These in turn must be balanced against the interests of other States in exercising and ensuing the integrity of their sovereignty and jurisdiction extending over and from their respective territories. In establishing the layered system of maritime zones appurtenant to all coastal states, UNCLOS establishes a sophisticated legal regime for navigation and overflight for the benefit of user states and thereby strikes a balance between their respective interests. To lay out this elaborate system in detail will take an entirely separate volume of work, thus for the purposes of this article it is only necessary to describe it in broad strokes.

The basic elements of this regime are comprised of the guaranteed passage rights which may be exercised in the jurisdiction of coastal states outside of internal waters. The customary right of innocent passage within the 12 nm territorial sea,[5] through straits used for international navigation,[6] and any archipelagic waters enclosed by them[7] (made applicable in accordance with UNCLOS) are at the foundation of this system of guarantees meant to ensure seamless mobility across oceans and seas between States. Unimpeded passage through constrained straits enclosed within the territorial waters of bordering States, as well as through archipelagic waters of archipelagic States, are additionally guaranteed by the treaty-based and similar rights of transit passage[8] and archipelagic sea lanes passage,[9] respectively. Outside the territorial sea, foreign ships are entitled to exercise high seas freedoms in both the EEZ and the high seas beyond,[10] although the 12 to 24 nm contiguous zone is additionally subject to specific coastal state jurisdiction over customs, immigration, fiscal and sanitary regulation.[11]

Generally, user states exercising these passage rights have duties to comply with reasonable rules of the coastal state meant to ensure the latter's interests in matters such as security, safety and resources,[12] while coastal states are recognized to be able to reasonably regulate foreign passage to the extent that, and for as long as, they do not actually hinder or impede such passage.[13] However, the regulatory jurisdiction of coastal states is limited to legislation and rule-making in specified instances, as unilateral enforcement jurisdiction needs to be positively recognized in UNCLOS or customary law in order to be effective.[14]

Where recognized, coastal state enforcement must contend with the inherent limitation established by the principle of sovereign immunity of other States' warships and other vessels or aircraft in government service.[15] It is also obliged to carry out enforcement using only warships or ships in the government service, especially in the high seas beyond national jurisdiction.[16] Furthermore, the exercise of enforcement against foreign vessels must be undertaken in a manner that does not endanger the safety of navigation or otherwise create any hazard to a vessel, or bring it to an unsafe port or anchorage, or expose the marine environment to unreasonable risk.[17]

In the absence of recognition of the coastal state's ability to unilaterally enforce laws or rules, the principle of flag State jurisdiction usually prevails and coastal states must therefore call upon the flag States' responsibility and cooperation in the enforcement of the former's laws and rules. This is on account of the restrictions on the criminal and civil jurisdiction of coastal states over merchant and sovereign vessels in their waters.[18] These restrictions remain the starting point and must be constantly considered in relation to any proposed exercise of coastal state jurisdiction. Otherwise, the unilateral exercise of coastal state jurisdiction over foreign flag vessels is recognized only in very limited instances such as suppression of piracy in the high seas, slave-trading, illicit traffic in narcotic drugs, and unauthorized broadcasting.[19]

Apart from flag State jurisdiction, three other principles dominate the balancing of user and coastal state interests. One is the principle of non-interference, in which the coastal state should not exercise its jurisdiction in ways that have the practical effect of denying or impairing passage.[20] The other is the principle of non-discrimination, which means that coastal states in the recognition of user state rights should not discriminate in form or in fact against any State, ships, or cargoes.[21] These are particularly emphatic for passage within the territorial sea and straits used for international navigation. The third principle is emerging as the most contestable, the principle of due regard that States are bound to observe in favor of each other;[22] this may be owed by the user state to the coastal state, or to another user state, within any given maritime zone. There is no specific and clear definition of "due regard" and what it entitles, although it may be understood as a kind of Golden Rule, or rule of reciprocity, as commonly observed in international law.

The elaborate system of rules in UNCLOS governing navigation and overflight is by no means perfect. It is generally accepted that apart from the provisions relating to passage rights and sovereign immunity, UNCLOS does not otherwise regulate military activities, vessels or aircraft in the maritime arena. Such activities comprise one of the most important historical, continuing, and controversial uses of the oceans. This, however, has not prevented coastal states from invoking their jurisdictions against military activities, vessels or aircraft, and the constant exchange of assertions and denials is no more frequent than in incidents in the EEZ, where the exclusive sovereign rights and jurisdictions to natural resources, regulation of marine scientific research, as well as the principle of reservation of the oceans and high seas for peaceful uses, are pitted against the practical effects of military activities.[23]

Incidents in the SCS since 2009

The year 2009 is a significant milestone in the downward trend in the SCS disputes, beginning with the *USNS Impeccable* incident wherein five Chinese government and civilian vessels converged upon the unarmed US Navy ship carrying out an ocean surveillance mission 75 nautical miles off Hainan Island.[24] The vessels interfered with the ship's safe navigation by coming within twenty-five feet and stopping in front of the *USNS Impeccable*, forcing emergency maneuvers to prevent collision.[25] The US protested the actions as "reckless, unprofessional, and unlawful" but China argued that the ship was conducting illegal activities under Chinese and international law.[26] Similar incidents also took place involving other US Navy ships in the Yellow Sea, at least four events in the two seas off the coast of China were recorded in May 2009.[27] These incidents became the subject of special high-level meetings between US and PRC officials.[28] China maintained that its EEZ was off-limits to foreign intelligence-gathering, while the US insisted that the EEZ was deemed part of international waters subject to all uses other than for economic purposes.[29] Both sides acknowledged differing views on the interpretation of international law in this area but deemed it necessary to discuss operational issues of interaction between their ships.[30] The high-level dialogues apparently addressed the matter in the short term, the incidents between military ships were not repeated the following year.

The following month in June 2009, Vietnam reported that its fishing vessels had been attacked and sunk while fishing near the Spratly and Paracel islands; Vietnamese fishermen would have been lost at sea had they not been rescued by other fishing vessels.[31] Just days later, a Chinese submarine collided with the towed sonar array of the *USS John S. McCain* at an unspecified location some 140 nautical miles from Subic Bay, Philippines adjacent to the South China Sea.[32]

In March 2011, two Chinese patrol boats ordered a seismic exploration ship contracted by the Philippines surveying waters near the Spratly islands to leave the area and even threatened to ram it.[33] In May, two Chinese MiG-29s reportedly entered the airspace above the Philippine-claimed Kalayaan Islands and buzzed two Philippine Air Force OV-10 Broncos on a routine surveillance mission over Reed Bank.[34] This was followed by a serious incident off Vietnam in June 2011, when Chinese patrol ships approached a Vietnamese seismic survey vessel at high speeds and deliberately cut its seismic exploration cables.[35] The following month, the Indian Navy ship *INS Airavat* was hailed through radio by a Chinese officer who demanded that the ship explain its presence despite the fact that the ship was within the Vietnamese EEZ heading toward Haiphong in Vietnam; this was said to be typical of the Chinese approach to vessels operating in the SCS.[36] In October, a Philippine Navy ship investigating a Chinese trawler towing about 35 smaller vessels through the Reed Bank area accidentally collided with one of the smaller vessels.[37] The trawler left and abandoned 25 small vessels entangled with the Philippine ship.[38]

The year 2012 was marked primarily by a tense stand-off between Philippine and Chinese vessels sparked by the attempted arrest of Chinese fishermen at

Scarborough Shoal, which China calls Huangyan Island, located 124 nautical miles from the Philippine island of Luzon. As the stand-off ensued from April to July, two navigational incidents occurred. One involved a Philippine research vessel attempting to resume marine archaeological research at Scarborough Shoal; Chinese aircraft reportedly buzzed the vessel and the China alleged that it was conducting "illegal salvage archaeology" of an ancient Chinese shipwreck and demanded its departure.[39] Another involved a Chinese Navy frigate that ran aground on Half Moon Shoal while preventing Philippine fishing boats from approaching.[40] Months later in November, the cables of a Vietnamese seismic exploration vessel conducting surveys were severed by Chinese fishing vessels.[41]

The culmination of events in the Scarborough Shoal incident led the Philippines to initiate an arbitration case against China in January 2013, pursuant to UNCLOS Part XV and Annex VII.[42] The proceedings led China to put even greater pressure to bear on the Philippines in the months that followed as relations between the two countries reached an absolute low. The following March 2013, Malaysia lodged a diplomatic protest with China over the conduct of exercises in James Shoal, some 50 nautical miles from Malaysia, by four Chinese warships.[43] In May, the Philippines lodged protests with China over the presence of warships, surveillance vessels, and numerous fishing boats around Second Thomas Shoal, located about 105 nautical miles from the Philippine island of Palawan, occupied by a small contingent of Philippine marines onboard a grounded ship.[44] In December, a Chinese Navy ship placed itself in front of the guided missile cruiser *USS Cowpens* near an area where the Chinese aircraft carrier *Liaoning* was undergoing sea trials.[45]

In January 2014, Malaysia lodged another diplomatic protest over Chinese patrols in the vicinity of James Shoal.[46] The following month, the Philippines sent a protest against China's use of water cannon against small Philippine fishing vessels attempting to shelter at Scarborough Shoal.[47] In March, Chinese vessels prevented two civilian supply ships from reaching the contingent on Second Thomas Shoal, accusing the Philippines of attempting to build structures there.[48] Another crisis erupted in May when China sent its new offshore oil rig the HY-981 to conduct exploratory drilling near the Paracels some 120 nautical miles from the Vietnamese coast.[49] This led to numerous collision incidents between Vietnamese and Chinese ships, as the former attempted to interfere with the drilling and the latter cordoned them off from the oil rig.[50] The stand-off continued well into July, until China withdrew the rig.

In August, the US announced that dangerous encounters had actually taken to the air, with the interception by Chinese aircraft of US surveillance planes operating in the region. Aerial interceptions took place in March, April, and May, but the US did not publicize them until after another incident in August when a Chinese J-11 fighter buzzed an American P-8 maritime patrol aircraft off Hainan Island.[51] The US complained of dangerous maneuvers by the J-11, coming to within 9 meters of the wing, and at one point doing a barrel roll over the P-8.[52] China denied any wrongdoing and lay blame on the US for undertaking "large-scale and highly frequent close-in reconnaissance."[53]

Aerial navigation became the central focus the following year. In early May 2015, the Armed Forces of the Philippines revealed that Philippine aircraft conducting routine surveillance began receiving radio warnings and demands to leave the disputed areas around Philippine positions in the Spratlys.[54] The warnings began as China continued unabatedly with reclamation activities started the previous year to create artificial islands out of the seven reefs it occupied in the SCS.[55] Concerns were raised that these warnings foreshadowed the declaration of an Air Defense Identification Zone (ADIZ) in the SCS, recalling tensions in the East China Sea where China declared an ADIZ in 2013.[56] Regardless, it was clear that the warnings were intended to discourage surveillance of China's artificial island-building activities at the time. Later that month, the US revealed that its own P-8 surveillance aircraft were subjected to repeated warnings to stay away from unannounced Chinese "military alert zones" around the artificial islands.[57]

China's attempts to constrain US surveillance flights through such zones prompted a more serious response. The US ramped up from unannounced surveillance to publicized freedom of navigation operations (FONOPs) in October, beginning with a voyage by the guided missile destroyer *USS Lassen* to within 12 nautical miles of China-held Mischief and Subi Reefs.[58] The US asserted that it was the first of a series of FONOP that would become more frequent; China described the operation as a "coercive action that seeks to militarize the SCS region" and an "abuse" of freedom of navigation under international law.[59]

The second FONOP took place in January 2016, when the *USS Curtis Wilbur* sailed within 12 nautical miles of Triton Island in the Paracels without notifying either China or Vietnam.[60] The following month, it was revealed that the Royal Australian Air Force had also been conducting its own FONOPs since the previous year.[61] A third US FONOP took place in May 2016, with the *USS William P Lawrence* passing within 12 nautical miles of Fiery Cross Reef.[62]

Tensions rose sharply in July 2016 when the Annex VII tribunal handed out its decision on the merits in the *Philippines v. China* case, in which the Philippines won almost all of its submissions. Immediately, China initiated combat air patrols over Scarborough Shoal using an HK-6 nuclear bomber.[63] But a change in leadership in the Philippines broke the upward trend of tensions when the new Philippine President introduced a radical foreign policy shift of friendliness toward China and open disdain for the US. In later October, Filipino fishermen were able to resume fishing in Scarborough Shoal without interference from Chinese law enforcement vessels even though they remained on station.[64] In the same month, as the regional atmosphere relaxed, the US conducted a new FONOP, this time with the *USS Decatur* traversing the waters between the Paracel Islands.[65] As the year drew to a close, China seized an underwater drone while it was being recovered by the US survey ship *USS Bowditch* just 50nm northwest of Subic Bay in the Philippines.[66] The drone was returned to the US after the latter protested the action.

In February 2017, it was also reported that a US EP-3 maritime patrol craft and Chinese KJ-200 AWACS aircraft had an unexpected and unsafe encounter in the air in the vicinity of Scarborough Shoal.[67] The aerial incident marks a new year of possibly more unexpected encounters between ships and aircraft operating in the region.

US policy on freedom of navigation and overflight operations

The current US policy on freedom of navigation and overflight, and the program to assert them, have been in place since March 1979.[68] These are rooted in US positions during the negotiations for the UN Convention on the Law of the Sea, and articulated as specific national security policy as early as 1982, making it clear that despite the impending conclusion of the negotiations, "[t]he United States will also continue to exercise its rights with respect to navigation and overflight against claims that the United States does not recognize."[69] Maintenance of navigation and overflight rights were therefore at the heart of US concerns about the breadth of the territorial sea and the then-proposed exclusive economic zone. Although the relevant provisions of UNCLOS were eventually deemed acceptable and consistent with US interests, the decision was made to not sign it, and "review the US navigation and overflight program focusing on protecting US rights and directing the practice of states toward the US interpretation of the navigation and overflight provisions of the Law of the Sea Convention."[70] The US considers the navigation and overflight regimes established by UNCLOS for the territorial sea, contiguous zone, EEZ and continental shelf, and high seas as representing an agreed and acceptable balance of rights and freedoms between coastal states and user states.

The establishment of the Freedom of Navigation and Overflight Program in 1982 was intended to "continue to protect US navigation, overflight, and related security interests in the seas through the vigorous exercise of its rights against excessive maritime claims" due to continuing uncertainty in the law of the sea and US decision not to become a party at the time.[71] The program was to protect US interests against a detailed list of what were deemed excessive maritime claims:[72]

1. Those historic bay/historic water claims not recognized by the United States.
2. Those continental territorial sea baseline claims not drawn in accordance with the LOS Convention.
3. Those territorial seas claims exceeding three miles but not exceeding twelve miles in breadth that:
   a. overlap straits used for international navigation and do not permit transit passage in conformance with the LOS Convention, including submerged transit of submarines, overflight of military aircraft, and surface transit of warships/naval auxiliaries, without prior notification or authorization; or
   b. contain requirements for advance notification or authorization for warships/naval auxiliaries or apply discriminatory requirements to such vessels; or

  c. apply special requirements, not recognized by international law, to nuclear-powered warships or to warships/naval auxiliaries carrying nuclear weapons on specific cargoes.
4. Territorial sea claims in excess of twelve miles.
5. Other claims to jurisdiction over maritime areas in excess of twelve miles, such as exclusive economic zones or security zones, which purport to restrict non-resource related high seas freedoms.
6. Those archipelagic claims that:
  a. are not in conformance with the LOS Convention, or
  b. do not permit archipelagic sea lanes passage in conformance with the LOS Convention, including submerged passage of submarines and overflight of military aircraft, including transit in a manner of deployment consistent with the security of the forces involved.

The Freedom of Navigation and Overflight Program directed both operational assertions by the Department of Defense and diplomatic protests by the Department of State. Despite being a non-party, the US attempted to trade the recognition of its navigation and overflight interests by coastal states for US recognition of the latter's maritime entitlements and jurisdictions:

> The United States is prepared to accept and act in accordance with the balance of interests reflected in the Law of the Sea Convention relating to traditional uses of the oceans, such as navigation and overflight. In this respect, the United States will (1) recognize the rights of other states in the waters off their coasts, as reflected in the Law of the Sea Convention, so long as the rights and freedoms of the United States and others under international law are recognized by such coastal states; and (2) as indicated in National Security Decision Directive 72, the United States will exercise and assert its navigation and overflight rights and freedoms in a manner that is consistent with the results reflected in the Convention.

After several years, the program was again adjusted to "strive for a balanced challenge program which contests the excessive claims or illegal regimes of allied or friendly states, inimical powers, and neutral states alike" with special emphasis given to challenging "claims which have no record of prior challenge."[73] Since then, the program has continuously been implemented, with each year's operational assertions regularly reported and publicized by the Department of State.[74]

With respect to the SCS, historically the US remained aloof to the disputes, emphasizing its neutrality over competing claims and preference that the claimants settle their disputes peacefully, despite attempts by its treaty ally the Philippines to get it more involved in the 1970s and 1980s.[75] Such neutrality remained in place despite Philippine concerns with China's activities in Mischief Reef and Scarborough Shoal in the 1990s. The *modus vivendi* reached in the 2002 Declaration of Conduct of the Parties in the South China Sea seemed to satisfy all the parties that the region was on a trajectory toward proper management of the disputes.

However, in 2010, due to the notable increase in incidents and absence of progress in efforts to manage and resolve the disputes, US Secretary of State Hillary Clinton declared US policy principles toward the SCS as including freedom of navigation, unimpeded commerce, recognition of maritime rights only in accordance with UNCLOS, preference for a collaborative (apparently multi-lateral) diplomatic process among claimants to resolve territorial claims, and encouragement of the negotiation of a Code of Conduct.[76] This drew a sharp rebuke from China, which saw the statement as interference in its affairs, and set the stage for increasingly sharp exchanges over the SCS between China and the US in the years that followed.

As China increasingly asserted its claimed prerogatives against Southeast Asian littoral states, the latter reacted by seeking greater US involvement in the SCS as a foil against Chinese behavior. The US perceived a disturbing pattern of intimidation and coercive behavior against the smaller States' interests in the maritime arena that, left unchecked, could lead toward eventual restriction of the US' own interests in unhindered military mobility and maritime commerce. The US began to be more vocal about its freedom of navigation and overflight interests in published statements and policies toward the SCS. Most recently, the US continuing insistence on freedom of navigation and overflight in the SCS, in the context of the ongoing disputes, were summarized and reiterated by Assistant Secretary Daniel Russell as follows:

> For us, it's not about the rocks and shoals in the South China Sea or the resources in and under it, it's about the rules and it's about the kind of neighborhood we all want to live in. So, we will continue to defend the rules, and encourage others to do so as well.[77]

This signaled a subtle shift in US attitudes toward the SCS; from absolute neutrality and relative detachment to a slightly more active intercession. Russell stressed the point more pointedly in the following manner: 'We are not neutral when it comes to adhering to international law. We will come down forcefully when it comes to following the rules.'[78]

He also laid out in very clear terms what the specific interests of the US were in the context of the disputes:

> Protecting unimpeded freedom of navigation and overflight and other lawful uses of the sea by all, not just the US Navy;
>
> Honoring our alliance and security commitments, and retaining the full confidence of our partners and the region in the United States;
>
> Aiding the development of effective regional institutions, including a unified ASEAN;
>
> Promoting responsible marine environmental practices;

> Fostering China's peaceful rise in a manner that promotes economic growth and regional stability, including through consistency with international law and standards;
>
> And more generally, an international order based on compliance with international law and the peaceful settlement of disputes without the threat or use of force.[79]

The turning point for the US shift was apparently China's artificial island-building activities in the SCS in 2014. The following year, China began warning away aircraft on approach vectors to its new islands, signaling a new phase of active interference in overflight in the region. Navigation and overflight freedoms were again highlighted subsequently in the published US strategy for the Asia-Pacific that prominently featured China's new artificial islands and their implications to the regional order.[80]

US policies regarding navigation and overflight are a known quantity: they have been well-documented and in place for a very long time prior to the flare-up in the SCS tensions in 2013–2016. On account of clarity in its policy, its actions and decisions on how to protect its interests are relatively predictable even if their exact timing are not. The conduct of FONOPs in the SCS, in light of the marked change in China's actions and accompanying rhetoric, was a foreseeable event and there is no reason to not expect that further FONOPs in the SCS will continue to be conducted well into the future.

China's emergent policies on freedom of navigation and overflight

China's policies on freedom of navigation and overflight have been officially articulated in more detail relatively recently, but is complicated by the fact that it has done so in connection with the ongoing disputes in the South China Sea. But it does also have a older lineage. In 1974, John Norton Moore, the US' lead negotiator for UNCLOS, met with officials of China's Permanent Mission to the United Nations led by Counselor Madame Ho Hi-Liang and First Secretary Tang Hsing-Po. The report on the discussions between Mdm. Ho and Mr. Moore states:

> On territorial sea, she said that in PRC view each country can set limit to territorial sea according to its geographic, economic and security conditions. Breadth of territorial sea should be reasonable. She stressed that PRC claims 12 miles and asked whether US could accept 12 miles. Moore said US could accept 12-mile limit as part of satisfactory overall comprehensive LOS Treaty including unimpeded transit of straits…
>
> On straits, Madame Ho stated PRC believes innocent passage regime should apply even in international straits. Further, there should be advance notification to coastal states of passage of warships through straits. PRC interest, she

> said, was to maintain international security and peace. She expressed concern with deployment of warships in areas far from home countries, specifically mentioning Mediterranean, China Sea, and Pacific Ocean...
>
> Madame Ho concluded discussion of straits with remark that US and PRC views on passage of warships differ ... PRC considers that warships of one nation should not be permitted to approach close to the shores of another country without the latter's consent.
>
> Madame Ho said that PRC supports establishment of economic zone beyond the territorial sea for a maximum distance of 200 miles except possibly for continental shelf. Within zone there should be no distinction between jurisdiction over living and non-living resources and there should no exploitation of resource within zone without consent of coastal state. She stressed that coastal states should have exclusive and not preferential rights. In PRC view, there would be freedom of navigation and overflight in economic zone...
>
> Madame Ho emphasized that scientific research in zone should be carried out only with consent of coastal state. Moore noted US flag State approach and indicated importance for all mankind of protecting freedom of scientific research.[81]

Subsequently at the Caracas Session of UNCLOS III, China's head of delegation Chai Shu-fan formally stated in plenary that

> coastal states have the right to regulate international straits and formulate necessary rules and regulations in accordance with their security needs, while taking into account the convenience of international navigation and some reasonable international[82] standards. Non-military ships should have right of innocent passage while military ships would be subject to coastal state regulations and prior notification.

However, these original policies appear to have changed in step with China's expanding maritime capabilities since then. While it maintains its original strict policy for the territorial sea that denies the right of innocent passage by military ships and requires prior consent to enter,[83] its restrictive attitude has extended outward to the EEZ. Although it acknowledges that any States may enjoy freedom of navigation and overflight in China's EEZ, it may do so only if such State "observes international law and the law and regulations of the People's Republic of China."[84] This conditional recognition essentially attempts to reserve in favor of China the jurisdiction to regulate activities of foreign ships and aircraft.

Debates over the issue of military activities in the EEZ were re-ignited in 2001 on account of several incidents involving US, Chinese, Vietnamese, Japanese, and Korean ships and aircraft operating in EEZs, and although these were never officially resolved (such resolution would probably require clarificatory amendments to the LOS Convention),[85] nonetheless they marked historical junctures during which China deliberately reconsidered its position with respect to navigation and overflight in the EEZ.[86] A decade later, China perceived an additional need to assert its territorial and maritime claims against those of smaller Southeast Asian littoral states and embarked on a maritime rights protection and law enforcement program using its civilian maritime law enforcement forces that steadily ramped up its presence and patrols in the SCS.[87] These operations inevitably led to even more incidents implicating navigation and overflight rights.

Insofar as the SCS is concerned, China's policies toward navigation and overflight are somewhat fuzzy. On one hand, China continues to assure the international community that it guarantees and respects freedom of navigation and overflight through the SCS. Despite issues raised by the Philippines' claim that China's actions and posture posed a threat to freedom of navigation and overflight in the SCS, in December 2014 China expressly stated publicly: "It should be particularly emphasized that China always respects the freedom of navigation and overflight enjoyed by all States in the South China Sea in accordance with international law."[88]

After the Annex VII tribunal issued its Award, China released a white paper thereon, maintaining its opposition and refusal to recognize the tribunal and the award, but seeking to again assure the international community by devoting an entire section expressly stating its position on navigation and overflight:

> 136. China is committed to upholding the freedom of navigation and overflight enjoyed by all states under international law, and ensuring the safety of sea lanes of communication.
>
> 137. The South China Sea is home to a number of important sea lanes, which are among the main navigation routes for China's foreign trade and energy import. Ensuring freedom of navigation and overflight and safety of sea lanes in the South China Sea is crucial to China. Over the years, China has worked with ASEAN Member States to ensure unimpeded access to and safety of the sea lanes in the South China Sea and made important contribution to this collective endeavor. The freedom of navigation and overflight enjoyed by all states in the South China Sea under international law has never been a problem.
>
> 138. China has actively provided international public goods and made every effort to provide services, such as navigation and navigational aids, search and rescue, as well as sea conditions and meteorological forecast, through capacity building in various areas, so as to uphold and promote the safety of sea lanes in the South China Sea.
>
> 139. China maintains that, when exercising freedom of navigation and overflight in the South China Sea, relevant parties shall fully respect the sovereignty and security interests of coastal states and abide by the laws and regulations enacted by coastal states in accordance with UNCLOS and other rules of international law.

China highlights the exclusive sovereign rights of a coastal state in its EEZ, and considers foreign military activities such as those conducted by the US to be in derogation of the coastal states' exclusive sovereign rights and therefore inherently illegal. This applies specifically to foreign military activities, vessels and aircraft in the EEZ, and is in line with its earlier reservation of coastal state jurisdiction in the EEZ. The requirement for compliance with international law "and the laws and regulations" of China provides the foundation for contesting practically all kinds of foreign military activities.

China subsumes military survey activities such as hydrographic surveys under the broader category of marine scientific research, and therefore insists that the former cannot be undertaken without the express consent of the coastal state in accordance with UNCLOS Part XIII.[89] To this end it invokes its EEZ legislation prohibiting marine scientific research without its consent.[90] More overtly military activities in the EEZ such as naval patrols and reconnaissance are considered to be serious infringements of coastal state security interests, and not legitimate exercises of freedom of navigation and overflight.[91] China does not consider the EEZ to be the high seas subject to high seas freedoms, but even if it were, the high seas are "reserved for peaceful purposes" and therefore still do not allow for military activities.[92] Moreover, it considers foreign military activities in the EEZ as contrary to flag State obligations to ensure its actions are harmless, undertaken in good faith, do not abuse its rights, and gives due regard to the rights of the coastal state.[93]

In addition, China's formerly ambivalent claims to the SCS on the basis of historic rights, represented by its so-called nine dashed lines map[94] and previously argued to cover a range of possible prerogatives from territorial rights to special rights to natural resources,[95] appear to have been used to justify activities carried out against vessels and aircraft. The conflation of claims to "indisputable and indivisible" sovereignty over the islands, rocks, and other maritime features based on historic rights within the nine dashed lines[96] with the claims to maritime jurisdiction under UNCLOS[97] meld China's policy over the territorial sea with its policy over the EEZ, and applies it to much of the SCS. Thus, China has rejected and warned against the conduct of freedom of navigation operations by the US, Japan, and Australia.[98] In response to a recent deployment of a carrier battle group to the SCS, China declared:

> China always respects the freedom of navigation and overflight that countries enjoy in the South China Sea under international law. But we oppose relevant countries threatening and undermining the sovereignty and security of coastal states under the pretext of such freedom. We hope that relevant countries can do more for regional peace and stability.[99]

The problem now lies with China's practice. By invoking and conflating EEZ and territorial claims and asserting rights throughout the entire area of the nine dashed lines, other States interpret China's actions as attempts to assert full and absolute sovereignty indiscriminately through the entire SCS. Even if China insists that it respects freedom of navigation and overflight, it is still subject to the reservation of jurisdiction found in Chinese law which may be asserted at any time in the future. In the absence of unqualified recognition of navigation and overflight freedoms beyond the territorial sea in the SCS, China's position will therefore always be looked upon with suspicion and equal reservation on the part of neighboring and external States.

Caught in between: The Philippines and other littoral states

The smaller Southeast Asian littoral states' interests in navigation and overflight have traditionally been limited to their perceived nearshore areas, either straits, and/or the inter-island waters of archipelagoes. At the time of negotiations for UNCLOS, these States did not have any significant maritime naval capabilities, and thus had generally viewed foreign military presence in their waters adversely. Their respective starting points for negotiation about navigation and overflight at the UNCLOS conferences were, like China, restrictive as they sought to protect themselves from perceived threat of gunboat diplomacy and foreign intervention that characterized their colonial past. These manifested in claims to larger areas of sovereignty over water, and to greater regulatory prerogative over the entry and passage of vessels and aircraft.

The former was exemplified by the archipelagic State claims of the Philippines and Indonesia, the two largest Southeast Asian archipelagoes. In 1972, they submitted to the Seabed Committee a statement of archipelagic principles[100] that included the recognition of the archipelagic State concept and basic passage rights in favor of foreign vessels within archipelagic waters:

> 3. Innocent passage of foreign vessels through the waters of the archipelagic State shall be allowed in accordance with national legislation, having regard to the existing rules of international law. Such passage shall be through sea lanes as may be designated for that purpose by the archipelagic State.

This was elaborated into draft articles on archipelagoes, containing five detailed articles with numerous sections.[101] Passage rights in favor of foreign vessels were proposed to be recognized "in sea lanes suitable for the safe and expeditious passage of ships through its archipelagic waters" and the archipelagic State "may restrict the innocent passage by foreign ships through those waters to those sea lanes."[102] The original intention of the archipelagic States here may be properly described as restrictive, and rang alarm bells for the maritime powers in view of their obvious potential impact on submarine and carrier group operations. In the years that followed, a flurry of diplomatic activity, particularly between the US and Indonesia in 1974, over the text submitted by the "archipelago group" introduced at the joint session of the Seabed Committee in Caracas,[103] led to the formulation and finalization of text that became Part IV of UNCLOS. Part IV establishes two passage regimes for navigation and overflight applicable to archipelagic waters: innocent passage for ships, and archipelagic sea lanes passages for both ships and aircraft.

Current Philippine and Indonesian official practice, however, indicates that neither archipelagic State has fully given up on the claim to regulatory prerogatives over foreign vessels and aircraft in their archipelagic waters. In the case of the Philippines, technically it still holds on to its original position at the UNCLOS negotiations that denies foreign vessels and aircraft innocent passage rights through its archipelagic waters despite its declared position in the *Philippines v. China* arbitration. As a civil law country, Philippine statutes are binding until they are amended or repealed, and as of this writing the standing legislation still establishes a restrictive policy against foreign vessels and aircraft passage. Although the Philippines enacted UNCLOS-compliant archipelagic baselines in 2009,[104] it did not expressly repeal the provisions of the previous baselines law that characterizes as "internal" all waters within the baselines, and "territorial" all waters beyond the baselines up to the irregular rectangular lines formed by the early twentieth-century cession treaties that identified the islands of the Philippine archipelago.[105] Legislation to expressly establish an UNCLOS-compliant territorial sea have yet to be passed.

The Philippines' prospective attitude toward archipelagic sea lanes and archipelagic sea lanes passage further may be gleaned from examination of the text of proposed archipelagic sea lanes legislation originally filed in 2011, namely House Bill no. 4153 and its counterpart Senate Bill no. 2738.[106] The archipelagic sea lanes bill purports to unilaterally designate three sea lanes through the archipelago and expressly attempts to limit all foreign vessel passage to only those three sea lanes. This designation was to be legislated without the requisite consultation with the International Maritime Organization. The bill repeatedly stalled in Congress and had not been passed as of this writing, but the latest version eliminates the unilateral designation of sea lanes and instead merely authorizes the President to carry out the designation process.[107] However, the legislative intent appears to be to ensure that the Philippines is, like Indonesia, able to limit foreign vessel passage to only the designated sea lanes. Speaking on the passage of the bill on Third Reading at the sixteenth Congress, sponsor Congressman Ace Acedillo is quoted that "[t]he ASL law will now delimit maritime areas that foreign ships can pass through without inviting suspicion," and leaves it to the President to define the sea routes where foreign vessels can pass through.[108] The draft law also expressly attempts to regulate the exercise of the right of archipelagic sea lane passage by specifying the rights and obligations of vessels and aircraft exercising archipelagic sea lanes passage right.

In addition, the Philippines holds similarly restrictive views against the passage of fishing vessels and cargo vessels carrying toxic substances or hazardous and nuclear wastes. The Fisheries Code establishes an evidentiary *prima facie* presumption against foreign fishing vessels found in any of its waters, including the EEZ; such vessels are presumed to be carrying out illegal fishing and therefore subject to arrest, detention, and criminal and administrative sanctions.[109] And the Toxic Substances and Hazardous or Nuclear Wastes Control Act penalizes the entry and transit of such prohibited substances into the Philippine territorial limits (which are maritime in nature).[110] The Philippines does not have a specific law or policy against military activities, vessels and aircraft of other States transiting or operating in its EEZ.

In Indonesia's case, despite the partial designation of archipelagic sea lanes under Part IV of UNCLOS, Indonesian Government Regulation No. 37 issued in 2002 elaborates on the rights and obligations of foreign ships and aircraft exercising the right of archipelagic sea lanes passage and specifies that such right can only be exercised in an archipelagic sea lane designated for that purpose.[111] It is even more specific that after the regulation takes effect, "foreign ships and aircraft can exercise the right of archipelagic sea lanes passage only through the designated Indonesian archipelagic sea lanes."[112] It thus appears that Indonesia considers all archipelagic waters to be subject to the innocent passage regime by default, and that the right of archipelagic sea lanes passage can be asserted only after archipelagic sea lanes have been designated in specific areas of its archipelagic waters. This is in contrast with UNCLOS Article 53(12) which posits that the archipelagic sea lanes passage regime exists in archipelagic waters particularly in the absence of a sea lane designation. A subsequent clarification explained that the right of archipelagic sea lanes passage may be used by foreign ships seeking to sail through Indonesian waters from one part of the EEZ or high seas to another part of the EEZ/high seas; in contrast, all other ships entering Indonesian waters intending to call or anchor at Indonesian ports are to observe the innocent passage regime, even as they traverse the archipelagic sea lanes.[113] Again, this indicates that Indonesia's position on navigation and overflight through its waters are not as liberal as UNCLOS prescribes.

During the UNCLOS negotiations, Malaysia's positions on navigation and overflight were defined primarily in relation to its interests in the strategic Strait of Malacca. On one hand, this aligned closely with Indonesian positions since the latter also shared portions of the Strait of Malacca, as well as controlled several other strategic straits elsewhere in the Indonesian archipelago. On the other hand, its restrictive view was presented more clearly as arising from its concerns over pollution emitted by thousands of vessels passing each year. In 1976, Malaysia tabled the draft articles to strengthen control over navigation and overflight and protect interests vis-à-vis pollution.[114] Its principal concerns centered around tanker traffic in the Strait of Malacca, and it sought to establish unilateral regulatory and enforcement rights over vessel traffic.[115] Eventually, it was satisfied with the concessions now contained in the regulatory provisions in favor of bordering States contained in UNCLOS Part III.

Instead of military vessels and activities in the EEZ, however, Malaysia discriminates against fishing vessels. Although it generally allows foreign fishing vessels to enter and transit Malaysian waters, including the EEZ, it legally requires prior notification for such entry and transit.[116] The stringent policy against fishing vessels particularly led to sometimes fatal incidents between Malaysian law enforcement and Thai fishing vessels in the 1970s and 1980s.[117]

Vietnam recently passed legislation to streamline applicable rules to Vietnamese maritime zones. While it recognizes the right of innocent passage in favor of foreign vessels in its territorial sea, it requires prior notice for entry and transit of foreign military vessels.[118] Otherwise, its policies are generally consistent with UNCLOS; and it recognizes freedom of navigation and overflight in its EEZ so long as such navigation and overflight operations "are not detrimental to the sovereign rights, jurisdiction and national maritime interests of Vietnam."[119] This qualification, unlike China's, is more general and ambivalent, but performs a similar function of reserving coastal state jurisdiction although in a less obvious manner. No doubt this reservation is more directly relevant against its powerful neighbor, which has been conducting civilian and military maritime operations of all kinds in contested waters adjacent to Vietnam.

On the surface, the Southeast Asian littoral states' restrictive views on passage through the territorial sea mirror China's own restrictive and discriminatory position of denying such rights in favor of military vessels and aircraft, while their respective stances on the EEZ clearly differ. In practice, however, China's loose and expansive interpretation through action of the scope of its territorial waters on historic grounds is a cause for concern among the smaller littoral states, which are conscious of its implication of denying them of huge portions of their EEZ under UNCLOS. Chinese civilian or military activities in their EEZs are therefore viewed with extreme suspicion, which is not at all helped by China's own ambiguity through conflation of territorial and EEZ rights in the SCS.

As China continues to try to expand and consolidate its control and influence over the SCS, the Southeast Asian States will face increasing pressure. Their current restrictive and discriminatory policies, particularly against fishing vessels, indicate that they will be more inclined to harden their positions against navigation and overflight in order to protect themselves. Since China's maritime access to the oceans of the world partly begins with the SCS, this will in turn tend to make China push back even harder, i.e., become even more assertive and demanding of pre-emptory status for purposes of navigation and overflight. This will then make the smaller States choose between either surrendering their maritime interests to China in exchange for some other consideration, or balancing against China by seeking alliance and cooperative partnerships with stronger external powers.

Impact of the *Philippines v. China* arbitration

A key number of issues brought by the Philippines before the Annex VII tribunal in the case it initiated against China[120] concerned the latter's actions, some of them punitive, against Philippine vessels and aircraft as the proceedings progressed.

Submission no. 13 particularly complained that China operated its law enforcement vessels in a dangerous manner against Philippine private and government vessels.[121] These involved incidents of near-collision between two small Philippine and much large Chinese Fishery Law Enforcement Command ships,[122] and a small Philippine fisheries patrol vessel and much larger China Maritime Surveillance ships,[123] both near Scarborough Shoal. The Philippines essentially argued that in the first instance, the Chinese ships deliberately maneuvered to make high speed passes at the stationary Philippine vessel at close range while the latter was transferring personnel from two rubber boats, and in the second instance, the Chinese ships repeatedly "crossed the bow" (i.e., it passed directly in front) of the smaller Philippine ship and tried to block its progress toward the shoal. Upon review of the facts and consideration of an independent experts' report,[124] the tribunal deemed China to have acted contrary to the provisions of the Rules 2, 6, 7, 8, 15, and 16 COLREGS which represented "generally accepted international regulations" concerning measures necessary to ensure maritime safety, which in turn could be also considered as a violation of UNCLOS Art. 94.[125]

In doing so, the tribunal accepted the characterization of the Chinese ships closing in on stationary vessels, making close high-speed passes, nearly ramming vessels, and high-speed blocking maneuvers against moving vessels to be irresponsible and in "total disregard of good seamanship and neglect of precaution."[126] Notwithstanding its acceptance that China took actions as law enforcement activities in relation to its claim to sovereign territory, nevertheless, China was still under an obligation to carry out such actions in a manner consistent with conventions to ensure and promote the safety of life and property at sea such as COLREGS.[127] China's actions were deemed inexcusable and not attended by any mitigating circumstances.[128]

The tribunal's rebuke sends a strong signal to China, and possibly Vietnam, which have engaged in similar uses of their respective vessels against each other, most especially during the HY981 incident in 2014 in which Chinese and Vietnamese ships practically engaged in a running sea-battle. From a broader perspective, it is an unmistakable signal that international law does not countenance, even in cases of disputed maritime space, that claimant States should use their respective maritime assets in ways short of the use or threat of use of force, but which definitely cause danger to life and property at sea and are intended to deliberately intimidate smaller ships.

Air defense identification zone concerns

China's controversial establishment of an air defense identification zone (ADIZ) over the East China Sea in 2013 raised concerns that it would do the same for the South China Sea.[129] Although the issue seemed to recede into the background, concern was revived after China began challenging commercial flights and warning away military reconnaissance aircraft from unspecified and undefined "military alert zones" in or around its artificial island building activities sometime in 2015. The publicized incident involving the US P-8A Poseidon aircraft[130] was only the tip of the iceberg, as subsequent news coverage indicated that all aircraft transiting in or near the Spratly Islands region were being subjected to the same challenges and warnings.

Although most observers agree that it is unlikely under current conditions,[131] persistent worries that China might decide to go ahead and declare an ADIZ in the

South China Sea have instigated academic discussions about its legal implications for the disputes. Unlike nuanced passage rights for ships, there are no overflight rights for aircraft over territorial airspace co-extensive with the 12 nm limit of the territorial sea; aircraft must seek coastal state consent to enter it in accordance with international aviation law. Freedom of overflight exists only outside territorial airspace. The imposition of ADIZ is therefore feared to be a means of advancing territorial claims, and acceptance thereof might be seen as binding acquiescence.

A distinction should be made between ADIZ, the future establishment of which observers fret over, and military exclusion zones, which are practically already operational in the SCS. ADIZ are incidentally dealt with in the International Convention of the Civil Aviation Organization (ICAO), which recognizes that ADIZ may be established by States for purposes of management of airspace. ICAO Annex 15 describes how ADIZ may be managed, monitored and enforced. Enforcement of an ADIZ generally does not authorize the use of force against civilian aircraft, and the prohibition against the use of force against civil aviation is thought to be part of customary international law codified in the Chicago Convention.[132]

ADIZ are founded on ICAO Art. 11 and 13, which allow a State to lay down such requirements or conditions for entry or admission of civilian aircraft into its airspace.[133] ADIZ *per se* should not be controversial, but China's apparent use of ADIZ meets with disapproval particularly because it is apparently employed to justify China's exercise of jurisdictions over contested maritime space by posing as civilian administrative control over areas that are either disputed or beyond national jurisdiction. Other States will find it necessary to object to any future Chinese ADIZ in the SCS to ensure that it does not buttress China's territorial claims, whether or not they are actual claimants or external powers.

However, much of the discussions seem to omit the fact that China has already attempted to establish, even if it has yet to enforce, military exclusion zones in the South China Sea. Chinese Navy warnings in P-8A incident and others that followed expressly mention or refer to the aircraft on approach to unspecified "military alert zones" and demand the latter to avoid them. These essentially evidence the existence of military exclusion zones not governed by any specific provisions of international law, raising the specter of potential air-to-air or ground-to-air engagements. The latter would certainly be even more worrisome should China elevate the status of its unenforced military alert zones into full-fledged air defense zones, a not improbable idea given its preparations to install hefty anti-aircraft weapons on its artificial islands.[134] The legality of military alert zones, as well as any prospective air defense zone, are certainly beyond the scope of UNCLOS and its dispute settlement mechanisms. Indeed, *Philippine v. China* also ruled that the existence of "a quintessentially military situation, involving the military forces of one side and a combination of military and paramilitary forces on the other, arrayed in opposition to one another," was sufficient to deprive the tribunal of jurisdiction. Between prospective ADIZ and existing announced military exclusion zones or future air defense zones, the latter two certainly represent much more serious potential sources of instability and conflict in the SCS.

China's establishment of military exclusion zones sometime in 2015 was clearly an attempt to ward off and discourage aerial surveillance and reconnaissance of its new artificial islands. The unspecified extent of the zone represents a potential obstacle to navigation and overflight; in the absence of a formal announcement and appropriate information it is impossible to determine exactly where the military alert zone is located. On one reconnaissance mission, a US P-8A Poseidon aircraft was warned while it was still 30 minutes away from Fiery Cross Reef; considering the aircraft's cruising speed, this means the two may have been about 200 km apart at the time of the first warning.[135] Even if such zones are directed only against military aircraft, the potential for confusion and misunderstanding in the busy airways are clear: during the same incident, civilian airline pilots hastily responded to Chinese warnings against the US aircraft thinking the warnings were directed at them.[136]

Synthesis

The freedom of navigation and overflight regime in UNCLOS, comprised of a detailed set of special legal rules corresponding the territorial sea, contiguous zone, straits used for international navigation, archipelagic waters, EEZ, and high seas, are being sorely tested in the confined waters of the SCS. This occurs partly due to the conflation of activities and arenas within the highly contentious area, that melds abstract and general navigation and overflight freedoms, rights, and interests with practical and specific individual assertions of rights and claims. The SCS is a large body of water with relatively tiny patches of dry land subject to competing claims by the surrounding coastal states. Navigation and overflight are therefore absolutely necessary and incidental to any of their actions in support of the prosecution of their claims to exclusive rights and jurisdiction: they need to reach the contested areas by sea or air in order to demonstrate it. Hence, between 2009 and 2016 many of the encounters between claimant States necessarily include some degree of interference with navigation and overflight rights and freedoms.

This raises a fair question of whether navigation and overflight rights and freedoms can be reasonably separated from activities to assert and protect territorial and jurisdictional claims. Stated in other ways, at what point does a claimant State go beyond the lawful exercise of its navigation and overflight rights and freedoms and should be considered as acting not to exercise them but rather to pursue its claims against another claimant State? Conversely, at what point should a claimant State not be considered as acting legitimately and only to protect its own claims, but rather threatening or violating navigation and overflight rights and freedoms *per se*?

This may not be so easy to answer, given the history and conduct of the parties over the past decades of the disputes. But perhaps the key lies in the consideration of equity that may be derived from the moderating impact of all States due regard obligations in the exercise of their maritime rights. The balance of rights between coastal and user states in UNCLOS may be assumed to be premised on the need to ensure that neither one gains an undue advantage over the other by virtue of the invocation of legal norms. Coastal States may be expected to guard their exclusive jurisdictions just as zealously as user states could be expected to protect their navigation and overflight rights and freedoms. In the context of the SCS, this principle of due regard, interpreted or implemented as to not give undue advantage, would then be able to discriminate between acts in abuse of rights or acts in legitimate protection of interests in relation to the SCS disputes are concerned.

This approach would be similar to that taken by the Annex VII tribunal in deciding on the legitimacy of China's law enforcement actions against Philippine vessels in Scarborough Shoal, as explained above; in that case, the tribunal made its decision based on standing obligations of all States, regardless of context, to ensure safety and avoid undue harm. In the same way, assessments could be made about actions involving arrest of, or taken against, fishing vessels; interference with law enforcement actions; intervention with petroleum operations; and other incidents already experienced. While parties remain free to pursue or protect their interests, they must do so without essentially abusing their rights or over-extending their prerogatives, as those would imply they are not only acting in accordance with their respective sides of the dispute but are also acting directly against broader norms no longer necessarily connected with the dispute. Each claimant State must realize that if their actions against another claimant State, even if discriminating and specific but carried out in a way that undermines broader navigation and overflight rights and freedoms, the international community has no assurance that such actions will not be carried out against non-parties to the disputes in the future. All States have an interest in maintaining freedom of navigation and overflight as a global and non-discriminatory regime; it is essential to world commerce, inter-connectivity and inter-dependence that all States now depend on for their national existence. Every effort must therefore be undertaken to ensure that the navigation and overflight regime remains in place without derogation.

Another reason why the navigation and overflight regime in the SCS is increasingly challenged is the nested overlap of two competitive arenas: the first between the littoral states themselves trying to either expand their claimed regulatory reach or to consolidate and protect their existing territorial and jurisdictional prerogatives, and the second between the littoral states and external powers (most prominently China and the US). These arenas are nested in the sense that they concern different legal contests applicable within the same maritime space. It is necessary to disentangle these contests to better appreciate their impact on the navigation and overflight regime and anticipate areas of continuing contests or reconciliation.

Between the littoral states of the SCS, the problem arises from the conflation of territorial and jurisdictional claims, most visibly demonstrated by China's nine dashed lines claim that overlaps with the 200nm EEZ claims and island territorial claims of neighboring and smaller Southeast Asian States. In this context, clarity of the basis for unilateral assertion of rights and claims is absolutely essential not only to avoid misunderstanding but also to promote the gradual process of building trust and confidence that paves the way toward settlement of disputes. Trust and confidence between claimant States cannot be generated by ambivalence and legal sleight-of-hand implied by an inability to firmly clarify the factual and legal basis of claimed rights. Neither furtive acts nor inconsistent conduct and statements can give rise to defensible rights. This is similar to the legal principle derived from the Roman concept of *usucapio* that clandestine possession cannot give rise to ownership.

Determining which among the claimant States is favored with legitimacy in any of the given incidents between 2009–2016 above will therefore depend on the more careful appreciation of the claimant State's legal justification for its actions, specially when it also apparently transgresses specific norms of the navigation and overflight regime. Analyzing each incident through this lens will especially help non-parties to the dispute to decide whether or not their own interests are particularly affected, and whether they have any real reason to be concerned or to intercede. In this connection, the Award on the Merits in *Philippines v. China* bears special significance: it is thus far the only attempt by any of the disputing States to precisely disentangle the nested and conflated claims created by China's insistence on rights other than those expressly recognized in UNCLOS. To date, China maintains its refusal to recognize the jurisdiction of the Annex VII tribunal, and Chinese scholars continue to attack the validity, legitimacy, and logic of the decision. Doing so necessarily maintains the nested legal arenas that prevents a reasonable legal and equitable allocation of sovereignty, rights and jurisdictions in the SCS, and over the long term, will not be welcoming of firm and fair resolution among the different disputing parties because it will remain the source of reasons for lack of trust and confidence in any prospective negotiated solution.

It is important that all claimant States in the SCS should agree and act on ensuring the equal protection of navigation and overflight rights and freedoms in accordance with what has already been agreed in UNCLOS. Attempts to suppress such rights and freedoms will only tend to provoke coastal states to assert them even more. As noted above, most of the claimant States are already poised with restrictive and discriminatory domestic rules against foreign navigation and overflight in their waters. Should the UNCLOS regime break down, these States will have even more reason to tighten controls on their respective maritime areas against other States to whom that breakdown is attributed. Even a regional superpower China would be hard-pressed to maintain its influence in the face of a hostile regional neighborhood.

Finally, as between claimant States and external powers such as the US, Japan, Australia, India, and Russia, the issue takes on a different complexion. The question raised is whether such external actors are legitimately acting in accordance with their common interest in navigation and overflight, or are either intervening in favor of one or some claimants or acting to pursue nothing more than their own interests against the latter. In the more frequent diplomatic tussles between China and the US on account of the latter's freedom of navigation operations, for example, incidents may be assessed on the basis of whether the actions of one party are of the needed scale to preserve and protect the guarantees of navigation and overflight under law, or go beyond it to comprise direct and undue interference in the sovereignty and jurisdiction of a claimant State. In appreciating such incidents, it must be considered whether each side's actions relate only to the preservation of their respective legal rights, or go beyond it.

It is accepted that this approach will be even more difficult in practice. The extent to which the actions of one party actually impact adversely or undermine a State's sovereignty and jurisdiction tend to be self-defined and self-determined by the affected claimant State because it is a function of that State's sense of security and confidence in the integrity and resilience of its own governance. To put it simply, the greater the insecurity and lack of confidence a coastal state has in its ability to maintain its sovereignty and jurisdiction, the more threatened it feels by any action, however innocuous, by another State. The State's sense of danger, especially in the SCS, is often quite disproportionate to the actual source, whether it is the presence of one military aircraft or the transit of an entire fleet. Thus, China's complaints about US surveillance flights in the SCS, which it has described as anywhere from merely intrusive to dangerously provocative, should be considered with their geo-political competition in mind and the legal aspects take on a secondary role. Ultimately, how claimant States relate with external States will be determined not by factual findings or legal arguments, but by the overall state of their relations with each other.

This does not mean, however, that incidents between China and the US or other external powers should be dismissed as little more than political maneuvering. Just as how claimants States in the SCS disputes treat each other should be seen as how they will potentially treat other States elsewhere, how external powers interact with some claimant States should also be viewed as models of how such powers and States will interact with the other claimant States. The extent to which States demonstrate impartial and non-discriminatory adherence to legal principles and compliance with legal norms and standards such as those enshrined in UNCLOS tend to be good gauges of their future behavior and reliability in the course of diplomatic relations. Transactional politics and perceived lack of good faith will ultimately reflect very badly on the State whose actions and decisions are characterized by it, which in turn undermines its ability to have good working relations with others and diminish its power and standing over the long term.

This highlights the importance of adherence to the rules of international law, as plainly expressed in UNCLOS or related maritime conventions, as the primary benchmark for assessing the legitimacy of the conduct of States. Despite its flaws, international law does establish certain obligations that maintain a sense of international civility and protect common interests, such as the interest in maritime safety and protection of the marine environment regardless of the maritime zone in which it is located. These ground rules should be made the minimum standards of conduct in States' prosecution or protection of their claims in the SCS. Thus, the Annex VII tribunal's judgment on the Philippines' submission no. 13 is in fact a good and useful starting point to reiterate norms to moderate the disputing States' behavior so that the regional atmosphere does not spiral toward tensions and potential conflict, and instead kept on an even keel that promotes sanguine discussions and negotiations.

Where the law can admit of arguable interpretation, such as in the specific definition and application of "due regard" obligations, or the proper scope and interpretation of "marine scientific research," the preferable course of action is not to insist on unilateral, self-serving, and *a priori* justification of one's own conduct. Rather, States should commit to openness to avail of negotiations or other peaceful disputes settlement modes as provided in UNCLOS Part XV to settle their differences. Continuing with unilateral assertions are not only potentially dangerous, but also tend to further complicate and extend the disputes. While *Philippines v. China* may not have been a good experience for the respondent, it should nonetheless be seen as an important opportunity to learn and adapt to an increasingly complex and globalized international community that requires institutional mechanisms to firmly and fairly settle disputes, whether holistically or incrementally. Just as UNCLOS was not expected to encompass the entirety of maritime international law, neither should the process of adjustment of relations and settlement of disputes be expected to be accomplished in one stroke.

Conclusion

In sum, whether the interests of coastal states and user states concerning navigational rights, freedoms, and interests in the SCS can be reconciled depends partly on will and partly on law. International law performs an important function of providing a basic standard of legitimacy and illegitimacy in States' actions to pursue and protect their specific interests in the tangled arena of the SCS. The rise in incidents concerning navigation and overflight in the SCS is symptomatic of an upheaval in relations between claimant States and external powers as new adjustments are being made to what used to be the status quo after the 2002 Declaration of Conduct of the Parties in the South China Sea.

With the major incremental changes introduced between 2013 and 2016, in the legal sphere through the *Philippines v. China* arbitration and in the maritime arena through the construction of artificial islands, the evolution of the SCS disputes are at a veritable crossroads. The arbitration has laid one option, that of allocating maritime jurisdictions in a more conservative manner in line with the existing practice of the smaller Southeast Asian States, that actually provides an opening for engaging the multiple duties to cooperate in ocean management enshrined in UNCLOS and actually encourages multi-lateral cooperation and management of the disputes that presumably holds promise for future resolution. The artificial islands symbolize another option, that of unilateral action on a large scale but essentially in stride with a trend of unilateral actions in various forms taken by claimant States since 2009.

Navigation and overflight rights, freedoms and interests are only one of the many subjects of the SCS disputes, but a possible means of considering and balancing the various claimant and external States interests in these have been indicated. Ultimately it will be up to these same States to determine how a balance will be struck; hopefully it will be reached primarily by careful assessment and deliberate resort to principles of UNCLOS and international law, no matter how long the solution may take. "A clash of civilizations" is not unavoidable, if the parties agree to begin with acknowledging and observing at least some ground rules for the pursuit and protection of their respective maritime interests.

Notes

1 See Samuel P. Huntington, *The Clash of Civilizations and the Remaking of World Order* (New York: Simon & Schuster, 2011); also Samuel P. Huntington, "The Clash of Civilizations?," *Foreign Affairs* 72, no. 3 (Summer 1993): 22–49, www.jstor.org/stable/20045621.
2 See Michael Pillsbury, *The Hundred-Year Marathon: China's Secret Strategy to Replace America as the Global Superpower* (New York: Henry Holt and Co., 2015).
3 See Alfred Thayer Mahan, *The Influence of Sea Power Upon History, 1660–1783* (Project Gutenberg, 2004), www.gutenberg.org/ebooks/13529.
4 ASEAN-China Declaration on the Conduct of Parties in the South China Sea. Center for International Law, February 17, 2017, https://cil.nus.edu.sg/rp/pdf/2002%20Declaration%20on%20the%20Conduct%20of%20Parties%20in%20the%20South%20China%20Sea-pdf.pdf
5 UNCLOS, Art. 17–18.
6 UNCLOS, Art. 45.
7 UNCLOS, Art. 52.
8 UNCLOS, Art. 37–38.
9 UNCLOS, Art. 53.
10 UNCLOS, Art. 58, 87.
11 UNCLOS, Art. 33.
12 UNCLOS, Art. 19–20, 30, 39–40, 54, 58, 78.
13 UNCLOS, Art. 21–26, 33, 41–44, 54, 56, 60, 73, 78, 80.
14 See for example, UNCLOS Art. 21(1) and 22, which specify the subjects or areas that coastal States may regulate that user States are bound to comply with, in relation to the exercise of innocent passage in the territorial sea. See also UNCLOS Art. 73, which recognizes and describes coastal State enforcement in the EEZ.
15 UNCLOS, Art. 32, 95–96.
16 UNCLOS, Art. 224.
17 UNCLOS, Art. 225.
18 See UNCLOS, Art. 27–32, 91–97.
19 See UNCLOS, Art. 99–109.
20 UNCLOS, Art. 24(a), 42(2).
21 UNCLOS, Art. 24(b), 25(3), 42(2), 52(2), 53(2), 87.
22 UNCLOS, Art. 27, 39, 56(2), 58(3), 60(3), 87, 234.
23 Possibly the best record of diametrically opposed positions on these matters can be drawn from the dialogue between civil and military officials of China and the US, contained in Peter Dutton (Ed.). *Military Activities in the EEZ: A US-China dialogue on security and international law in the maritime commons.* (Newport: China Maritime Studies Institute and US Naval War College, 2010).
24 Raul Pedrozo, *Close encounters at sea: The USNS Impeccable incident.* 62:3 Naval War College Review 101–11 (2009), at 101–2.
25 Ibid.
26 Ibid.
27 BBC News. Pentagon warns over Chinese boats. *BBC News*, May 5, 2009 (February 17, 2017), http://news.bbc.co.uk/2/hi/asia-pacific/8034385.stm

28 Ian Johnson, US, China talk defense: High-level meetings to focus on run-ins between two navies. *Wall Street Journal*, June 24, 2009 (February 17, 2017), www.wsj.com/articles/SB124584004195946677.

29 Ibid.

30 Ibid.

31 Thang Long. Vietnam urges China to cancel fishing ban. *Vietnam in the News*, June 8, 2009, http://vietnaminthenews.blogspot.com/2009/06/hanoi-vietnam-is-urging-china-to-cancel.html

32 CNN. Sub collides with sonar array towed by US Navy ship. *CNN*, June 12, 2009, http://edition.cnn.com/2009/US/06/12/china.submarine/

33 BBC News. Philippines halts tests after China patrol challenge. *BBC News*, March 8, 2011, www.bbc.com/news/world-asia-pacific-12672889

34 Chinese jets buzz Philippine patrol planes. *The Peninsula*, May 20, 2011, http://thepeninsulaqatar.com/news/asia/152900/chinese-jets-buzz-philippine-patrol-planes

35 Alex Watts. Tensions rise as Vietnam accuses China of sabotage. *Sydney Morning Herald*, June 2, 2011, www.smh.com.au/world/tensions-rise-as-vietnam-accuses-china-of-sabotage-20110601-1fgno.html

36 Indrani Bagchi, China harasses Indian naval ship on South China Sea. *The Times of India*, September 2, 2016, http://timesofindia.indiatimes.com/india/China-harasses-Indian-naval-ship-on-South-China-Sea/articleshow/9829900.cms

37 Associated Press. Philippines apologizes to China over sea incident. *Philippine Daily Inquirer*, October 19, 2011, http://globalnation.inquirer.net/15803/philippines-apologizes-to-china-over-sea-accident

38 Ibid.

39 Andreo Calonzo, China wants PHL archaeological vessel out of Panatag Shoal. *GMA News Online*, April 17, 2012, www.gmanetwork.com/news/story/255208/news/nation/china-wants-phl-archaeological-vessel-out-of-panatag-shoal

40 Tania Branigan, Chinese frigate runs aground in disputed part of South China Sea. *Guardian*, July 13, 2012, www.theguardian.com/world/2012/jul/13/chinese-frigate-runs-aground-sea

41 Jeremy Page, Vietnam accuses Chinese ships. *Wall Street Journal*, December 3, 2012, www.wsj.com/articles/SB10001424127887323717004578157033857113510

42 *PCA Case No. 2013–19. In the matter of the South China Sea arbitration. Philippines v. China, Award on the Merits*, July 12, 2016, https://pca-cpa.org/wp-content/uploads/sites/175/2016/07/PH-CN-20160712-Award.pdf [Award on the Merits, Philippines v. China]

43 Chinese ships approach Malaysia. *Wall Street Journal*, March 27, 2013, www.wsj.com/articles/SB10001424127887324685104578386052690151508

44 Michaela Del Callar, *PH files diplomatic protest vs China's 'provocative, illegal presence' in Ayungin Reef. Interaksyon*, May 21, 2013, http://interaksyon.com/article/62292/ph-files-diplomatic-protest-vs-chinas-provocative-illegal-presence-in-ayungin-reef

45 BBC. China confirms US warship near-collision. *BBC News*, December 18, 2016, www.bbc.com/news/world-asia-25426245

46 Reuters. Chinese ships patrol area contested by Malaysia. January 26, 2014, http://uk.reuters.com/article/uk-china-malaysia-idUKBREA0P06X20140126

47 Reuters. Philippines protests over South China Sea water cannon incident. February 25, 2014, www.reuters.com/article/us-philippines-southchinasea-idUSBREA1O09P20140225

48 Manuel Mogato, Manila air-drops supplies to troops on disputed reef. *Reuters*, March 12, 2014, www.reuters.com/article/us-china-philippines-idUSBREA2B1IL20140312

49 Scott Neuman, China, Vietnam spar over oil rig in South China Sea. *National Public Radio*, May 7, 2014, www.npr.org/sections/thetwo-way/2014/05/07/310488736/china-vietnam-spar-over-oil-rig-in-south-china-sea

50 Associated Press. Vietnam: Chinese ships ram vessels near oil rig. *Associated Press*, May 8, 2014, www.dailymail.co.uk/wires/ap/article-2622387/Vietnam-Chinese-ships-ram-vessels-near-oil-rig.html
51 Phil Stewart and David Brunnstorm. US, Chinese officials to meet at Pentagon after jet intercept. *Reuters*, August 26, 2014, www.reuters.com/article/us-usa-china-military-idUSKBN0GP20G20140826
52 Ibid.
53 Ibid.
54 Manuel Mogato, China warns Philippine military planes away from disputed sea area: Manila. *Reuters*, May 7, 2015, www.reuters.com/article/us-southchinasea-philippines-idUSKBN0NS0GN20150507
55 Ibid.
56 Ibid.
57 John Sciutto, China warns US surveillance plane. *CNN*, May 21, 2015, http://edition.cnn.com/2015/05/20/politics/south-china-sea-navy-flight/
58 Reuters. Angry China shadows US warship near man-made islands. *Reuters*, October 27, 2015, www.reuters.com/article/southchinasea-usa-idUSL1N12Q1L720151027
59 Ibid.
60 Sam LaGrone, US destroyer challenges more Chinese South China Sea claims in new freedom of navigation operation. *USNI News*, January 30, 2016, https://news.usni.org/2016/01/30/u-s-destroyer-challenges-more-chinese-south-china-sea-claims-in-new-freedom-of-navigation-operation
61 Andrew Greene, RAAF patrols over disputed South China Sea facing more regular resistance from Chinese military. *ABC News*, February 3, 2016, www.abc.net.au/news/2016-02-03/raaf-patrol-flights-facing-more-regular-resistance-from-chinese/7138100
62 Ankit Panda, South China Sea: US Navy destroyer asserts freedom of navigation near Fiery Cross Reef. *The Diplomat*, May 10, 2016, http://thediplomat.com/2016/05/south-china-sea-us-navy-destroyer-asserts-freedom-of-navigation-near-fiery-cross-reef/
63 China's air force conducts combat air patrol in South China Sea. *Xinhua*, July 18, 2016, http://news.xinhuanet.com/english/2016-07/18/c_135522387.htm; Michael Forsythe, China begins air patrols over disputed area of the South China Sea. *New York Times*, July 15, 2016, www.nytimes.com/2016/07/19/world/asia/china-sea-air-patrols.html?_r=0
64 Philippine fishermen back from Panatag Shoal with big catch. *Philippine Daily Inquirer*, October 30, 2016, http://globalnation.inquirer.net/148316/filipino-fishermen-back-from-panatag-shoal-with-big-catch
65 Indrees Ali and Matt Spetalnick. A US warship was shadowed by three CHiense vessels during a freedom-of-navigation exercise in the South China Sea. *Business Insider*, October 21, 2016, www.businessinsider.com/us-warship-freedom-of-navigation-exercise-south-china-sea-2016-10; Sam LaGrone, *US warship conducts South China Sea freedom of navigation operation*. US Naval Institute, October 21, 2016, https://news.usni.org/2016/10/21/u-s-warship-conducts-south-china-sea-freedom-navigation-operation.
66 Chinese warship seizes US underwater drone in international waters. *The Guardian*, December 16, 2016, www.theguardian.com/world/2016/dec/16/china-seizes-us-underwater-drone-south-china-sea
67 Ryan Browne, Chinese and US aircraft in unsafe encounter. *CNN*, February 10, 2017, http://edition.cnn.com/2017/02/09/politics/us-china-aircraft-unsafe-encounter/
68 US Department of Defense. *Freedom of Navigation Fact Sheet*. US Department of Defense, March 2015, http://policy.defense.gov/Portals/11/Documents/gsa/cwmd/DoD%20FON%20Program%20--%20Fact%20Sheet%20(March%202015).pdf
69 *United States Law of the Sea Policy. National Security Decision Directive No. 20, 29 January 1982*, February 17, 2017, https://reaganlibrary.archives.gov/archives/reference/Scanned%20NSDDS/NSDD20.pdf

70 *United States Law of the Sea Policy. National Security Decision Directive No. 43, 09 July 1982.* February 17, 2017, https://reaganlibrary.archives.gov/archives/reference/Scanned%20NSDDS/NSDD43.pdf

71 *United States Program for the Exercise of Navigation and Overflight Rights at Sea. National Security Decision Directive No. 72, 13 December 1982.* February 17, 2017, https://reaganlibrary.archives.gov/archives/reference/Scanned%20NSDDS/NSDD72.pdf

72 Ibid at 1–2.

73 *Freedom of Navigation Program. National Security Decision Directive No. 265, 16 March 1987.* February 17, 2017, https://reaganlibrary.archives.gov/archives/reference/Scanned%20NSDDS/NSDD265.pdf

74 See *DoD Annual Freedom of Navigation (FON) Reports.* Undersecretary of Defense for Policy, US Department of Defense, February 18, 2017, http://policy.defense.gov/OUSDP-Offices/FON/

75 See Jay L. Batongbacal, *The Kalayaan Islands and the American Asia-Pacific Order under Challenge: Retrospective and Prospects.* In M. S. Camacho and B. R. Churchill (Eds.). Selected Papers of the 24th Annual Manila Studies Conference, De La Salle University-College of St. Benilde, August 24–27, 2015. (Manila: National Commission for Culture and the Arts, 2015) at 254–91.

76 US Department of State. *Comments by Secretary Hillary R. Clinton in Hanoi, Vietnam,* February 18, 2017, http://iipdigital.usembassy.gov/st/english/text-trans/2010/07/20100723164658su0.491289.html

77 *Remarks at the Fifth Annual South China Sea Conference, 21 July 2015.* Center for Strategic and International Studies, January 16, 2017, www.state.gov/p/eap/rls/rm/2015/07/245142.htm.

78 Pranath Parameswaran, US not 'neutral' in South China Sea disputes: Top US diplomat. *The Diplomat,* July 22, 2015 (January 16, 2017), http://thediplomat.com/2015/07/us-not-neutral-in-south-china-sea-disputes-top-us-diplomat/

79 Ibid.

80 Department of Defense. *The Asia-Pacific Maritime Security Strategy: Achieving US National Security Objectives in a Changing Environment* (Washington DC: Department of Defense, 2015).

81 NARA Access to Archives Database [AAD]. Doc 1974STATE08375, Secretary to State to US Mission New York and US Liaison Office Peking, April 26, 1974.

82 NARA Access to Archives Database [AAD]. Doc 1974STATE150383, Secretary to State to US Liaison Office Peking, July 11, 1974.

83 Peoples' Republic of China. *Law on the Territorial Sea and the Contiguous Zone of 25 February 1992.* February 17, 2017, www.un.org/depts/los/LEGISLATIONANDTREATIES/PDFFILES/CHN_1992_Law.pdf

84 People's Republic of China. *Exclusive Economic Zone and Continental Shelf Act of 26 June 1998,* February 2017, www.un.org/depts/los/LEGISLATIONANDTREATIES/PDFFILES/chn_1998_eez_act.pdf [EEZ and Continental Shelf Act], at Art. 11, 13. 17.

85 It is accepted that the issue of military activities in the EEZ are not directly governed by UNCLOS. See Kaye, S. *Freedom of navigation, surveillance and security: Legal issues surrounding the collection of intelligence from beyond the littoral.* 24 *Australian Yearbook of International Law* 93 (2005), www.austlii.edu.au/au/journals/AUYrBkIntLaw/2005/7.html

86 Mark Valencia, and Kazumine Akimoto. Guidelines for navigation and overflight in the exclusive economic zone. 30 *Marine Policy* 704–11 (2006), at 704.

87 *Journey in the South China Sea,* Episode 8: Guardian of the Eighth Lanjiang. CCTV 4 Documentary. Online, www.youtube.com/watch?v=kaVdwLcNYY4; See also Li Minjiang, *Reconciling assertiveness and cooperation? China's changing approach to the South China Sea dispute.* 6:2 Security Challenges 49–68 (2010) at 61.

88 Ministry of Foreign Affairs of the Peoples' Republic of China. *Position paper of the Government of the Peoples' Republic of China on the Matter of Jurisdiction in the South China Sea Arbitration initiated by the Republic of the Philippines*, February 17, 2017, www.fmprc.gov.cn/mfa_eng/zxxx_662805/t1217147.shtml at para. 28.
89 See Ji Wu, *The concept of marine scientific research*. In P. Dutton (Ed.). Military Activities in the EEZ: A US-China dialogue on security and international law in the maritime commons (Newport: China Maritime Studies Institute and US Naval War College, 2010) at 65–73.
90 *EEZ and Continental Shelf Act*, Art. 9.
91 Zhou Bo, Freedom of navigation: an old issue and new approaches. *China-US Focus*. October 24, 2014, www.chinausfocus.com/peace-security/freedom-of-navigation-an-old-issue-and-new-approaches
92 Peng G. *China's maritime rights and interests*. In Peter Dutton (Ed.). Military Activities in the EEZ: A US-China dialogue on security and international law in the maritime commons (Newport: China Maritime Studies Institute and US Naval War College, 2010), 15–22 at 20–21.
93 Ibid.
94 See People's Republic of China. *Note Verbale CML/18/2009*, May 7, 2009, www.un.org/depts/los/clcs_new/submissions_files/vnm37_09/chn_2009re_vnm.pdf. The Annex VII tribunal in the *Philippines v. China* arbitration, however, interpreted China's claim to be one limited only to living and non-living resources on the basis of historic rights within the area encompassed within the so-called nine dashed lines, and did not include more extensive rights based on title or sovereignty. Such claims were deemed inconsistent with UNCLOS. Award on the Merits, Philippines v. China, at 97, 111–15.
95 Zhiguo Gao and Bing Bing Jia. *The nine-dash line in the South China Sea: History, status and implications*. 107:1. *American Journal of International Law*, 98–124 (2013).
96 *Understanding China's position on the South China Sea*. Institute for Security and Development Policy, June 2016, http://isdp.eu/publication/understanding-chinas-position-south-china-sea-disputes/
97 *Law on the Territorial Sea and the Contiguous Zone of 25 February 1992*, February 17, 2017, www.un.org/depts/los/LEGISLATIONANDTREATIES/PDFFILES/CHN_1992_Law.pdf; *Declaration of the Government of the People's Republic of China on the baselines of the territorial sea*, May 15, 1996, February 17, 2017, www.un.org/depts/los/LEGISLATIONANDTREATIES/PDFFILES/CHN_1996_Declaration.pdf; Exclusive Economic Zone and Continental Shelf Act of 28 June 1998, February 17, 2017, www.un.org/depts/los/LEGISLATIONANDTREATIES/PDFFILES/chn_1998_eez_act.pdf
98 Tyler Durden, China opposes 'threatening and damaging' US carrier patrols in the South China Sea. *Zero Hedge*, February 17, 2017, www.zerohedge.com/news/2017-02-21/china-opposes-threatening-and-damaging-us-carrier-patrols-south-china-sea; Red line: China warned Japan against joining US freedom of navigation stunts. *Financial Times*, August 22, 2016, www.rt.com/news/356695-china-warns-japan-red-line/; Ben Blanchard, *China protests Australia's South China Sea freedom of navigation comment*. February 22, 2017, www.thestar.com.my/news/world/2016/07/14/china-protests-australias-south-china-sea-freedom-of-navigation-comment/
99 *Foreign ministry spokesperson Geng Shuang's regular Press Conference on February 21, 2017*, February 22, 2017, www.fmprc.gov.cn/mfa_eng/xwfw_665399/s2510_665401/t1440264.shtml
100 UN Doc A/AC.138/SC.II/L.15.
101 UN Doc A/AC.138/SC.II/L.48.
102 Ibid., draft Article V.
103 UN Doc A/CONF. 62/C.2/L.49.

104 Republic of the Philippines. Republic Act No. 9522, An Act to amend certain provisions of Republic Act No. 3046, as amended by Republic Act No. 5446, to define the archipelagic baselines of the Philippines, and for other purposes.
105 These cession treaties refer to the 1898 Treaty of Paris and the 1900 Treaty of Washington between the United States and Spain, both of which identified the archipelago that comprised the Philippine Islands, and the 1930 Convention between the United States and Great Britain that separated the islands of the Philippines from the island of North Borneo which formed part of Malaysian and Indonesian territory.
106 The bills, not having passed, were subsequently re-filed in subsequent Congresses. At the start of the seventeenth Congress in June 2016, the archipelagic sea lanes bill has been re-filed as Senate Bill no. 92 and House Bill no. 3285, and the maritime zone bill as Senate Bill no. 93 and House Bill no. 3286.
107 See House of Representatives. House Bill no 3285, January 13, 2017, www.congress.gov.ph/legisdocs/basic_17/HB03285.pdf
108 House bill assigning routes for foreign ships, planes approved on 2nd reading. *Businessworld online*, March 23, 2015, www.cab.gov.ph/news/2250-house-bill-assigning-routes-for-foreign-ships-planes-approved-on-2nd-reading
109 Republic of the Philippines. Rep. Act No. 8550 (1998), The Fisheries Code of 1998 as amended by Rep. Act No. 10654 (2014), s. 91 punishes the offense of "poaching in Philippine waters."
110 Republic of the Philippines. Rep. Act No. 6969 (1990).
111 Republic of Indonesia. Government Regulation No. 37 (2002), Art. 3.
112 Ibid. Art. 15.
113 Republic of Indonesia. Clarification of Government Regulation No. 3 (2002), Art. 2.
114 NARA AAD. Doc 1976USUNN03795, US Delegation LOS to US Secretary of State, September 17, 1976.
115 NARA AAD. Doc 1977STATE081604, US Secretary of State to American Embassies, April 14, 1977. See also Saravanamuttu, J. Malaysia's Foreign Policy, the First 50 Years: Alignment, Neutralism, Islamism. Singapore: ISEAS, 2010 at 145.
116 Federation of Malaysia. Act 317. Fisheries Act 1985, sec. 16.
117 Mark Valencia, *Conflict over Resources in Southeast Asia and the Pacific* (Tokyo: United Nations University, 1990). Online, http://archive.unu.edu/unupress/unupbooks/80a04e/80A04E0a.htm#4.2 Common threads in the pattern of conflict.
118 Socialist Republic of Vietnam. Law of the Sea of Vietnam of July 2, 2012, Art. 12.
119 Ibid., Art. 18.
120 Award on the Merits, *Philippines v. China*, supra.
121 Ibid., at 417–35.
122 Ibid, at 418.
123 Ibid., at 418–21.
124 Captain Gurpreet Singhota, *Report of the International Navigational Safety Expert appointed by the Permanent Court of Arbitration, The Hauge, The Netherlands. 15 Apr 2016.* February 17, 2017, www.pcacases.com/web/sendAttach/1810
125 Award on the Merits, *Philippines v. China*, at 435.
126 Ibid., at 431.
127 Ibid., at 432.
128 Ibid., at 435.
129 Zhu Feng, *China's first ADIZ decision: One year later.* CSIS Asia Maritime Transparency Initiative, November 25, 2014, https://amti.csis.org/chinas-first-adiz-decision-one-year-later/
130 Reuters and T. Thornhill. This is Chinese navy, you go! China issues EIGHT warnings to US surveillance planes to get away from disputed man-made islands. *Mail Online*, May 21, 2015 (January 16, 2016), www.dailymail.co.uk/news/article-3090728/China-navy-warns-U-S-spy-plane-disputed-South-China-Sea-CNN.html

131 See Zhu Feng, supra.; also Ankit Panda, Is China really about to announce a South China Sea air defense identification zone? Maybe. *The Diplomat*, June 1, 2016, http://thediplomat.com/2016/06/is-china-really-about-to-announce-a-south-china-sea-air-defense-identification-zone-maybe/; Ralph Jennings, China ponders ADIZ in disputed sea. *Voice of America*, November 30, 2016, www.voanews.com/a/china-ponders-adiz-in-disputed-sea/3617133.html.

132 See *Chicago Convention on International Civil Aviation of 7 December 1944*, and more particularly the Protocol adopted at the occasion of the 25th (Extraordinary) Session of the Assembly on May 10, 1984 introducing art 3 bis on the non-use of weapons against civil aircraft in flight. This amendment entered into force on October 1, 1998. ICAO, February 17, 2017, www.icao.int/publications/Documents/7300_cons.pdf [ICAO]. See also International Convention on International Civil Aviation: Annexes 1–18, ICAO, February 17, 2017, www.icao.int/safety/airnavigation/nationalitymarks/annexes_booklet_en.pdf.

133 ICAO Art. 11, 13.

134 Asia Maritime Transparency Initiative. *China's new Spratly Islands defenses.* Center for Strategic and International Studies, December 13, 2016, https://amti.csis.org/chinas-new-spratly-island-defenses/

135 John Schiutto, *Exclusive: China warns US surveillance plane.* CNN, September 15, 2015, http://edition.cnn.com/2015/05/20/politics/south-china-sea-navy-flight/

136 Ibid.

5 Indonesia

An archipelagic state's perspectives on the law of the sea

Etty R. Agoes

Indonesia's maritime interests are best viewed through the lens of the national archipelagic outlook called *Wawasan Nusantara*, which emphasizes the importance of Indonesia's national unity and territorial integrity. The special geographical position of Indonesia, a country comprised of more than 13,000 islands, and long combined coastlines, brings with it special needs and imperatives relating to its national existence. Under these special needs and imperatives, Indonesia has to ensure and safeguard its national economic, social and political integrity as well as territorial integrity since its status as an archipelago has important consequences both for its identity as a nation and for its character as a State.

Indonesia articulates its maritime interest in the process of UNCLOS negotiation and how its rights are reflected in its domestic regulation, for example, its archipelagic regime. Indonesia's attention to the law of the sea has been centered on the acceptance by the international community of its status as an archipelagic State, which requires a special regime under the law of the sea. In his presentation at the Seventh Annual Conference of the Law of the Sea Institute, Mochtar Kusumaatmadja explained the condition at the time, as follows:

> While a state of uncertainty envelops most matters of the law of the sea which until quite recently were considered beyond dispute, the subject I have been asked to speak on today has the additional difficulty of having been neglected under existing international law.[1]

He was referring to the legal regime of archipelagoes. As it may be recalled, Indonesia submitted a special proposal for archipelagoes at the Second United Nations Conference on the Law of the Sea in 1960. However due to lack of support, it withdrew the proposal.

Historically, the seas between and around the Indonesian islands have played a significant role in economic, political, social and defense. To mention an example Sriwijaya and Majapahit, two former Indonesian kingdoms, have used the waters between and around the islands as bridges for territorial unity.[2] Alternatively, colonial powers had used them as routes for conquest, which in the end became elements to divide and dominate Indonesia.

The country of Indonesia, located between the Indian and Pacific oceans and comprising of more than 13,000 islands, with a combined coastline almost equal to or even longer than the equator, brings with it special needs and imperatives relating to its national existence. In addition, Indonesia has special responsibilities relating to the interests of the international community.[3] Therefore, Indonesia has to ensure and safeguard her national and political unity as well as its territorial integrity.

Consequently, Indonesia declared itself an archipelagic State by the proclamation of December 13, 1957, which is known as the Djuanda Declaration. This was followed by revising or more precisely replacing the 1939 colonial Ordinance on the Territorial Sea and Maritime District. The Djuanda Declaration pronounced that Indonesia apply straight baselines connecting the outermost points of its outermost islands. Furthermore, it also declared that waters within these baselines and connecting and surrounding these islands became Indonesia's territorial waters. The Indonesian territorial sea would then be measured 12 nautical miles from the said straight baselines. The Djuanda Declaration noted the uniqueness of the Indonesian archipelago consisting of thousands of islands and the waters connecting them as one total unit by declaring that:

> all waters surrounding, between and connecting the islands or parts of islands belonging to the Indonesian archipelago, irrespective of their width or dimensions, are the natural appurtenances of its land territory of the Republic of Indonesia and, therefore, form part of the internal and national waters which are under the absolute sovereignty of Indonesia.

This legal and geographical outlook later known as *Wawasan Nusantara*, literally translated means the archipelagic outlook. Compared with the archipelagic State doctrine, *Wawasan Nusantara* is a political concept which departs from a territorial concept. Mochtar Kusumaatmadja described the difference as follows:

> Whenever it is asked what is its *(Wawasan Nusantara)* relationship with the archipelagic state principle, which in the international law of the sea exists as a conception of an island state or an archipelagic state (the Indonesian islands) the answer is that whereas the archipelagic state principle is a concept of national territory, the *Nusantara* concept is a way of looking at the political unity of a nation and people that subsumes the national geographic reality of an archipelagic state. It can also be said that the conception of the unity of land and seas contained in the concept of the archipelagic state constitutes the *physical forum* for the archipelago's development.[4]

The Djuanda Declaration noted the need to accommodate the international community's navigation through these internal waters by guaranteeing innocent passage for foreign ships, "as long as and in so far as it is not contrary to or disturb the sovereignty or the security of Indonesia."

The Indonesian archipelagic concept, as envisaged by the Djuanda Declaration, was proposed during the first United Nations Conference on the Law of the Sea in Geneva in 1958, however, many objections and criticisms were raised about the concept. Before a decision was made on the proposal, Indonesia withdrew it primarily because it was not considered to be ready for international consideration and recognition.

Meanwhile, the reaction of states, in particular the Netherlands and major maritime powers, was very strong. They accused Indonesia of violating international law, regarding it as an encroachment on the principle of freedom of navigation. Notwithstanding such reactions, Indonesia proceeded with the enactment of Law No. 4 of 1960 concerning Indonesian Territorial Waters. Law No. 4 of 1960 as the ultimate legal form of the Djuanda Declaration, which gives a legal and territorial meaning of the national outlook.

Indonesia is one of the archipelagic countries that had submitted various draft articles on archipelagic State at the Third United Nations Conference on the Law of the Sea. Indonesia, together with Fiji, Mauritius, and the Philippines had submitted draft principles concerning the archipelagic State concept to the UN Sea-bed Committee.[5] Some of the basic elements of the concept are:

> Firstly, for the reason of its national unity, territorial integrity, political and economic stability, an archipelagic State shall have right to draw straight baselines connecting the outermost points of the outermost islands and drying reef of the archipelago.
>
> Secondly, the archipelagic State exercises sovereignty over the waters within the baselines, the airspace above these waters, the water column, the seabed and the subsoil thereof as well as over the resource contained therein.
>
> Thirdly, the extent of the territorial sea, economic and other jurisdiction of the State with regard to the sea around it shall be measured from these baselines.
>
> Fourthly, the legitimate interests of the international community for passage through the archipelagic waters for the purpose of transit from the high seas to high seas shall be respected on the basis of innocent passage through archipelagic waters or through designated sea-lanes, taking into account that the passage shall not prejudice the peace, good order and security of the archipelagic State.[6]

Indonesia persisted in charting a long and lonely course to begin a 25-year struggle for recognition as an archipelagic State. During these years the Indonesian delegates to the Third United Nations Conference on the Law of the Sea lobbied the international community. Indonesia argued that as an archipelago it should deserve special rights in international law, particularly in the law of the sea. For this, Mochtar Kusumaatmadja argues:

> It might be interesting for the conference to know that the Indonesian language equivalent to the word "fatherland", "patrie", "patria", is *"tanah air"*,

> meaning "land and water", thereby indicating how inseparable the relationship is between water and land to the Indonesian people. The seas, to our mind, do not separate but connect our islands. More than that, these waters unify our nations.[7]

Indonesia's efforts finally bore fruit in December 1982, when the special provisions on the archipelagic State principles were included in Part IV of the 1982 United Nations Convention on the Law of the Sea.[8] Under these provisions Indonesia is entitled to draw straight archipelagic baselines around its archipelago and may designate archipelagic sea-lanes to accommodate foreign ships, especially foreign military vessels, to transit through the archipelago. It should be noted, however, that in the process Indonesia has consulted its neighboring states affected by those baselines and designated sea lanes for ships that normally transit Indonesian waters. The waters enclosed by the baselines is then called archipelagic waters where Indonesia holds full sovereignty but "archipelagic sea lanes" may be designated for foreign vessels for navigation in the normal mode.

Indonesia also played an active role in extensive discussions at other fora such as the Asian African Legal Consultative Committee and various academic gatherings such as the Law of the Sea Institute. Efforts to gain recognition of its status as an archipelagic State were also carried out through negotiations on maritime boundaries with its neighboring countries.

Foreign military activities in Indonesia's exclusive economic zone

The 1982 UNCLOS provisions on exclusive economic zone attempts to balance the differing interests of coastal and maritime states but is silent or ambiguous on the legality of military operations in foreign exclusive economic zones. Coastal states seek to assert increasing control over their maritime zones while maritime states prioritize the freedom of navigation. As far as States other than the coastal state, Article 56 paragraph 2 guaranteed that in exercising and performing its rights and duties in the exclusive economic zone, coastal states shall have due regard to the rights and duties of other States and shall act in a manner compatible with the provisions of the 1982 UNCLOS. It is important to note that "sovereign rights" is not the same as sovereignty.

Article 58 of the 1982 UNCLOS provides that all States, whether coastal or land-locked and whether subject to the relevant provisions of this Convention, enjoy the freedoms such as those in the high seas. This is referred to in Article 87 of navigation and overflight, and of the laying of submarine cables and pipelines, and other internationally lawful uses of the sea related to these freedoms such as those associated with the operation of ships, aircraft, and submarine cables and pipelines, and compatible with the other provisions of this Convention. Furthermore, paragraph 2 of this Article stated that Articles 88 to 115 and other pertinent rules of international law apply to the exclusive economic zone in so far as they are not incompatible with this Part VI of UNCLOS.

In addition, paragraph 3 of the same Article provides limitation in exercising what has been stated in paragraph 1 and 2, by stating that States shall have due regard to the rights and duties of the coastal state which mainly includes sovereign rights for exploring and exploiting, conserving, and managing living or non-living resources, and also for other activities for the economic exploitation and exploration of the zone. The coastal State also has jurisdiction with regard to the establishment and use of artificial islands, installations and structures, marine scientific research, and the protection and preservation of the marine environment. Furthermore, States shall comply with the laws and regulations adopted by the coastal state in accordance with the provisions of the 1982 UNCLOS and other rules of international law in so far as they are not incompatible with the provisions of Part V.

In case conflict arises where the 1982 UNCLOS does not attribute rights or jurisdiction in the exclusive economic zone to the coastal state or other States, according to Article 59 conflict should be resolved on the basis of equity and in the light of all the relevant circumstances, taking into account the importance of the interests involved both to the parties as well as to the international community.

A compromise to balance the differing interests of coastal states and maritime powers has resulted in ambiguity and lack of clarity in those provisions. It should also be noted that these provisions were formulated more than three decades ago in different political and technological circumstances than what exists at present.

Such misunderstanding regarding activities within the exclusive economic zone that are not clearly regulated by Part V of the 1982 UNCLOS, came in various forms of interpretation. A noticeable example concerns military activities in foreign exclusive economic zones. The issue remains controversial in state practice. As has been indicated before, coastal states seek to assert increasing control over their maritime zones while maritime states adhere to the principle of freedom of navigation.

An example of States practice occurred in March 2009 when Chinese vessels surrounded an unarmed United States (US) navy surveillance vessel, the *Impeccable*, in the South China Sea about 75 nautical miles south of China's Hainan Island, while it was conducting routine seabed mapping and tracking submarines.[9] The vessel retreated from the area but returned later accompanied by a US guided missile destroyer for its protection.[10] This incident raised tensions in Sino-American relations as both accused the other of violating international law.[11] The US protested the Chinese vessel's harassment while Beijing accused the US ship of operating illegally in China's exclusive economic zone.[12] This confrontation is a good example of the uncertainty and controversy regarding the legality of military operations in the EEZ. Did the US have the right to conduct activities in China's claimed EEZ? Was China out of line to require prior notification and permission? What does the 1982 UNCLOS permit and prohibit in terms of military activities in the EEZ? Unfortunately, the issue of the military uses of the oceans in peacetime raises many contentious questions and very few answers.

A recent incident not involving military activities took place in the South China Sea whereby Indonesian authorities attempted to capture a Chinese trawler on Saturday, 19 March 2016 and arrest the Chinese crew. They were stopped by a Chinese coast guard boat that reportedly prevented Indonesia from securing the fishing vessel and pushed it back into the South China Sea. A report said Indonesia has the crew in custody.[13]

China disputes Indonesia's version of events and said the fishing vessel was operating in "traditional Chinese fishing grounds" before it was "attacked and harassed by an armed Indonesian ship," prompting the Chinese coast guard to offer assistance, and demand that the fishermen be released.

The Indonesian Minister for Maritime Affairs and Fisheries said that the incident occurred well inside Indonesia's exclusive economic zone. She indicated that while Indonesia wants to avoid a more serious incident only by arresting the eight crew members, Indonesia also must maintain its sovereignty.

Such an incident happened before. At that time Indonesia tried to keep the maritime clashes quiet, apparently concerned about disrupting Indonesian–Chinese relations. In 2010, a Chinese maritime enforcement vessel compelled an Indonesian patrol boat to release another illegal Chinese trawler. Similarly in March 2013, armed Chinese vessels confronted an Indonesian fisheries patrol boat and demanded the release of Chinese fishermen who had been apprehended in Natuna waters. This time, Indonesia's foreign minister has protested to China against what it described as a breach by the Chinese coastguard of Indonesia's sovereign rights near a disputed area of the South China Sea.

China and Indonesia do not contest the sovereignty of the Natuna islands and the seas around them and both agree they are part of Indonesia's Riau Province. Nevertheless, the entire South China Sea – a strategic shipping corridor rich in fish and natural gas – is claimed by China and several Southeast Asian countries who have overlapping claims. Indonesia's role in the South China Sea dispute is not as a mediator, since the conflict is not yet at the mediation stage. Indonesia has put lots of effort into confidence-building measures, as indicated by Arif Havas Oegroseno:

> Indonesia's relentless facilitation in the second track approach, known as the Workshop on Managing Potential Conflict in the South China Sea, is not intended to position Indonesia as a mediator. It is a confidence-building measure to enhance understanding and mutual trust. [14]

Notwithstanding the current situation, as a state that has geostrategic importance in Southeast Asia, Indonesia uses maritime diplomacy as a means of establishing cooperative regional relationships including settling maritime disputes. This achieves two objectives: Firstly, ensuring its security; and secondly, by actively resolving its maritime disputes – demonstrating its leadership credentials to mediate interstate maritime disputes in the region.

Indonesia's experience of harmonizing its domestic interest with international law, including UNCLOS

There is no doubt that the archipelagic principles of the 1982 UNCLOS are considered to be one of Indonesia's noticeable experience in harmonizing its domestic interest with international law, particularly with the international law of the sea. In its efforts to fulfill the international obligations arising out of its ratification of the 1982 UNCLOS, Indonesia analyzed existing related laws and regulations, attempting to harmonize them with the new international law. In its efforts Indonesia has enacted and revised a number of laws and regulations.

As part of the first effort toward the implementation of the 1982 UNCLOS, Indonesia has enacted a new Law No. 6 of 1996 on the Indonesian Territorial Waters.[15] The new Law, revised Law No. 4 of 1960, adopted principles embodied in the 1982 United Nations Convention on the Law of the Sea. Basically the new Law upholds some old principles like the one on the breadth of the territorial sea of 12 nautical miles.

The old provision of straight baselines from point to point is adjusted accordingly with a new provision on straight archipelagic baselines. The Indonesian Navy's Hydrographic Office had conducted a preliminary study on the exact base points where the new baselines can be drawn upon. An illustrative map is attached to the Law showing the possible new baselines, the territorial sea, outer limit of the exclusive economic zones, and special lines showing the unfinished or still negotiated boundaries with Indonesia's neighboring countries.

Several new concepts, such as the right of transit passage, the right of archipelagic sea-lanes passage, and the right of access and communication, are also included. The provisions on the right of innocent passage are adjusted to the new concept embodied in the 1982 UNCLOS.

When Indonesia established its position as an archipelagic State through the enactment of Law No. 4 of 1960, it was not in a position to carry out a thorough survey on the locations of the base points. Geographical coordinates were listed and an illustrative map at a small scale was annexed to that Law. Meanwhile, Article 47 paragraph 2 of the 1982 UNCLOS provides that an archipelagic State may draw baselines that shall not exceed 100 nautical miles, and that an exception may exceed that length up to a maximum length of 125 miles for up to 3 percent of the total number of baselines.

Taking into account these facts and situations, during the period of 1989–1995 Indonesia began its endeavor to carry out a survey of all existing base points. In the course of this survey new base points were located and new baselines were established. As a result of the survey 233 possible base points were located, out of which 231 baselines can be drawn. To take the benefit of the provision of Article 47 paragraph 2, these baselines can be reduced to a number of 189, where 187 baselines can be drawn, out of which five baselines of 100 to 125 nautical miles in length can be drawn.

It is based on this survey that on 28 June 2002 the government finally decided to enact Government Regulation No. 38 of 2002 concerning List of Geographical Coordinates of the Base points of the Indonesian Straight Archipelagic Baselines.[16] With the independence of East Timor, Indonesia has revised some of the base points and baselines already drawn in the area of the Timor Sea, and Government Regulation No. 37 of 2008 on the Revision of Government Regulation No. 38

of 2002 concerning List of Geographical Coordinates of the Base points of the Indonesian Straight Archipelagic Baselines.

Before Indonesia ratified the 1982 UNCLOS, Indonesia made its claim to a 200-mile exclusive economic zone on March 21, 1980, by the promulgation of a Declaration on the Indonesian Exclusive Economic Zone. It was soon followed by the enactment of Law No. 5 on the Indonesian Exclusive Economic Zone on October 18, 1983. This law grants Indonesia sovereign rights for the purpose of exploring and exploiting, and conserving and managing the natural resources of its exclusive economic zone.

This Law also provides for foreign legal entities or governments a guaranteed access to the surplus of the allowable catch. The provisions of this Law also contains an obligation to take the necessary measures to prevent, reduce, and control pollution of the marine environment. It also contains provisions on liability for any act which contravenes Indonesian laws and regulations, and in the case of marine scientific research, rules of international law. Strict liability shall be imposed on any activity resulting in the pollution of the marine environment or damage to the natural resources.

As an implementation of this law, on June 29, 1984, Government Regulation No. 14 of 1984 was enacted. Basically, it contains provisions regarding the utilization and conservation of the living resources in the Indonesian exclusive economic zone, procedures for obtaining licenses, and sanctions for any violation of these provisions. This Regulation was issued under a consideration that Indonesia needs to develop its fishing industry.

On September 19, 1997, a new Law No. 23 of 1997 concerning the Management of the Living Environment was passed to replace Law No. 4 of 1982. The 1997 law lays out in Article 3, the basis, objective, and target of the law – "environmental management consistent with national responsibility and sustainable development" and "exploitation within the framework of the holistic development of the Indonesian individual and community in its entirety."

Chapter III goes on to elaborate upon the right of every person to a healthy environment and the obligation to preserve environmental functions and combat environmental pollution. Chapter IV serves as the implementation of Article 33 paragraph 3 of the 1945 Indonesian Constitution whereby it is provided that natural resources are controlled by the state, and are to be developed by the government for the greatest possible public welfare. Article 11 in Chapter IV reposes the tasks of environmental management in an institutional instrument, coordinated by the Office of the State Minister of the Environment.

The 1997 law proceeds to provide for the delegation of authority to provincial governments. Chapter V on the Preservation of Environmental Functions prohibits every business and/or activity from breaching environmental quality standards and criteria. Projects that would create impacts on the environment must possess an environmental impact analysis, further elucidation of which will be carried out through the enactment of Government Regulations. Businesses and activities must manage their wastes, including hazardous and toxic wastes. The law also contains provisions on supervision, compliance control, environmental audits, and administrative sanctions at provincial and district levels. The latter includes sanctions in the form of revocation of business licenses.

Chapter VII of this law provides for environmental dispute settlement either through judicial or extra-judicial means. Judicial settlement anticipates the payment of compensation and the issuance of orders to carry out certain actions. Two very significant features of the 1997 Law appear in this Chapter – first, strict liability is prescribed for violations involving hazardous and toxic materials, which cause significant impact to the environment; and second, following recent decisions in the courts, community, and environmental organizations are explicitly given judicial standing to bring class actions, and/or to report on environmental violations. One of the enabling instruments of this law is Government Regulation No. 18 of 1999 regarding the Control of Pollution of and/or Damage to the Marine Environment.

On 13 October 1992 Indonesia enacted Law No. 24 of 1992 concerning Spatial Planning. This law governs the utilization, planning, and control of the national territory as an archipelagic State for development purposes, including areas outside of national territory where Indonesia may exercise its law under sovereign rights for the management of natural resources, or under other legitimate rights govern by international law.

Basically this law can be described through the following points of the Indonesian territory as an archipelagic State with its diversified ecosystem or ecology; coordination and integration; pattern of sustainable development; and ability to accommodate further development. Among the principles used in this law there are regulations regarding planning (formulation and determination of development programs, including formulation of action plans for each program); utilization (through issuance of permits, evaluation and actual use of space); and control (through surveillance and regulation).

Through the People's Consultative Assembly (MPR) Decision No. XV/MPR/1998, the government is instructed to establish laws and regulations concerning autonomous regional administration. On May 7, 1999 the government enacted Law No. 22 of 1999 concerning Regional Government.

Article 2 paragraph 1 of this law stipulates that the Indonesian territory is divided into three autonomous regional territories of provinces, municipalities, and regencies. Furthermore, Article 3 provided that the territory of a province consists of land areas and a sea area of 12 nautical miles measured from the "coastline" toward the high seas and/or toward the archipelagic waters.[17] Meanwhile the territory of the municipalities and regencies is set to be one third of that assigned to the provinces, or a belt of four nautical miles, assumed to be measured in the same manner as that of the provinces.

This assignment of territories is accompanied with a corresponding rights for the regional governments in the following areas:[18] exploration, exploitation, conservation, and management of marine resources within the assigned territory; regulation of administrative matters; regulation of spatial planning; enforcement of the regional and national laws and regulations; and assisting the government in the enhancement of security and sovereignty of the State.

On 6 October 2004 Indonesia enacted a new Law No. 31 of 2004 concerning Fisheries to replace Law No. 9 of 1985, which was considered not to have sufficient provisions on management and conservation of living resources. Basic provisions of the 1982 UNCLOS concerning management and conservation of living resources were elaborated in this new Law. According to Melda Kamil Ariadno, this Law, which was later revised by Law No. 45 of 2009:

> has stipulated almost all relevant principles and management tools which are believed compatible with national needs and could be implemented effectively in the fishing activity. This new law has clearly identified that fisheries management in Indonesia has to achieve continuous productivity (article 1 point 7) and optimal as well as sustainable use of fisheries resource (article 6 paragraph 1). In achieving this aim, the adapt law and local knowledge should be observed, and the role of local community should be taken into account (article 6 paragraph 2).[19]

Indonesia has also tried to revise its Law No. 1 of 1983 on the Indonesian Continental Shelf by trying to make the best available option for determining the outer limits of its continental shelf beyond 200 nautical miles. On June 16, 2008 based on Article 76 paragraph 8, Indonesia submitted to the United Nations Commission on the Limits of the Continental Shelf, a partial submission on the outer limit of the extended continental shelf in the area of North West of Sumatra. Later, on March 28, 2011 the Commission decided a "Recommendations of the Commission on the Limits of the Continental Shelf in regard to the submission made by Indonesia in respect of the area North West of Sumatra on 16 June 2008." At present, the revision is still in progress at the Ministry of Justice.

These are only few examples on how Indonesia has tried to implement the 1982 UNCLOS by harmonizing it with the existing relevant laws and regulations. It is clear that there are still many things to be done in terms of implementation as well as harmonizing its national interests with its international obligations under the 1982 UNCLOS.

UNCLOS' role in addressing the maritime dispute in the South China Sea

Many of the maritime disputes today represent a competing interest of two groups, coastal states (new regime of EEZ and continental shelf), and user states (freedom of navigation, innocent passages). It also reflects the interpretation of UNCLOS (for instance, the interpretation of article 121 (3) and rights of submarines and government vessels while exercising innocent passages, etc.).

According to Arif Havas Oegroseno of the Coordinating Minister for Maritime Affairs the very essence of the South China Sea dispute is, in simple terms, about who owns over hundreds of islands, rocks, reefs, low-tide elevations and sandbanks in the Spratlys and the Paracels.[20] Since the inception of the 1957

Djuanda Declaration and moreover since its independence in 1945, Indonesia has never lay any claim to any of those hundreds of features in the South China Sea. Neither the 1945 Declaration of Independence nor the 1957 Djuanda Declaration, included the Spratlys and Paracels as parts of Indonesian territory.

Unlike other Southeast Asian states such as Brunei, China, Malaysia, the Philippines, and Vietnam, Indonesia never laid any territorial claim in the islands and other features in the South China Sea. It was for that reason that Indonesia never regarded itself as claimant. On the other hand, Indonesia has keen interests in the management of the potential conflicts in the South China Sea, and put lots of effort transforming it into potential for cooperation.

Indonesia even took the informal initiative to convene a series of workshops among participants from the ASEAN member countries, which later expanded to also include Vietnam and China. Through these workshops the participants, initiated by Indonesia, attempted to identify possible areas for cooperation and agreed to discuss the following areas: First, shipping, navigation, and communication; second, environment and marine scientific research; third, management of the resources.

In conclusion, Indonesia is not a claimant state to the islands and other features in the South China Sea, but maintains its rights to the territorial sea under international law – including the contiguous zone, the exclusive economic zone, and the continental shelf measured from its straight archipelagic baselines as has already been registered with the United Nations.

Notes

1 Mochtar Kusumaatmadja, "The Legal Regime of Archipelagoes: Problems and Issues," (paper presented at the Seventh Annual Conference of the Law of the Sea Institute, University of Rhode Island, Kingston, R.I., 1972).
2 Hasjim Djalal, "The Development of the Archipelagic Concept (1975)," in *Indonesia and the Law of the Sea*, Hasjim Djalal (Centre for Strategic and International Studies, Jakarta, 1955) 336.
3 "Statement made by H. E. Prof. Dr. Mochtar Kusumaatmadja, Minster of Justice and Leader of the Indonesian Delegation to the Third United Nations Conference on the Law of the Sea, Caracas, July, 1974," in Mochtar Kusumaatmadja, *Bunga Rampai Hukum Laut* (Penerbit Binacipta, Bandung, 1978), 92.
4 Mochtar Kusumaatmadja, "The Concept of the Indonesian Archipelago," *Indonesian Quarterly X*, No. 4: 23, as is quoted in Dino Patti Djalal, *The Geopolitics of Indonesia's Maritime Territorial Policy*, (Centre for Strategic and Internationl Studies, Jakarta, 1996), 68.
5 UN Doc. A/AC.138/SC.II/L.15 of 14 March 1973, A/AC.138/SC II/L.48 of 6 August 1973, and A/CONF. 62/C.2/L. 49 of 1974.
6 "Statement made by H. E. Prof. Dr. Mochtar Kusumaatmadja, Minster of Justice and Leader of the Indonesian Delegation to the Third United Nations Conference on the Law of the Sea, Caracas, July, 1974," in Mochtar Kusumaatmadja, *Bunga Rampai Hukum Laut* (Penerbit Binacipta, Bandung, 1978), 93–94.
7 Dino Patti Djalal, *The Geopolitics of Indonesia's Maritime Territorial Policy*, (Centre for Strategic and Internationl Studies, Jakarta, 1996, 70). Translated from a publication by the National Defence Council, "Pokok-pokok Pengertian dan Sejarah Pengembangan Wawasan Nusantara," 1982.

8 Hereinafter shall be referred to as the "1982 UNCLOS."

9 C. Rahman and M. Tsamenyi, "A Strategic Perspective on Security and Naval Issues in the South China Sea" (2010) 41 *Ocean Dev and Int'l L* 315, 326.

10 R. Pedrozo, "Close Encounters at Sea: The USNS *Impeccable* Incident" (2009) 62 *Naval War Col Rev* 101.

11 V. England, "Who's right in South China Sea spat?" *BBC News* (London, 13 March 2009) http://news.bbc.co.uk/2/hi/asia-pacific/7941425.stm (accessed January 30, 2012).

12 *Ibid.*

13 "South China Sea: Indonesia summons Chinese ambassador as fishing dispute escalates," *The Guardian*, Monday, March 21, 2016, theguardian.com, accessed on March 23, 2016, at 11.00 a.m.

14 Arif Havas Oegroseno, "Indonesia, South China Sea and the 11/10/9-dash lines," *Jakarta Post*, April 9, 2014, www.thejakartapost.com/news/2014/04/09/indonesia-south-china-sea-and-11109-dashed-lines.html#sthash.L92zy2Dr.dpuf, accessed March 24, 2016.

15 State Gazette No. 73 of 1996, Additional State Gazette No. 3647 of 1996.

16 In 1998 as a first trial, Indonesia drew straight baselines around the Natuna Sea. Government Regulation No. 61 of 1998 on the straight baselines in the Natuna Sea was enacted. This Government Regulation was then replaced by Government Regulation No. 38 of 2002.

17 The use of the term "coastline" has been challenged by many as an indication that the drafter of this Law is ignorant of the existence of methods used to measure maritime zones according to the 1982 UNCLOS which Indonesia has ratified in 1985.

18 Article 10 paragraph 2.

19 Melda Kamil Ariadno. "Sustainable Fisheries in Southeast Asia", journal.ui.ac.id/index.php/ilrev/article/view/2834, accessed on April 25, 2016.

20 See more at: www.thejakartapost.com/news/2014/04/09/indonesia-south-china-sea-and-11109-dashed-lines.html#sthash.L92zy2Dr.dpuf

6 Balancing the rights of coastal states and user states in the post-UNCLOS age

Vietnam and navigational rights

*Hao Duy Phan**

Vietnam and UNCLOS: an overview

Pre-UNCLOS period

Being a maritime nation, Vietnam has a long coastline, stretching for 3,444 kilometres (km) from the Gulf of Tokin to the Gulf of Thailand.[1] Its sea area is about three times larger than its land area[2] and is considered rich in fishery and oil and gas resources. The seacoast provides an important natural communication link to the outside world.[3] Moreover, the coastal areas are where more than half of the country's population reside and more than half of its major cities are located.[4]

Given its maritime geography, it is not surprising that Vietnam started paying attention to the development of the international law of the sea quite early. Delegations under the name of Vietnam, either the Democratic Republic of Vietnam, the Republic of Vietnam or the Socialist Republic of Vietnam, were seated at all three United Nations conferences on the law of the sea.[5] Because of its status as a member of the UN specialized agencies, the Republic of Vietnam was able to attend the first conference (UNCLOS I) and the second conference (UNCLOS II). For a variety of political reasons, the Democratic Republic of Vietnam was excluded from both UNCLOS I and UNCLOS II.[6]

When the third United Nations Conference on the Law of the Sea (UNCLOS III) started on 3 December 1973,[7] both the Republic of Vietnam and the Democratic Republic of Vietnam were invited to attend. However, as they were preoccupied with the war at that time, their participation in the initial sessions of UNCLOS III was very limited.[8] The Democratic Republic of Vietnam did not even participate in the first few sessions of the Conference.[9]

After the war in Vietnam ended, the Socialist Republic of Vietnam became a unified state and once again became involved with the development of the international law of the sea. First, it entered UNCLOS III at the sixth session in 1977 when the Conference was moving toward an informal composite negotiating text of the Convention (ICNT).[10] At UNCLOS III, Vietnam generally supported the positions of the Group of 77 and the Non-Aligned Movement, especially when it comes to seabed mining issues and the Area under Committee I and marine scientific research, protection of the marine environment, and transfer of technology under Committee III.[11]

Second, also in 1977, the Socialist Republic of Vietnam issued the Statement on the Territorial Sea, the Contiguous Zones, the Exclusive Economic Zone (EEZ) and the Continental Shelf (CS – the 1977 Statement) – its first official statement on the law of the sea as a newly unified state.[12] Most of the claims in the 1977 Statement reflected the progress and the expected outcome of the negotiation of UNCLOS III. However, some provisions were subject to criticism for using a straight baseline system that 'links the furthest seaward points of the coast and the outermost point of Vietnamese offshore islands'[13] and the use of the contiguous zone for security purposes.[14]

In 1980, when UNCLOS III was in its final stage and the Draft Convention on the Law of the Sea (Informal Text) was reached,[15] Vietnam adopted Decree No. 30 on Regulations for Foreign Ships Operating in Vietnamese Maritime Zones (the 1980 Decree). The 1980 Decree consists of 26 articles divided into three chapters on general provisions; specific regulations for foreign ships operating in Vietnamese maritime zones and control and measures of application.[16] Several provisions in the 1980 Decree were considered by maritime powers and legal experts as limiting navigational rights of user states in Vietnamese maritime zones.

Finally, in November 1982 when UNCLOS was only one month away from being adopted, Vietnam issued the Statement on the Territorial Sea Baseline (the 1982 Statement), announcing the specific coordinates to the straight baseline system it claimed back in 1977.[17] The 1982 Statement, however, was viewed as not meeting the geographical criteria for the use of straight baselines as provided in Article 7 of UNCLOS and was subject to protest from a number of states.[18]

Vietnam continued its participation at UNCLOS III until the adoption of the Convention in 1982.[19] Together with 129 other states, it voted in favour of the Convention and its related resolutions and decisions.[20] It signed UNCLOS on the day the Convention was opened for signature on 10 December 1982 in Montego Bay, Jamaica.[21]

Post-UNCLOS period

It took Vietnam more than a decade to ratify UNCLOS. During the 1980s, most of its attention was focused on much more pressing issues, including its internal problems, the conflict in Cambodia, tension with China, the US-led isolation, and sanctions regime against the country and its relationship with the Soviet Union. By the late 1980s, Vietnam began to adopt a new foreign policy approach. Its external relations were no longer confined to the Soviet Union-led socialist bloc but rather expanded for diversification and multilateralization. On 23 June 1994, the National Assembly of Vietnam adopted a resolution to ratify UNCLOS (the 1994 Resolution).[22] The 1994 Resolution makes clear that, by ratifying UNCLOS, Vietnam is '[determined] to join the international community in establishing an equitable legal order and promoting maritime development and cooperation'.[23]

In the wake of its UNCLOS ratification, Vietnam took various steps both domestically and on the international plane to implement the treaty. At the international level, it actively participated in the negotiation of the 1994 Agreement relating to the Implementation of Part XI of UNCLOS.[24] It eventually ratified the 1994 Agreement in 2006.[25] It has sent delegations to all meetings of the state parties to UNCLOS[26] and has also complied with the financial provisions under UNCLOS in making annual contributions to foster the operation of the bodies established therein.[27] In accordance with Article 76 of UNCLOS, it submitted information on the limits of the continental shelf beyond 200 nautical miles (nm) to the Commission on the Limits of the Continental Shelf, which included a joint submission with Malaysia.[28] It was elected as a member of the Council the International Seabed Authority in 2013 and 2014.[29] It has on many occasions expressed its support for the enhanced activities of the Commission on the Limits of the Continental Shelf and the judicial function of the International Tribunal for the Law of the Sea.[30]

A review of the status of the conventions under International Maritime Organization (IMO) indicates that Vietnam has also ratified many treaties on navigation and shipping. The list includes, among others, the 1965 Convention on Facilitation of International Maritime Traffic, the 1966 International Convention on Load Lines, the 1973 International Convention for the Prevention of Pollution from Ships and the 1978 Supplemented Protocol (MARPOL 73/78), the 1969 International Convention on Tonnage Measurement of Ships, the 1972 International Regulations for Preventing Collisions at Sea, the 1974 International Convention for the Safety of Life at Sea, the 1978 International Convention on the Standards of Training, Certification and Watch-keeping for Crew Members, the 1979 International Convention on Maritime Search and Rescue, the 1988 Convention for the Suppression of Unlawful Acts Against the Safety of Maritime Navigation, and the 1988 Protocol for the Suppression of Unlawful Acts Against the Safety of Fixed Platforms Located on the Continental Shelf.[31]

At the regional level, Vietnam is a member of the Association of Southeast Asian Nations (ASEAN)[32] and has participated in the negotiation of all ASEAN instruments since 1995. Among many ASEAN instruments relevant to navigation and shipping, Vietnam has signed or ratified the 1975 Agreement for the Facilitation of Search of Ships in Distress and Rescue of Survivors of Ship Accidents, the 2005 ASEAN Framework Agreement on Multimodal Transport, the 2007 ASEAN Counter-Terrorism Convention, the 2009 ASEAN Framework Agreement on the Facilitation of Goods in Transit, and the 2009 ASEAN Framework Agreement on the Facilitation of Inter-state Transport.[33] It has also ratified the 2004 Regional Cooperation Agreement on Combating Piracy and Armed Robbery against Ships in Asia (ReCAAP) and participated in the work of the Information Sharing Centre established under the Agreement.[34]

When Vietnam's National Assembly decided to ratify UNCLOS, it asked the government to review all relevant national legislation to consider necessary promulgation and amendments of legislation in conformity with UNCLOS.[35]

Many laws since then have been enacted to implement different provisions of UNCLOS, including the 2003 Law on National Border, the 2004 Fishery Law, the 2005 Maritime Code, the 2014 Environment Protection Law, and the 2015 Law on Sea and Island Natural Resources and Environment.[36]

In particular significance is the Vietnam Law of the Sea (the 2012 Law) that the National Assembly adopted on 21 June 2012, which is the country's most comprehensive piece of legislation on the law of the sea. It covers all major aspects of the management and use of the sea, including the scope and regime of internal waters, territorial sea, contiguous zone, EEZ, continental shelf, regime of islands, archipelagos, activities in the Vietnamese sea areas, search and rescue, protection of marine resources and environment, marine scientific research, development of maritime economy, sea patrol and control, and maritime international cooperation.[37] The 2012 Law also clarifies many of Vietnam's legal positions on several issues. This law has brought Vietnamese legislation much closer to UNCLOS. The shift in Vietnam's regulations on navigational rights reflects its efforts to strike a balance between its rights as a coastal state and the rights of other user states in its maritime zones. It also reveals an evolution in the country's policies toward UNCLOS and its overall perception of the international maritime order in general. The case of navigational rights in Vietnamese law and policies in relation to UNCLOS will be the focus of the next section.

Vietnam and navigational rights before and after the ratification of UNCLOS: A paradigm shift

Navigation under UNCLOS

Navigation is one of the most important areas in the law of the sea.[38] It also represented one of the most difficult issues during the negotiation of UNCLOS.[39] There were many alliances and state groupings at UNCLOS III and they did not share the same views or common interests regarding the issue of navigation. The Maritime States Group and the Great Maritime Powers Group, for example, sought to protect their fleets' freedom of movement and objected to any attempts to limit their traditional navigational practice.[40] For members of the Coastal States Group, the aim was to promote their cause for extended coastal states jurisdiction in their maritime zones.[41] Within the Coastal States Group, there was a Territorialist Sub-group that was fighting for a territorial sea of more than 12 nm. This Sub-group also espoused a strong view, claiming that the proposed 200 nm EEZ conforms as closely as possible to their territorialist concept, according to which the coastal states would have more jurisdictional and regulatory powers in their EEZs.[42] In addition, the Group of Archipelagic States and the Group of Straits States were seeking to adopt a common position in the legal regime on passage through straits on archipelagic waters.[43] It was certainly not unusual for a state to belong to several groups since a state could have more than one vital area of interest.[44] The outcome of this group system and the complex negotiation structure is a delicate balance in UNCLOS between the interests of the maritime powers in maintaining their traditional rights of navigation and those of coastal states, straits states, and archipelagic states in exercising their sovereignty over their territorial sea or archipelagic waters as well as their sovereign rights over their EEZ and continental shelf.[45]

The Convention, for example, recognizes that every state has the right to establish a territorial sea of 12 nm over which it has sovereignty, but it also retains for naval and merchant ships the right of innocent passage through the territorial sea of a coastal state.[46] Article 19 of the Convention provides that passage is innocent so long as it is not prejudicial to the peace, good order, or security of the coastal state. It further provides that passage shall be considered to be prejudicial to the peace, good order, or security of the coastal states if it engages in (i) any threat or use of force against the sovereignty, territorial integrity or political independence of the coastal states; (ii) any exercise or practice with weapons of any kind; (iii) any act aimed at collecting information to the prejudice of the defence or security of the coastal states; (iv) any act of propaganda aimed at affecting the defence or security of the coastal states; (v) the launching, landing, or taking on board of any aircraft; (vi) the launching, landing, or taking on board of any military device; (vii) the loading or unloading of any commodity, currency, or person contrary to the customs, fiscal, immigration, or sanitary laws and regulations of the coastal states; (viii) any act of wilful and serious pollution; (ix) any fishing activities; (x) the carrying out of research or survey activities; (xi) any act aimed at interfering with any systems of communication or any other facilities or installations of the coastal state; and (xii) any other activity not having a direct bearing on passage.[47] In the territorial sea, submarines are required to navigate on the surface and to show their flag.[48] The coastal states may prevent passage that is not innocent or temporarily suspend passage without discrimination among foreign ships in specified areas of its territorial sea essential for the protection of its security, including weapons exercises.[49] The coastal states shall not hamper the innocent passage of foreign ships through the territorial sea except in accordance with the Convention.[50]

Under UNCLOS, archipelagic states have sovereignty over archipelagic waters; similarly, states bordering straits used for international navigation have sovereignty over the straits.[51] However, to ensure that the navigational rights of the maritime states would not be negatively affected, the Convention provides that the sovereignty or jurisdiction of archipelagic states or states bordering straits must be exercised in accordance with two newly established passage regimes, namely, *archipelagic sea lanes passage* through archipelagic waters and *transit passage* in straits used for international navigation.[52] Archipelagic sea lanes passage means the exercise of the rights of navigation and overflight in the normal mode solely for the purpose of continuous, expeditious, and unobstructed transit between one part of the high seas or an EEZ and another part of the high seas or an EEZ.[53] Transit passage means the exercise of the freedom of navigation and overflight solely for the purpose of continuous and expeditious transit of the strait between one part of the high seas or an EEZ and another part of the high seas or an EEZ.[54] In straits used for international navigation, ships can sail in their normal modes[55] and states bordering straits shall not hamper transit passage or suspend transit passage.[56]

UNCLOS allows the coastal states to have a contiguous zone of 24 nm from the baselines.[57] Within the contiguous zone, the coastal states may only exercise the control related to customs, fiscal, immigration, or sanitary laws and regulations.[58] This means that the contiguous zone is neither part of the territorial sea nor under the coastal state's sovereignty. Thus, the high seas freedom of navigation is applicable in it.[59]

UNCLOS creates a new maritime zone, that is, the EEZ of 200 nm in which the coastal states have the sovereign rights to explore, exploit, conserve, and manage the natural resources of the waters superjacent to the seabed and to the seabed and its subsoil.[60] However, it also provides that in the EEZ of the coastal states, all other states enjoy the freedoms of navigation and overflight, of the laying of submarine cables and pipelines, and other internationally lawful uses of the sea related to these freedoms as long as they have due regard to the rights and duties of the coastal states and comply with the laws and regulations adopted by the coastal states in accordance with the Convention.[61] Any conflicts arising in cases where the Convention does not attribute specific rights or jurisdiction to the coastal states or to other states within the EEZ should be resolved on the basis of equity and in the light of all the relevant circumstances, 'taking into account the respective importance of the interests involved to the parties as well as to the international community as a whole'.[62]

Last but not least, UNCLOS provides that the coastal states have sovereign rights over the continental shelf for the purpose of exploring and exploiting its natural resources.[63] The right of the coastal states over the continental shelf, however, do not affect the legal status of the superjacent waters and the air space above those waters and the exercise of the rights of the coastal state over the continental shelf must not infringe or result in any unjustifiable interference with navigation and other rights and freedoms of other states.[64]

Navigational rights under Vietnam's law

Pre-UNCLOS period

The Socialist Republic of Vietnam issued its first instrument on the law of the sea in 1977 in the form of the Statement on the Territorial Sea, the Contiguous Zones, the Exclusive Economic Zone and the Continental Shelf, which was approved by the Standing Committee of the National Assembly.[65] The 1977 Statement claims a territorial sea of 12 nm, a contiguous zone of 24 nm, an EEZ of 200 nm and a CS to the outer edge of the continental margin or to a distance of 200 nm where the outer edge of the continental margin does not extend up to that distance.[66] These claims are in accordance with the progress and expected outcome of the negotiation at UNCLOS III. With the 1977 Statement, Vietnam became one of the pioneering states in establishing the EEZ in light of the negotiation progress at UNCLOS III, thus contributing to the development and consolidation of the practice of states in this regard.[67]

The 1977 Statement, however, also raises some concerns over Vietnam's possible use of the contiguous zone for security purposes.[68] While UNCLOS only allows the coastal states to exercise control necessary to prevent and punish infringement of its customs, fiscal, immigration, or sanitary laws within its territory or territorial sea, the 1977 Statement claims that Vietnam shall also exercise 'necessary control in its contiguous zone in order to see to *its security*' in addition to the permissible control over customs, immigration, sanitation, and fiscal matters.[69] It should be noted that during the negotiation of UNCLOS, a number of states proposed that security be included in the list of activities over which coastal states would have enforcement jurisdiction in their contiguous zones. These proposals were not accepted for inclusion in Article 33 of UNCLOS.[70]

In 1980, the Vietnamese government adopted Decree No. 30 on Regulations for Foreign Ships Operating in Vietnamese Maritime Zones. The 1980 Decree raised concerns as well over a number of provisions related to the navigational rights of other states in Vietnam's territorial sea and contiguous zone. First, the 1980 Decree specifies the 1977 Statement on the use of the contiguous zone for security purposes by requiring foreign military ships to seek permission to enter the contiguous zones at least 30 days in advance and, after permission is granted, to notify the Vietnamese Ministry of Communications and Transport 48 hours before actually entering the zone.[71] Before entering the contiguous zone, all ships must have their weapons in a 'non-operative position', with ammunition locked away and gun barrels covered.[72] Foreign submarines when entering Vietnam's contiguous zone have to surface and hoist the flag of the country of their nationality.[73] These provisions do not appear to conform to Article 33 of UNCLOS on the contiguous zone.

Second, the 1980 Decree puts forward many conditions for foreign military ships when entering Vietnam's territorial sea that go beyond what is provided under UNCLOS. For example, it states that no more than three warships of the same nationality may be in the territorial sea of Vietnam at the same time. It also provides that the maximum stay of each ship in the territorial sea of Vietnam is one week.[74] Such requirements do not exist in UNCLOS provisions on the territorial sea.

Third, under the 1980 Decree, foreign ships must move along assigned routes and corridors and must not enter forbidden areas in the territorial sea of Vietnam.[75] There is no indication, however, whether the assigned routes follows the guidelines and criteria for establishment of sea lanes set out in Article 22 of UNCLOS.[76]

Fourth, the 1980 Decree prohibits foreign ships from engaging in a list of activities that largely corresponds to the list in Article 19 of UNCLOS. It should be noted, however, that while the list in UNCLOS is applicable only in the territorial sea, the geographical scope for a number of forbidden activities under the 1980 Decree is extended to the contiguous zone.[77]

To implement the 1980 Decree, in 1986, the Vietnamese government's Council of Ministers issued Decision No. 13 on Strengthening the Protection of Vietnam's Sovereignty and Security in Vietnam's Maritime Zones (the 1986 Decision). The 1986 Decision lists a series of measures to strengthen the coordination between relevant agencies of Vietnam to enforce the 1980 Decree. In 1988, the Chairman of the Council of Ministers further issued Order No. 85 (the 1988 Order), which specifies measures to settle violations by foreign ships in the maritime zones of Vietnam as provided by the 1980 Decree.

Together the 1977 Statement, the 1980 Decree, the 1986 Decision, and the 1988 Order were perceived as limiting navigational rights of other states in Vietnam's maritime zones contrary to international law of the sea.[78] The fact that Vietnam had not ratified UNCLOS at that time does not release it from the obligation to refrain from acts which would defeat the object and purpose of the Convention,[79] not to mention that several provisions on navigation in UNCLOS were considered as reflecting customary international law. The United States protested in 1982 and repeatedly conducted operational assertions against these provisions in 1982, 1983, 1985, 1986, 1996 through 2002, and 2010 through 2012.[80]

Post-UNCLOS period

Vietnam started to open its door in the late 1980s and early 1990s. It finally decided to ratify UNCLOS in 1994.[81] In 1996, it issued Decree No. 55 on Visits of Foreign Military Ships (the 1996 Decree), which is its first domestic legal document that refers to UNCLOS as a legal basis.[82] The 1996 Decree only regulates activities of foreign military ships visiting Vietnam and does not deal with military ships exercising navigational rights through Vietnam's maritime zones. Included in the 1996 Decree is a provision that prohibits foreign ships from engaging in a list of activities that largely corresponds to the list in Article 19 of UNCLOS; however, unlike the 1980 Decree, the list in the 1996 Decree is only applicable to vessels anchoring or operating within licensed harbours of Vietnam, and not to vessels passing through Vietnam's maritime zones.[83]

In 2001, the government adopted Decree No. 41 on Activities of the Vietnam's Sea Police Forces (the 2001 Decree), which also has several references to international law of the sea. The 2001 Decree provides that enforcement activities of the Vietnam's Sea Police Forces in Vietnam's maritime zone will be conducted in accordance with international treaties to which Vietnam is a party.[84] It further provides that the Ministry of Foreign Affairs of Vietnam has the responsibility to advise Vietnam's Sea Police Forces to settle violations committed in Vietnam's maritime zones as provided in international treaties to which the country is a party.[85]

Another step forward was made in 2003 when the National Assembly adopted the Law of National Boundaries (the 2003 Law). The 2003 Law states in Article 2 that the legal regimes concerning the contiguous zone, the EEZ and the CS are regulated in accordance with UNCLOS. The 2003 Law also, for the first time, acknowledges that vessels of all states has the *right of innocent passage* through Vietnam's territorial sea.[86] It further provides that passage is innocent so long as it is not prejudicial to the peace, good order, security, and marine environment of Vietnam as provided in Vietnamese law and UNCLOS.[87] This is the country's first legal document on law of the sea that requires that, if there is a conflict between the 2003 Law and an international treaty on the same subject to which Vietnam is a party, relevant authorities, agencies, and individuals shall implement the provisions of the international treaty.[88] A similar provision on the primary status of international treaties over domestic law is also found in the 2005 Maritime Code.[89]

This process of oceans legislation reform culminated in 2012 with the adoption of the Law of the Sea (the 2012 Law). Under this law, UNCLOS becomes a guiding principle for the management and protection of the sea.[90] International law, international treaties and UNCLOS are referred to in 40 provisions of the 2012 Law.[91] It is also clearly stated in this law that Vietnam shall respect and protect the rights and interests of foreign vessels in its maritime zones in conformity with international treaties to which the state is a party.[92] The 2012 Law reaffirms the primary role of UNCLOS in case there are differences between its provisions and those under UNCLOS.[93] It also clarifies the relationship between its provisions and those in previous legal documents on the same matters, stating that in case there are differences the 2012 Law shall prevail.[94] It, therefore, could be argued that in the Vietnamese legal hierarchy, the 2012 Law of the Sea ranks below UNCLOS but above all other domestic legal documents on the same matters. This demonstrates the important role of UNCLOS in Vietnam's maritime legal order and maritime policy.

Like UNCLOS, the 2012 Law of the Sea regulates navigation activities of foreign vessels by maritime zones. The Law provides that, in its EEZ, Vietnam 'respects *freedoms of navigation and overflight*, the right of the laying of submarine cables and pipelines and *lawful uses of the sea by other states*' in accordance with this Law and international treaties to which the state is a party, including UNCLOS.[95] This marks the first time a Vietnamese legal document formally acknowledges freedom of navigation and overflight in the EEZ. Article 37 of the 2012 Law includes a list of activities that are not permitted to be undertaken in Vietnam's exclusive zone, most of which are consistent with UNCLOS such as piracy, illegal exploitation of living resources, illegal construction of artificial islands, unlawful marine scientific research, and pollution of the marine environment. The only provision on the EEZ in the 2012 Law that has been subject to criticism is the requirement that, when exercising the freedoms of navigation and overflight in the exclusive economic zone of Vietnam, organizations or individuals are not permitted to conduct acts against Vietnam's sovereignty, defence, and security. The United States protested against this provision in 2013.[96]

In the contiguous zone, the 2012 Law provides that, in addition to the rights and jurisdiction over natural resources as provided in UNCLOS, Vietnam can only exercise control to prevent and punish acts of infringement of its legislation on customs, tariff, health, or immigration committed in the territory or the territorial sea of Vietnam.[97] This provision is consistent with Article 33 of UNCLOS. It is worth noting that, unlike the 1980 Decree, the 2012 Law of the Sea makes no reference to claims over security matters in the contiguous zone. As the Law supersedes previous legal documents on the same matters, it in effect terminates the provisions regulating military activities in the contiguous zone in the 1980 Decree.[98]

The 2012 Law also makes clear that Vietnam's sovereignty in its territorial sea shall be exercised in accordance with UNCLOS,[99] according to which vessels of all states shall enjoy the right of innocent passage.[100] Innocent passage of foreign vessels shall be conducted on the basis of international treaties to which Vietnam is a party, including UNCLOS.[101] The specific requirement in the 1980 Decree that all ships must have their weapons in a 'non-operative position' in the territorial sea of Vietnam no longer exists. There is also no requirement that only up to three warships of the same nationality be in the territorial sea of Vietnam at the same time or that the maximum stay be only one week.

The 2012 Law requires that foreign submarines surface and fly their national flags[102] and foreign nuclear-powered ships carry documents and observe special precautionary measures established for such ships under international law when entering the country's territorial sea.[103] These requirements are consistent with UNCLOS provisions.[104] The 2012 Law also provides that Vietnam may temporarily suspend the exercise of innocent passage in specified areas in Vietnam's territorial sea if such suspension is essential for the protection of its security,[105] which is again allowed under UNCLOS.[106] It further specifies that the temporary suspension shall be made public domestically and internationally on the 'Maritime Notice' in accordance with international maritime practice at least 15 days before the temporary suspension.[107] The 2012 Law has a list of activities that could be construed as prejudicial to Vietnam's peace, good order, and security, which is almost identical to the list in Article 19 of UNCLOS.[108] Unlike the 1980 Decree, the list in the 2012 Law is only applicable in the territorial sea, and not in the contiguous zone.

The only provision on navigation in the territorial sea in the 2012 Law that arguably goes further than UNCLOS is Article 12(2), which requires foreign military vessels exercising the right of innocent passage through Vietnam's territorial sea to give *prior notice* to the Vietnamese competent authorities before entering the state's territorial sea.[109] Compared to Article 3(c) of the 1980 Decree, which requires foreign military ships to seek permission from the Vietnamese government 30 days in advance before entering the contiguous zone, Article 12(2) of the 2012 Law of the Sea is a step forward in a more open direction as it does not require permission and is not applicable to the contiguous zone. Still, one could argue that the prior notice requirement is not entirely consistent with UNCLOS as it might affect the right of innocent passage of foreign military vessels.

The National Assembly of Vietnam, when adopting the Law, did have a debate on this requirement.[110] Several members of the National Assembly suggested that the Law should require foreign military vessels to obtain permission before entering the territorial sea of Vietnam. Some even suggested the Law should provide a specific timeline for submitting and granting permission that foreign military ships can follow. The National Assembly Standing Committee, however, made the case that a requirement for permission in advance could be understood as violating the right innocent passage under UNCLOS. As a compromise, it proposed instead that the Law would follow the practice of a number of other states in requiring foreign military ships to merely give a prior notice, the purpose of which is mainly to ensure the safety of navigation for ships moving in the territorial sea of Vietnam and to assist the competent authorities of Vietnam to manage the state's territorial sea. The provision, however, does not specify the period of notice as many members of the National Assembly had urged due to a concern such a specification would, contrary to UNCLOS, set more restrictive conditions for foreign military ships to exercise the right of innocent passage. Eventually, the view of the Standing Committee prevailed in arguing that a prior notice requirement without a specific timeline would represent a balance between the rights of Vietnam as the coastal state and those of user states in its territorial sea.

In practice, though, the prior notice requirement does not seem to be enforced. The United States' acts of challenge by repeatedly dispatching its military vessels to the territorial sea of Vietnam without prior notification, for example, have never led to any official protests from Vietnam. In January 2016, for example, when the United States USS Curtis Wilbur, an Arleigh Burke-class guided missile destroyer, sailed without any notification within the territorial sea of Triton Island, which is part of the Paracel Islands occupied by China but claimed by Vietnam,[111] Vietnam did not file any protest. In fact, it even issued a statement supporting the United States' acts and saying that Vietnam respects the right of innocent passage through the territorial sea conducted in accordance with relevant rules of international law, in particular Article 17 of UNCLOS.[112] The statement conveniently makes no reference to either Article 12 of the 2012 Law of the Sea on prior notice or Article 37 on acts that can affect Vietnam's security.[113]

Conclusion: UNCLOS in Vietnam's perception of the international maritime order

Evidence from Vietnam's behaviours in recent years indicates that there has been a major change in Vietnam's perception of UNCLOS and the role of UNCLOS in the international maritime order. Specifically, the state has paid more attention to the impact of UNCLOS while formulating its foreign policy. It has also relied more on UNCLOS to buffet its maritime claims and referred to the treaty with some regularity as a source of guidance in drafting its domestic law.

At the international level, Vietnam continues to highlight the significance of UNCLOS in maintaining the world's maritime order. It actively participates in various instruments that have been adopted to implement UNCLOS. It is worth noting that the state has repeatedly touted UNCLOS as the most important law of the sea document that has met the desire and expectations of the international community for a fair international legal order of the oceans.[114] The government's representative has also called for a full implementation of UNCLOS, which includes the respect for the rights the coastal states have in their maritime zones.[115] Also, the country has frequently emphasized the importance of the 'comprehensive and effective dispute settlement system which offers States Parties important peaceful means for the settlement of their maritime disputes, thus protecting their legitimate interests as well as the interest of the international community'.[116] This is a clear departure from the position it took in the negotiation of UNCLOS in which it 'firmly opposed' any compulsory third-party settlement because that would violate 'the principle of the sovereign equality of states'.[117]

At the domestic level, Vietnam has established a relatively comprehensive domestic legal framework to facilitate its implementation of UNCLOS. Recent laws, including the 2003 Law on National Border, the 2004 Fishery Law, the 2005 Maritime Code, the 2014 Environment Protection Law, the 2015 Law on Sea and Island Natural Resources and Environment and, in particular, the 2012 Law of the Sea have helped to bring the country's legislation much closer to UNCLOS. The old legal documents adopted in the pre-UNCLOS period have all been replaced and superseded. The picture is not perfect though, as one can still argue that a few provisions in Vietnamese laws, including the straight baselines system, are not consistent with international law and UNCLOS. But it is clear that UNCLOS plays an increasingly prominent role in Vietnam's domestic legal order. Article 2 of the 2012 Law of the Sea, for example, states that in case there are differences between the provisions of the Law on the one hand and those of an international treaty to which Vietnam is a party on the other hand, then provisions of the international treaty shall prevail.[118] This is in accordance with the new Constitution of Vietnam which provides that Vietnam shall comply with all treaties to which it is a party.[119] This is also in accordance with the 2016 Treaty Law, which provides that when a domestic legal document and a treaty to which the state is a party contain incompatible provisions on the same matter, the treaty shall prevail;[120] and the 2016 Law on Promulgation of Legal Normative Documents, which provides that the promulgation of domestic legal documents shall not create any obstacles to the implementation of treaties to which Vietnam is a party.[121]

Vietnam's policy change and legislative evolution in the area of maritime issues and navigational rights in particular are the result of its own reassessment of geopolitical realities and national interests. The adoption of the 1977 Statement and the 1980 Decree reflected Vietnam's heightened sensitivity and overwhelming preoccupation with national security in the midst of the Cold War. The country was stretching to cope with the aftermath of the Vietnam war, the military confrontation from the Pol Pot regime in Cambodia, the isolation and sanctions imposed by the United States and its allies, and the suspicions, tension, and rivalries in its relationships with China and many ASEAN member states.[122] Toward the end of the Cold War, Vietnam began to re-evaluate its security environment and reassess its foreign policy in response to the changing context both domestically and internationally. Along that line, Vietnam has concluded that UNCLOS would offer or facilitate a more level playing field for all states, especially small ones, to protect their legal rights in the oceans, including the rights to explore and exploit natural resources for economic development, and peacefully settle their disputes. It has, therefore, become increasingly interested in promoting the role of UNCLOS as a 'constitutive multilateral treaty' on the oceans in laying the legal foundation for the establishment of all major maritime areas.[123] Given its evolving perception of international law, its priority and desire for a peaceful environment and economic development and in the context of the South China Sea disputes with its neighbours, it is expected that Vietnam will continue to rely more heavily on international law and UNCLOS in its foreign and oceans policy in the years to come.

Notes

* The views expressed in this chapter are those of the author and do not necessarily represent the position of his affiliations.

1 *See* Central Intelligence Agency, *The World Facebook: Vietnam*, available at www.cia.gov/library/publications/the-world-factbook/geos/vm.html (last visited 1 April 2016).

2 Nguyen Chu Hoi and Hoang Ngoc Giao, 'National Maritime Policy: A Vietnamese Case Study' in *Routledge Handbook of National and Regional Oceans Policy* edited by Bilianca Cicin-Sain, David Vanderzwaag and Miriam Balgos (New York: Routledge, 2015), 444–61, at 444.

3 Epsey Cooke Farrell, *The Socialist Republic of Vietnam and the Law of the Sea: An Analysis of Vietnamese Behavior within the Emerging International Oceans Regime* (The Hague: Nijhoff, 1998), 7.

4 Nguyen Chu Hoi and Hoang Ngoc Giao, 'National Maritime Policy: A Vietnamese Case Study' in *Routledge Handbook of National and Regional Oceans Policy* edited by Bilianca Cicin-Sain, David Vanderzwaag and Miriam Balgos (New York: Routledge, 2015), 444–61, at 446.

5 Epsey Cooke Farrell, *The Socialist Republic of Vietnam and the Law of the Sea: An Analysis of Vietnamese Behavior within the Emerging International Oceans Regime* (The Hague: Nijhoff, 1998), 7.

6 The Soviet Union led the protest against the omission of the Democratic Republic of Vietnam at UNCLOS I and UNCLOS II; the protest, however, did not succeed. See Epsey Cooke Farrell, *The Socialist Republic of Vietnam and the Law of the Sea: An Analysis of Vietnamese Behavior within the Emerging International Oceans Regime* (The Hague: Nijhoff, 1998), 33.

7 *See* United Nations, *Third Conference on the Law of the Sea, Volume I, Summary Records of Plenary Meetings of the First (New York, 3–15 December 1973) and Second (Caracas, 20 June to 29 August 1974) Sessions, and of Meetings of the General Committee, Second Session*, available at http://legal.un.org/diplomaticconferences/lawofthesea-1982/Vol1.html (last visited 1 April 2016).

8 For an overview of the Vietnam war, see Spencer C. Tucker (ed.), *The Encyclopedia of the Vietnam War: A Political, Social, and Military History* (2nd edn, ABC-CLIO, 2011).

9 The Democratic Republic of Vietnam did not want to attend the initial sessions also because it protested against the exclusion of the Provisional Revolutionary Government of South Vietnam at UNCLOS III. *See* Epsey Cooke Farrell, *The Socialist Republic of Vietnam and the Law of the Sea: An Analysis of Vietnamese Behavior within the Emerging International Oceans Regime* (The Hague: Nijhoff, 1998), 33–39.

10 *See* Myron H. Nordquist, *United Nations Convention on the Law of the Sea 1982: A Commentary – Volume I*, Martinus Nijhoff Publishers (Dordrecht/Boston/Lancaster, 1985), 121–30.

11 *See* Epsey Cooke Farrell, *The Socialist Republic of Vietnam and the Law of the Sea: An Analysis of Vietnamese Behavior within the Emerging International Oceans Regime* (The Hague: Nijhoff, 1998), 33–39. For information on the membership

and common interests of the traditional groups at the Conference, see Myron H. Nordquist, *United Nations Convention on the Law of the Sea 1982: A Commentary – Volume I*, Martinus Nijhoff Publishers (Dordrecht/Boston/Lancaster, 1985), 81–85.

12 *See* Statement on the Territorial Sea, the Contiguous Zone, the Exclusive Economic Zone and the Continental Shelf of 12 May 1977, available at www.un.org/depts/los/LEGISLATIONANDTREATIES/STATEFILES/VNM.htm (last visited 1 April 2016) (hereinafter '1977 Statement').

13 Statement on the Territorial Sea, the Contiguous Zone, the Exclusive Economic Zone and the Continental Shelf of 12 May 1977, paragraph 1, available at www.un.org/depts/los/LEGISLATIONANDTREATIES/STATEFILES/VNM.htm (last visited 1 April 2016).

14 Statement on the Territorial Sea, the Contiguous Zone, the Exclusive Economic Zone and the Continental Shelf of 12 May 1977, paragraph 2, available at www.un.org/depts/los/LEGISLATIONANDTREATIES/STATEFILES/VNM.htm (last visited 1 April 2016).

15 For an overview of the draft Convention (informal text), *see* Myron H. Nordquist, *United Nations Convention on the Law of the Sea 1982: A Commentary – Volume I* (Dordrecht/Boston/Lancaster: Martinus Nijhoff Publishers, 1985), 130.

16 Decree No. 30 of the Government Council of the Socialist Republic of Vietnam on Regulations for Foreign Ships Operating in Vietnamese Maritime Zones, adopted 29 January 1980, available at http://faolex.fao.org/docs/pdf/vie4470.pdf (last visited 1 April 2016).

17 Statement of 12 November 1982 by the Government of the Socialist Republic of Vietnam on the Territorial Sea Baseline of Vietnam, available at www.un.org/depts/los/LEGISLATIONANDTREATIES/STATEFILES/VNM.htm (last visited 1 April 2016).

18 Vietnam argued that the Vietnamese coast meets both the geographical criteria for the use of straight baselines – a "deeply indented" coast or "a fringe of islands along the coast in its immediate vicinity" and that it base points "[do] not deviate in any way from the general 's-shaped' direction" of the coast. Many states and observers, however, maintain that the Vietnamese baselines do not meet the criteria and depart to an appreciable extent from the general direction of its coast. *See*, for example, United States Department of States, *Limits in the Sea No. 99 – Straight Baselines: Vietnam* (Washington D.C., 1983) available at www.state.gov/documents/organization/58573.pdf (last visited 1 April 2016).

19 For an overview of the adoption of the Convention, *see* Myron H. Nordquist, *United Nations Convention on the Law of the Sea 1982: A Commentary – Volume I*, Martinus Nijhoff Publishers (Dordrecht/Boston/Lancaster, 1985), 132–34.

20 *See* Myron H. Nordquist, *United Nations Convention on the Law of the Sea 1982: A Commentary* (Dordrecht/Boston/Lancaster: Martinus Nijhoff Publishers, 1985), 133–34.

21 See Epsey Cooke Farrell, *The Socialist Republic of Vietnam and the Law of the Sea: An Analysis of Vietnamese Behavior within the Emerging International Oceans Regime* (The Hague: Nijhoff, 1998), Chapter 2. See also United Nations Treaty Collection, *Status of the United Nations Convention on the Law of the Sea*, available at https://treaties.un.org/pages/ViewDetailsIII.aspx?src=TREATY&mtdsg_no=XXI-6&chapter=21&Temp=mtdsg3&lang=en (last visited 1 April 2016).

22 See United Nations Treaty Collection, *Status of the United Nations Convention on the Law of the Sea*, available at https://treaties.un.org/pages/ViewDetailsIII.aspx?src=TREATY&mtdsg_no=XXI-6&chapter=21&Temp=mtdsg3&lang=en(lastvisited 1 April 2016).

23 See United Nations Treaty Collection, *Status of the United Nations Convention on the Law of the Sea*, available at https://treaties.un.org/pages/ViewDetailsIII.aspx?src=TREATY&mtdsg_no=XXI-6&chapter=21&Temp=mtdsg3&lang=en(lastvisited 1 April 2016).

24 The Agreement relating to the implementation of Part XI of the United Nations Convention on the Law of the Sea of 10 December 1982 was adopted on 28 July 1994 to address certain difficulties with the seabed mining provisions contained in Part XI. The Agreement entered into force on 28 July 1996 and, as of 28 March 2016, has 147 parties. See United Nations Oceans and Law of the Sea, The Agreement relating to the implementation of Part XI of the United Nations Convention on the Law of the Sea of 10 December 1982: Overview, www.un.org/depts/los/convention_agreements/convention_overview_part_xi.htm (last visited 1 April 2016). See Epsey Cooke Farrell, *The Socialist Republic of Vietnam and the Law of the Sea: An Analysis of Vietnamese Behavior within the Emerging International Oceans Regime* (The Hague: Nijhoff, 1998), Chapter 2.

25 See United Nations Treaty Collection, *Status of the United Nations Convention on the Law of the Sea*, available at https://treaties.un.org/pages/ViewDetailsIII.aspx?src=TREATY&mtdsg_no=XXI-6&chapter=21&Temp=mtdsg3&lang=en (last visited 1 April 2016).

26 'Viet Nam circulates report on UNCLOS implementation', *Viet Nam News*, available at http://vietnamnews.vn/politics-laws/233975/viet-nam-circulates-report-on-unclos-implementation.html (last visited 1 April 2016). See also Statement by H.E. Ho Xuan Son, Deputy Foreign Minister of Vietnam, 'Vietnam Upholds UNCLOS Significance', available at http://english.vietnamnet.vn/fms/government/54502/vietnam-upholds-unclos-significance.html (last visited 1 April 2016).

27 'Viet Nam circulates report on UNCLOS implementation', *Viet Nam News*, available at http://vietnamnews.vn/politics-laws/233975/viet-nam-circulates-report-on-unclos-implementation.html (last visited 1 April 2016). See also Statement by H.E. Ho Xuan Son, Deputy Foreign Minister of Vietnam, 'Vietnam Upholds UNCLOS Significance', available at http://english.vietnamnet.vn/fms/government/54502/vietnam-upholds-unclos-significance.html (last visited 1 April 2016).

28 United Nations, *Commission on the Limits of the Continental Shelf (CLCS) Outer limits of the continental shelf beyond 200 nautical miles from the baselines: Submissions to the Commission: Joint submission by Malaysia and the Socialist Republic of Viet Nam*, available at www.un.org/depts/los/clcs_new/submissions_files/submission_mysvnm_33_2009.htm (last visited 1 April 2016).

29 International Seabed Authority, *Council Members*, available at www.isa.org.jm/authority/council-members (last visited 1 April 2016).

30 *See* 'Viet Nam circulates report on UNCLOS implementation', *Viet Nam News*, available at http://vietnamnews.vn/politics-laws/233975/viet-nam-circulates-report-on-unclos-implementation.html (last visited 1 April 2016). *See* also Statement by H.E. Ho Xuan Son, Deputy Foreign Minister of Vietnam, 'Vietnam Upholds UNCLOS Significance', available at http://english.vietnamnet.vn/fms/government/54502/vietnam-upholds-unclos-significance.html (last visited 1 April 2016).

31 *See* International Maritime Organization, *Status of Conventions*, available at www.imo.org/en/About/Conventions/StatusOfConventions/Pages/Default.aspx (last visited 1 April 2016).

32 The Association of Southeast Asian Nations (ASEAN) was established in 1967 by the Bangkok Declaration. It consists of Brunei, Cambodia, Indonesia, Laos, Malaysia, Myanmar, the Philippines, Singapore, Thailand and Viet Nam.

33 For the list, text and status of ASEAN instruments, see ASEAN, ASEAN Legal Instruments, available at http://agreement.asean.org/ (last visited 1 April 2016).

34 2004 Regional Cooperation Agreement on Combating Piracy and Armed Robbery against Ships in Asia, available at http://cil.nus.edu.sg/2004/2004-regional-cooperation-agreement-on-combating-piracy-and-armed-robbery-against-ships-in-asia/ (last visited 1 April 2016). For information on the Information Sharing Centre's activities, *see* http://www.recaap.org/ (last visited 1 April 2016).

35 United Nations Treaty Collection, *Status of the United Nations Convention on the Law of the Sea*, available at https://treaties.un.org/pages/ViewDetailsIII.aspx?src=TREATY&mtdsg_no=XXI-6&chapter=21&Temp=mtdsg3&lang=en (last visited 1 April 2016).

36 For full texts of Vietnamese legal documents in Vietnamese, see Government of Vietnam, *Legal Documents*, available at http://vanban.chinhphu.vn/ (last visited 1 April 2016).

37 2012 Law of the Sea dated 21 June 2012 (hereinafter '2012 Law of the Sea'), Article 1.

38 *See* Division for Ocean Affairs and the Law of the Sea, Office of Legal Affairs, United Nations, 'The United Nations Convention on the Law of the Sea: A Historical Perspective', available at www.un.org/depts/los/convention_agreements/convention_historical_perspective.htm (last visited 7 March 2016).

39 *See* Division for Ocean Affairs and the Law of the Sea, Office of Legal Affairs, United Nations, 'The United Nations Convention on the Law of the Sea: A Historical Perspective', available at www.un.org/depts/los/convention_agreements/convention_historical_perspective.htm (last visited 7 March 2016).

40 For the list of members of the Maritime State Group and Great Maritime Powers Group, *see* Myron H. Nordquist, *United Nations Convention on the Law of the Sea 1982: A Commentary – Volume I*, Martinus Nijhoff Publishers (Dordrecht/Boston/Lancaster, 1985), 79–80.

41 For the list of members of the Coastal States Group and their positions, *see* Myron H. Nordquist, *United Nations Convention on the Law of the Sea 1982: A Commentary – Volume I*, Martinus Nijhoff Publishers (Dordrecht/Boston/Lancaster, 1985), 70–71.

42 For the list of members of the Territorialist Group and their positions, *see* Myron H. Nordquist, *United Nations Convention on the Law of the Sea 1982: A Commentary – Volume I*, Martinus Nijhoff Publishers (Dordrecht/Boston/Lancaster, 1985), 76–77.

43 For the list of members of the Straits States Group and the Archipelagic States Group, *see* Myron H. Nordquist, *United Nations Convention on the Law of the Sea 1982: A Commentary – Volume I*, Martinus Nijhoff Publishers. (Dordrecht/Boston/Lancaster, 1985), 71–78.

44 *See* Myron H. Nordquist, *United Nations Convention on the Law of the Sea 1982: A Commentary – Volume I* (Dordrecht/Boston/Lancaster: Martinus Nijhoff Publishers, 1985), 69.

45 *See* Division for Ocean Affairs and the Law of the Sea, Office of Legal Affairs, United Nations, *The United Nations Convention on the Law of the Sea: A Historical Perspective*, available at www.un.org/depts/los/convention_agreements/convention_historical_perspective.htm (last visited 7 March 2016).

46 UNCLOS, Articles 3, 18 and 19. *See* Division for Ocean Affairs and the Law of the Sea, Office of Legal Affairs, United Nations, *The United Nations Convention on the Law of the Sea: A Historical Perspective*, available at www.un.org/depts/los/convention_agreements/convention_historical_perspective.htm (last visited 7 March 2016).

47 UNCLOS, Article 19.

48 UNCLOS, Article 20.

49 UNCLOS, Article 25.

50 UNCLOS, Article 24.

51 UNCLOS, articles 34 and 49.

52 UNCLOS, parts III and IV.

53 UNCLOS, Article 53(4).

54 UNCLOS, Article 38(2).

55 UNCLOS, Article 39(1).

56 UNCLOS, Article 44(1).

57 UNCLOS, Article 33.

58 UNCLOS, Article 33.

59 Myron H. Nordquist, *United Nations Convention on the Law of the Sea 1982: A Commentary – Volume II* (Dordrecht/Boston/Lancaster: Martinus Nijhoff Publishers, 1993), 267.
60 UNCLOS, Article 56.
61 UNCLOS, Article 58.
62 UNCLOS, Article 59. Major naval powers and the coastal states, for example, do not agree on whether states can engage in military activities in foreign exclusive economic zones. For further details on the debate between the United States and China on military activities in exclusive economic zones, see Raul (Pete) Pedrozo, Preserving Navigational Rights and Freedoms: The Right to Conduct Military Activities in China's Exclusive Economic Zone, 9 *Chinese Journal of International Law* (2010), 9–29; Zhang Haiwen, Is It Safeguarding the Freedom of Navigation or Maritime Hegemony of the United States? – Comments on Raul (Pete) Pedrozo's Article on Military Activities in the EEZ, 9 *Chinese Journal of International Law* (2010), 31–47; and Erik Franckx, American and Chinese Views on Navigational Rights of Warships, 10 *Chinese Journal of International Law* (2011), 187–206.
63 UNCLOS, Article 77.
64 UNCLOS, Article 78.
65 Statement on the Territorial Sea, the Contiguous Zone, the Exclusive Economic Zone and the Continental Shelf of 12 May 1977, available at www.un.org/depts/los/LEGISLATIONANDTREATIES/STATEFILES/VNM.htm (last visited 1 April 2016).
66 Statement on the Territorial Sea, the Contiguous Zone, the Exclusive Economic Zone and the Continental Shelf of 12 May 1977, available at www.un.org/depts/los/LEGISLATIONANDTREATIES/STATEFILES/VNM.htm (last visited 1 April 2016).
67 *See* 'Viet Nam circulates report on UNCLOS implementation', *Viet Nam News*, available at http://vietnamnews.vn/politics-laws/233975/viet-nam-circulates-report-on-unclos-implementation.html (last visited 1 April 2016).
68 Statement on the Territorial Sea, the Contiguous Zone, the Exclusive Economic Zone and the Continental Shelf of 12 May 1977, available at www.un.org/depts/los/LEGISLATIONANDTREATIES/STATEFILES/VNM.htm (last visited 1 April 2016).
69 Statement on the Territorial Sea, the Contiguous Zone, the Exclusive Economic Zone and the Continental Shelf of 12 May 1977, available at www.un.org/depts/los/LEGISLATIONANDTREATIES/STATEFILES/VNM.htm (last visited 1 April 2016) (emphasis added).
70 Myron H. Nordquist, *United Nations Convention on the Law of the Sea 1982: A Commentary – Volume II* (Dordrecht/Boston/Lancaster: Martinus Nijhoff Publishers, 1993), 273.
71 Decree No. 30 of the Government Council of the Socialist Republic of Vietnam on Regulations for Foreign Ships Operating in Vietnamese Maritime Zones, adopted 29 January 1930, Article 3(c), available at http://faolex.fao.org/docs/pdf/vie4470.pdf (last visited 1 April 2016).
72 Decree No. 30 of the Government Council of the Socialist Republic of Vietnam on Regulations for Foreign Ships Operating in Vietnamese Maritime Zones, adopted 29 January 1930, Article 14, available at http://faolex.fao.org/docs/pdf/vie4470.pdf (last visited 1 April 2016).
73 Decree No. 30 of the Government Council of the Socialist Republic of Vietnam on Regulations for Foreign Ships Operating in Vietnamese Maritime Zones, adopted 29 January 1930, Article 10, available at http://faolex.fao.org/docs/pdf/vie4470.pdf (last visited 1 April 2016).
74 Decree No. 30 of the Government Council of the Socialist Republic of Vietnam on Regulations for Foreign Ships Operating in Vietnamese Maritime Zones, adopted 29

January 1930, Article 5, available at http://faolex.fao.org/docs/pdf/vie4470.pdf (last visited 1 April 2016).

75 Decree No. 30 of the Government Council of the Socialist Republic of Vietnam on Regulations for Foreign Ships Operating in Vietnamese Maritime Zones, adopted 29 January 1930, Article 9, available at http://faolex.fao.org/docs/pdf/vie4470.pdf (last visited 1 April 2016).

76 Epsey Cooke Farrell, *The Socialist Republic of Vietnam and the Law of the Sea: An Analysis of Vietnamese Behavior within the Emerging International Oceans Regime* (The Hague: Nijhoff, 1998), 86.

77 *See* Epsey Cooke Farrell, *The Socialist Republic of Vietnam and the Law of the Sea: An Analysis of Vietnamese Behavior within the Emerging International Oceans Regime* (The Hague: Nijhoff, 1998).

78 Epsey Cooke Farrell, *The Socialist Republic of Vietnam and the Law of the Sea: An Analysis of Vietnamese Behavior within the Emerging International Oceans Regime* (The Hague: Nijhoff, 1998), 86.

79 The Vienna Convention on the Law of Treaty, Article 18(1) provides that a state is obliged to refrain from acts which would defeat the object and purpose of a treaty when it has signed the treaty or has exchanged instruments constituting the treaty subject to ratification, acceptance or approval, until it shall have made its intention clear not to become a party to the treaty.

80 US Department of Defense, 'Maritime Claims Reference Manuals: Vietnam 2016', available at www.jag.navy.mil/organization/documents/mcrm/Vietnam2016.pdf (last visited 1 April 2016).

81 *See* United Nations Treaty Collection, *Status of the United Nations Convention on the Law of the Sea*, available at https://treaties.un.org/pages/ViewDetailsIII.aspx?src=TREATY&mtdsg_no=XXI-6&chapter=21&Temp=mtdsg3&lang=en (last visited 1 April 2016).

82 Decree No. 55 dated 1 October 1996 on Activities of Foreign Military Vessels Visiting Vietnam.

83 Decree No. 55 dated 1 October 1996 on Activities of Foreign Military Vessels Visiting Vietnam, preamble.

84 Decree No. 41 dated 24 July 2001 on Activities of the Vietnam's Sea Patrol Forces, Article 7.

85 Decree No. 41 dated 24 July 2001 on Activities of the Vietnam's Sea Patrol Forces, Article 10.

86 2003 Law on National Boundaries, adopted 17 June 2003, Article 4(9), emphasis added.

87 2003 Law on National Boundaries, Article 4(9).

88 2003 Law on National Boundaries, Article 3.

89 2005 Maritime Code, adopted 14 June 2005, Article 2.

90 2012 Law of the Sea, Article 2(1).

91 'International law' is referred to in 15 provisions, including articles 4(3), 5(3), 5(4), 6(1), 16(1), 22(1), 22(3), 28, 32, 33(3), 33(6), 35(1), 35(4), 36(2) and 37(9). 'International treaties' is referred to in 21 provisions, including articles 4(1), 5(4), 12(3), 12(4), 16(2), 16(3), 18(4), 18(5), 22(1), 23(1), 30(4), 33(7), 35(4), 35(5), 39(2) and 48(b). 'UNCLOS' is referred to in three provisions, including articles 3(1), 4(3) and 12(1). The 'Charter of the United Nations' is referred to in Article 4(1).

92 2012 Law of the Sea, Article 22(2).

93 2012 Law of the Sea, Article 2(1).

94 2012 Law of the Sea, Article 2(1).

95 2012 Law of the Sea, Article 16(2), emphasis added.

96 US Department of Defense, 'Maritime Claims Reference Manuals: Vietnam 2016', available at www.jag.navy.mil/organization/documents/mcrm/Vietnam2016.pdf (last visited 1 April 2016).

97 2012 Law of the Sea, Article 14(2).
98 2012 Law of the Sea, Article 2(1).
99 2012 Law of the Sea, Article 12(1).
100 2012 Law of the Sea, Article 12(2).
101 2012 Law of the Sea, Article 12(3).
102 2012 Law of the Sea, Article 29.
103 2012 Law of the Sea, Article 23.
104 UNCLOS, articles 20 and 23.
105 2012 Law of the Sea, Article 26.
106 UNCLOS, Article 25.
107 2012 Law of the Sea, Article 26.
108 The major difference is that while the UNCLOS does not consider that threat or use of force against other countries would render passage in the territorial sea not innocent, Article 12(3) of the 2012 Law of the Sea of Vietnam does.
109 2012 Law of the Sea, Article 23 (3)
110 *See* The Standing Committee of the National Assembly of Vietnam, Report on Summarization, Giving of Explanations to Acceptance of Opinions on the Draft Law of the Sea, June 2012.
111 CNN, 'US Navy sends ship near disputed island in South China Sea', http://edition.cnn.com/2016/01/30/asia/us-navy-south-china-sea/ (last visited 9 March 2016).
112 Ministry of Foreign Affairs of Vietnam, 'Remarks by MOFA Spokesperson Le Hai Binh on US Navy's FONOP', www.mofa.gov.vn/en/tt_baochi/pbnfn/ns160131221102 (last visited 9 March 2016).
113 Ministry of Foreign Affairs of Vietnam, 'Remarks by MOFA Spokesperson Le Hai Binh on US Navy's FONOP', www.mofa.gov.vn/en/tt_baochi/pbnfn/ns160131221102 (last visited 9 March 2016).
114 *See* Statement by H.E. Nguyen Phuong Nga, Permanent Representative of Vietnam to the United Nations at the general debate at the 69th General Assembly Session on Agenda Items 'Oceans Law and Policy' (9 December 2014).
115 Statement by H.E. Nguyen Phuong Nga, Permanent Representative of Vietnam to the United Nations at the general debate at the 69th General Assembly Session on Agenda Items 'Oceans Law and Policy' (9 December 2014).
116 Statement by H.E. Nguyen Phuong Nga, Permanent Representative of Vietnam to the United Nations at the general debate at the 69th General Assembly Session on Agenda Items 'Oceans Law and Policy' (9 December 2014).
117 Epsey Cooke Farrell, *The Socialist Republic of Vietnam and the Law of the Sea: An Analysis of Vietnamese Behavior within the Emerging International Oceans Regime* (The Hague: Nijhoff, 1998), 120.
118 2012 Law of the Sea, Article 1.
119 2013 Constitution of the Socialist Republic of Vietnam, Article 12, available at www.chinhphu.vn/portal/page/portal/chinhphu/NuocCHXHCNVietNam/ThongTinTongHop/hienphapnam2013 (last visited 1 April 2016).
120 2016 Treaty Law, Article 6(1).
121 2015 Law on Promulgation of Legal Documents, Article 5(5).
122 *See* Jorn Dosch, '*Vietnam's ASEAN Membership Revisited: Golden Opportunity or Golden Cage?*', *Contemporary Southeast Asia* 28 (2006), 234–58.
123 'Viet Nam circulates report on UNCLOS implementation', *Viet Nam News*, available at http://vietnamnews.vn/politics-laws/233975/viet-nam-circulates-report-on-unclos-implementation.html (last visited 1 April 2016). See also Statement by H.E. Ho Xuan Son, Deputy Foreign Minister of Vietnam, 'Vietnam Upholds UNCLOS Significance', available at http://english.vietnamnet.vn/fms/government/54502/vietnam-upholds-unclos-significance.html (last visited 1 April 2016).

7 The United States and accession to UNCLOS

A case of how domestic political polarization results in free ridership

Anastasia Telesetsky

From 1973 until early 1982, United States representatives led by the US Department of State participated actively in negotiations for the UN Convention on the Law of the Sea (UNCLOS). In April 1982, irreconcilable political differences emerged over the deep seabed mining provisions of the treaty perceived as a restriction to future US mining enterprise and a curtailment of the freedom of the seas.[1] An interagency review of the US ocean policy conducted in 1982 when Ronald Reagan became President determined that while the treaty's provisions on most of the jurisdictional provisions, freedom of navigation, marine research, and the environment were acceptable to the United States as both a coastal state and a user state, the treaty's deep sea mining provisions were unreasonable.[2]

So what did the US decide to do in light of its concerns? The US announced that it would return to the multilateral negotiating table prepared to create a mutually acceptable document. When other countries did not agree to the US amendments and adopted the UNCLOS text in April 1982, President Reagan announced that the US pursue an alternative 'club' agreement with France, the United Kingdom and the Federal Republic of Germany to create an alternative minilateral regime for efficient exploration and exploitation of the ocean seabed that did not require transfers of technology and a treaty amendment process based on majority vote.[3] The US deployed a number of diplomats to garner support for its positions outside of the UNCLOS treaty negotiation framework.

This 1982 'I'll do it my way' incident highlights a particular pattern in US foreign policy regarding ocean management.[4] Even though the United States complies with the substance of much of UNCLOS, it continues to remain estranged from the UNCLOS institutional regime. The reasons for this are not intuitive in light of the repeated support by both Democratic and Republic leaders in the United States over the last couple decades.

This chapter will start with an explanation of how US ocean policy conforms with UNCLOS obligations as a coastal state and as a user of global ocean resources. Concluding that US ocean policy is largely in conformity with UNCLOS treaty obligations, it will then pose the question of whether the United States is operating as a free rider within the treaty regime, e.g. receiving benefits without accepting concurrent duties. The chapter concludes with an attempt to explain why the United States continues to remain an outlier to the UNCLOS regime in spite of repeated accession efforts by senior members of the US Congress and the executive department. Specifically, the chapter suggests that the accession to UNCLOS has become a rhetorical rallying call within domestic politics for certain populist groups who have used the UNCLOS treaty as a means to promote a specific political agenda that has very little to do with the substance of UNCLOS. Regrettably for international partners who would like to see the United States become a party to UNCLOS, the failure to accede is no longer about international substantive matters but rather is a reflection of a nation that has become deeply domestically divided.

United States adherence to UNCLOS commitments as a non-party

It is axiomatic that a non-party to a treaty does not have obligations under the treaty. Yet paradoxically, in spite of the rejection of UNCLOS text by the United States in 1982, the United States acts largely in adherence with UNCLOS duties and calls attention to this in official documents even though the US does not have treaty legal obligations under UNCLOS. For example, in a routine email from an official in the US Department of State to an official in the US Maritime Administration regarding an application for a private company to construct a deepwater port 16 miles off the coast of Louisiana, the Department of State concludes that the language 'subject to recognized principles of international law' in the US statute being analysed must be interpreted to refer to particular sections of UNCLOS regarding sea lanes, artificial islands in the exclusive economic zone, and pollution from vessels.[5] This explicit reference to UNCLOS within internal communication between government agencies in contrast to a reference to 'customary international law' as the source of law that defines 'recognized principles of international law' reveals an operational understanding that the US has domesticated UNCLOS as relevant US law. In practice, the United States need never mention UNCLOS as the US has no obligations under UNCLOS, but agencies involved in marine matters frequently refer to governing principles from UNCLOS.

The US has defined its marine jurisdictions on the basis of UNCLOS by designating a territorial sea, a contiguous zone, and an exclusive economic zone.[6] The US has defined for itself fishing management obligations that closely parallel UNCLOS obligations.[7] 'International conservation and management measures' are understood in the US Code as measures 'to refer to that are adopted and applied in accordance with the relevant rules of international law, as reflected in the 1982 United nations Convention on the Law of the Sea, and that are recognized by the United States'.[8] In keeping with the expectations detailed in UNCLOS Article 117, Article 118, and Article 119 that States will cooperatively adopt conservation and management measures for nationals operating on the high seas, the US is a member of regional fisheries management organization.[9] In tackling marine pollution, the US as a coastal state is implementing laws that conform with expectations under UNCLOS.[10] In some cases, language from the UNCLOS is even incorporated by reference into US law.[11]

Even on the controversial issue of deep seabed mining, the United States Congress in its statutes anticipated that the US would eventually become subject to the UNCLOS regime. In its 1980 Deep Seabed Hard Mineral Resource Act, Congress incorporated a finding that 'It is in the national interest of the United States and other nations to encourage a widely acceptable Law of the Sea Treaty, which will provide a new legal order for the oceans covering a broad range of ocean interests, including exploration for and commercial recovery of hard mineral resources of the deep seabed.'[12] The Act was understood as 'transitional' to a binding international agreement.[13]

Given the track record of the United States as a nation that has closely aligned its laws and regulations to conform with expectations under UNCLOS for both coastal and user states and as a State that interprets its laws in the context of UNCLOS even though it has no obligation to do so, it is puzzling that the US does not formally become a Party to the treaty. The United States Executive Branch in both Republican and Democratic led-administrations has unequivocally expressed its intention to become a Party to UNCLOS once the President has received advice and consent from the US Senate to proceed with accession to the treaty.[14] The Department of State who supports the President in his foreign policy work and represents US positions to the world has become increasingly outspoken in its support of the treaty.[15] The Governors of US States expressed their support for the treaty.[16] Major US trade associations have expressed their support of accession to the treaty.[17] With all of these factors weighing in favour of the US becoming a party, why does the US continue in its status as a non-party? One answer that makes theoretical sense but raises moral quandaries for the US who proclaims itself as an international leader is that the United States is operating as a free-rider.

United States as a treaty free-rider

A free-rider refers to an individual or, in the case of politics, a State who receives benefits (e.g. positive externalities) without contributing to the economic or political costs associated with generating those benefits. In recent rhetoric, some political analysts urge the United States not to become a member of UNCLOS, because there is no value added for the US in becoming a party beyond what the United States has already identified as customary law. As one author writes, 'all of the important provisions of UNCLOS dealing with freedom of movement, such as the rights of innocent passage, transit passage, archipelagic sea lanes passage, and high seas freedoms seaward of the territorial sea, are considered by virtually all nations as a reflection of customary international law that is binding on all nations.'[18]

Other examples exist to validate the point that the United States can benefit from the treaty regime without becoming a party. For example, with over 95% of data and voice transfer communications speeding along submarine cables, the ability to lay cable is essential for participation in the global economic regime.[19]

The United States lays undersea cable systems across its continental shelf and the high seas bed without any contestation from other States not just for communication but also energy transmission. The Department of the Interior's Bureau of Ocean Energy Management has been authorized by the US Congress to provide oversight for laying cables set down in 'support [of the] production, transportation, or transmission of energy from sources other than oil and gas' on the US outer continental shelf.[20]

Is the United States taking advantage of adherence and compliance to UNCLOS by other parties without actually investing in a long-term treaty framework? It is certainly in the US's interest that other States adhere to UNCLOS by defining their boundaries in harmonious fashions, protecting freedom of navigation rights, implementing conservation and management measures, and reducing marine pollution.

The US participates in an active observer status. Even though the US is not a party to the treaty, it has submitted objections to the UN Commission on the Limits of the Continental Shelf (CLCS) protesting portions of the Russian claim associated with the Alpha-Mendeleev and Lomonosov mid-ocean ridges.[21] The US has also submitted objections to other extended continental shelf submissions.[22] The US free ridership is particularly pronounced in the case of defining an extended continental shelf. While opponents of US accession suggest that the purported benefits of accession are already reflected in customary international law that has been merely codified by UNCLOS, the modern concept of an extended continental shelf and the rules associated with defining such a shelf are an example of UNCLOS's contribution to progressive law and not just a restatement of existing customary practice. While the United States is a party to the 1958 Convention on the Continental Shelf, the US today officially relies upon the renegotiated definitions of the limits of extended continental shelf as reflected in UNCLOS. As noted on the Department of State's website as part of the US Extended Continental Shelf Project,

> The rules for defining the ECS are based in international law, specifically Article 76 of the Convention on the Law of the Sea… A coastal Country can use one of two formulas in any combination to determine the edge of its ECS. The Convention also provides two constraint lines that those two formulas cannot go past. Here, too, a country can use any combination of those constraint lines to maximize its shelf.[23]

In an approach that might be appropriately characterized as cherry-picking, the US claims that not just the general principle of what constitutes an extended continental shelf in Article 76(1) is customary international law as recognized by the International Court of Justice but also Article 76(2) through Article 76(7) can be considered provisions that 'reflect customary international law'.[24] The US does not claim, however, that Article 76(8) is customary international law which requires coastal states to submit for review the outer limits of their continental shelf to the CLCS which when established on the basis of the CLCS's recommendations is 'final and binding'. To the extent that Articles 76(2) through Article 76(7) reflect customary international law, State practice by 77 coastal states including some of the largest coastal states and *opinio juris* in relation to Article 76(8) also seem to 'reflect customary international law'. Yet, the United States has not made a submission or even indicated that it intends to make a submission in spite of undertaking a great deal of national effort to collect bathymetric and seismic data.[25] Arguably, the US can point to Annex II Article 4 which indicates that a coastal state need only make a submission within 10 years of the Convention entering into force 'for that State' indicating that there is no positive obligation to make a submission until the US becomes a party. It seems arbitrary that Article 76(2) through Article 76(7) can be considered to 'reflect customary international law' while Article 76(8) is not considered to have the same legal status even though all of Article 76 really should be considered to reflect the practice and opinio juris of coastal states.

Why would the US make this distinction? One explanation could be free-ridership whereby the US expects other States to potentially changes limits on the basis of CLCS's recommendations but is unwilling to submit the US to the same process. The US benefits from the predictability associated with other States making submissions without limiting its own options in spite of its declaration that it understands Article 76(1) through Article 76(7) to reflect customary international law. The same free-ridership explanation might elucidate why the US is content with other States binding themselves to some form of mandatory dispute settlement while the US claims to adhere to UNCLOS but is not subject to any accompanying accountability mechanism.[26]

One legal commentator opposed to US accession sums up the attractiveness of defection that is always implicit when a State is free-riding on other State's commitments. Rabkin writes:

> So the treaty [UNCLOS] can be acceptable if interpreted as we want it to be interpreted. But if we commit to the treaty, we are, by its terms, leaving ultimate interpretations to be determined by international tribunals, which may not agree with our interpretations… if we ratify the treaty, we will, as a practical matter, find it very awkward (to say the least) to reject the interpretations that emerge from international arbitration of its disputed points.[27]

Yet the US expects other States to accept and adhere to international tribunal interpretations.[28]

Even for rights and obligations for which there is no customary international law claim, there are commentators who expound the rights for the US to participate in free-ridership by allowing its US nationals to use private international law mechanisms to avoid public international law responsibilities for the US. Grove explains, 'if a US company insists on engaging in mining only under the convention's auspices despite the inequities associated with the UNCLOS regime', it can do so by incorporating 'a subsidiary entity in a country that is party to the convention' and thereby 'apply for an exploration contract under the sponsorship of the foreign country and engage in seabed mining through the convention's regime'.[29] This suggestion of using tools of corporate international law mechanisms to avoid the US needing to join UNCLOS raises the possibility of US nationals intentionally seeking to operate under 'flags of convenience' to avoid scrutiny of environmental, safety, or labour practices. The presence of flags of convenience in so many maritime activities are classic examples of 'free ridership' where one State encourages another State to accept responsibility and liability associated with supervising a given vessel that may exceed its operational capacities. As the ITLOS Seabed Disputes Chamber has advised, a State sponsoring a private entity operating within the Area has due diligence responsibilities and obligations including creating and implementing a system of legal oversight to ensure compliance by those entities with seabed mining protections.[30] Where a State fails to exercise adequate due diligence in undertaking its responsibilities and obligations, it may become liable if damages occur.[31] States with an already weak rule of law due to a lack of resources or endemic corruption or other complex social reasons may find non-nationals abusing their already weak legal structures. Subsidiary companies can be notoriously difficult to trace ownership to even where there is the legal right to pierce a corporate veil thereby exposing a sponsoring State to both financial and political risks.

Free ridership on a treaty's benefits is not a legal issue because States cannot be compelled to join a treaty regime. Free ridership is, however, a political and moral issue as long as the US is benefiting from collective action without fully contributing to the institutions that support the collective action. Whether free ridership is rational as might be argued by international relations theorists and opponents to US accession to UNCLOS, the current free ridership of the US compromises the political legitimacy of the United States to be a spokesperson for other international legal regimes for which the US is urging broader ratifications such as the Port States Measures Agreement.[32] While the US because of its size may be in a better economic position to free-ride than other States, the practice of free-riding in one arena of international law by the US (e.g. Law of the Sea) could lead to institutional destabilization in other arenas of international law if other States take the same position as the US that they are adhering to treaty principles without actually joining a treaty. The final section of this paper suggests that US freeriding is unlikely to come to an end as long as US domestic politics remain sharply divided on the basis of ideological differences. The bipartisanship that the US has depended upon to reach previous political agreements that benefit the US public is at an all-time low. The final section of this paper argues that UNCLOS is being used as a rallying call for various domestic politicians at the expense of the US's international reputation.

UNCLOS as a rhetorical sword for polarization in contemporary US domestic politics

In a 2007 op-ed by Ken Adelman, a former diplomat under the Reagan administration who was involved in lobbying for changes to the original UNCLOS treaty to reflect US interests, Adelman calls for the immediate accession by the US to

UNCLOS.[33] He observes that after the deep sea bed mining regime was revised to address US concerns about global socialism and world federalism, the US should accede to the treaty because it reflects free market principles, no 'bulk-up of multilateral institutions', no seabed mining decisionmaking without US participation, and no requirements for technology transfer.[34] LOS accession has also been vocally supported by prominent conservatives including former Secretary of State Henry Kissinger, George Schultz, James Baker, Colin Powell, and Condoleezza Rice and the Joint Chiefs of Staff from the US Department of Defense.[35]

Yet, the US Congress remains paralyzed in any effort to provide its two-third vote to give advice and consent to the President to accede to the treaty. The problem as highlighted in the first section of this chapter is no longer a problem of a lack of implementing legislations to ensure that the treaty is properly executed. Many aspects of UNCLOS are already implemented in existing United States statutes. Rather the problem is that UNCLOS has become a foil for domestic politics that reflects the breakdown of bipartisanship within the United States and the rise of a certain strain of anti-governance populism. The failure to accede to UNCLOS is a concrete example of the internal fracturing of American politics that is then reflected to the rest of the world as American exceptionalism and non-cooperation.

In the last decade, populism of a particular flavour has emerged that focuses exclusively on reducing government spending and stalling government. In the United States, when the US reached a debt ceiling in late 2013, populists in the House of Representatives and Senate almost succeeded in shutting down the government by resisting passage of any appropriation act to fund the government and extend the debt ceiling.[36] Part of the governance meltdown was attributed to parties voting strictly along party lines with no seeming ability to compromise.[37]

The very same dynamics at play in the US budget impasse are also present in efforts to seek accession to the Law of the Sea. The failure to become a Party has little to do with the US perspectives on its role as a port state, a coastal state, or a state seeking to exercise its global freedom of navigation, but has everything to do with the fragmentation and factionalism that reflect existing US political interactions. In 2012, the Senate Foreign Relations Committee Chairman John Kerry held hearings on acceding to the Law of the Sea. Secretary of State Hillary Clinton spelled out the case for US accession which included re-confirmation of the Convention's 'favourable freedom of navigation provisions' for all US vessels including commercial ships involved in global trade, recognition of US sovereignty over natural resources within both the EEZ and the extended continental shelf, and tenure security to mine sites in areas beyond national jurisdiction.[38] After the hearings, the Republican majority in the Senate rejected the treaty before it was put to a vote with a number of the Senators offering enigmatic statements such as 'no international organization owns the sea' as their reasons for opposing accession. This type of reasoning highlights the use of the UNCLOS accession as symbolic of a particular type of domestic political resistance that pervades US policymaking.[39] UNCLOS is a victim of larger political forces that are thrashing about the United States.

It is important to recognize that polarization between ideological groups has become a defining feature of US domestic politics. Members who identify with the Democrats and Republicans are more ideologically divided than in the past.[40] According to the Pew Research Center, the number of Americans who express consistently conservative or consistently liberal opinions has doubled from 10 per cent in 1994 to 21 per cent in 2014 with increasing partisan animosity where these citizens consider the political party that they do not affiliate with as a 'threat to the nation's well-being'.[41] These consistently conservative or consistently liberal citizens are often political players with 'the most ideologically oriented and politically rancorous Americans' making 'their voices heard through greater participation in every stage of the political process'.[42] Increasingly polarization is critical to understanding non-accession to UNCLOS.

The rhetoric around UNCLOS accession particularly for opponents to accession is not specific to the content of UNCLOS but is part of a much broader project by populists such as the Tea Party, a libertarian faction of the Republican party, designed to build a political identity emphasizing American 'freedoms' and exceptionalism. Opponents of UNCLOS accession emphasize two lines of reasoning to reject the treaty with the rhetoric designed to increase the polarization gap by appealing to certain deeply held values including a push to reduce taxes and to 'protect' America.

The first line of reasoning focuses on financial costs associated with becoming a member. Opponents argue that UNCLOS accession will be expensive for the United States because it will have to pay into institutional budgets such as the Seabed Authority and US companies may have to 'forego' a fraction of royalty benefits.[43] This line of reasoning resonates with strongly held beliefs by some citizens that the government is exercising excessive taxing powers. The second line of reasoning is that the US is ceding its sovereignty by joining UNCLOS.[44] With the revisions made to UNCLOS to address US national interests in 1994, the current concern over sovereignty seems misplaced. While becoming a Party to UNCLOS might be viewed by many as an exercise of state sovereignty, those who consider it a relinquishment of sovereignty do so because they view politics as a 'winner takes all' enterprise and not an 'art of the possible'. Opponents of UNCLOS accession perceive themselves as protecting the US constitutional system from an over-reaching international organization and an over-reaching executive branch.

The non-accession of UNCLOS is simply another symptom of the US deep political polarization. In spite of the US major contribution to the drafting of the treaty and its ongoing commitment to adhere to the treaty, the US will not become a party as long as there remain ongoing domestic rifts among political active Americans. The polarization has been particularly pronounced in 2016 with the President-to-be seeking to extract the US from institutions, rules and relationships that have 'facilitated restraint, commitment, reciprocity, and legitimacy.'[45]

Conclusion

While there are palpable tensions between coastal states and user states over core rights such as navigational rights, these tensions are not the current basis for the US not acceding to the treaty. The US benefits from the UNCLOS regime but will not become a member to the Treaty until there is internal reconciliation within US domestic politics and return to genuine bipartisanship. There is some hope for ultimate accession in the future. In spite of the lack of advice and consent given by the Senate in 2012, the failure to accede to UNCLOS is not a choice by the majority of Americans. In 2014, the Pew Research Center observed that even though there is an increasing amount of polarization within America which are 'over-represented in the political process', these individuals 'do not make up the majority of voters, donors, or campaign activists'.[46] It may just be matter of time before the majority of voters, donors, and campaign activists become engaged again to support treaties that protect the US's national interests, reflect the US's commitment to rule of law, and enhance the US's international reputation.

Notes

1 T. Kronmiller, The Lawfulness of Deep Seabed Mining 176 (1980). (Arguing that mining on the seabed floor of the high seas must be deemed a 'high seas freedom'.)

2 James Malone, The United States and the Law of the Sea After UNCLOS III, 46 Law and Contemporary Problems.

3 Agreement Concerning Interim Arrangements Relating to Polymetallic Nodules of the Deep Sea Bed, 21 I.L.M. 950, 950–62 (1982); *see* UNCLOS, 21 I.L.M. 1261 (1982) Article 155 ('If, five years after its commencement, the Review Conference has not reached agreement on the system of exploration and exploitation of the resources of the Area, it may decide during the ensuing 12 months, by a three-fourths majority of the States Parties, to adopt and submit to the States Parties for ratification or accession such amendments changing or modifying the system as it determines necessary and appropriate. Such amendments shall enter into force for all States Parties 12 months after the deposit of instruments of ratification or accession by three fourths of the States Parties.') and Article 316(5).

4 The 'Sinatra Doctrine' has historically referred to the Union of Soviet Socialist Republic's willingness to allow other Warsaw Pact countries to govern their own internal affairs. The term was coined in 1989 by USSR Foreign Ministry spokesperson.

5 Department of State Bureau of Oceans and International Environmental and Scientific Affairs Letter Concerning Deepwater Port in the Gulf of Mexico, Digest of United States Practice in International Law (2005). Available at www.state.gov/s/l/2005/87227.htm?goMobile=0 (accessed 20 March 2016).

6 President Ronald Reagan Executive Order 1988 (Territorial Sea); President William Clinton Executive Order 1999 (Contiguous Zone); President Ronald Reagan Executive Order 1983 (Exclusive Economic Zone).

7 High Seas Fishing Compliance Act 16 USC. Section 5501 et al.

8 16 USC. Section 5502.

9 The United States is a party to the Convention for the Conservation of Salmon in the North Atlantic Ocean, the Convention on Future Multilateral Cooperation in the Northwest Atlantic Fisheries, the International Commission for the Conservation of Atlantic Tuna, the Convention for the Conservation of Anadromous Stocks in the North Pacific Ocean, the Convention for the Establishment of an Inter-American Tropical Tuna Commission, the Convention for the Conservation and Management of Highly Migratory Fish Stocks in the Western and Central Pacific Ocean, and the Convention on the Conservation of Antarctic Marine Living Resources.

10 Clean Water Act 33 USC. § 1251 *et seq*; *Coastal Zone Management Act* 16 USC. §§1451–1465, Shore Protection Act 33 USC. §2601 et seq. Article 211- Pollution from Vessels Act to Prevent Pollution from Ships 33 USC Section 1905 et seq.
11 See e.g. Ballast Waste Management for Control of Nonindigenous Species in Waters of the United States, 33 CFR 151.2005. (Providing that 'unless otherwise stated in this section the definitions in [several statutory sections] and the United Nations Convention on the Law of the Sea apply.')
12 30 U.S.C. Section 1401.
13 30 U.S.C. Section 1441.
14 *See e.g*. President George W. Bush National Security Presidential Directive and Homeland Security Presidential Directive (9 January 2009): Section C.4. http://georgewbush-whitehouse.archives.gov/news/releases/2009/01/20090112-3.html (accessed 26 March 2016). (Observing that 'The Senate should act favorably on U.S. accession to the U.N. Convention on the Law of the Sea promptly, to protect and advance U.S. interests, including with respect to the Arctic. Joining will serve the national security interests of the United States, including the maritime mobility of our Armed Forces worldwide. It will secure U.S. sovereign rights over extensive marine areas, including the valuable natural resources they contain. Accession will promote U.S. interests in the environmental health of the oceans. And it will give the United States a seat at the table when the rights that are vital to our interests are debated and interpreted.')
15 See e.g. United States Department of State Fact Sheets- The Law of the Sea Convention (Treaty Doc. 103–39): The U.S. National Security and Strategic Imperatives for Ratification (23 May 2012); Why the United States Needs to Join the Law of the Sea Convention Now (21 March 2012); The Law of the Sea Convention Helps American Business (1 July 2011); The Law of the Sea Convention- In Our national Security Interest (1 July 2011).
16 Letter from Governor Sarah Palin and Governor Martin O'Malley, National Governors Association to U.S. President (15 June 2009) www.nga.org/cms/home/federal-relations/nga-letters/natural-resources-committee-lett/col2-content/main-content-list/title_june-15-2009-l.html (accessed 25 March 2016) ('Until the United States is a full party to the Convention, we are hindered in accessing ocean resources, establishing and promoting environmental protections, and curtailed from participating in continuing debate on sovereign rights. Therefore, Governors urge the swift ratification of the U.N. Convention on the Law of the Sea.')
17 Thomas J. Donohue, U.S. Chamber of Commerce, Letter in Support of the Law of the Sea Treaty (26 June 2012) www.uschamber.com/letter/letter-support-law-sea-treaty (accessed 25 March 2016) ('Law of the Sea would grant American business the stability, predictability, and clear legal rights that business needs before making multi-billion-dollar investments in deep seabed resource recovery. Ratification would unleash an investment boom in the development of vast untapped oil, natural gas, and strategic mineral resources – including vital rare earth minerals – off America's shores. Failure to ratify would leave U.S. business on the sidelines. With ratification, America would gain exclusive resource sovereignty over 4.1 million square miles of subsea territory, an area greater than the contiguous 48 states. Securing international recognition for U.S. sovereign rights over this territory – and defending against encroachment by other nations – is vital to American prosperity.')
18 Raul Pedrozo. 'Is it Time for the United States to Join the Law of the Sea Convention', *Journal of Maritime Law and Commerce*, Vol. 41, No. 2 (April 2010): 151–66.
19 U.N. Env't Programme World Conserv'n Monitoring Ctr., *Submarine Cables and the Oceans: Connecting the World*, UNEP-WCMC Biodiversity Series No. 31: 3.
20 Energy Policy Act of 2005 43 U.S.C. § 1337(p)(1)(C).
21 United States of America: Notification Regarding the Submission Made by the Russian Federation to the Commission on the Limits of the Continental Shelf, Ref. No. CLCS.01.2001.LOS/USA (18 March 2002).

22 United State of America: Notification Regarding the Submission made by Brazil to the Commission on the Limits of the Continental Shelf, Ref. No. CLCS.02.2004 LOS/USA (8 September 2004) www.un.org/Depts/los/clcs_new/submissions_files/bra04/clcs_02_2004_los_usatext.pdf (accessed 5 April 2016).
23 U.S. department of State, Defining the Limit of the U.S. Continental Shelf, www.state.gov/e/oes/continentalshelf/ (Accessed 5 April 2016); See also U.S. Extended Continental Shelf Project, FAQ www.continentalshelf.gov/faq/index.htm (Accessed 5 April 2016). (Indicating that 'the rules for defining the outer limits of the ECS come from Article 76 of the Law of the Sea Convention' and that 'sovereign rights and jurisdiction of a coastal State are reflected in the Law of the Sea Convention.')
24 U.S. Extended Continental Shelf Project, FAQ www.continentalshelf.gov/faq/index.htm (accessed 5 April 2016).
25 U.S. Extended Continental Shelf Project, Missions and Data, www.continentalshelf.gov/missions_data/index.htm (accessed 5 April 2016).
26 The International Court of Justice subsequent to the 1986 *Nicaragua v. United States* case no longer has compulsory jurisdiction to resolve international disputes involving the United States.
27 Jeremy Rabkin, How Many Lawyers Does it Take to Sink the U.S. Navy?, *Weekly Standard* (10 September 2007). (Arguing that some of the United States commitments under the Proliferation Security Initiative could be challenged by ITLOS under its review of prompt release cases.)
28 See e.g. Joint Statement for Whaling and Safety at Sea, Government of Australia, the Netherlands, New Zealand, and the United States (11 January 2016) ('We do not believe that Japan has sufficiently demonstrated that it has given due regard to the guidance found in the 2014 International Court of Justice judgment on ensuring that lethal research whaling is consistent with the obligations under the International Convention for the Regulation of Whaling. On December 7, 2015, our Governments joined 29 other nations to protest Japan's decision.')
29 Steven Groves, The U.S. Can Mine the Deep Seabed Without Joining the U.N. Convention on the Law of the Sea, Heritage Foundation: Washington, D.C., (4 December 2012).
30 ITLOS, Seabed Disputes Chamber, Responsibilities and Obligations of States Sponsoring Persons and Entities with Respect to Activities in the Area, Case No. 17 (1 February 2011).
31 Id.
32 U.S. Secretary of State, John Kerry, Port State Measures Agreement Ratification (11 February 2016) www.state.gov/secretary/remarks/2016/02/252366.htm (accessed 20 April 2016). ('By joining the Port State Measures Agreement, the United States commits to work together with other nations to prevent illegally caught fish from entering into commerce worldwide by reducing the number of ports where these fishing products can be unloaded and making it harder for bad actors to do business. I hope other countries around the world will work urgently to ratify this vital Agreement as well.')
33 Ken Adelman, Sea Law Turbulence, *Washington Times* (12 December 2007) www.washingtontimes.com/article/20071212/COMMENTARY/112120011 (accessed 25 March 2016).
34 Id.
35 Henry Kissinger, George Schultz, James Baker III, Colin Powell, and Condoleezza Rice, Time to Join the Law of the Sea Treaty, *The Wall Street Journal* (May 30, 2012).
36 Jonathan Weisman and Jeremy Peters, Government Shuts Down in Budget Impasse, *New York Times*, (September 30, 2013) http://www.nytimes.com/2013/10/01/us/politics/congress-shutdown-debate.html?_r=0 (accessed April 20, 2016).
37 Id.

38 Written Testimony of Hillary Rodham Clinton, Secretary U.S. Department of State Before the Senate Foreign Relations Committee on 23 May 2012, Accession to the 1982 Law of the Sea Convention and Ratification of the 1994 Agreement Amending Part XI of the Law of the Sea Convention, www.foreign.senate.gov/imo/media/doc/REVISED_Secretary_Clinton_Testimony.pdf (accessed April 15, 2016)
39 Austin Wright, Law of the Sea Treaty Sinks in Senate, Politico (16 July 2012), www.politico.com/story/2012/07/law-of-the-sea-treaty-sinks-in-senate-078568 (accessed 20 April 2016).
40 Pew Research Center, Political Polarization in the American Public: How Increasing Ideological Uniformity and Partisan Antipathy Affects Politics, Compromise and Everyday Life (12 June 2014) www.people-press.org/files/2014/06/6-12-2014-Political-Polarization-Release.pdf (accessed 25 March 2016).
41 Id. at 6–7.
42 Id. at 8.
43 Steven Groves, The law of the Sea: Costs of U.S. Accession to UNCLOS, Hearing Before the United States Senate Committee on Foreign Relations (14 June 2012); www.heritage.org/research/testimony/2012/06/the-law-of-the-sea-convention-treaty-doc-103–39 (accessed 20 April 2016); National Public Radio, Jackie Northam, Senate Pressured to Ratify 'Law of the Sea' (24 July 2012) (Quoting Senator Risch R-Idaho 'Why, oh why, oh why, do we, as Americans, give up our taxing authority, handing money over to the United Nations?')
44 Groves supra note 43.
45 Will Moreland, World Order Under Donald Trump, The National Interest (14 April 2016) (Quoting John Ikenberry) http://nationalinterest.org/blog/the-buzz/world-order-under-donald-trump-15774 (accessed 25 April 2016).
46 Pew Research Center, supra note 40 at 77.

Part III

Navigation related issues and UNCLOS

8 Freedom of navigation and the UNCLOS order

Mira Rapp-Hooper

Introduction

Freedom of navigation has become perhaps the central concern in the South China Sea disputes as tensions have peaked in recent years. The South China Sea sovereignty disputes involve six regional claimants and the United States has long maintained a neutral stance on the territories. Following several incidents at sea in 2010, however, Secretary of State Hillary Clinton articulated a US national interest in freedom of navigation in this waterway at the ASEAN Regional Forum in Hanoi.[1]

The principle has garnered uncommon attention from analysts and policymakers since 2015, when China constructed seven artificial islands atop former reefs and rocks in the Spratly Island group, creating 3,000 acres of new land. Artificial island building itself is not expressly illegal under UNCLOS unless it occurs in another state's exclusive economic zone. China has claimed that the islands are in its sovereign territory and it is free to develop them as it wishes. Beijing has not, however, clarified the maritime and airspace claims it is making from those islands. Leaders in the region and in the United States have grown concerned that China is treating the water and airspace around these artificial islands as though it is sovereign, which contravenes the Law of the Sea in the case of several features. Because spurious claims to water and airspace necessarily close off pieces of the global commons that otherwise would have been open, US and regional officials have begun to emphasize the principle of freedom of navigation as a central South China Sea concern.

In mid-2015, US policymakers began to articulate their freedom of navigation position using what might be termed the Carter Formulation, for the Secretary of Defense who first used it, "The United States will fly, sail, and operate wherever international law allows."[2] In late 2015, the United States resumed its use of Freedom of Navigation Operations (FONOPs) in the South China Sea after a multi-year hiatus. The US Freedom of Navigation program contests claims to water and airspace that are inconsistent with the UN Convention on the Law of the Sea. By conducting FONOPs around Chinese-held features, the United States has sought to signal that Chinese claims to water and airspace do not comport with international law.

For their part, however, Chinese officials deny that freedom of navigation is at issue in the South China Sea. In addition to arguing that Chinese-occupied features are China's sovereign territory, senior officials have argued that China values freedom of navigation in the South China Sea "more than any other country in the world."[3] What lies at the heart of the disagreement between the United States and China when it comes to freedom of navigation in the South China Sea? Is it substance or mere semantics? To answer this question we must consider more closely how each country defines and employs the principle.

Defining freedom of navigation

Freedom of navigation is the right, recognized in international law, for transiting vessels not to suffer interference by other states. Put simply, it is the right of vessels to transit from point A to point B. When the United States has conducted Freedom of Navigation Operations, it has explained that these assertions "serve to protect the rights, freedoms, and lawful uses of the sea and airspace guaranteed to all nations under international law."[4] Top US officials have pointed to the fact that China has begun to regularly warn away aircraft and vessels from its artificial islands, thereby impeding freedom of navigation.

Chinese President Xi Jinping, however, has argued that China "respects and safeguards the freedom of navigation and overflight other countries are entitled to under international law."[5] Chinese Foreign Minister Wang Yi insists that China has not obstructed freedom of navigation:

> And there have not been any problems with regard to freedom of navigation in the South China Sea, and recently many ship owners or insurers have said that they do not feel there are any problems in this regard, and insurance premium has not gone up. And no commercial vessel has encountered any problem in the area of freedom of navigation.[6]

Similarly, a Chinese scholar argues, "civilian and commercial freedom of navigation in the South China Sea has never been sabotaged by China's military forces." It is the United States' "*military* 'freedom of navigation' in the South China Sea that could be limited by China," according to this scholar.[7] Herein lies the central point of disagreement: the United States, and most other countries, understand freedom of navigation to apply to military as well as civilian and commercial vessels; China does not, or at least does not in all circumstances. These divergent definitions are based on each country's interpretation of key provisions of the UN Convention on the Law of the Sea.

Freedom of navigation under UNCLOS

The United States and China were each active participants in the Third United Nations Conference on the Law of the Sea. China has ratified UNCLOS; the United States has not, but observes its provisions as customary international law. Shortly after UNCLOS opened for signature, Ambassador Tommy Koh of Singapore, the President of the Third UN Conference on the Law of the Sea, gave a speech entitled "A Constitution for the Oceans." In it, he detailed the role that freedom of navigation played in the Convention, noting that this principle was not guaranteed by any one specific provision, but rather through a set of related understandings:

> The world community's interest in the freedom of navigation will be facilitated by the important compromises on the status of the exclusive economic zone, by the regime of innocent passage through the territorial sea, by the regime of transit passage through straits used for international navigation and by the regime of archipelagic sea lanes passage.[8]

Koh went on to note that these provisions essentially constitute a grand bargain on freedom of navigation that required a holistic embrace: "The provisions of the convention are closely interrelated and form an integral package. Thus, it is not possible for a state to pick what it likes and what it does not like."[9] When it comes to freedom of navigation, UNCLOS contains rights and obligations that go hand-in-hand.

As Koh noted, freedom of navigation is comprised of certain rights and obligations that apply to the territorial sea, and others that apply to the exclusive economic zone (EEZ). The rights and obligations that prevail in the territorial sea and EEZ were purposefully designed to balance the interest of the coastal states whose waters may be transited with those of the user states, who have an abiding interest in unimpeded passage. The central disagreement between the United States and China is on the rights of military vessels in each of these zones. These disagreements hardly belong to the United States and China alone: the US view is shared by the majority of UNCLOS signatories, but China's is held by approximately 27 other states.[10] China has also codified its own interpretation through domestic law.

Innocent passage and the territorial sea

The first component of freedom of navigation under UNCLOS is the rights and obligations relating to the innocent passage in the territorial sea. The territorial sea is the zone extending 12 nautical miles from a coastal state's baselines. This zone is generally considered to be the sovereign waters of the coastal state, with some specific exceptions, most notably innocent passage. Innocent passage is the movement by vessels on the surface of the ocean for the purpose of "continuous and expeditious" transit. Passage is innocent if it does not prejudice the "peace, good order, or security of the coastal state."[11]

Under UNCLOS, aircraft do not enjoy innocent passage within the territorial sea, and vessels that do must conduct it consistent with certain criteria. Submarines must surface if they seek to enjoy innocent passage in a territorial sea. But aside from these designations, innocent passage is not determined by the vessel type, but rather, decided based on the behavior of that vessel. According to Article 19, vessels cannot make threats or use force against the sovereignty or territorial integrity of the coastal state or otherwise violate the UN Charter; they cannot exercise or practice with weapons; they cannot conduct intelligence or surveillance that may prejudice coastal state security; they cannot launch or land aircraft or other military devices; they cannot interfere with communications systems. There are also several prohibitions related to fishing, research and survey activities, and pollution.[12]

UNCLOS does not establish any conditions for innocent passage, so long as vessels comply with these aforementioned behavioral expectations. China is one of several states, however, that requires warships to give prior notification before entering its territorial sea. Within Asia, Vietnam, Taiwan, and Indonesia, place similar restrictions. According to China and others, warships cannot enjoy innocent passage unless they give this notification. This is one fundamental freedom of navigation disagreement between the United States and China.

Military activities in the Exclusive Economic Zone

The United States and China also hold differing interpretations of the military activities that are permissible in a coastal state's exclusive economic zone (EEZ). Unlike the territorial sea, in which rights mostly accrue to the coastal state with the innocent passage exception for user states, the balance is reversed in the EEZ. This is because EEZs make up one-third of the world's high seas. The EEZ did not exist until UNCLOS III, and its codification put a huge percentage of the world's oceans under national administration for the first time. At the Third UNCLOS Conference, then, it was decided that the EEZ would be a form of the high seas, with some special rights granted to the coastal state, such as resource extraction. In the EEZ, most rights and interests accrue to user states.[13]

Three principle UNCLOS provisions govern the EEZ: Article 56, Article 58, and Article 87. Article 56 guarantees to the coastal state "sovereign rights" in the EEZ for the purposes of resource exploration and extraction. Article 58 codifies the rights of user states in the EEZ. It reserves for all states the rights of freedom of navigation and freedom of overflight stated in Article 87.

Article 87 governs "Freedom of the High Seas" and declares the high seas open to all states, whether coastal or land-locked. According to Article 87, high seas freedoms comprise: freedom of navigation; freedom of overflight; freedom to lay submarine cables and pipelines; freedom to construct artificial islands; freedom of fishing; freedom of scientific research. Taking Article 58 and Article 87 together, then, UNCLOS reserves to all states in the EEZ the same rights of freedom of navigation and freedom of overflight that they enjoy on the high seas. Airspace beyond 12 nautical miles is also considered international airspace.

Historically, China had objected to some military activities that other countries – particularly, the United States – may conduct in its EEZ. Namely, it has actively opposed the activities of intelligence, surveillance, and reconnaissance aircraft (EP-3 and P-8 aircraft), as well as those of US Navy vessels. This difference of position has led to several serious close encounters between US and Chinese craft, including the EP-3 incident in 2001 and incidents involving the *Bowditch*, *Impeccable* and *Cowpens* vessels. But China's position is not limited to US activities – it has issued warnings to Australian and Indian ships and aircraft operating in the South China Sea.[14] Once again, however, China is not the only country that places restrictions on some foreign military activities in its EEZ and territorial sea. In Asia alone, India, Malaysia, and Thailand also object to foreign military activities in their EEZs.

Two years after UNCLOS opened for signature, Ambassador Koh acknowledged that the text of the Convention did not clearly state whether or not a third party could conduct military activities in the EEZ of a coastal state. He went on to note, however, that during the convention's negotiations, the parties had agreed that military activities would be permitted in the EEZ.[15] China, however, holds the view that the high seas freedoms of navigation and overflight for military craft apply somewhat differently in the EEZ. China's domestic law seeks to further codify its freedom of navigation positions.

China: Domestic law and the nine-dash line

China has two domestic laws relating to the restrictions it places on innocent passage in the territorial sea and military activities in the EEZ. Article 6 of China's 1992 Law on the Territorial Sea and Contiguous Zone declares:

> Non-military foreign ships enjoy the right of innocent passage through the territorial sea of the People's Republic of China according to law. To enter the territorial sea of the People's Republic of China, foreign military ships must obtain permission from the Government of the People's Republic of China.

Article 2 states that the law applies to China's mainland as well as its offshore islands, including Taiwan, the Senkaku/Diaoyu Islands, and the Spratly and Paracel Islands. It is therefore unsurprising that China insists that foreign warships must obtain permission to enter within 12 nautical miles of land features it holds in the South China Sea – although the United States and many other members of the international community do not recognize these as Chinese sovereign territory.

China's freedom of navigation position is also represented by its 1998 Exclusive Economic Zone and Continental Shelf Act. Article 11 of that law declares that other states enjoy freedom of navigation and overflight in China's EEZ so long as they observe "international law and the laws and regulations of the People's Republic of China." As one Chinese scholar explains, however, China's interpretation is that the EEZ is not equivalent to the high seas when it comes to navigation and overflight, and that they may therefore place greater restrictions on military activities.[16]

One further complication is China's so-called Nine-Dash Line – its maritime boundary encompassing some 90 percent of the South China Sea, which its leaders have never explained or defined. Some statements by Chinese officials suggest that they may consider the line to represent Chinese internal waters or a massive exclusive economic zone.[17] If the former were true, this could serve as a basis to restrict freedom of navigation, as the international community is not entitled to innocent passage in internal waters. But China's leaders have not made the case that the South China Sea should be considered as such and the 2016 Permanent Court of Arbitration decision undermines any such claim.[18] If the latter were true, Chinese leaders would presumably see this as justification for rejecting the rights of other countries to conduct military activities in much of the South China Sea, based on their general objection to military activities in the EEZ. They do not, however, object to *all* military activities that are conducted in the South China Sea. China's Nine-Dash Line is neither a territorial sea nor an EEZ under UNCLOS, but another demarcation that may somehow figure in to the way China's leaders interpret freedom of navigation in their near seas.

China's efforts to codify exceptions to freedom of navigation for military vessels are problematic where international law is concerned. A basic principle of international law is that it supersedes domestic legislation for those parties who accede to it. If it did not, it would have no real purpose. Moreover, UNCLOS in particular binds signatory states to the treaty as a whole. Indeed, this is the primary reason why US President Ronald Reagan did not sign the treaty at the convention's conclusion and opted instead to implement piecemeal domestic oceans legislation. American lawmakers who continue to oppose UNCLOS ratification do so with a similar rationale, hypocritical as that may seem.[19]

China's 1982 signature to UNCLOS predates its Territorial Sea law by a decade, and it made no special declarations or statements at the time of signature. Upon its ratification of the Convention in 1996, China deposited a declaration reiterating the substance of its 1992 Territorial Sea law.[20] According to UNCLOS provision 310, however, such a declaration cannot modify the legal effect of the Convention. Moreover, China's domestic law applies to China proper, which does include its territorial sea, but certainly not its EEZ. From an international legal perspective, then, the content of China's domestic laws does not change its UNCLOS obligations.

The United States: Freedom of the seas and freedom of navigation

China's view of freedom of navigation may be unduly narrow when it comes to the transit of military vessels. But the US interpretation, shared by many other states, is also more expansive than the phrase "freedom of navigation" implies. As defined at the outset of this chapter, freedom of navigation is the right under international law for a vessel to transit unimpeded from point A to point B. But insofar as UNCLOS grants to military ships and aircraft high seas freedoms inside the EEZ, this is more than just unimpeded transit between two points. Indeed, freedom of the seas – a broader concept that subsumes freedom of navigation – includes the right to dispatch aircraft on reconnaissance missions, to conduct underwater surveys, and more.

US policymakers often refer to the national interest in freedom of navigation when they really mean freedom of the seas.[21] The terminological difference is not semantic: it may allow Chinese leaders to insist that there is no danger to freedom of navigation, defined as transit, when US leaders are really objecting to Chinese interference with military activities in the EEZ. The US interest in freedom of the seas, however, long predates UNCLOS and its interactions with Chinese interlocutors in the Pacific. It also helps to explain why UNCLOS appears to enshrine rights consistent with the broader principle of freedom of the seas.

The 2015 *Asia-Pacific Maritime Security Strategy* states that the United States has advocated for freedom of the seas throughout its history, and defines "freedom of the seas" as "all of the rights, freedoms, and lawful uses of the sea and airspace, including for military ships and aircraft, recognized under international law."[22] Freedom of the seas is not actually defined in international law. The concept of freedom of the seas was popularized by the Dutch jurist and philosopher, Hugo Grotius, in his international legal text *Mare Liberum*, and publicized by the Dutch East India Company, for whom Grotius served as counsel.[23]

For several hundred years, freedom of the seas was defined in terms of free transit and was held as a national interest by many seafaring powers with commercial interests, particularly in the west. During the Quasi-War with France in 1798–1800, the United States insisted on "freedom of the seas," which emphasized free peacetime transit as well as the right of neutral states to trade in wartime.[24] In 1801–1805, an embryonic US Navy action protecting American overseas commercial interests in the Barbary Wars, when pirates demanded that the Jefferson administration pay tribute so that merchant ships could pass through the Mediterranean Sea.[25] Of President Woodrow Wilson's Fourteen Points, the second was freedom of the seas, or "absolute freedom of navigation upon the seas outside territorial waters, alike in peace and in war."[26] Members of the League of Nations promised to enshrine and protect the principle in the Versailles Treaty.[27] The 1941 Atlantic Charter declared, "peace should enable all men to traverse the high seas and oceans without hindrance," and the signatories of the 1942 Declaration of United Nations signed on to its principles.[28] By the time the United Nations was formed, there was a growing international consensus behind the free movement of vessels outside of the territorial sea.

It was not until 1979, however, that the United States became the first (and to date, only) country to formalize a freedom of the seas mission with its Freedom of Navigation Program under President Jimmy Carter. The US FON program was developed in conjunction with UNCLOS and was officially established a year later. Although Washington is not a signatory to UNCLOS, the goal of the FON program is to promote international adherence to it. The FON program does so by challenging "excessive claims" to maritime and air space that do not conform with the convention.[29]

The Department of State and Department of Defense jointly oversee the FON program, which has three major components. The State Department files diplomatic protests of excessive claims; State and Defense consult with their international counterparts on claims' consistency with international law and work with them through military-to-military engagements; and Defense conducts what it calls "operational assertions," through which it demonstrates physically the United States' non-recognition of excessive claims. The purpose of the program is to reinforce UNCLOS and customary international law and is motivated by the belief that the failure to challenge inconsistent or illegal claims will allow them to crystallize over time.[30] Operational assertions are generally conducted with one or two vessels or aircraft and are generally not considered to be major military operations. Rather, they are intended to send a specific legal message. The United States, then, not only has a long history of espousing freedom of the seas beyond simple transit: it has a lengthy record of contesting the claims of countries, be they friend or foe, if it believes they do not comport with freedom of the seas – not just freedom of navigation.

The Department of Defense conducts dozens of Freedom of Navigation Operations (FONOPs) each year, many of them in Asia. But the program has garnered a great deal of public attention due to its role in responding to China's island building in the South China Sea. This returns us to the heart of the matter: how do two very different understandings of freedom of navigation, or freedom of the seas, intersect in the South China Sea?

Navigating the South China Sea

It is hardly a novel finding that the United States and China hold differing interpretations of innocent passage in the territorial sea and permissible military activities in the EEZ. So why has freedom of navigation been thrust to the fore in these disputed waters? The crux of the problem is the relationship between China's recent island building and broader access to the global commons. After several years of heightened tensions, the United States and many regional countries were alarmed to discover that China was quickly building artificial islands on the Spratly Islands features it holds. The lightening-quick, systematic nature of the island building campaign and Chinese officials' lack of transparency about their intentions caused great concern that China was attempting to close off parts of the global commons with its new atolls.

China's artificial islands are built atop former reefs and rocks in the eyes of most international legal experts and the legal status of these land features determines the airspace and water they can claim: rocks are entitled to a 12 nautical mile territorial sea and airspace; reefs are entitled to no airspace or water whatsoever, and are not even subject to sovereignty claims. US officials turned to the Freedom of Navigation Program as a tool to contest what they saw as one of the most problematic results of China's new outposts: spurious legal claims. Beyond the countries' different interpretations of freedom of navigation, however, there have been at least two major problems to date with pointing to freedom of navigation as being in jeopardy in the South China Sea, and to using the Freedom of Navigation Program to trying to rectify it.

First, Chinese officials have not clearly stated what air or maritime entitlements they claiming from the artificial islands. Some Chinese-held features are entitled to territorial seas, but China's leaders have expressly avoided using legal terminology. Instead, they have been known to refer to the air and water around their islands as "military alert zones" – a concept that has no meaning or force under international law.[31] US, Philippines, and Australian ships and vessels have all been warned away from the islands, which does indeed pose a risk to freedom of navigation if the relevant features are not entitled to water or airspace, but China's ambiguity about its own claims makes it very difficult for the United States and others to push back using legal instruments.

Second, when the United States has used its Freedom of Navigation Program in this context it has not always calibrated its operations to its legal objections. If the general concern is that China is closing off parts of the global commons through spurious claims to water and air then the most logical type of operation for the United States to conduct is one that demonstrates the non-recognition of a territorial sea or airspace around a feature that should be entitled to none under UNCLOS. Such an operation would require the US Navy to conduct normal military operations inside of 12 nautical miles of a former reef, as opposed to transiting a feature in a manner consistent with innocent passage.

The United States, however, resumed FONOPs in the South China Sea in late 2015 after a two-year hiatus. As of mid-2016, it had conducted three FONOPs. All three have contested the maritime claims of multiple claimants – not just China. All three operations were conducted consistent with innocent passage. Rather than contesting the legal status of China's features via its maritime entitlements, however, US operations have been contesting a longstanding point of FON disagreement: China's requirement that military vessels give prior notification before to conducting an innocent passage. These operations do indeed push back against a point of FON contention, but not the one that stems from China's artificial island building. The United States government may have been selecting its FON messages especially carefully as the Permanent Court of Arbitration prepared to make a ruling in the *Philippines vs. China* case. Indeed, since Spring 2017, the Trump Administration has conducted FONOPS at a relatively higher frequency and sent some clearer signals.

Freedom of navigation and freedom of the seas are clearly quite relevant to the current tensions in the South China Sea. Managing and solving these disputes is not a matter of reconciling legal definitions, as these caveats imply.

Is freedom of navigation lost in translation?

It may be tempting to depict the issue of freedom of navigation in the South China Sea as a matter of longstanding, competing UNCLOS interpretations between China, a coastal state, and the United States, a user state. This chapter has sought to demonstrate that the relationship is far more complex than that.

First, while China is indeed a coastal state, and therefore may see an interest in limiting the rights of military vessels in its territorial sea and EEZ, it is also a coastal state that is simultaneously trying to expand its administrative rights over sea and airspace. Since signing UNCLOS, it has adopted more restrictive views and policies on freedom of navigation, while also extending its reach through the pursuit of island claims. International (and domestic) law may be a means by which China articulates its interests in the seas and skies, but the ends are geostrategic.

Second, while the United States is a user state, it is also a coastal state, and has viewed military and commercial freedom of navigation as inextricable for as long as it has had a navy. Its interest in freedom of the seas was not predicated on great power status, although its rise as a global leader allowed it to enshrine the principle in multilateral agreements and institutions.

Furthermore, the fact that it developed its Freedom of Navigation Program alongside UNCLOS but in advance of its signature, and that it remains the only country to support such a program despite its non-ratification of the Convention, suggests that its investment in this principle is not strictly derivative of UNCLOS. That the US endorsement of the principle was most vocal in wartime and in postwar peace settlements underscores the fact that freedom of the seas itself is a geostrategic end for the United States.

Third, if we reduce states' support for freedom of navigation to their coastal or user state status, we ignore the fact that these positions may change over time alongside state interests. Until very recently, China was, of course, predominantly a land power. As it has developed its own blue water navy, China's own actions have contradicted its objections to military activities in the EEZ. In 2014, China was invited to participate in the multilateral Rim of the Pacific (RIMPAC) naval exercise, off the coast of Hawaii, to which it dispatched an uninvited surveillance vessel.[32] In 2015, following a naval exercise with Russia, five Chinese warships transited US territorial waters along the Aleutian island chain consistent with (unannounced) innocent passage.[33] China's military also operates freely in its neighbors' EEZs.[34]

All three of these examples suggest that, as China continues to grow its ability to project naval power, it will likely see an interest in exercising its right to exercise innocent passage without prior notification and to conduct military activities in other states' EEZs. This is especially so given that China is "zone-locked," meaning that it cannot reach the high seas without transiting its neighbors' EEZs. If China does amend its positions, another question is whether China will simply cease objecting to other countries' activities in its EEZ and territorial seas, or whether it will insist that it can exercise full freedom of the seas in its own activities while restricting it near its shores, using its domestic law as justification.

Other regional states may also change their views on freedom of navigation and the Law of the Sea as China's power projection capabilities expand. Like China, Vietnam has had a longstanding requirement of notification prior to innocent passage. Following a US FONOP in the Vietnam-claimed Paracel Islands, which gave no prior notice, it voiced only support for the operation, presumably because it saw an interest in contesting China's claims.[35] Similarly, the Association of Southeast Asian Nations (ASEAN) has not traditionally placed freedom of navigation high on its agenda, but the principle has featured prominently in some of its recent statements.[36]

The fact that freedom of navigation may play an instrumental role in broader strategic debates does not detract from its importance. International law serves to define the boundaries of the international order. The reason that freedom of navigation – or freedom of the seas – has become a central point of major power contention and regional concern is not, as we have seen, because the actors' differing legal interpretations are new. Rather, it is because a more powerful China now has the capabilities to match the alternative view it has long held, and the Law of the Sea gives us an appropriate vocabulary with which to describe the resultant changes that are taking place in the maritime domain. In the years to come, freedom of navigation and freedom of the seas will almost certainly remain touchstone principles in Asia – but this will not be because coastal and user states are grappling with competing UNCLOS interpretations. Rather, it will be because the question of what constitutes the high seas and who has access to them has become a paramount geostrategic question of the twenty-first century.

Notes

1 Mark Landler, "Offering to Aid Talks, US Challenges China on Disputed Islands," *New York Times*, July 23, 2016, www.nytimes.com/2010/07/24/world/asia/24diplo.html
2 Secretary of Defense Ash Carter, "A Regional Security Architecture Where Everyone Rises," IISS Shangir-La Dialogue, May 30, 2015.
3 "China Values Free Navigation in the South China Sea More than any Other Country," *Xinhua*, accessed June 3, 2016, http://news.xinhuanet.com/english/2016-05/13/c_135355157.htm
4 Gordon Lubold, "U.S. Navy Tests China Over Sea Claims," *Wall Street Journal*, October 27, 2015, accessed June 3, 2016, www.wsj.com/articles/china-says-it-warned-u-s-warship-in-south-china-sea-1445928223
5 "Xi Says China Will Defend its South China Sea Sovereignty," *Reuters*, March 31, 2016, accessed June 3, 2016, www.reuters.com/article/us-nuclear-summit-usa-china-southchinase-idUSKCN0WX2WQ
6 "Remarks with Chinese Foreign Minister Wang Yi," February 23, 2016, accessed June 3, 2016, www.state.gov/secretary/remarks/2016/02/253164.htm
7 Jin Kai, "5 Myths About China's Missile Deployment on Woody Island," *The Diplomat*, February 20, 2016, accessed June 3, 2016, http://thediplomat.com/2016/02/5-myths-about-chinas-missile-deployment-on-woody-island/
8 Tommy T.B. Koh, "A Constitution for the Oceans," accessed June 3, 2016, www.un.org/depts/los/convention_agreements/texts/koh_english.pdf
9 Tommy T.B. Koh, "A Constitution for the Oceans," accessed June 3, 2016, www.un.org/depts/los/convention_agreements/texts/koh_english.pdf

10 Ronald O'Rourke, "Maritime Territorial and Exclusive Economic Zone Issues Involving China: Issues for Congress," Congressional Research Service, May 31, 2016, p. 11, accessed on June 10, 2016: www.fas.org/sgp/crs/row/R42784.pdf
11 UN Convention on the Law of the Sea, Article 19, accessed June 3, 2016, www.un.org/depts/los/convention_agreements/texts/unclos/unclos_e.pdf
12 UN Convention on the Law of the Sea, Article 19, accessed June 3, 2016, www.un.org/depts/los/convention_agreements/texts/unclos/unclos_e.pdf
13 James Kraska, *Maritime Power and the Law of the Sea: Expeditionary Operations in World Politics* (Oxford: Oxford University Press, 2010), p. 141.
14 Raul Pedrozo and James Kraska, "Will China Decide to Reduce Tensions in the South Cina Sea?" *Straits Times*, May 31, 2016, accessed on June 2, 2016: www.straitstimes.com/opinion/will-china-decide-to-reduce-tension-in-the-south-china-sea
15 Ambassador Tommy Koh, as cited in Jon M. Van Dyke, "Military Ships and Planes Operating in the Exclusive Economic one of Another Country," *Marine Policy*, Vol. 28. No. 1 (2004), p. 31.
16 Guifang Xue, "China and the Law of the Sea: An Update," *International Law Studies*, Volume 84, U.S. Naval War College, p. 105.
17 See, e.g., Julian Ku, "Is the Nine-Dash Line a Super-Sized Exclusive Economic Zone?," *Lawfare*, March 25, 2016.
18 "China: Maritime Claims in the South China Sea," *Limits in the Seas No. 143*, Department of State, December 5, 2014, pp. 10–11, accessed June 3, 2016: www.state.gov/documents/organization/234936.pdf
19 Patricia C. Bauerlein, The United Nations Convention on the Law of the Sea & U.S. Ocean Environmental Practice, *Loyola Marymount University Law Review*, pp. 899–902.
20 United Nations Division for Ocean Affairs and Law of the Sea, Declarations and Statements, accessed June 3, 2016, www.un.org/depts/los/convention_agreements/convention_declarations.htm#China%20Upon%20ratification
21 James R. Holmes, "Obama and Abe Must Defend 'Freedom of the Seas,'" *Real Clear Defense*, May 1, 2015, accessed on June 3, 2016, www.realcleardefense.com/articles/2015/05/01/obama_and_abe_must_defend_freedom_of_the_sea_107906.html
22 Asia-Pacific Maritime Security Strategy, Department of Defense, August 2015, pp. 2–3, accessed June 3, 2016: www.defense.gov/Portals/1/Documents/pubs/NDAA%20A-P_Maritime_SecuritY_Strategy-08142015-1300-FINALFORMAT.PDF.
23 James Kraska, *Maritime Power and the Law of the Sea: Expeditionary Operations in World Politics* (Oxford: Oxford University Press, 2010), p. 50.
24 Kraska, p. 61.
25 Mira Rapp-Hooper, "All in Good FON: Why Freedom of Navigation is Business is Usual in the South China Sea," *Foreign Affairs*, October 12, 2015, accessed June 3, 2016: www.foreignaffairs.com/articles/united-states/2015-10-12/all-good-fon
26 President Woodrow Wilson's Fourteen Points, January 8, 1918, accessed on June 3, 2016, http://avalon.law.yale.edu/20th_century/wilson14.asp
27 Covenant of the League of Nations, Part I of the Versailles Peace Treaty of 1919, as cited in Kraska, p. 81
28 Atlantic Charter, August 14, 1941, accessed June 3, 2016 http://avalon.law.yale.edu/wwii/atlantic.asp; Declaration by the United Nations, January 1, 1942, accessed June 3, 2016 http://avalon.law.yale.edu/20th_century/decade03.asp
29 Rapp-Hooper, "All in Good FON."
30 Rapp-Hooper, "All in Good FON."
31 Ankit Panda, "China Issues 8 Warning to U.S. Surveillance Plane in South China Sea," *The Diplomat*, May 21, 2015, accessed June 2, 2016: http://thediplomat.com/2015/05/china-issues-8-warnings-to-us-surveillance-plane-in-south-china-sea/

32 Sam LaGrone, "China Sends an Uninvited Spy Ship to RIMPAC," *USNI News*, July 18, 2014, accessed on June 2, 2016: https://news.usni.org/2014/07/18/china-sends-uninvited-spy-ship-rimpac
33 Sam LaGrone, "Chinese Warships Made 'Innocent Passage' Through U.S. Territorial Waters Off Alaska," *USN News*, September 3, 2015, accessed on June 2, 2016: https://news.usni.org/2015/09/03/chinese-warships-made-innocent-passage-through-u-s-territorial-waters-off-alaska
34 Raul Pedrozo and James Kraska, "Will China Decide to Reduce Tensions in the South China Sea?" *Straits Times*, May 31, 2016, accessed on June 2, 2016: www.straitstimes.com/opinion/will-china-decide-to-reduce-tension-in-the-south-china-sea
35 Alan Bjerga, "U.S. Enters Waters Claimed by China Without Approval," *Bloomberg News*, January 20, 2015, accessed June 3, 2016: www.bloomberg.com/news/articles/2016-01-30/u-s-warship-enters-waters-claimed-by-china-without-approval
36 Chairman's Statement of the 26th ASEAN Summit, April 27, 2015, accessed June 3, 2016: www.miti.gov.my/miti/resources/fileupload/Chairman%20Statement%2026th%20ASEAN%20Summit.pdf

9 The prior notification issue of military activities in EEZ

Ying Yang

Introduction

The main focus of the disputes between ocean powers, represented by the US, and developing countries, represented by China, is whether warship of foreign States should provide prior notification to the coastal states before entering the exclusive economic zone (EEZ) of coastal states. In addition, the "*Impeccable*" incident also stirred up concern regarding the problem of the legal status of EEZ. There is an ongoing question of whether the EEZ represents waters with national security interests or international waters where every country enjoys freedom of navigation. The *Impeccable* incident also stirred up concerns about the legal status of EEZ. China, in this incident, held that activities of the USNS *Impeccable* were within the range of the jurisdictional waters of China, therefore the *Impeccable* should have provided prior notification to China. The United States held that the *Impeccable* was operating in international waters, meaning that the ship enjoyed the right to freedom of navigation – and did not require prior permission to do so. This difference of interpretation was debated between Sino-US scholars in the ninth edition (2010) of the *Chinese Journal of International Law*.[1] Who is right, and who is wrong? Given that the provisions are indeterminate, it is challenging to resolve the discord regarding prior notification of military activities such as military exercises, military intelligence-gathering, military surveys, and so on. The reasoning presented by both sides of this debate will be discussed from a dialectical perspective and solutions to this issue will be proposed.

Legal status of EEZ

Before the conclusion of the 1982 United Nations Convention on the Law of the Sea (UNCLOS), the legal status of EEZ was the focus of debate of the international community. Concerned about the issue of the *Creeping jurisdiction*, many maritime countries thought that EEZs should be in the category of high seas. The rules state that any activity that is not conducted by a coastal state should be subject to the provisions of the high seas regime. However, other State parties of UNCLOS did not agree with this interpretation. Article 55[2] and

Article 86[3] of UNCLOS clearly state that EEZs do not have the characteristics of both high seas and territorial seas, and therefore any activity, conducted by a non-coastal state, should fall under the jurisdiction of the relevant coastal state.

In conclusion, there are three main views about the legal status of EEZs: The first view is the *theory of national field*, which states that the coastal state enjoys complete jurisdiction in its EEZ. The main proponents of this view are Argentina, Brazil, Peru, Panama. The second view is represented by the *theory of priority privilege*, under which coastal states enjoy certain priority rights or special authorization in their EEZ. This interpretation is advocated by Japan. The third view is the *theory of economic waters*, which holds that EEZs are not only different from territorial waters, but also differ from the definition of high seas. EEZs are their own entity, an ocean space with special properties. The main proponent of this view is Kenya.

Although there are various viewpoints, the international community has already reached a consensus that EEZs are not to be considered part of the territorial sea of the coastal state. Rather, they are waters that grant the coastal state jurisdiction over the resources and economy within them, as stipulated by the third United Nations Conference on the Law of the Sea. Establishment of EEZ of the coastal state, however, does not, and cannot affect the freedom right of navigation of foreign State within this region.

According to Article 55 and Article 86 of UNCLOS, EEZs encompass the characteristics of territorial seas and high seas. It is the sea area of *sui generis* which has three characteristics. The first is that UNCLOS grants rights and obligations to the coastal states; the second is that UNCLOS grants rights and obligations to the other States; and the third is that UNCLOS has special regulations to adjust activities in this area of the sea. The activities within this region are different from the activities in territorial seas and in high seas.

John A. Rolls, Vice-Chairman of the United States Marine Program, observed that,

> one of the greatest achievements of UNCLOS is the establishment of EEZ, the coastal state enjoys sovereignty rights on exploration and exploitation of resources in the sea area of 200 nautical miles. This new legal sea area is between the territorial sea and the high seas, but not belong to them. Rapid development of fishing techniques is the most important impetus of the primary change in international maritime policy.[4]

The legal status of EEZ, a new area established by UNCLOS, is different not only with territorial seas but also with high seas. It is the sea area of *sui generis.*

The difference between EEZs and territorial seas is that EEZs do not constitute territory of the coastal states. The coastal states only enjoy sovereign rights over natural resources and jurisdiction with regard to the establishment and use of artificial island and structures, marine scientific research, protection and preservation of the marine environment, but do not have the sole authority over navigation in their EEZ. Any state can use these waters under the freedom of navigation clause of UNCLOS.

The difference between EEZs and high seas is that all States not only have the right to freely navigate the high seas, but also to lay submarine cables and pipelines.[5] Coastal states retain certain exclusive jurisdictions listed in Article 56.[6] Other States could carry out these activities, e.g. marine scientific research only after getting permission from the coastal states. Rights, freedoms, and jurisdictions of States, whether coastal states have an EEZ or not, are all stipulated in UNCLOS. They have no additional rights beyond the scope of UNCLOS, therefore coastal states can restrict the relevant activities of other States in their EEZ.

National security claims regarding the EEZ

The maritime powers represented by the United States think that EEZs are a part of international waters, and therefore every State enjoys the right to freedom of navigation in EEZs. Other States do not need to provide prior notification before entering the EEZ of a coastal state. However, some developing countries, represented by China, consider EEZs to be vital to their national security interests, and therefore foreign warships should provide prior notification to the coastal state before entering their EEZs. For example, Cape Verde has the following point of view,

> In the EEZ, the enjoyment of the freedoms of international communication, in conformity with its definition and with other relevant provisions of the Convention, excludes any non-peaceful use without the consent of the coastal state, such as exercises with weapons or other activities which may affect the rights or interests of the coastal States; and it also excludes the threat or use of force against the territorial integrity, political independence, peace, or security of the coastal states.[7]

Presently, 25 coastal states lay claim to national security jurisdiction over their EEZs.[8] They include Brazil, Bangladesh, Burma, Cambodia, Cape Verde, China, India, Egypt, Iran, Kenya, Malaysia, Maldives, Mauritania, Mauritius, Nicaragua, North Korea, Pakistan, Peru, Saudi Arabia, Sudan, Syria, Uruguay, Venezuela Vietnam, and Yemen.[9] Although the specific claims are different, all of them claim to have national security interest related to jurisdiction over their EEZs. For example, Egypt claims security jurisdiction out to 24nm; India allows military exercises or maneuvers in its EEZ or on its continental shelf, and claims security jurisdiction out to 24nm; Iran prohibits foreign military "activities and practices" in its EEZs; China allows other States to lay submarine cables and pipelines, but strictly enforces security laws in its EEZ, and fails to recognize airspace above its EEZ as "international airspace."[10]

Because some states claim national security interests over their EEZ, the issue of whether foreign warships should provide prior notification to the coastal states before entering its EEZ is contentious. For example, because of the pollution risks to marine environments, posed by refueling activities in the high seas, Spain and Mexico proposed that States should consider amending the *International Convention for the Prevention of Pollution from Ships* in 2004.[11] In subsequent years, the State parties of the *International Convention for the Prevention of Pollution from Ships*[12] considered limiting such activities. The Marine Environment Protection Committee eventually formulated various restrictive conditions at the fifty-eighth conference in October 2008.[13] One of these restrictive conditions is that the States must provide a minimum of 48 hours notice of refueling activity in the EEZ of a coastal state. Although the United States strongly opposed the measure, this convention entered into force on January 1, 2011.[14]

We can conclude that if a State holds the opinion that its national security interests give it jurisdiction over its EEZ, foreign warships must provide prior notification before entering the EEZ of the coastal state. However, if a State adheres to the notion that all EEZs represent international water, and that coastal states only enjoy economic jurisdiction in these areas, it would not require prior notification, because national security interests have no impact on the economic jurisdiction of the coastal state. Other States can then enjoy the full freedom of navigation and overflight in the coastal state's EEZ.

Issue of prior notification of military activities in EEZ

Military exercises

Maritime powers believe that the principles of freedom of navigation should apply to military activities in EEZs as well as in High Seas. This is supported by Article 58 and Article 87 of UNCLOS.

It should be noted that during signing and ratification of UNCLOS, some States including "Bangladesh, Brazil, Cape Verde, Pakistan, Malaysia, and Uruguay declared that if foreign State doesn't get prior permission of the coastal state, such military activities must not be engaged in EEZ"[15] and that "Germany, Italy, Netherlands, and United Kingdom proposed sharp and opposing declaration."[16] The United States also thinks that military activities in EEZs are already a part of international customary law according to Article 58 of UNCLOS. Consequently, the United States holds that the freedoms in EEZs should be the same as in high seas.

The issue about whether military activities can be carried out in EEZs is a disputed focus between some coastal states and maritime powers. The maritime powers think that these activities should be a part of the freedom of navigation rights that are granted by Article 58 of UNCLOS. The freedoms that every state enjoys in EEZs are the same in high seas, except for the sovereign rights and economic jurisdictions that belong to the coastal states.

Some coastal states hold that the provisions about these issues are undefined in UNCLOS, and therefore EEZs are dictated by the national security interests of the relevant coastal state. Under this interpretation, other States cannot engage in military activities in an EEZ before getting permission from the coastal state.[17] For example, China holds that foreign warships and military aircraft should not be permitted to carry out military activities in its EEZ before getting permission from China.

As to whether foreign States can carry out military activities in China's EEZ, the occurrence of conflicts and confrontation is inevitable due to the different interpretations of UNCLOS. For example, the location of joint military exercises between the United States and South Korea in the Yellow Sea in 2010 was only 170 kilometers off the coast of Shandong Peninsula, China. China thought that the distance was close enough to affect the coastal defense and security of its borders.

According to such national practices and in addition to the strong protest and the statement, the coastal states can solve this issue through bilateral meetings, continuing to accumulate State practices.

In summary, the following measures are incorporated by coastal states regarding State practices of foreign warships carrying out military exercises in EEZs. First, a strong protest is issued. Second, an attempt is made to negotiate a settlement through bilateral dialogue – hoping to impress upon the offending State – to respect all rights of the coastal state including its national security interests in its EEZ. Third, the coastal state excludes the mandatory procedures of UNCLOS through written statement; both parties agree to develop a cooperative relationship, and to encourage analogous agreements preventing maritime accidents – all based on the mechanism of maritime security consultation while seeking understanding and cooperation. Fourth, the timely application of other measures including sanctions to make the offending state realize that "cooperation benefits both, while confrontation benefits no-one." Implementing these four steps will then lead them to adjust their corresponding tactics. These four steps provide a limited solution in terms of the response of coastal states to the military exercises of foreign States in their EEZs. A more suitable solution will need to be found by the international community.

Military survey activities

Article 56 (1) of UNCLOS stipulates that coastal states enjoy the exclusive jurisdiction to marine science research in their EEZ. Other States must therefore get prior permission of the coastal states before carrying out marine science research in the EEZs of the coastal states. Article 9 of *Law of the People's Republic of China on the Exclusive Economic Zone and the Continental Shelf* clearly stipulates that every international organization, foreign organization, or individual must get prior approval from the competent authorities and abide by the laws of China before carrying out marine science research in the EEZ and continental shelf of China.

The main focus of issue regarding the limitation of marine science research on military activities is whether military surveys can be considered as marine science research. The "*Bowditch*," an American military surveillance ship, entered the EEZ of the Yellow Sea on September 19, 2002, which is only 100km away from the Chinese coast. Another incident occurred on March 8, 2009, when the "*Impeccable*," also an American military surveillance ship, was expelled by a Chinese ship about 120km away from the south of Hainan Island. These incidents sparked a major controversy regarding the issue of military survey activities in EEZs between China and the United States.

There are no specific and clear definitions for "marine science research" and "military survey" in UNCLOS, but there are some relevant provisions of these terms. For example: Article 19(2) (j) stipulates that "the carrying out of research or survey activities" shall be considered to be prejudicial to the innocent passage; Article 21(1) (g) regulates that "the coastal state may adopt laws and regulations of the marine scientific research and hydrographic surveys"; Article 40 regulates that "marine scientific research and hydrographic survey ships may not carry out any research or survey activities without the prior authorization of the States bordering straits"; Article 56(1) stipulates that the coastal state has the jurisdiction with regard to the marine science research in the exclusive economic zone; Article 143 regulates that the cooperation of the marine science research in the area; and the Part XIII regulates all aspects of the marine science research.

Although there are special provisions on marine science research in UNCLOS, the United States believes that there are differences between marine science research activities and military survey activities. That is because marine science research is "the general term most often used to describe those activities undertaken in the ocean and coastal waters to expand scientific knowledge of the marine environment and its processes."[18] Military surveys refer to activities undertaken in the ocean and coastal waters involving marine data collection. The United States accepts that although the means of data collection used in military surveys is often similar to that used in marine science research, the purpose of information derived from such activities is used for military purposes. Military survey activities are therefore inherently different from marine science research. The United States believes that military surveys should not be subject to the jurisdiction and restrictions of the coastal states and should belong to the other internationally lawful uses of the sea, while China does not agree with this opinion.

Different opinions such as these are reasons why some primary conflicts have occurred. The examples mentioned previously were 2001 EP-3, *Bowditch*, and the 2009 *Impeccable incident*. The question is whether or not military surveys in EEZs can be categorized as Marine Science Research, or if they can be restricted and managed by the coastal states.

Raul (Pete) Pedrozo,[19] a US scholar, discussed that Article 56 "specifically grants coastal states jurisdiction over 'research' activities in the EEZ. It does not, however, provide for jurisdiction over "survey" activities... various provisions of the Convention (i.e. Articles 19, 40, 52, 54 and 56 and Part XIII) discussed clearly distinguish between "research" and "survey" activities. Similarly, Article 56 does not provide security interests for coastal states in an EEZ. While UNCLOS does place certain limitations on military activities at sea, none of these restrictions applies in the EEZ."[20] Pedrozo illustrated these restrictions using examples, such as the threat or use of force and intelligence gathering. Pedrozo drew a conclusion from the principles of the Lotus case that "States may lawfully engage in intelligence collection and other military activities in the EEZ."[21]

This paper immediately drew rebuttal and comments from scholars of other States, such as Zhang Haiwen[22] and Seiho Yee[23] of China, and Sam Bateman[24] of Australia. Bateman directly refuted the view of Pedrozo about the relationship between marine scientific research, military data collection, and hydrographic surveys. Bateman said that "it is no longer possible to argue that hydrographic surveys are just about the safety of navigation and thus covered by the freedoms of navigation available in an EEZ."[25] He also observed that "Any hydrographic data, regardless of how they are collected, have economic value to the coastal state, and is important for the effective management of its EEZ. Despite what Pedrozo argues, there is no such thing as hydrographic data collected in an EEZ that only has utility to the military, or for the safety of navigation."[26] Bateman also discussed the relationship between hydrographic surveys and marine science research. He concluded that hydrographic surveys should be considered as marine science research. Therefore hydrographic surveys should be subject to the jurisdiction of the coastal state.

The main purpose of hydrographic survey is to determine and survey the data related with the bodies of water. "A hydrographic survey may consist of the determination of one or several of the following classes of data: depth of water, configuration and nature of the bottom; directions and force of currents; heights and times of tide and water stages; and location of topographic features and fixed objects for survey and navigation purposes."[27]

Marine science research is a general designation for the research activities regarding marine environments. Marine science research activities should include the research activities of hydrographic surveys. The data produced by hydrographic surveys is mainly used to provide facilitation, ensure the security of navigation, and is often provided to personnel involved in marine environment research such as oceanographers, biologists and environmental scientists.

Military survey activities relate to the collection of marine data for military purposes. In essence, hydrographic surveys and military surveys use the same process – activities involving detection and collection of data. There is only one difference between them – the ultimate purpose for collecting the data. Military surveys are only used for military purposes accompanied by military security factors. It should be considered as a part of marine science research, and should not change its nature just because of different purpose of using the surveying data.

According to this logic, military surveys should be placed in the same category as marine science research. Both should be subject to the restrictions stipulated in UNCLOS which dictates that coastal states have control over military surveying activities in their EEZ. Foreign surveying ships and aircraft should provide prior notification to the coastal states before engaging in military survey activities in the EEZs of coastal states.

Military intelligence-gathering activities

Given that intelligence-gathering activities are considered to be part of the freedoms of high seas in traditional law of sea, ocean powers believe that Article 58(1) of UNCLOS grants foreign state with the right to conduct intelligence-gathering activities in EEZ. They think that these intelligence-gathering activities do not affect the rights of the coastal states in their territorial sea and in the air space over the territorial sea.[28] Ocean powers have routinely conducted such activities in EEZs without protest from the coastal states, unless these activities are provocative in nature.[29] The US Navy also believes that these activities belong to a part of the freedoms of high seas and can be carried out in EEZs.[30] According to Article 19 of UNCLOS, the United States thinks that intelligence-gathering activities can "be considered to be prejudicial to the peace, good order or security of the coastal state,"[31] but the same regulation does not appear in part V of UNCLOS, therefore, according to Article 58 (1) of UNCLOS, such intelligence-gathering activities are not subject to the obligation to obtain the prior permission of a coastal state before conducting military intelligence gathering in its EEZ.

Alternatively, China considers that intelligence-gathering activities of foreign warships and military aircraft in the EEZ of the coastal states are activities threatening to national security and peaceful maritime order of the coastal states. The intelligence-gathering activities violate the basic principle of the international law – mutual respect for sovereignty and territorial integrity. For example, China strongly protested the 2001EP-3 incident. Although Article 58 (1) of UNCLOS regulates that other States enjoy the freedoms of navigation and overflight in the EEZ of coastal states, Article 58 (3) also regulates that:

> In exercising their rights and performing their duties… in the EEZ, States shall have due regard to the rights and duties of the coastal state and shall comply with the laws and regulations adopted by the coastal state in accordance with the provisions of this Convention and other rules of international law in so far as they are not incompatible with this Part.

Article 11 of the *Law on the Exclusive Economic Zone and the Continental Shelf of the People's Republic of China* stipulates that "All states shall, on the premise that they comply with international law and the laws and regulations of the People's Republic of China, enjoy the freedom of navigation in and flight over its exclusive economic zone…" China enjoys the rights of monitoring, surveillance and controlling in EEZ, believing that they have legal right to request foreign warships and military aircraft to provide the prior notification before engaging in military intelligence-gathering activities its EEZ.

New developments in science and technology have permitted a proliferation of supporting weapons, such as satellites, aircraft carriers, submarines, and missiles to greatly increase the scope and accuracy of military intelligence-gathering activities. UNCLOS does not provide detailed regulations on how warships and military aircraft use this new technology to improve the ability of electronic warfare, information warfare, and intelligence gathering. In addition, these new types of military activities are also not clearly defined as the "other internationally lawful uses of the sea" related to the rights of freedom of navigation and overflight.

The issue of prior notification

Dialectic analysis of the issue of prior notification

The issue of prior notification in EEZs can be discussed from the dialectic perspective.

Chinese scholars, Zhou Jianmin and Wang Hailiang, systematically elaborated on the connotation of national great strategy in their article, *National Great Strategy, National Security Strategy and National Interests.*[32] They discussed the national great strategy which:

> includes not only national development strategy but also national security strategy and national unified strategy... the core of national development strategy is public interests, for example, economic development, scientific and technological development, social development, culture development, and reforming development – all of which belong to the public interests... diplomatic strategy and national defense strategy belong to the national interests, national defense strategy mainly refers to maintenance of national security.[33]

The issue of prior notification in EEZs is mainly related to national security interests. The reason why developing countries represented by China require foreign warships to provide prior notification before entering their EEZ is their consideration of national security interests.

Of course, for the government of every State, national interests, like other interests, will also change with the changes of various internal or external elements. Examples include development of its own strength, passage of time, changes of the surrounding environment, and so on. National interests can also be divided into various areas: long-term interests, short-term interests and even medium-term interests. Difference between long-term interests and short-term interests are just like the different stages of economic development of a State. The government of every State could make a future economic developing framework that includes the targets of various stages of economic development, such as the targets of long-term development, medium-term development and short-term development. If the economic development of a State is in a beneficial trend and moving forward, the economy of this State must attain the developing targets of every stage within a certain timeframe.

Just like the establishment of the World Trade Organization (WTO), when the economic strength of a State is not strong, this State will set up barriers to import trade and investment, such as tariffs and foreign currency control. The purpose of establishment of these barriers is to protect the country's economy and its national industries from competition. After the economy of a State develops to a certain stage, this State will realize that its own economic development is closely related to the economic development of the world.

When States established the WTO to promote a global economy, they gradually abolished various barriers – enhancing import trade and investment. This demonstrated that when countries are strong economically, they support free trade and thus bring in more economic development to the countries involved.

How does this relate to national security interests? National security interests are different from economic interests although there are similarities in their development models. The countries claiming national security interest jurisdictions over their EEZ are developing countries, while the countries accepting the freedom of sea are ocean powers. Why does such phenomenon appear? The United States has explained that its national security interest is to maintain the presence of the US as a stabilizing power, and to ensure the fundamental institutions and values of international law will not be violated.[34] Hans J. Morgenthau elaborated on such a view in his book, *In Defense of the National Interest.* He states that the fundamental interest of a country is national survival. While national strength, such as industrial strength and military strength, is the basis of survival and development of a country, a weaker country must be repressed and restricted by powerful country.[35] Just like the view of Morgenthau, when economic strength and military strength of a country are not developed, the primary task of this country is to maintain survival and its own security. This is the only way to improve national strength and also the only way to create a favorable external environment to develop strength.

Let us try to imagine the situation of a small weak developing coastal state whose EEZ is completely open. The warships and military aircraft of marine powers can enter the EEZ of the weak country as they please and conduct a variety of military activities. This coastal state would be in a constant state of anxiety, fearing that the marine powers could attack them because the military strength of this coastal state is not enough to confront the ocean powers.

Similarly, the reason why marine powers insist upon the unrestricted freedom of navigation in EEZs is also out of the consideration of their strength. They do not need to worry about whether foreign warships can enter their EEZ. Why? First, because of their military strength, other States seldom or never have large pelagic warships that can enter the EEZ of their States. Second, if the warships of a small weak countries do manage to enter the EEZ of an ocean power, that ocean power need not fear because of its military strength, which would overpower the smaller country. In contrast, small developing coastal states need to be on constant alert.

China needs to create a favorable external environment to develop its economic and military strength. Even though its economic strength has made great progress over the years, there are also major gaps between China and ocean powers.

For the benefit of its short-term national security interest, China should emphasize the national security interests in its EEZ. For its long-term national security interest, China may need to change this point of view and accept a more unrestricted freedom of navigation principle in its EEZ. This will be particularly significant when the development of China's economic and military strength advance to the point that it can confront the strength of ocean powers.

Another scenario is that China could evolve like the WTO where the economic development of every country is linked together forming global economic integration, therefore establishing security interest at sea.

When countries are weak, they need to strengthen their offshore interests. Stronger countries, however, need to be concerned about their pelagic interest and limit their offshore interest consciously. Since ocean interests are global, this would bring together the greater maritime interests while promoting the freedoms of the sea. There is no doubt that, in the international arena, the game between countries is not just the game of rules, but also the game of strength of a country's policy, economy and military.

The settlement of issue of prior notification

With regard to the controversial issue of prior notification in EEZs, and lack of solutions, how can this be resolved in order to maintain the security at sea and the peace of the international community? There are two ways to settle this issue: First, form the international customary law. There are 25 developing countries, represented by China, that claim to have national security interest jurisdiction over their EEZs.[36] Even though the concrete claims are different, these countries require foreign warships to provide prior notification to the coastal states.

According to the formation of international customary law, this process requires two conditions. The first is an objective condition repeated by every country that requires a number of countries to repeat certain practice activities over a certain period of time. The generality not only requires the consistency and stability of such practice activities, but also requires that such practice activities have long been respected and recognized as obligatory by many countries. The second is a subjective condition known as *Opinio Juris*, in which countries recognize this rule as legally binding. If the issue of prior notification in EEZ is to be recognized by many countries, it is possible to form an international customary law.

Second, convene an international conference. Ocean powers emphasize the freedom of navigation in EEZ while coastal states claim national security interest jurisdiction in their EEZs. Under such conflicting conditions, it is recommended that the international community convene an international conference on this issue. This should be modeled after the Third United Nations Conference on the Law of the Sea, where numerous disputes were resolved through negotiations.

In addition, convening an international conference to discuss the issue of prior notification in EEZ is similar to discussing the provision of the deep seabed mining of Part XI of UNCLOS after the 1982 UNCLOS came into force. The international community finally made a conclusion of the *Agreement Relating to the Implementation to Part XI of the United Nations Convention of the Law of the Sea* in 1994.

Participating countries in this special international conference should be limited to the coastal states that have ratified UNCLOS. If all coastal states voiced their opinions on this complex issue through negotiation and repeated discussions, it is likely that a satisfactory solution would be concluded at last.

Although this process may be long and full of contradictions and conflicts, it is worthy of pursuing the long road of negotiation in order to maintain stability and security at sea, and the peace of the international community. It is also worth remembering that it took ten years of negotiations before UNCLOS went into force. The entire world is better off because of it. Human conflicts and two world wars should teach us the significant meanings about the pursuit of peace forever because wars will only bring untold sorrow to mankind.[37]

Notes

1 Zhang Haiwen, Is It Safeguarding the Freedom of Navigation or Maritime Hegemony of the United States? – Comments on Raul (Pete) Pedrozo's Article on Military Activities in the EEZ, 9 *Chinese JIL* (2010), pp. 31–47.Raul (Pete) Pedrozo, Preserving Navigational Rights and Freedoms: The Right to Conduct Military Activities in China's Exclusive Economic Zone, *9 Chinese JIL* (2010), pp. 9–29.Raul (Pete) Pedrozo, Responding to Ms. Zhang's Talking Points on the EEZ, 10 *Chinese JIL* (2011), pp. 207–23.

2 The Article 55 of UNCLOS is "the Exclusive Economic Zone... subject to the special legal regime... the rights and jurisdiction of the coastal States and the rights and freedoms of other States are governed by the relevant provisions of this Conventions."

3 The Article 86 of UNCLOS is "The provisions of (the high seas) apply to all parts of the sea that are not included in the EEZ..."

4 Zhou, Zhonghai, *Technology and the Law of Sea*, Taishan Press, 1998, p. 29.

5 Article 58 of UNCLOS regulates that all States, whether coastal or land-locked, enjoy the freedoms of navigation and overflight and of the laying of submarine cables and pipelines.

6 Article 56 of UNCLOS regulates that the coastal State not only has sovereign rights for the purpose of exploring and exploiting, conserving and managing the natural resources, but also has exclusive jurisdiction with regard to the establishment and use of artificial islands, installations and structures; marine science research; the protection and preservation of marine environment and other rights and duties.

7 Declaration made at the signature of UNCLOS and reaffirmed at ratification on August 10, 1987.

8 James Kraska, *Maritime Power and the law of the sea, expeditionary operations in world politics*, Oxford University Press, 2011, p. 303.

9 Id. p. 303.

10 James Kraska, *Maritime Power and the law of the sea, expeditionary operations in world politics*, Oxford University Press, 2011, p. 303.

11 International Convention for the Prevention of Pollution from Ships, November 2, 1973, 94 Stat. 2297, 1340 U.N.T.S. 184, reprinted in 12 I.L.M. 1319, amended by Protocol of 1978 Relating to the International Convention for the Prevention of Pollution from Ships, adopted February 17, 1978, 1340 U.N.T.S. 61, reprinted in 17 I.L.M. 546.

12 International Convention for the Prevention of Pollution From Ships.

13 IMO, International Maritime Organization, report of the marine environment protection committee at 58th conference, MEPC 58/23 (Oct.16,2008),see: www.imo.org/ourwork/environment/pollutionprevention/airpollution/documents/23-add-1.pdf.

14 James W. Houck, Alone on a Wide Wide Sea:A National Security Rational for Joining the Law of the Sea Convention, *Penn State Journal of Law & International Affairs*, Volume 1, Issue 1, April 2012, p. 12.
15 G. Galdorisi and A. Kaufman, Military activities in the exclusive economic zone: Preventing uncertainly and defusing conflicts, *California Western International Law Journal*, Vol. 32, 2002, p. 272.
16 Id, pp. 274–75.
17 25 countries have claimed the national security interest over the EEZ. see: James Kraska, *Maritime Power and the Law of the Sea- Expeditionary Operations in world Politics*, Oxford University Press, 2011, p. 303.
18 J. Ashley Roach, Marine Scientific Research and the New Law of the Sea, *Ocean Development & International Law*, 1996, V.27, p. 60.
19 Raul (Pete) Pedrozo, Preserving Navigational Rights and Freedoms: The Right to Conduct Military Activities in China's Exclusive Economic Zone, *Chinese Journal of International Law*, 2010, pp. 9–29.
20 Id. p. 11.
21 Id. p. 12.
22 Zhang Haiwen, Is It Safeguarding the Freedom of Navigation or Maritime Hegemony of the United States? – Comments on Raul (Pete) Pedrozo's Article on Military Activities in the EEZ, *Chinese Journal of International Law*, 2010, pp. 31–47.
23 Sienho Yee, Agora: Military Activities in the EEZ – Sketching the Debate on Military Activities in the EEZ: An Editorial Comment, *Chinese Journal of International Law*, 2010, pp. 1–7.
24 Sam Bateman, A Response to Pedrozo: The Wider Utility of Hydrographic Surveys, *Chinese Journal of International Law*, 2011, pp. 177–86.
25 Id. p. 178.
26 Id. p. 178.
27 International Hydrographic Bureau (IHB), International Hydrographic Dictionary [online] (5th edn., Monaco: IHB, 1994) [cited 23 September 2002]: Special publication S-32 (www.iho-wms.net:8080/hydrodic/en/index.php/hydrographic survey) quoted from Sam Bateman, A Response to Pedrozo: The Wider Utility of Hydrographic Surveys, *Chinese Journal of International Law*, 2011, p.179.
28 Raul (Pete) Pedrozo, Preserving Navigational Rights and Freedoms: The Right to Conduct Military Activities in China's Exclusive Economic Zone, *Chinese Journal of International Law*, 2010, p. 25.
29 Id. p. 25.
30 Department of the Navy, *The Commander's Handbook on the Law of Naval Operations (Norfolk, 1995)*, Sections 2.4.2. and 2.4.3.
31 Article19 of UNCLOS.
32 Zhou Jianmin, Wang Hailiang: National great Strategy, National Security Strategy and National Interests, *the Journal of World Economics and Politics*, No. 4, 2001, pp. 21–26.
33 Id. p. 22.
34 Peter G. Peterson and James K. Sebenius, "The Primacy of the Domestic Agenda," in Graham Allison and Gregory F. Trevert on (eds.), *Rethinking America's Security:Beyond Cold War to New World Order* (New York: Norton, 1992), p. 57.
35 Hans J. Morgenthau, *In Defense of the National Interest:A Critical Examination of American Foreign Policy*, New York:Alfred A. Knopf, 1951.
36 James Kraska, *Maritime Power and the law of the sea, expeditionary operations in world politics*, Oxford University Press, 2011, p. 303.
37 UN Charter, preface.

10 Maritime confidence-building measures

Assessing China–US MOU on notification of major military activities and rules of behavior

Yan Yan

In recent years, China and the United States (US) have taken many actions to reduce the risks of miscalculations of close encounter between naval ships and aircrafts. On November 10, 2014, in order to prevent accidental incidents at sea, the Department of Defense in the US and China signed two maritime confidence-building measures (CBMs): the Memorandum of Understanding on Notification of Major Military Activities and the Memorandum of Understanding Regarding the Rules of Behavior for Safety of Air and Maritime Encounters (hereinafter referred to as "Memorandum"). In September 2015, the two governments concluded on the supplemented military crisis notification attached to the notification agreement and the air-to-air annex in the MOU. The military crisis notification provided rules governing the use of a military crisis hotline, aiming to enhance top-level communication, and ensuring a broad scope in the air encounter behavior attachment, setting rules from the appropriate physical behaviors to use during crises to the right radio frequencies to use during distress calls. The MOU, and annexes, is a new confidence-building mechanism aiming to establish rules of close encounter while stabilizing the military relationship between the two states.

Preventive diplomacy and CBMs are widely discussed in the security discourse, especially in the maritime domain. In order to increase transparency and reduce the risk of potential conflicts in the South and East China Sea, China and the US have been working on establishing mechanisms to prevent incidents between military forces for years, but their fundamental differences remain. In January 1998, China's Ministry of National Defense and US Department of Defense signed The Agreement on Establishing a Consultation Mechanism (MMCA) to Strengthen Military Maritime Safety. Regardless, the EP-3 incidents occurred three years later. In addition to bilateral channels, the two militaries have also worked more closely under the framework of the Asia-Pacific multilateral security dialogue mechanism. At the fourteenth annual meeting of the Western Pacific Naval Symposium hosted by China in April 2014, they worked together for the adoption of Code for Unplanned Encounters at Sea (CUES), which had been discussed for 16 years. CUES stipulates maritime security procedure, communication program, signal and code, basic maneuvering instructions, legal status of the Code, and scope of application, etc.

A widely cited example of a practical CBM is the 1972 Agreement on the Prevention of Incidents on and Over the High Seas (often referred to as INCSEA Agreement) between the US and the Soviet Union over the high seas, which stood the test of demanding naval operational experience during the Cold War. The Prevention of Dangerous Military Activities (DMAA) agreement is another important CBM between the two to address most sensitive and dangerous military activities between the two.

In this article, there is an exploration of the previous maritime and air incidents between China and the United Sates, the security dilemma the two face in the South China Sea, and the models of confidence building in the history between the US and the Union of Soviet Socialist Republics (USSR), particularly the agreements that prevented serious maritime incidents during the Cold War. In this article, there is also an assessment of the current MOU of Rules of Behavior with a study of the case of the US naval vessel trespassing in waters within close distance of China's control. There is also a discussion of the South China Sea under the Freedom of Navigation Program and an identification of generic problems and possible policy implications of the agreement.

China–US sea and air close encounters: From 2000 to present

Following several dangerous maritime encounters between the China and US navies, the two countries started consultation of managing the potential crisis at sea. Therefore, in January 1998, the two countries signed the Military Maritime Consultation Agreement (MMCA) as a "mechanism to strengthen military maritime safety, which will enable their maritime and air forces to avoid accidents, misunderstandings or miscalculations." The MMCA established three levels of dialogue channels: annual meeting, working group meeting, and special meetings to discuss specific issues of military activities in the sea and air. By December 2015, the two navies had held 12 annual conferences, 21 working group meetings, and two special meetings.[1]

The MMCA is successful in terms of facilitating consultations between the two Departments of Defense, but it failed to prevent close encounters and incidents between military aircrafts and vessels. In April 2001, a US Ep-3 reconnaissance aircraft collided with a Chinese F-8 fighter jet in the airspace near the Hainan Island and resulted in the casualty of the Chinese pilot Wang Wei. The EP-3 had an emergency landing at the Lingshui Airport of Hainan province, and the local government held the crew for seven days. The September MMCA meeting in Guam and the December meeting in Beijing addressed this incident specifically.[2]

In March 2009, three Chinese law enforcement vessels approached the US surveillance ships USNS Impeccable and Victorious when conducting similar intelligence-gathering activities without the approval of the Chinese government. Later in May, two Chinese vessels approached USNS Victorious for the same reason. The USNS Victorious used its water hose towards the Chinese vessel. In December 2013, the USS missile cruiser Cowpens conducted surveillance activities[3] near China's aircraft carrier Liaoning task group in the South China Sea, despite a warning from the Chinese. In August 2015, the US Navy Poseiden sub-hunter and Chinese J-11 fighter jet close encountered over the South China Sea air space.

The Impeccable, Bowditch, and Victorious are all civilian-manned units of the US special Missions Program of the Military Sealift Command (MSC), but their missions are different. The Bowditch is an "oceanographic survey ship," while the Impeccable and Victorious are "ocean surveillance vessels." Apparently, the surveillance vessels were conducting intelligence-gathering activities for military purposes, but the Bowditch was conducting survey activity. There is significant controversy as to whether or not the coastal state should have regulated such activity. China protested that the activities of US naval ship Bowditch were conducting in China's Exclusive economic zone were in contravention of international law, while the US argued that it was an oceanographic research vessel, not naval, and asserted a right of free passage and survey activities in "international waters."[4] They were part of the high seas freedoms of navigation preserved by the UNCLOS in Article 58. The two states also differ on the interpretation of terms in the UNCLOS, such as "peaceful purpose," "abuse of rights," "survey," and "marine scientific research."

Before China started land reclamation projects in the South China Sea, most of the incidents were about the US conducting surveillance and intelligence-gathering activities in the waters of China's jurisdiction. In recent years, the US has increased the number of FON operations in the South China Sea, and the focus changed from surveillance to challenging China's law and practice of innocent passage and reclamation work in the South China Sea. On October 27, 2015, the US Navy sent its Arleigh Burke-class guided missile destroyer "Lassen" to provocatively patrol within 12 nautical miles off Zhubi Reef of Nansha Islands without the permission from China, and, as a result, China sent warships to monitor, follow, and warn "Lassen." On December 10, two US Air Force B-52 strategic bombers trespassed in the airspace near China's Nansha Islands and Reefs without authorization. The Chinese army maintained a close surveillance on the two bombers, gave warnings, and expelled them. On January 30, 2016, without notification and authorization, the US Navy dispatched Arleigh Burke-class guided missile destroyer "Curtis Wilbur" to navigate within the adjacent waters of Zhongjian Island of the Xisha Islands. China's force on the island gave warnings and expelled it from the waters. On May 10, 2016, the US Navy missile destroyer "Lawrence" sailed into the adjacent waters of Yongshu Reef of the Nansha Islands without the permission from China. The Chinese monitored, followed, gave warnings to the US ship, and finally expelled it.

The US Department of Defense asserted that the operations conducted by "Lassen," "Curtis Wilbur," and "Lawrence" were regular activities to maintain "freedom of navigation."[5] The Chinese foreign ministry responded by saying that the US sent military vessels and aircraft one after another to the relevant waters and airspace of the South China Sea to flex its military muscle and create tensions, and that such activities had constituted serious military provocations.[6] China holds the opinion that these operations posed a threat to the safety of the facilities and personnel on the islands and reefs, as well as a threat to China's sovereignty and security interests, which could lead to militarization in the South China Sea and undermine regional peace and stability.

Unlike previous FON operations, it is still not clear what excessive maritime claims the Lassen operation was challenging, and US scholars have different competing views on the topic. Bonnie Glaser from the CSIS and Peter Dutton from the US Naval War College argued that this FON operation was based on the UNCLOS and the geography of the Spratly Island. Subi Reef is located within 12 nm of Sandy Cay, and can be used as a base point for Sandy Cay's territorial sea. There is a 12 nautical mile territorial sea around Subi Reef, generated by Sandy Cay. Therefore, unlike many experts' assertions, the intension of the Lassen operation is not to challenge the territorial sea around Subi Reef. Rather, the intent of the operation was to exercise freedom of navigation consistent with international law, and to demonstrate that China's building of artificial islands will not change how the US operates in the waters and airspace of the South China Sea. Additionally, contrary to international law, Chinese domestic law requires prior notification for warships to exercise innocent passage.[7]

Glaser and Dutton tried to make a reasonable explanation for the behavior of the US Navy from the perspective of international law, but their views were contradictory, failing to explain the deeds of the US Navy. In the article "The US Asserts Freedom of Navigation in the South China Sea" co-authored by Glaser, Michael Green and Gregory Poling on October 27, 2015, the authors remarked that this particular operation was intended to assert that the US does not recognize a 12 nm territorial sea, or any other maritime entitlements generated by reefs that were originally submerged on which China has built artificial islands. Later Bonnie Glaser and Peter Dutton tried to find rationale for innocent passage by arguing that there is a 12 nautical mile territorial sea around Subi Reef, generated by Sandy Cay, and so high seas freedoms do not apply around the built-up low-tide elevations.[8] According to this latter view, the previous article should have pointed out the lack of international law basis of the FON operation.

What is also worth mentioning is that the US recent patrols and navigations near the China-controlled features have been declared high profile and with a lot of media hype, a phenomenon that has never been seen in any waters and in any country. For example, before USS Lassen sailed within the adjacent waters of Zhubi Reef, US anti-submarine patrol aircraft P-8A carried CNN reporters in its patrol in the South China Sea in May 2015, and relevant video and recording were released to the public. In October 2015, Admiral Harry Harris, Commander of the US Pacific Command, said in his interview with Japan's NHK that under order from the US President Barack Obama, the US Navy had made everything ready for patrolling within 12 nautical miles of China's Nansha islands and reefs. He also stated that this was the most direct counter-measure against China's ongoing island construction activities. After "Lassen" sailed within the adjacent waters of Zhubi Reef, the US Department of Defense immediately released information to relevant media, announcing that "Lassen" had entered the adjacent waters of Zhubi Reef in the South China Sea and that the patrol would last a few hours. These practices have been very different from the usual practice of implementing the FON program.

Cooperative security and confidence-building measures (CBMs)

Prevention of maritime crisis is under the umbrella of CBMs, an important instrument both in theory and in practice for managing international crisis. The history of international relations shows that it is difficult for a state to bolster its own chance of survival without threatening the survival of other states. Even if a state only pursues its own security, and means no harm to its neighbors, other countries may still feel unsafe. Actions taken by a state to heighten its security can lead other states to respond with similar measures, producing increased tensions that create conflict, even when no side really desires it. This creates a "security dilemma."[9] At a symposium in 1988 entitled "Cooperative security in the Pacific Basin," the concept of "cooperative security" was introduced.[10] It indicates that two or more sides should work together to reduce risks and avoid attrition of national strength. Canadian scholar David Dewitt thinks that the key to cooperative security theory is to cultivate the habit of dialogue and pursue an inclusive approach to all participants.[11] "Cooperative security" has three-fold meanings. First, the term is inclusive and emphasizes that both state actors and non-state actors, as well as both like-minded and non-like-minded actors, can be engaged in the process of cooperative security. Second, the participating actors should cultivate the habit of dialogue. They should have dialogue on a regular basis because formal dialogue will bring about long-term interests. Third, security should arise through cooperation. Because of the manifold security problems in the current world, such as transnational crimes and environmental issues, that have transcended national boundaries and cannot be resolved through unilateral actions, there needs to be a concerted effort of international and domestic actors.[12]

There has not been a universally accepted definition of cooperative security. One famous definition is "a commitment to regulate the size, technical composition, investment patterns, and operational practices of all military forces by mutual consent for mutual benefit."[13] Some American scholars have expanded the connotation of security cooperation to incorporate cooperation among major powers. For example, they once proposed that the US and the former Soviet Union should establish cooperative security to ensure stability and security of the third world and reduce the risks of conflict.[14] Some scholars from Southeast Asian countries argue that the cooperative security should be designed to prevent, contain, and handle differences and disputes, promote regional dynamics, as well as finally realize international common security through regional cooperation and peaceful means.[15]

Therefore, the cooperative security theory is an inevitable outcome of the background of balance of terror and does not come into being by chance.[16] One prerequisite of cooperative security is that all states hope to avoid war, but in the actual operational process, cooperative security requires all states to gradually build confidence, which mainly entails making the right judgment on other countries' military intentions. In addition, while promoting international mutual confidence, cooperative security theory also stresses that international systems and institutions can be used to guarantee this confidence and prevent collapse. Judging by the current international relations practice, incorporating sources of potential threat into the framework of cooperative security helps to promote international confidence and may be more effective than military alliance in safeguarding the security of a state.

As defined by the Center for Strategic and International Studies (CSIS), CBMs are broadly defined as measures that address, prevent, or resolve uncertainties among states.[17] Designed to prevent wanted and especially unwanted escalations of hostilities and build mutual trust, CBMs can be formal or informal, unilateral, bilateral, or multilateral, military or political, and can be state-to-state or non-governmental. They are particularly pertinent in addressing and working towards the resolution of long-term political stalemates.

Belgium and Italy first proposed the concept of confidence-building measures (CBMs), and the 1973–1975 Helsinki Conference on Security and Cooperation in Europe adopted the concept.[18] States dealt with CBMs in a small section of the 1975 Helsinki Final Act, which was entitled "Document on Confidence-Building Measures and Certain Aspects of Security and Disarmament."[19] Originally, NATO in 1975 used CBMs at the Helsinki Conference on Security and Cooperation in Europe as a means to counter the Soviet Union, but officials of Western countries soon diminished the military utility of CBMs, thinking that the CBMs could only have political and psychological impacts.[20] For lack of a clear political orientation, there were different interpretations on the targets of CBMs. Eventually, Europe, as the front of the West–East face-off, became the birthplace of CBMs. Because in Europe military activities were strictly confidential, they could have been mistaken for a potential hostile act, triggering confrontation or military conflict. Instead, following the rules of the routine military activities can reduce the risk of conflict, and "help distinguish definite hostility from casual, ongoing military activities."[21]

CBMs are the first step from crisis management to security cooperation. Military exchanges take various shapes, and the levels of cooperation are different. As a security cooperation mechanism, states mainly design CBMs to avoid conflicts. The most significant function of CBMs is to reduce tensions and avoid the risk of conflict. The CBMs, either in unwritten understandings or written agreements between hostile states, must be able to ensure or strengthen the safety of relevant states, promote military transparency, and help identify the intent or threat of potential adversaries. Exchanging military observers can make one state have a more thorough understanding of the intention of another state's military activities, and enhance the level of the military exchanges. Commonly banning or restricting certain military activities is very important to limiting the risk of conflict and the improvement of bilateral relations. Limiting the number and scale of certain military actions of potential threats helps reduce the possibility of conflict. Banning certain military actions in sensitive areas could also reduce the risk of triggering preemptive strikes. However, limiting, restricting, or banning military activities usually comes as the second phase of CBMs implementation process after more moderate measures have been tried. All the above measures are designed to create the right atmosphere to achieve the main targets of CBMs, including arms control and disarmament. These expectations for CBMs require all relevant sides to give up confrontation, and ensure each side conducts their military activities for peaceful purposes. These expectations also confirm the fact that states can change their thinking on security.

From a strategic level, states intend CBMs to help eliminate mutual suspicion, give up the concept of deterrence via arms race, and finally realize common security as well as peaceful and friendly coexistence. Therefore, CBMs at political and military levels are a strategic target that serves as the foundation of stable international relations. Of course, in today's fast-globalized world, available time determines the ability of states to build confidence at official, track-II, and people-to-people levels. In practice, CBMs can go from the military domain and the security domain (including releasing defense white paper, national defense policy, and military strategy, etc.), and then rise to the international level. Therefore, the areas where states can practice CBMs expand from the military domain to other varied domains of different states.

Most scholars would not define the 1998 MMCA mechanism as a successful CBM model. First, it does not contain any substantial provisions on military maneuvers. Compared with the 1972 US–Soviet Union INCSEA Agreement and other maritime CBMs, the most significant feature of the 1998 China–US MMCA is that it simply creates a consultation mechanism and makes provisions regarding the channels of communication, the personnel to be involved, and the agenda to be set and other details. The 1998 MMCA does not, however, put forward any specific measures to address specific issues, such as how Chinese and US military ships and aircraft should act when they encounter each other, what rules they should follow, and how they should communicate. The most conspicuous role of the 1998 China–US MMCA is to establish a platform for direct military exchanges between China and the US for the first time, establishing a preliminary basis for bolstering military mutual trust. In essence, it is more like an initial – rather than final – agreement on Sino-US military confidence building. So far, more than 10 years of discussions have not yielded any substantial results. This stagnant mechanism has resulted in a lack of sound mechanism to prevent maritime incidents, and the military aircraft and ships do not have operable rules to follow in the course of interaction in case of an unintentional encounter.

Second, the 1998 China–US MMCA does not produce a regular mechanism and is susceptible to political factors. After signing the INCSEA Agreement in 1972, the US and the Soviet Union never halted the annual meeting mechanism under its framework, in spite of disagreement in the bilateral relations and the suspension of strategic arms limitation talks and other military consultation mechanisms. This regularized mechanism helped the two sides build a long-term cooperative relationship, bolstering trust and helping to dispel suspicions in case of a crisis. Annual meetings served as a window for the two sides to conduct military exchanges, avoid miscalculations, and manage crises. By contrast, political events such as the US arms sales to Taiwan have always interfered with the China–US military maritime consultation mechanism.

Third, the 1998 China–US MMCA plays a relatively limited role in improving military mutual trust and military relations. China–US military exchanges and cooperation are still at a low level. During the past consultations, the two sides mainly reaffirmed their respective positions and even accused each other. The US repeatedly accused the Chinese military ships and aircraft of taking risky measures, threatening the safety of US military personnel, while China stressed that the root cause of the air and maritime incidents was the US close-in reconnaissance. This situation is not in line with the fundamental purpose of CBMs.

Since the US declared its "Rebalancing" strategy towards the Asia-Pacific in 2010, China and the US have been in an emerging security dilemma. Driven by the "rebalancing" strategy, the US has gradually built up its troop deployments, forward presence, and military activities in the region, and has focused on increasing military cooperation with its regional allies and partners such as Japan, the Philippines, Vietnam, and Malaysia. It seems from its official strategic report series that the US will continue to increase troop deployment and forward presence in the Philippines, Singapore, Malaysia and other ASEAN countries, and will bolster military activities in the South China Sea waters and surrounding areas.[22]

Chinese President Xi Jinping called for establishing a "new type of military relations" on November 12, 2014 during a meeting with US President Barack Obama in the US.[23] To build such a relationship under the framework of the new model of major-country relations is an integral part of China's US policy in the new era. This new military-to-military relationship echoes and compliments the principles of "non-conflict, non-confrontation, mutual respect, and win-win cooperation" in the new model of relationship. However, it is widely believed in China that the "rebalancing" strategy aims to contain and restrain China's rise, but the US perceives an increasingly aggressive rising China, with a desire to explore maritime rights excessively. However, on the other side, the military relationship between the two is quite stable and predictable. The two governments pay close attention to maintaining and developing military-to-military exchanges and cooperation with each other in recent years, and such exchanges and cooperation is an essential component of its relations with China and its Asia-Pacific strategy. In particular, the two states have made efforts in conducting bilateral and multilateral practical cooperation in non-traditional security fields, such as counter-piracy, maritime search and rescue, humanitarian aid, and disaster prevention and mitigation, as well as in key areas in Asia-Pacific and beyond. The purpose of engaging China in these activities is essentially three-fold: first, maintain smooth communication channels with the Chinese military at a high level in order to expeditiously convey messages in times of emergency or contingency, and to manage crisis and differences; second, directly learn the progress of China's military modernization and new military reform, and improve the US perception of the Chinese military strengths; and third, maintain the positive side of US–China relations to serve the strategic needs of the US engagement policy with China.

INCSEA And DMAA agreement between US and USSR

The Prevention of Incidents on and over the High Seas (INCSEA) agreement signed in 1972 between the US and the USSR is the most quoted treaty in the study of CBMs and collision prevention. During the Cold War, both the US and USSR conducted dangerous operations at sea and in the air, and caused several serious incidents. In 1968, the USS Essex collided with a Soviet TU-16 Badger bomber in the Norwegian Sea, resulted in the death of all the crew.[24] Additionally, a number of such collisions happen during that period. The US initiated the idea of this agreement in 1967 when the frequency and severity of maritime incidents between navies were increasing.[25] The two states then started negotiation in 1971, with the first round in Moscow, and second round in Washington, D.C. The INCSEA agreement was immediately entered into force after signature. Although the Convention on the International Regulations for Preventing Collisions at Sea (COLREGs) was not yet in force, the agreement requires that ship commanders should observe the spirit and letter of it strictly. Article III of the INCSEA Agreement describes what behavior commanders should take during close encounter:

1. In all cases ships operating in proximity to each other shall remain well clear to avoid risk of collision;
2. Ships meeting or operating in the vicinity of a formation of the other party shall avoid maneuvering in a manner which would hinder the evolutions of the formation;
3. Formations shall not conduct maneuvers through areas of heavy traffic where internationally recognized traffic separation schemes are in effect;
4. Ships engaged in surveillance of other ships shall stay at a distance which avoids the risk of collision and also shall avoid executing maneuvers embarrassing or endangering the ships under surveillance;
5. When maneuvering in sight of one another, such signals (flag, sound, and light) as are prescribed by the Rules of the Road, the International Code of Signals, or other mutually agreed signals, shall be adhered to for signaling operations and intentions;
6. Ships shall not simulate attacks by aiming guns, missile launchers, torpedo tubes, and other weapons in the direction of a passing ship of the other party, not launch any object in the direction of passing ships of the other party, and not use searchlights or other powerful illumination devices to illuminate the navigation bridges of passing ships of the other party;
7. When conducting exercises with submerged submarines, exercising ships shall show the appropriate signals prescribed by the International Code of Signals to warn ships of the presence of submarines in the area; and
8. When approaching ships of the other Party conducting operations and particularly ships engaged in launching or landing aircraft as well as ships engaged in replenishment underway, shall take appropriate measures not to hinder maneuvers of such ships and shall remain well clear.[26]

The unique features of the INCSEA agreement is that it confirms the importance of the COLREGs, specifies clearly that each side should avoid conducting dangerous maneuvers and provides rules to follow, as well as an annual review set out in Article IX. The annual review article was later concluded in many bilateral and multilateral arms control agreements, for its success in creating a communication channel for US and USSR navies to build trust and confidence, through the review of implementation of the agreement and exchange of other information.[27] During the war in the Middle East in 1973, the INCSEA agreement was tested, in which 150 US and USSR naval vessels were crowded into the eastern Mediterranean seas, creating a highly tense atmosphere.[28] Thanks to the implementation of the agreement, the crisis did not burst into military conflict between the two navies. In the second half of the 1980s, the US and USSR relationship again became exacerbated, and the military leaders started to exchange views outside the INCSEA structure, with a focus on issues such as the use of lasers, establishing caution areas around ships, and others.[29] On June 12, 1989, the two states signed the Agreement between the Government of the United States of America and the Government of the Union of Soviet Socialist Republics on the Prevention of Dangerous Military Activities (DMAA) in Moscow.[30]

The specific military issues in the DMAA include entering the other state's national territory either unintentionally or by force majeure; the use of laser to damage equipment or hurt personnel of the other party; prohibition of the other party's activities in a special caution area; and interference with the control and command networks.[31] The DMAA for the first time covered certain military activities on land. Its Articles III-IV further elaborates on the four kinds of military activities. For example, it requires military personnel of the parties to have great caution and prudence while operating within close proximity to the national territory of the other party. Article IV outlines the use of lasers, requiring notification to the opposing party before using a laser.

Although the US–USSR agreement is a successful model of CBMs, negotiating one between China and the US is a different story. The disparity of sea power and strategic needs is the most significant obstacle. The success of negotiation is dependent on equal bargain. One reason why the US and the Soviet Union were able to agree on specific measures to prevent maritime incidents was that the two sides were relatively equal sea powers and had common interests on formulating a code of conduct. In the early years of the Cold War, the US took an absolute lead in gathering intelligence via aircraft and ships because of its extensive network of military bases in Europe and Asia. The Soviet Navy, however, did not possess the capability to conduct in-depth surveillance on the homeland of the US or US military presence outside its homeland, and it was not able to counter effectively the close-in reconnaissance conducted by the US. Because the US received large benefits from this disparity, it was natural for it to engage in negotiation with the Soviet Union. The Soviet Union, refusing to make concessions in close-in reconnaissance, was also reluctant to negotiate with the US. In the 1960s, however, the Soviet Union put into service a large number of intelligence-gathering ships and Tu-95 warplanes, thus greatly improving its intelligence-gathering capabilities. Its operations covered the areas off the US coast, the North American Air Defense Identification Zone, and US naval units around the globe.[32] As a result, incidents at sea began to become more frequent. According to a 1972 US report, 32 out of 79 incidents at sea in the previous six years were related to espionage vessels. Such incidents made the US feel the urgent need to restrict Soviet Union's maneuvers via negotiation.[33] From one perspective, equal surveillance capability of the Soviet Union qualified itself as a counterpart with the US at the negotiating table. Conversely, the Soviet Union, with enhanced capability, hoped to continue its maneuvers by ensuring its safety. Therefore, the two sides' negotiating positions gradually converged.

However, relatively inferior naval capabilities do not enable China to negotiate with the US on an equal basis. Although the Chinese navy has made great strides because of China's much improved comprehensive national strength and Chinese military modernization, it still lags far behind the US Navy. In addition, the Chinese navy is primarily focused on maintaining territorial sovereignty and maritime rights, and has no intention of conducting reconnaissance maneuvers in the exclusive economic zone of the US. Besides, the 1972 US–Soviet Union INCSEA Agreement included clauses granting extra protection to aircraft carriers on which aircraft were taking off or landing and warships being replenished. If these were applied to Chinese and naval forces, they would be obviously in favor of the US Navy. The US commands an absolute advantage at sea, so it does not feel the urgent need to negotiate with China, which could undermine the freedom enjoyed by its navy.

Some scholars advocate a similar INCSEA agreement to avoid incidents between China and the US, while the US naval scholars do not support this. Pete Pedrozo (2012) listed six reasons why there is no need for such an agreement between the two states. He argues that first, the Chinese navy is far from being a "blue water" navy compared to the Soviet navy. Signing such an agreement means upgrading the Chinese navy, which is not the US interest. Second, unlike the US and the USSR, China and the US do not have a common interest in freedom of navigation; therefore, the different legal interpretation on some of the law of the sea rules would not be reconciled. Third, most of the incidents between China and the US are not navy-to-navy but navy-to-law enforcement vessels or fishing vessels, so a navy-to-navy agreement would not help. Fourth, the INCSEA agreement is a Cold War product, and it is not appropriate to define the China–US relationship in such terms. Fifth, he characterizes China as a "non-responsible" state actor, as not reliable since it breaks promises and conducts aggressive actions towards its neighbors. Finally, there exist widely recognized rules and documents on the prevention of incidents such as the COLREGs, so there is no need for a new one.[34] In stating that another new agreement between the two is a duplicate of COLREGS, Kraska (2011) expresses the same opinion, highlighting the sense of rivalry among the two countries.[35]

It is true that the Chinese navy is still not yet a blue-water navy as the USSR, and the tension and incidents between the two are not complete as well. Compared to the US–USSR maritime incidents, the maritime standoffs between

China and the US have been relatively controllable. In the 1960s, maritime incidents between the US and the Soviet Union happened throughout the globe, even averaging at more than 40 each year. In the recent 10 years, despite occasional frictions between China and the US, the frequency is far lower than that in the Cold War. In most cases, there have been no casualties, and the incidents have mainly occurred in China's coastal waters. A Chinese scholar summarized China–US maritime incidents as "non-intentional, non-violent, non-strategic and non-challenging," and further argued that they were mostly infrequent, low-level accidents between non-hostile countries, neither of which intended to stir up maritime conflicts to challenge the other's core interests. Therefore, most of the maritime conflicts between China and the US have ended within a short period, and these did not cause any long-lasting outcomes. Therefore, creating the same INCSEA Agreement as the US and USSR has not been an urgent priority.

However, to not support a bilateral agreement between the two most important maritime states is an overconfident position that could undermine regional stability. It is also a shortsighted view considering the escalation of the South China Sea issue. Written in 2012, these papers represent the thinking of US naval scholars at that time, when the US just applied its Pivot to Asia strategy and China's Aircraft Carrier Liaoning had not yet set out for sea trials.[36] Driven by the Pivot to Asia strategy, the US has gradually built up its troop deployments, forward presence, and military activities in the region, and has increased military cooperation with its regional allies and partners, such as Japan, the Philippines, Vietnam, and Malaysia. Establishing such agreements will benefit not just the military-to-military relationship but also peace and stability in the South China Sea region.

The law of collision and the 1972 COLREGs and Codes For Unplanned Encounter at Sea (CUES)

Most of the rules of behavior in the 2014 China–US MOU are drawn from the technical specifics of the 1972 Convention on the International Regulations for Preventing Collisions at Sea (COLREGs). Therefore, it is necessary to review the law of collision to see the deficiencies in the application of these rules. The Black's Law Dictionary defines the term "collision" as "the act of ships or vessels striking together."[37] Maritime law also uses this definition. The origins of collision law are still obscure.[38] L. Aquilio Gallo drafted the first Roman law on this subject, Lex Aquilia, in 467 A. D.[39] Later in 1360, the English Admiralty Court is widely seen as the originator of the law when the civil maritime cases were started under the Lord High Admiral's jurisdiction. In the 1815, Woodrop-Sims case, two vessels, the Woodrop-Sims and Industry, crashed into each other off the South Foreland. Sir William Scott established four principles of collision law in his judgment: (1) in an inevitable accident such as in a storm, none of the vessels is to blame; (2) both vessels are to blame if require due diligence; (3) the suffering vessel must bear its own cost if the reason is its misconduct; (4) and when the fault is clearly on one side, the injured vessel could get an entire compensation from the other side.[40] These principles remain largely true today.

During the nineteenth century, modern law of collision developed greatly due to the advent of steam and the promulgation of a set of navigation principles, as well as collision and pilot rules. The first conference on navigation rules was held in Washington in 1889, resulting in the birth of a set of rules, in 1897, that influenced the world.[41] In the later conferences, 1910 in Brussels, and 1948 and 1960 in London, participants made minor changes about these rules.[42]

States adopted the currently used navigational rules in the 1972 London Conference, initiated by the Intergovernmental Maritime Consultative Organization (IMCO); the organization later became the International Maritime Organization (IMO).[43] The states adopted the COLREGs on October 20, and entered into force on July 15, 1977,[44] with an aim to update and replace the collision regulations of 1960, and provide specific guidance to mariners on how to avoid maritime collision, as well as providing some rules of apportioning blame after incidents.

The COLREGS rules provide various guidelines for navigation officers regarding crossing, passing, and overtaking maneuvers, as well as the actions ships should take under certain circumstances. The COLREGs consist of 38 rules broken into five parts: Part A-General, Part B-Steering and Sailing, Part C-Lights and Shapes, Part D-Sound and Light Signals, and Part E-Exemptions. It sets a series of rules of behaviors with the aim of standardizing navigational practices, thus often referred to as "International Rules of the Road."[45] The COLREGs specifies responsibilities of mariners when maneuvering in close distance, general standards of prudent navigation, lightening configurations for vessels, and signals of danger or distress.

The annexes of maritime and air encounters directly use the rules in the COLREGs to which both China and the US are parties, but there are certain obstacles of applying COLREGs rules to the China–US situation. First, officials wrote the COLREGs with the assumption that the navigators on the vessel would have a complete understanding of the situation, know exactly which rules were in effect, and know the right course of action. Belcher holds that COLREGs operate in an environment of mutual respect, understanding, comprehension, and coordination, with clear steps that guarantee predictability and clarity.[46]

None of the maritime encounters in the South and East China Seas between China and the US have been unplanned. They are "purposeful and perhaps expected intercepts designed to send a message."[47] Therefore, it is unlikely for the naval captains to follow logical steps to ensure clarity and predictability. For example, in November 2013, the Chinese aircraft carrier Liaoning was conducting her first deployment from Qingdao to the South China Sea, accompanied by two destroyers, the Shijiazhuang and Shenyang, and two missile frigates, Weifang and Yantai. The guided missile cruiser USS Cowpens closely monitored the military drills in the South China Sea. On December 5, the Chinese naval vessel contacted the Cowpens through the radio and asked it to leave the drilling area, because it was trespassing in a "no-sail zone" in the South China Sea.[48] Reports indicate that the Cowpens entered within the inner defense layer of 45 kilometer of the Liaoning carrier group and was "tailing after and harassing the Liaoning formation,"[49] but the Cowpens decided not to leave, for "it was operating in international waters."[50] The US media reported that the Chinese Amphibious Dock Ship suddenly crossed its bow and the distance was less than 500 meters when it stopped. Clearly, the primary issue in this case was intentions not communication. Both were professional seafarers. They did apply the MOU rules Section III, ii of Annex 2, which was directly taken from the COLREGs, "when one side initiates a call, the other side should respond promptly,"[51] but this approach did not help prevent the close encounter and possible collision. Nonetheless, there are also other general problems with the COLREGs, such as the difficulty to apply the rules in different situations and locations at sea, the fact that officials have not updated some of its rules since 1972, and the inadequacy in using the rules with advanced-equipped vessels.

Another contributor of preventing miscalculation and misunderstanding is the Codes for Unplanned Encounters at Sea (CUES). The Western Pacific Naval Symposium (WPNS) is a meeting of the Pacific states established in 1987 to discuss naval matters held on a biennial basis.[52] It began to discuss the procedures to prevent maritime incidents between navies since 2000. In the 2014 Symposium, the CUES was finally signed by 21 member states, including Australia, Brunei, Cambodia, Canada, Chile, China, France, Indonesia, Japan, Malaysia, New Zealand, Papua New Guinea, Peru, the Philippines, Russia, Singapore, South Korea, Thailand, Tonga, the US, and Vietnam.[53] Bangladesh, India, Mexico, and Peru are observers to the WPNS mechanism.

Chinese People's Liberation Army Navy (PLAN) Commander Admiral Wu Shengli stated the 2014 symposium reached its goal of "broadening horizons, enhancing mutual understanding and deepening friendship."[54] The then Commander of the US Pacific Fleet, Admiral Harry Harris, appraised CUES as an important step forward in the prevention of tension on the sea.[55]

CUES is a voluntary agreement with no legal binding force. The agreement is a de-escalation mechanism that provides safety procedures and means of communication for navy commanders to eliminate uncertainty and miscalculation of close encounter. Part 2 contains standard safety procedures, such as a disabled ship should make at least six short blasts on the whistle and hoist two black balls to inform other ships; a single naval ships is suggested to adopt measures to stay away from a formation or convoy; and vessels are also required to keep a safe speed and distance as in the rules of COLREGs. Part 2 of CUES states that in joint exercises, surface vessels should display certain signals from the International Code of Signals to notify the presence of submarines in the water area.[56]

Part 3 of CUES describes standard communication procedures, and Annex A lists the basic maneuvering instructions and selected signals vocabulary.[57] Part 3 reaffirms the rules of COLREGs, specifying sailors should use sound, light, and flag signals when encountering others during maneuvers. Radio is also encouraged as the preferable method to communicate when encountering others. Also in Part 3 are call signs, voice procedures, exchange of key information, and tack line. In addition, the technical rules of the agreement are helpful to prevent collision. The CUES also serves as effective CBMs in the region, enabling navies to cooperate and de-conflict operations at sea. On April 24, 2015, China and the US Navy vessels, the PLA Amphibious Dock Landing Ship Jinggangshan and the USS Blue Ridge, conducted a joint military exercise practicing CUES. Later in November, after the USS Stethem finished a port visit in Wusong naval port, it conducted with the Chinese counterpart another communication exercises involving the use of CUES. Besides the China–US practice, CUES also calls for a joint exercise with ASEAN states, to enhance the use of its language and build confidence among the navies.

Given its success in confidence building and crisis prevention, some South China Sea States, such as Singapore, advocate expanding the CUES to law enforcement agencies in the region, to avoid possible future conflict between these vessels and defuse regional tension. After adoption, the Chinese and American navies conducted many exercises for implementing CUES.

Assessing the MOUs and China–US confidence building measures (CBMs)

The MOU on Notification of Major Military Activities contains four sections and two annexes. The preamble to the MOU stresses the desire of the two to reduce risk, reduce the potential for misunderstanding and miscalculation, and to develop a "new model of China-US military-to-military relations."[58] The preamble also mentions that the participants should conduct the activities "on the basis of the principles of constructive cooperation, mutual interest, mutual trust, mutual benefit, and reciprocity, consistent with accepted international norms of behavior."[59] Section III establishes an annual assessment working group meeting, under the framework of the Defense Policy Coordination Talks. Section IV stresses that it is a voluntary document, and that content of notifications should not be disclosed to third parties without written approval of the other side.

The three annexes of the military activities notification MOU are Notification of Major Security Policy and Strategy Developments, Observation of Military Exercises and Activities, and Military Crisis Notification Mechanism for Use of the Defense Telephone Link. Although a big step forward on military confidence building, the MOU may have limited contribution to preventing possible conflicts at sea. Conversely, unlike the INCSEA and DMAA, which deal directly with the most contentious issues between the two military forces during that time, such as intelligence gathering and use of lasers, the military notification MOU only includes the least sensitive and controversial issues. Therefore, the diverging views of China and the US regarding intelligence-gathering activities in the EEZ, innocent passage of warships, and the use of unmanned underwater vehicles in naval operations remains untouched. In contrast, all three annexes stress that the activities should be "voluntary," and that there is no punishment for not applying the rules. It seems that both countries do not want to have a legally binding agreement to restrain them from possible future dangerous activities at sea.

The Memorandum of Understanding on Notification of Major Military Activities and the Memorandum of Understanding Regarding the Rules of Behavior for Safety of Air and Maritime Encounters did not create new rules to apply during encounter. Instead, they rely on the existing multilateral agreements, including the International Regulations for Preventing Collision at Sea (COLREGs), the Code for Unplanned Encounters at Sea (CUES), the ICAO, and the UNCLOS.

The Rules of Behavior Memorandum contains five sections and two annexes. Section I of the memorandum stresses the desire of the two sides to improve navigation and aviation safety, as well as to establish a "new type of military-to-military relationship."[60] To that end, they commit themselves to apply the rules of behavior when countering the other party at sea or in the air. The three annexes, namely Terms of Reference of the Rules of Behavior for Safety of Air and Maritime Encounters, Rules of Behavior for Safety of Surface-to-Surface Encounters, and Rules of Behavior for Safety of Air-to-Air Encounters, finished in the 2015, provides guidance for captains of both sides when encountering the other party at sea.

Both China and the US praised the MOUs for playing a positive role in risk reduction in the maritime space, especially the South China Sea. The US sees it as a step forward for bringing China into the ruled-based maritime order, and China is satisfied with the US, agreeing to apply these rules while conducting close reconnaissance activities. However, for three reasons, the MOUs are still far from sufficient as an antidote for the potential danger. First, Section IV states that an annual assessment meeting should be conducted to review the application of this MOU in the previous year. This section expressly shows the two states' intention of not making this MOU a legally binding document, which to some extent implies the lack of confidence of applying it strictly. Though both documents are voluntary and have a non-binding nature, reports indicated that both states want to expand the scope of the agreement to include China's missile launches and US arms sales to Taiwan, but failed to reach consensus.[61]

Second, the Rules of Behavior MOU does not specify the corresponding maritime area. Parties must assume that the MOU is applicable in all maritime zones, including territorial sea, EEZ and the high seas, and the South China Sea. However, both parties might find applying the MOU difficult when the intent of the encounter is to send a message. In the Lassen case, Captain of the USS Lassen, Commander Robert Francis said that the vessel travelled within 6–7 nautical miles of the Subi reef and did not warn or notify China in advance. He also stated that the radars on the Lassen were operating during the operation.[62] Reports indicate that when the Chinese vessel asked the Lassen entering the adjacent waters of the Subi, "You are in Chinese waters. What is your intention?" Commander Francis responded that the Lassen was "operating in accordance with international law."[63] However, the Chinese Naval Chief Wu Shengli said that the Chinese naval vessel communicated to the Lassen several times using the language of CUES, but that the US ignored the communication.[64]

Thirdly, as some skeptical scholars stated, the MOUs does not deal with the differences between China and the US, such as intelligence-gathering activities in the coastal state's EEZ, interpretation of the UNCLOS term "peaceful purposes," "freedom of navigation," and "abuse of rights," thus will not be enough for preventing maritime incidents.[65] Indeed, while the MOUs received much praise, the fundamental differences between China and the US remains, as the 2014 MOU referred to "existing international law and norms" without explaining what they were. Lastly, the agreement states that the exchange of information between the two states should remain confidential, including the assessments of conduct. The confidential clause of the MOU makes it difficult for observers to evaluate the extent of its implementation.

Though many problems and unsolved issues exist, the MOU still contributes much to the confidence building between the two navies. In fact, China and the US have intensified military-to-military exchanges over the past years, relaxing the "security dilemma" between the two, despite the tensions in the South China Sea. In the 2016 China–US Strategic & Economic Dialogue Outcomes of the Strategic Track, China and the US reaffirmed the importance of the MOUs and committed to implement "the CBMs by incorporating exercises related to the Rules of Behavior for Safety of Air and Maritime Encounters in conjunction with agreed upon port visits and coordinate on discussions of additional annexes to the Notification of Major Military Activities MOU, including a mechanism for informing the other party of ballistic missile launches."[66] Joint exercise is one of the most important means of building trust between the two navies in recent years. From 2012 to 2016, in the field of non-traditional security, the two militaries expanded their exercises on search and rescue to counter-piracy, humanitarian aid, disaster prevention and mitigation, and other areas. In September 2012, the two militaries held a first joint counter-piracy exercise in the Gulf of Aden. In multilateral exercises, the RIMPAC 2014 invited the Chinese Navy for the first time. From June to September, the Chinese Navy sent missile destroyer "Haikou," missile frigate Yueyang, comprehensive supply ship Qiandaohu, and hospital ship Ark Peace as Formation 171 to Hawaii. Despite major differences between China and the US over some maritime issues, RIMPAC 2016 invited the Chinese navy again to participate.

Conclusion

The 2014 Notification of Major Military Activities and Rules of Behavior MOUs are military-to-military CBMs that mainly specify the rules of behavior for the pilots to maintain flight safety during air-to-air encounters between military aircraft. The MOUs also specify basic principles for communications, rules for establishing or announcing specially designated areas such as danger areas or warning areas, peacetime security assurance measures, and rules for emergency on-scene coordination. Instead of serving as an effective regime of preventing incidents, the MOUs contribute more to the confidence building between the two navies, trying to relax the "security dilemma" between the two, despite the tensions in the South China Sea.

With the many issues unresolved, such as military survey and marine scientific research, and new disagreements coming out, the annual review conferences established by the MOUs should be conducted as scheduled. The review could serve a platform to exchange views between the two. On December 16, 2016, a Chinese lifeboat identified a device – the Unmanned Underwater Vehicle (UUV) – in the South China Sea, and took it out of the water. After examination, the Chinese Navy returned the UUV to the US Navy. Though President Donald Trump labeled the event "unprecedented,"[67] it was resolved efficiently and peacefully within six days. However, the debate on the legal status of the UUV and military survey in the EEZ went on.[68] One could predict that states will deploy and use more UUVs in naval operations in the future. Considering discussing these issues in the regional security forums such as the WPNS may generate more tension, a more prudent approach is to discuss them within a bilateral forum like the assessing conference of the MOUs. Additionally, the two states should continue to negotiate new annexes of the Military Activities MOU, such as one governing the use of UUVs in naval operations, to use the mechanism to address real issues of divergence and to prevent miscalculation and conflict.

Notes

1 Report on the Military Presence of the United States of America in the Asia-Pacific Region 2016, *National Institute for South China Sea Studies, Current Affairs Press*, 2016, 69.
2 Pete Pedrozo, "The U.S.-China Incidents at Sea Agreement: A Recipe for Disaster," *Journal of National Security Law & Policy* 6 (2012).
3 http://edition.cnn.com/2013/12/13/politics/us-china-confrontation/
4 http://edition.cnn.com/2013/12/13/politics/us-china-confrontation/
5 https://news.usni.org/2016/01/30/u-s-destroyer-challenges-more-chinese-south-china-sea-claims-in-new-freedom-of-navigation-operation
6 http://www.fmprc.gov.cn/mfa_eng/xwfw_665399/s2510_665401/t1362106.shtml
7 http://nationalinterest.org/feature/the-us-navy%E2%80%99s-freedom-navigation-operation-around-subi-reef-14272
8 https://www.csis.org/analysis/us-asserts-freedom-navigation-south-china-sea
9 Kenneth Waltz, *Theory of International Politics* (Long Grove, IL: Waveland Press, 1979).
10 Su Hao, Cong Ya Ling Dao Gan Lan: Ya Tai He Zuo An Quan Mo Shi Fen Xi,World (Knowledge Press, 2003), 53.
11 David B. Dewitt, "Common, Comprehensive and Cooperative security," *The Pacific Review* 7, no.1 (1994): 9–10.
12 David B. Dewett and Amitay Acharya, Cooperative Security and Development Assistance, The Relationship Between Security and Development with Reference to Eastern Asia, *Eastern Asian Policy Paper, No. 16*, Toronto University of Tomonto-York, Joint Centre for Asia Pacific Studies.
13 Ashton B. Carter, William J. Perry, and John D. Steinbruner, *A New Concept of Cooperative Security* (Washington, DC: Brookings Institution, 1992), 6.
14 I. William Aartinan and Victor A. Krethenyuk, ed, *Cooperation Security: Reducing Third World War* (Syracuse, NY: Syracuse University Press, 1995), 289–312.
15 J. Soedjati Djiwondono, "Cooperative Security in the Asia-Pacific Region; An ASEAN Perspective," *The Indonesian Quarterly*, X XII/3 (1994), 203–4.
16 Ashton B. Carter, William J. Perry, and John D. Steinbruner, *A New Concept of Cooperative Security* (Washington, DC: Brookings Institution, 1992), p. 6.

17 www.csis.org/programs/international-security-program/international-security-program-archived-projects/asia-4
18 J.D. Toogood, Helskinki "What was Achieved in the Field of Confidence Building Measures?" *Canadian Defense Quarterly*, 5, no. 2 (1975): 29. For a similar observation almost ten years later, see Goetze, Security in Europe, page 78.
19 Jonathan Alford, The Usefulness and the Limitations of CBMs, in William Epstein and Bernard T. Feld (eds), *New Directions in Disarmament* (New York: Praeger, 1981), p. 135.
20 J.D. Toogood, Helskinki "What was Achieved in the Field of Confidence Building Measures?" *Canadian Defense Quarterly*, 5, no. 2 (1975): 29.
21 Jonathan Alford, "The Usefulness and the Limitations of CBMs," in William Epstein and Bernard T. Feld (eds.), *New Directions in Disarmament* (New York: Praeger, 1981), p. 135.
22 For example the Quadrennial Defense Review (QDR) 2014 states that the U.S. should increase the resiliency of U.S. forward posture and base infrastructure.
23 http://news.xinhuanet.com/english/china/2014-11/12/c_133784921.htm
24 Pete Pedrozo, "The U.S.-China Incidents at Sea Agreement: A Recipe for Disaster," *Journal of National Security Law & Policy* 6 (2012).
25 Ibid. 128.
26 Agreement Between the Government of the United States of America and the Government of the Union of Soviet Socialist Republics on the Prevention of Incidents On and Over the High Seas, Bureau of International Security and Nonproliferation, U.S. Department of State, www.state.gov/t/isn/4791.htm
27 John H. McNeil, "Chapter 43 Military-to-military Arrangements for the Prevention of U.S.-Russian Conflict," in *Naval War College Review, 1978–1994*, (eds.) John Norton Moore and Robert F. Turner, 576.
28 Ibid.
29 Ibid. 577.
30 Timothy J. Nagle, "The Dangerous Military Activities Agreement: Minimum Order and Superpower Relations on the World's Oceans." *Virginia Journal of International Law* 31 (1990): 125.
31 Full text available at: https://en.wikisource.org/wiki/Prevention_of_Dangerous_Military_Activities_Agreement
32 Fang Zhi Hai Shang Shi Jian Yu Zhong Mei Hai Shang Hu Xin Ji Zhi Jian She, Zhang Yuan, and Hu De Kun, *China International Studies* 2 (2014): 98.
33 David F. Winkler, "The Evolution and Significance of the 1972 Incidents at Sea Agreement," *The Journal of Strategic Studies*, 28, no. 2 (2005): 362; Mark E. Redden & Phillip C. Saunders, *Managing Sino-U.S. Air and Naval Interactions: Cold War Lessons and New Avenues of Approach* (Washington, D.C.: National Defense University Press, 2012), 14.
34 Pete Pedrozo, "The U.S.-China Incidents at Sea Agreement: A Recipe for Disaster," *Journal of National Security Law & Policy* 6 (2012): 207, 209.
35 James Kraska, *Maritime Power and the Law of the Sea* (Oxford: Oxford University Press, 2011), 230.
36 The Chinese aircraft carrier Liaoning is the first aircraft carrier commissioned into the PLAN. The carrier conducted its first sea trial on September 25, 2012.
37 Black's Law Dictionary.
38 Nicholas J. Healy and Joseph C. Sweeney, "Basic Principles of the Law of Collision," *Journal of Maritime Law and Commerce* 22, no. 3 (1991).
39 Ibid. 360
40 Susan Hodges, *Cases and Materials on Marine Insurance Law* (London, Routledge, 1999), 540.
41 D.R. Owen, "Origins and Development of Marine Collison Law," *Tul. L. Review* 51 (1977): 786.

42 Ibid.
43 Ibid.
44 IMO website: www.imo.org/en/About/conventions/listofconventions/pages/colreg.aspx. Accessed July 30, 2016.
45 Timothy J. Nagle, "The Dangerous Military Activities Agreement: Minimum Order and Superpower Relations on the World's Oceans." *Virginia Journal of International Law* 31 (1990): 125.
46 P. Belcher, "A Sociological Interpretation of the COLREGS," *The Journal of Navigation* 55, no. 213–14 (2002): 3.
47 Mark Valencia, "The US-China MOU on Air and Maritime Encounters," *The Diplomat*, November 17, 2014, http://thediplomat.com/2014/11/the-us-china-mou-on-air-and-maritime-encounters/
48 www.globaltimes.cn/content/832735.shtml
49 Ibid.
50 United States Department of State Daily Press Briefing, Deputy spokesperson Marie Harf.
51 Memorandum of Understanding Between the Department of Defense of the United States of America and the Ministry of National Defense of the People's Republic of China Regarding the Rules of Behavior for Safety of Air and Maritime Encounters, Annex 2, Section III.
52 www.mindef.gov.sg/imindef/press_room/official_releases/nr/2011/mar/25mar11_nr/25mar11_fs.html
53 www.abc.net.au/news/2014-04-22/an-asia-pacific-nations-agree-to-maritime-accord/5405104
54 http://thediplomat.com/2014/04/small-but-positive-signs-at-western-pacific-naval-symposium/
55 Ibid.
56 CUES Part 2.
57 Ibid.
58 MOU between the United States of America Department of Defense and the People's Republic of China Ministry of National Defense on Notification of Major Military Activities Confidence-Building Measures Mechanism, Paragraph 2 and 3 of the Preamble.
59 Ibid. Preamble paragraph 8.
60 Memorandum of understanding between the department of defense of the United States of America and the Ministry of National Defense of the People's Republic of China regarding the rules of behavior for safety of air and maritime encounters, Section I.
61 Mira Rapp-Hooper and Bonnie Glaser, "In Confidence: Will we know if US-China CBMs are Working?" http://amti.csis.org/in-confidence-will-we-know-if-us-china-cbms-are-working/
62 www.ft.com/content/8762e906-853c-11e5-9f8c-a8d619fa707c
63 Ibid.
64 www.reuters.com/article/us-southchinasea-usa-communications-idUSKCN0SO0E220151030
65 Mark Valencia, "The US-China MOU on Air and Maritime Encounters," *The Diplomat*, November 17, 2014, http://thediplomat.com/2014/11/the-us-china-mou-on-air-and-maritime-encounters/
66 www.state.gov/r/pa/prs/ps/2016/06/258146.htm
67 www.theguardian.com/us-news/2016/dec/17/donald-trump-china-unpresidented-act-us-navy-drone
68 www.ippreview.com/index.php/Home/Blog/single/id/315.html

Part IV

Maritime entitlement, delimitation and dispute settlement and UNCLOS

11 The Sino-Philippine arbitration on the South China Sea disputes

A preliminary assessment of the merits award

*Michael Sheng-ti Gau**

Introduction

After three and half years the Sino–Philippine Arbitration for the South China Sea ("SCS") Disputes finally ended on July 12, 2016, with a Merits Award totally in Philippine favor. As the respondent, China rejected this arbitration from day one and categorically opposes the Awards on Jurisdiction, Admissibility, and Merits. This paper serves as a preliminary assessment of the efficacy of this arbitration. The first section of this paper addresses the development of this arbitration. The following sections provide the possible reasons behind the non-compliance of China for the Merits Award. Finally, concluding remarks will be given in the last section.

Development of SCS arbitration

Philippine initiation of the arbitration

On January 22, 2013, the Philippines invoked Article 287 and Annex VII of the United Nations Convention on the Law of the Sea ("UNCLOS")[1] for initiating an arbitration against China.[2] The Notification and Statement of Claims ("the Notification") said that the goal was "to seek a peaceful and durable resolution of the dispute in the West Philippine Sea ('WPS'),"[3] by narrowing disputes to facilitate future negotiation.[4] The Philippines challenged China's maritime entitlements and claims, land reclamations, enforcement and military actions and omissions within WPS located in the eastern part of SCS enclosed by the U-Shaped Line ("USL").

Five groups of claims were presented by the Notification.[5] *First*, China's rights concerning SCS maritime areas are those established by UNCLOS only and consist of territorial sea, contiguous zone, Exclusive Economic Zone ("EEZ") and continental shelf; China's maritime claims therein based on USL contravene UNCLOS and are invalid. *Second*, Mischief, McKennan, Gaven and Subi Reefs are low-tide elevations ("LTEs"), instead of "islands" or "rocks" under Article 121. None of them are located in China's continental shelf. Mischief and McKennan Reefs are part of Philippine continental shelf. Thus, China's occupation of these four maritime features and construction activities thereon are unlawful and should be terminated. *Third*, Johnson, Cuarteron, and Fiery Cross Reefs as well as Scarborough Shoal are rocks under Article 121(3) which may generate territorial sea only. Having unlawfully claimed maritime entitlements beyond twelve nautical miles ("nm") from these features, China should refrain from preventing Philippine vessels from exploiting living resources in waters adjacent to Scarborough Shoal and Johnson Reef, and from undertaking other activities inconsistent with UNCLOS at or in the vicinity of these features. *Fourth*, the Philippines is entitled under UNCLOS to a 12-nm territorial sea, a 200 nm EEZ, and a continental shelf measured from its archipelagic baselines, which is WPS. China has unlawfully claimed and exploited the natural resources in this EEZ and continental shelf, and prevented the Philippines from exploiting the living and non-living resources therein. *Fifth*, China has unlawfully interfered with Philippine exercise of its navigational rights and other rights under UNCLOS within and beyond Philippine EEZ. China should desist from these unlawful activities.[6]

As China rejected the Philippines' arbitration request from day one,[7] its complaints against the Philippines were missing in the Submissions.[8] China's refusal was based on, *inter alia*, China's 2006 Declaration,[9] which from Chinese perspectives has covered the disputes submitted by the Philippines and deprived the Tribunal's jurisdiction to entertain the case. The default rules[10] were applied to appoint arbitrators and establish the arbitral tribunal.

On July 11, 2013, the Members of the Tribunal decided to use the Permanent Court of Arbitration ("PCA") as Registry.[11] The Tribunal soon adopted the PH-CN Rules of Procedure ("ROP") and fixed March 30, 2014 as the deadline for the Philippines to submit its Memorial. *Knowing* that China has jurisdictional objections, the Tribunal directed the Philippines to *fully* address the issues of jurisdiction, admissibility, and *merits* in the Memorial altogether.[12]

Philippine Memorial and further written arguments

The Philippines submitted the Memorial[13] largely corresponding to the structure of the Notification. The Memorial requested the Tribunal to adjudge and declare that:

(1) China's maritime entitlements in SCS, like those of the Philippines, may not extend beyond those permitted by UNCLOS;
(2) China's claims to sovereign rights and jurisdiction, and to 'historic rights', with respect to SCS maritime areas encompassed by USL are contrary to UNCLOS and without lawful effect to the extent that they exceed the geographic and substantive limits of China's maritime entitlements under UNCLOS;
(3) Scarborough Shoal generates no EEZ or continental shelf;
(4) Mischief Reef, Second Thomas Shoal and Subi Reef are LTEs incapable of generating territorial sea, EEZ or continental shelf, and incapable of appropriation by occupation or otherwise;

(5) Mischief Reef and Second Thomas Shoal are part of Philippine EEZ and continental shelf;
(6) Gaven and McKennan Reefs (including Hughes Reef) are LTEs incapable of generating territorial sea, EEZ or continental shelf, but their low-water line may be used to determine the baseline from which the breadth of territorial sea of Namyit and Sin Cowe, respectively, is measured;
(7) Johnson, Cuarteron and Fiery Cross Reefs generate no EEZ or continental shelf;
(8) China has unlawfully interfered with the enjoyment and exercise of Philippine sovereign rights with respect to the living and non-living resources of Philippine EEZ and continental shelf;
(9) China has unlawfully failed to prevent its nationals and vessels from exploiting the living resources in Philippine EEZ;
(10) China has unlawfully prevented Philippine fishermen from pursuing their livelihoods by interfering with traditional fishing activities at Scarborough Shoal;
(11) China has violated its UNCLOS obligations to protect and preserve the marine environment at Scarborough Shoal and Second Thomas Shoal;
(12) China's occupation of and construction activities on Mischief Reef: (a) violate UNCLOS provisions concerning artificial islands, installations, and structures; (b) violate China's UNCLOS duties to protect and preserve the marine environment; and (c) constitute unlawful act of attempted appropriation against UNCLOS;
(13) China has breached its UNCLOS obligation by operating its law enforcement vessels dangerously causing serious risk of collision to Philippine vessels navigating in the vicinity of Scarborough Shoal;
(14) Since the commencement of this arbitration in January 2013, China has unlawfully aggravated and extended the dispute by, *inter alia*: (a) interfering with Philippine rights of navigation in the waters at, and adjacent to, Second Thomas Shoal; (b) preventing the rotation and resupply of Philippine personnel stationed at Second Thomas Shoal; and (c) endangering the health and well-being of Philippine personnel stationed at Second Thomas Shoal.
(15) China shall desist from further unlawful claims and activities.[14]

On December 5, 2014, the Tribunal received "Statement of the Ministry of Foreign Affairs of Viet Nam for the attention of the Tribunal in the Proceedings between the Philippines and PRC,"[15] affirming the Tribunal's jurisdiction over the disputes before it.[16] On December 7, 2014, the "Position Paper of PRC Government on the Matter of Jurisdiction in the SCS Arbitration Initiated by the Philippines ("Position Paper")" was released. Denying the Tribunal's jurisdiction over the disputes presented by the Philippines, the Position Paper was neither meant to be a Counter-Memorial,[17] nor treated as such *initially*.[18] Article 25(2) of ROP[19] became applicable. Accordingly, the Tribunal gave the Philippines 26 questions to be answered before March 15, 2015 as "Further

Written Arguments." China is requested to comment by June 15, 2015.[20] China declined. The hearing took place on July 7–13, 2015 ("July Hearing") in the Peace Palace, to address the jurisdictional and admissibility issues.[21]

The Jurisdictional Award

On October 29, 2015 the PCA released the Award on Jurisdiction and Admissibility ("Jurisdictional Award"), moving all Philippine Submissions into the merits phase.[22] Submissions 1–4, 6–7 and 10–14 were held to reflect disputes concerning the interpretation or application of UNCLOS, while *not* relating to sovereignty or concerning sea boundary delimitation. Submissions 5 and 8–9 were held to reflect disputes while not relating to sovereignty. For Submissions 1–2, 5, 8–9, 12 and 14, there remain unresolved jurisdictional issues not of exclusively preliminary nature. The Tribunal decided to move these seven Submissions into Merits Phase to settle the remaining jurisdictional issues.[23]

Second hearing and the amended submissions

The second hearing was held on November 24–30, 2015 ("November Hearing") to discuss the remaining issues of jurisdiction and admissibility as well as the merits issues.[24] Without China's presence the Hearing ended with *extra* Final Submissions 11, 14(d) and 15 from the Philippines, primarily concerning island-building, environmental harms and aggravation of the disputes done by China in Mischief, Cuarteron, Fiery Cross, Gaven, Johnson, Hughes and Subi Reefs.[25]

The Merits Award

On July 12, 2016, the Merits Award was released.[26] Among the 15 Philippine Final Submissions, only Submissions 14(a) to (c) and 15 failed to surmount the thresholds of jurisdiction and admissibility. The Tribunal's rulings on the merits were totally in favor of the Philippines concerning (the remaining) Final Submissions 1–13 and 14(d). However, among China-occupied or controlled maritime features, six were held as rocks and five LTEs.[27] Moreover, none of the high-tide features in the Spratly Islands was held capable of generating EEZ and continental shelf under Article 121(3), as interpreted by the Tribunal.[28] Archipelagic or straight baselines may not be used to enclose the Spratly Islands as a unit.[29]

The erasure of the U-Shaped Line: Submissions 1–2

The object and purpose of Philippine Submissions 1–2 is to negate the legal foundations underpinning USL.[30] What USL confronts are all SCS littoral states. However, in this arbitration there is only one applicant, the Philippines.[31] Therefore, the disputed maritime area that this Tribunal may examine is confined to WPS, as explicitly requested by the Philippines itself.[32] In WPS that is the 200 nm region stretching from Philippine archipelagic baselines facing SCS, there are Sino-Philippine disputes concerning delimitation of their overlapping maritime claims. There are also the disputes concerning conflicts of law enforcement activities pending settlement of the maritime delimitation disputes. Underlying these disputes are the territorial disputes concerning Scarborough Shoal and maritime features within Kalayaan Islands Group (KIG), as part of the Spratly Islands. On top of these issues lie the disputes concerning many salient and disguised military activities necessitated by the unsettled territorial struggles.[33]

WPS does not cover all the dashes of USL. Only those three dashes within WPS may be entertained by the Tribunal when determining the legality of USL's foundations in this case. The legality of the foundations for the other dashes facing Vietnam, Indonesia, Malaysia, Brunei, and Island of Taiwan are beyond the Tribunal's jurisdiction. Consequently, China's legal positions supporting those dashes beyond WPS should not be prejudiced by the award of the Tribunal.

From Philippine perspectives, when USL or its legal foundations are held against international law, China should erase it from official maps. However, if China does so, it will be tantamount to China's abandonment of its SCS territorial and maritime claims, which is unlikely.

USL symbolizes China's territorial claims

USL first appeared in the 1947 Map of Location of the SCS Islands (南海諸島位置圖), representing *China's territorial claims* over the maritime features located within such dashed line.[34] People may feel assured that the arbitral award is without prejudice to China's SCS territorial claims, as the Philippines said that territorial disputes were not submitted for resolution here.[35] However, Philippine oral arguments flew in the face of such a disclaimer. The November Hearing saw a theory of *the undetermined legal status of the Spratly Islands and Paracel Islands*, i.e. the territorial sovereignty over the Spratly Islands and Paracel Islands does not pertain to China. At that time no arbitrator stopped the Philippine legal team from such deliberation beyond the Tribunal's mandate. Two arbitrators even engaged in the discussion eagerly, as indicated by the transcripts of the Hearing.[36]

If the Merits Award is interpreted as endorsing or accepting the above theory that was not supposed to be published,[37] such an Award would be easily regarded as dismissing China's SCS territorial claims, or accepting that the territorial claims of the other littoral states prevail over that of China. It would be equal to overruling USL as a territorial claim of China. Such an award would go beyond the Tribunal's jurisdiction and have no legal effects.

Even assuming such an award has legally binding force, it is still hard for China to implement. Given the situation that most maritime features in the Spratly Islands Group are under foreign occupation, USL symbolizes *China's national shame for stolen territories*. Erasing USL would mean the end of educating Chinese people with the integrity of SCS territories, and giving up national aspirations to recover those lost territories. In fact, the idea of China's territorial integrity in four SCS Islands Groups was forged at the latest by the 1935 Map of Chinese Islands in SCS (中國南海各島嶼圖),[38] which was published forty years earlier than Philippine territorial claims over KIG. Why should China abandon its much older and more comprehensive SCS territorial claims, which this Tribunal was powerless to negate?[39]

USL represents China's provisional maritime claims

If the Merits Award is interpreted as overruling the legality of USL as the outer limits of China's *maritime* claims[40] due to its inconsistency with UNCLOS, it is also unlikely for China to comply by deleting USL.

First of all, USL serves as a *provisional* maritime claim pending settlement of maritime delimitation issues between China and other SCS littoral states. As such, USL is China's first offer in such political negotiations. As such, USL is incapable of being disposed of by international judicial body or arbitral tribunal, especially when China refuses to appear. In fact, China and Vietnam once settled their territorial and maritime boundary delimitation disputes in the Gulf of Tonkin. The two dashes between (China's) Hainan Island and Vietnam were removed from China's official maps in the course of such bilateral negotiations.[41] Such a removal illustrates that USL was negotiable.[42] By the same token, when the Philippines returns to the negotiation table with China to draw SCS maritime boundaries those three dashes within WPS will be equally negotiable.

In this connection, to ask China to withdraw such provisional maritime claims before maritime boundary delimitation negotiation with, *inter alia*, the Philippines starts is to ask China to give up its important negotiation position. As the Tribunal has declared its lack of intentions to draw Sino-Philippine maritime boundaries in WPS,[43] the Merits Award is without prejudice to the Sino-Philippine positions concerning boundary delimitation negotiations. Why would China bear any obligation to abandon its negotiation positions concerning delimitation by deleting USL?

As a pleasant surprise, Figure 3.4[44] attached to the newly released Philippine Memorial provided *dotted* maritime boundaries to the north and the south of the Philippines, called "Provisional Equidistance Lines". The fact that the maritime boundaries in these two regions were not drawn by March 30, 2014 (when the Memorial was submitted) did not deter the Philippines from making *unilateral* maritime claims whose outer limits were obviously marked after the Chinese model. Such "*Provisional* Equidistance Lines" will be definitely removed after boundaries there are drawn. This practice signifies the lawfulness of USL when compared with such Philippine practice. The Philippines would apply double standards if demanding China to remove such "provisional" outer limits of its SCS maritime claims (i.e. USL) before starting Sino-Philippine maritime boundaries negotiation.

China's maritime claims based on historic rights: Submissions 1–2

China's "claim" on historic rights in Southern WPS is a moot issue

As already discussed, the geographic limits of the Tribunal's mandate in the present case are confined to WPS. The Tribunal lacked power to investigate the legality of China's maritime claims based on, *inter alia*, so-called "historic rights" *beyond* WPS. It follows that Figure 3 of the Merits Award, i.e. a map enclosed with China National Offshore Oil Corporation Press Release notifying Part of Open Blocks in Waters under Jurisdiction of the People's Republic of China, is improper, to say the least. Serving as evidence to prove China's maritime claims based on historic rights in SCS but outside WPS,[45] this map should have been deemed inadmissible and irrelevant.

Secondly, when examining whether China has relied on historic rights to justify its law enforcement activities in the WPS, the target area should be even smaller. China uses the Spratly Islands Group as a whole to claim EEZ and continental shelf, while the Philippines,[46] Malaysia[47] and Vietnam[48] have repeatedly implied that fully entitled "islands" exist in the Spratly Islands Group. Besides, the legality issue for China to use the Spratly Islands Group as a whole to claim EEZ and continental shelf was not included in Philippine Final Submissions to the Tribunal. Applying *Non Ultra Petita* Principle, the Tribunal's rulings would be without prejudice to such claims of China.[49] Under such circumstances, the only possible area for China to invoke historic rights is further narrowed down to the northern part of WPS, minus the EEZs and continental shelf generated by Islands of Taiwan and Pratas.

Whether China claimed historic rights in Northern WPS is unanswerable

It is clear that the northern part of the WPS, minus the EEZ generated by Taiwan Island, would be totally covered by the EEZ generated by Scarborough Shoal, should this feature be a fully entitled island. This way, there will be no need for China to invoke historic rights to justify its law enforcement activities in the northern part of the WPS. The Summer Fishing Ban in China, which can then be justified by China's sovereign rights and jurisdiction derived from its EEZ and continental shelf surrounding Scarborough Shoal, would be unable to prove China's invocation of historic rights there. Clearly, China's claim of historic rights in the northern part of WPS may not be real, unless Scarborough Shoal is held as a rock under Article 121(3).[50]

A fundamental question arises. If Submission 3 relating to the legal status of Scarborough Shoal cannot reflect any dispute or *concerns* regarding maritime boundary delimitation, the Tribunal would be powerless to decide if this maritime feature is a rock or an island. In separate papers this author pointed out the factual and legal errors hidden in the Jurisdictional Award that (i) Submission 3 was wrongfully held as capable of reflecting the dispute,[51] and (ii) the dispute to be reflected, if any, was wrongfully characterized as not concerning maritime boundary delimitation.[52] Consequently the legal status of Scarborough Shoal should remain unanswerable in this case, depriving the Tribunal of the legal foundations to determine whether, in the northern part of WPS, China really invoked historic rights to justify its law enforcement activities. Therefore, the Tribunal's declaration that China's maritime claims based on historic rights in WPS violated UNCLOS becomes *ultra vires* and questionable.

Legal status of nine maritime features: Submissions 3–4 and 6–7

The Philippines argued in its Submissions 3–4 and 6–7 that four of the nine maritime features occupied by China in WPS should be considered as rocks under Article 121(3) of UNCLOS, while the other five features only qualify as LTEs. Hence, China may not have maritime entitlements of EEZ and continental shelf in WPS. Seen totally in Philippine favor, the Merits Award declared that among those maritime features occupied by China in WPS, six (Scarborough Shoal, Gaven Reef (North), McKennan Reef, Johnson Reef, Cuarteron Reef, and Fiery Cross Reef) are rocks, five (Subi Reef, Gaven Reef (South), Hughes Reef, Mischief Reef, and Second Thomas Shoal) are LTEs.[53] Furthermore, the Merits Award said that no island exist in the Spratly Islands Group and in WPS. China is hence not entitled to claim EEZ or continental shelf in WPS. For the following reasons, it is nearly impossible for China to comply with such an Award assuming it has any legally binding force for China at all.

Compliance with Merits Award is pointless

First of all, China has never used any single SCS maritime feature to claim maritime entitlements of territorial waters, EEZ and continental shelf. This is evidenced by the official statements taken by the Jurisdictional Award, namely, the 2009 and 2011 NVs sent by Beijing Government to the Secretary-General of the United Nations.[54] As far as WPS is concerned, China is using the Spratly Islands Group *as a whole* to claim EEZ and continental shelf.[55] Philippine Submissions 3–4 and 6–7 contended that China may not use *those nine* maritime features to claim EEZ and continental shelf. The question is: what different actions should China take to comply with the Merits Award given in Philippine favor? Perhaps China can reiterate its positions declared in its 2009 and 2011 NVs to enlighten the Tribunal that Philippine Submissions 3–4 and 6–7 aimed at the wrong targets.

China's evacuation from LTEs means abandonment of territorial claims

It was the Philippine contention that those LTEs are not located in China's EEZ and continental shelf, while they are located in and constitute part of Philippine EEZ and continental shelf. Besides, LTEs are incapable of appropriation by occupation or otherwise. These positions were upheld by the Merits Award. It plainly means that those five LTEs may not be appropriated by China through the means of occupation or/and claim of territorial sovereignty.[56] However, it is very hard for China to implement such an award.

Since 1935 at the latest the Chinese Government has continuously and repeatedly declared its detailed and comprehensive territorial sovereignty claims over four groups of SCS islands,[57] embracing these LTEs. To ask China to "stop appropriation" of these LTEs regarded as part of Philippine EEZ and continental shelf is to ask China to evacuate. If so, these LTEs will be gladly taken over by the Philippines winning this arbitration. It also means that China abandons its territorial claims over these LTEs. Given the situation that the Tribunal was powerless to settle territorial disputes, China is not bound to change its positions in its territorial disputes with the Philippines, embracing, *inter alia*, these LTEs. Why should China waive its territorial claims that cannot be dismissed by the Tribunal by evacuating from these LTEs?

Besides, China is obviously using these five LTEs as military bases to defend its territorial integrity concerning, *inter alia*, those five China-occupied "rocks" in the Spratly Islands Group. Meanwhile, Vietnam, the Philippines, and Malaysia also claim territorial sovereignty over all or part of maritime features of the Spratly Islands Group. Those five China-occupied "rocks" are in constant danger of being taken by these claimants. How could China abandon its means to maintain territorial integrity in the Spratly Islands Group by implementing the Merits Award indirectly requesting it to evacuate from those LTEs?

Evacuation from LTEs means withdrawal of China's boundary delimitation positions

According to the Merits Award, there is no single maritime feature in the WPS qualified to generate EEZ and continental shelf according to Article 121(3) as interpreted by the Tribunal. Given the fact that China claims territorial sovereignty over Scarborough Shoal and all maritime features in the Spratly Islands Group, China is still not entitled to claim EEZ and continental shelf in WPS according to this ruling, without answering the question if China's territorial claims are better than the other contesting States. It follows that those five LTEs are not located in China's EEZ and continental shelf. However, the Tribunal's decision that no island exists in the Spratly Islands Group contradicts Philippine, Vietnamese, and Malaysian positions *implying* that islands exist in the Spratly Islands Group, as discussed already. Claiming all the maritime features in the Spratly Islands Group, China can of course use these "islands" to claim EEZ and continental shelf, which embrace those five LTEs. In other words, those five LTEs are situated in the overlapping EEZ and continental shelf claimed by China and, *inter alia*, the Philippines. Such position is strengthened by another fact that Philippine Final Submissions did not include the legality issue of China's using the Spratly Islands Group as a whole to claim territorial waters, EEZ and continental shelf. The application of *Non Ultra Petita* principle will prevent the Tribunal's Award from jeopardizing the legality of China's claim of this nature.[58]

Since the Tribunal is powerless to draw maritime boundaries, the Tribunal's Merits Award cannot deny that those five LTEs fall within China's side of territorial waters, EEZ and continental shelf. To ask China to accept such an impossible decision of the Tribunal that those LTEs are located in Philippine EEZ and continental shelf, instead of being situated in the Sino-Philippine overlapping EEZ and continental shelf, is to ask China to abandon its basic negotiation position concerning boundary delimitation with the Philippines, which is unlikely.

Not treating the "rocks" as islands means withdrawal of boundary delimitation positions

The Merits Award declared that six China-occupied maritime features are "rocks" within the meaning of Article 121(3) of UNCLOS. Accordingly they generate no entitlement to an EEZ or continental shelf for China. It implies that China shall stop claiming EEZ and continental shelf *from* each of these six "rocks." It also means that the law enforcement actions carried out by China in the areas beyond 12 nm *from* each of these "rocks" cannot be justified, given that China's maritime claims based on historic rights were overruled by the same award. In short, China must desist from taking such kind of law enforcement activities as a matter of compliance of the Merits Award.

However, such kind of decisions can hardly be implemented by China. As said already, China has never relied on any of these six "rocks" to claim EEZ and continental shelf. China uses the Spratly Islands Group *as a whole* to claim territorial waters, EEZ and continental shelf. Such position was not included in Philippine Final Submissions for the Tribunal to decide its legality. As a result, the Merits Award should be without prejudice to such position of China according to *Non Ultra Petita* Principle. Therefore, those law enforcement activities done by China in the waters beyond 12 nm from the five "rocks" would still be justified by China's sovereign rights and jurisdiction derived from its EEZ and continental shelf.[59] To ask China to quit its disputed law enforcement activities in the waters beyond 12 nm *from* these five "rocks" will mean asking China to admit that these areas are *not* located on China's side of territorial waters, EEZ and continental shelf. It is equivalent to China's abandonment of its positions concerning boundary delimitation negotiations with the Philippines in WPS. As mentioned above, China has no obligation to retreat from its negotiation positions which shall remain unaffected by any decisions of this Tribunal.

No evidence to prove that China considers Scarborough Shoal as an island

With respect to Scarborough Shoal that is not part of the Spratly Islands Group, Philippine Submission 3 essentially argued that China wrongfully used this maritime feature to claim EEZ and continental shelf. However, judging from the maritime confrontations identified by Philippine written and oral arguments in its Submissions 10, 11, and 13, all confrontations involving Scarborough Shoal occurred within 12 nm from this feature.[60] Apart from the Summer Fishing

Ban,[61] the evidence taken by the Jurisdictional Award failed to prove that China used Scarborough Shoal to claim maritime entitlement beyond territorial waters, not to mention EEZ and continental shelf.[62] Submission 3 should have been deemed hypothetical and *moot* in the eyes of law and held inadmissible by the Tribunal, leaving the issue of China's implementation of the Merits Award for this Submission out of the question.

Formulation of Submissions 3–4 and 6–7 fails to address the real issues

Most interestingly, Philippine Final Submissions, having undergone certain revisions, stuck to the original structure requesting the Tribunal to examine those individual features occupied by the Beijing Government, but not all the maritime features claimed by China in WPS which constitute the real basis for China to claim maritime entitlements of territorial waters, EEZ and continental shelf there. The Philippines clearly understood that getting all China-claimed maritime features on board means getting all SCS littoral states (i.e. Vietnam, Malaysia, and Brunei) on board. The situations would have become too complicated to handle.[63]

If adhering to the *Non Ultra Petita* Principle,[64] however, the Tribunal would not be able to address the real and critical issue dividing both Parties in this arbitration. During the July Hearing the Tribunal asked the Philippine legal team about the situations of *all* maritime features in the Spratly Islands Group. Obviously, the Tribunal was trying to *fix* Philippine Submissions, while the Philippine agent was reluctant to cooperate.[65] Later on, during the November Hearing the Philippines invited an internationally renowned scholar, Professor Clive Schofield,[66] who once opined that twelve islands exist in the Spratly Islands Group, to appear before the Arbitrators to deny his previous remarks. Professor Schofield then testified in the court room that no maritime feature in the Spratly Islands Group qualified for a fully entitled "island" within the meaning of Article 121 of UNCLOS.[67] The Merits Award finally endorsed this Philippine position, declaring that China is not entitled to claim EEZ or continental shelf by using the Spratly Islands Group as a whole.[68] China is also not justified to draw archipelagic or straight baselines surrounding the Spratly Islands Group.[69]

Leaving the Tribunal's problematic interpretation of Article 121(3) aside just for now, one question remains. Violating the *Non Ultra Petita* Principle,[70] such a ruling has doubtful legal effect. China's non-compliance becomes justified. What is worse, Malaysia was not a Party to this Arbitration and not bound by the Award. If Malaysia comes out to claim EEZ, continental shelf, and outer continental shelf using certain maritime features within the Spratly Islands Group deemed as "islands", as announced by its letter to the Tribunal,[71] what will become of the Merits Award?

China's trespass into Philippine EEZ and continental shelf: Submissions 8–9

The Philippines in its Submissions 8–9 contended that China trespassed into Philippine EEZ and continental shelf. Specifically, China interfered with the enjoyment and exercise of Philippine sovereign rights with respect to the living and non-living resources of its EEZ and continental shelf, in areas of Mischief Reef, Second Thomas Shoal, Reed Bank, Philippine Service Contracts (54, 14, 58, 63), and Areas 3–4 of Philippine Petroleum Blocks. Moreover, China failed to prevent its nationals and vessels from exploiting the living resources in Philippine EEZ, specifically in Second Thomas Shoal and Mischief Reef.

The Merits Award was given in Philippine favor for its claims against (i) China's interference with the enjoyment and exercise of Philippine sovereign rights over non-living resources of its continental shelf in Reed Bank, (ii) China's Summer Fishing Ban for SCS areas falling within Philippine EEZ, and (iii) China's failure to prevent its vessels from harvesting in Mischief Reef and Second Thomas Shoal.[72] However, this kind of award seems impossible for China to implement. This is because China also is entitled to claim EEZ and continental shelf in the relevant areas.[73] The actions complained of by the Philippines were the result of the enjoyment and exercise of China's sovereign rights and jurisdiction within its EEZ and continental shelf. Prior to the delimitation of Sino-Philippine maritime boundaries in their overlapping areas, such kind of maritime confrontations will continue.

From Philippine perspectives, "China does not have EEZ and continental shelf in the WPS." The Philippines argued that no WPS maritime features qualifies as a fully entitled "island" within the meaning of Article 121 of UNCLOS.[74] Moreover, the counsel of the Philippines during the November Hearing advanced a theory of "the undetermined legal status of the Spratly and Paracel Islands Groups," denying China's territorial claims over these two groups of islands.[75] Therefore, even if there exists islands in the Spratly Islands Group, the EEZ and continental shelf to be generated thereby will not accrue to China.

Are there no islands in the Spratly Islands Group? The answer is "No," as discussed already.[76] Does the territorial sovereignty over the Spratly Islands Group not belong to China? This issue is untouchable in this arbitration, not to mention to be endorsed by the Merits Award. At the outset when the Philippines initiated this arbitration, it said that no territorial disputes were submitted for settlement.[77] Even if territorial disputes were submitted to the Tribunal, such disputes cannot be resolved by this Tribunal, as such disputes are not the ones concerning the interpretation or application of UNCLOS. As a result, any award granted by this Tribunal will be without prejudice to China's SCS territorial claims. China has every right to reject (i) Philippine theory of the "undetermined legal status of the Spratly and Paracel Islands Group" which somehow was welcome and eagerly inquired by certain Arbitrators during the November Hearing,[78] and (ii) the *ultra vires* rulings of the Merits Award that directly or indirectly confirmed the value of such a theory.[79]

For the foregoing reasons, the denial of China's right to claim EEZ and continental shelf in WPS by the Merits Award is questionable. Given the fact that this Tribunal has no power to draw maritime boundaries, the Merits Award may impose upon China no obligation to accept that "the locations of those maritime confrontations identified by Philippine Submissions 8–9 fall within Philippine side of EEZ and continental shelf." For China, to accept such a position is to abandon its positions in its disputes with the Philippines concerning (i) territorial sovereignty over maritime features in KIG, and/or (ii) maritime boundaries delimitation for the overlapping EEZ and continental shelf claims in WPS. This perhaps can explain China's refusal to comply with the Merits Award.

Whether Mischief Reef and Second Thomas Shoal are part of Philippine EEZ and continental shelf: Submission 5

Philippine Submission 5 requested the Tribunal to declare that Mischief Reef and Second Thomas Shoal, as LTEs, constitute part of Philippine EEZ and continental shelf. The Merits Award for this Submission was given in favor of the Philippines.[80] However, it is hardly possible for China to comply with this ruling, for the following reasons:

Submission 5 suffers from mootness

In fact, Submission 5 does not reflect any Sino-Philippine dispute, as China has never doubted that these two maritime features are located in the EEZ and continental shelf that the Philippines may claim. In fact, the Philippines failed to prove that China ever challenged such a position during the arbitral proceedings. Since no Sino-Philippine dispute can be reflected by Submission 5, such a Submission should have been held by the Tribunal as inadmissible, and should have been barred from entering into the Merits Phase.

Interestingly, the real Sino-Philippine dispute was *not* submitted by the Philippines. What has been really disputed between these two Parties is *whether Mischief Reef and Second Thomas Shoal also constitute part of China's EEZ and continental shelf.* This is because the EEZ and continental shelf China may claim in the WPS also cover the locations of these two features. What the Philippines has been denying is that China may claim EEZ and continental shelf in WPS. According to the *Non Ultra Petita* Principle,[81] the Tribunal may not entertain the real dispute, as it was not submitted to the Tribunal by the Philippines in the first place.

The tribunal entertained a dispute not reflected by Submission 5

However, the Tribunal transformed the "hypothetical, moot, and inadmissible claim" into a "claim capable of reflecting real dispute." In Paragraph 172 of the Jurisdictional Award, the Tribunal kindly fixed the above-mentioned inherent problem with Submission 5 (i.e. reflecting no dispute) by "interpreting" what was meant by that Submission, turning this hypothetical claim into a new claim that can *apparently* reflect the real dispute.

> In Submission No. 5, however, the Philippines has asked not for a determination of the status of a particular feature, but for a declaration that Mischief Reef and Second Thomas Shoal as low-tide elevations "are part

> of the exclusive economic zone and continental shelf of the Philippines." In so doing, the Philippines has *in fact* presented a dispute concerning *the status of every maritime feature* claimed by China within 200 nautical miles of Mischief Reef and Second Thomas Shoal, at least to the extent of *whether such features are islands* capable of generating an entitlement to an exclusive economic zone and to a continental shelf.[82] [emphasis added]

Obviously, the Tribunal *enlarged* the scope of controversies conveyed by Submission 5, *switched* the direction of inquiry, and brought in a new dispute for investigation. Having been repaired, Submission 5 seems capable of reflecting Sino-Philippine disputes on the ground. Nevertheless, based on the same principle of *Non Ultra Petita*[83] international juridical body has an obligation to refrain from deciding what is *not* included in the final submissions of the parties. In the present arbitration, the Tribunal entertained a dispute which was not submitted by the Philippines and produced a decision *ultra vires*. What is worse, the new dispute as characterized by the Tribunal under para. 172 of the Jurisdictional Award is still artificial and unreal, as China does not use any individual maritime feature in the Spratly Islands Group to claim EEZ and continental Shelf.[84] It becomes justified for China to refrain from implementing such a ruling. Furthermore, to ask China to accept Mischief Reef and Second Thomas Shoal to be part of Philippine EEZ and continental shelf, instead of part of EEZ and continental shelf of both States, is to ask China to abandon its positions in maritime boundary delimitation negotiations with the Philippines, which is again unlikely.

Maritime confrontations around Scarborough Shoal: Submissions 10 and 13

One of the reasons for the Philippines to initiate this arbitration against China is because China obtained control over Scarborough Shoal since April 2012, at the cost of the Philippines. In this arbitration, the Philippines said that territorial dispute was not submitted for resolution. However, the maritime confrontations occurring in the waters surrounding Scarborough Shoal were submitted to the Tribunal to advance Philippine positions in this dispute over territorial sovereignty.[85]

Philippine traditional fishing rights in Scarborough Shoal are unreal

Philippine Submission 10 requested the Tribunal to declare that China has unlawfully prevented Philippine fishermen from pursuing their livelihoods by interfering with traditional fishing activities in the territorial waters of Scarborough Shoal. The Merits Award upheld Philippine claim.[86] Why is it hard for China to comply with such a ruling and to desist from its complained activities?

It is territorial sovereignty over Scarborough Shoal and its adjacent water that has been claimed by the Philippines before and after this arbitration. During this arbitration the Philippines abruptly switched its position and claimed traditional fishing rights in that water premised on the position that the territorial sovereignty over that water belongs to somebody else![87] In fact, the Philippines has not renounced its sovereignty over that water after winning this case. The reason is simple: this arbitration is without prejudice to territorial claims of both Parties. Under such a circumstance, how could the ruling upholding Philippine traditional fishing rights in that water make any sense? How should China implement such a groundless ruling? Fundamentally, the Philippines has never claimed traditional fishing rights in the territorial waters of Scarborough Shoal, making it impossible for China or any other States to reject or acquiesce. How could such so-called traditional fishing right regime ever be established in the first place? How would such a mirage of Philippine traditional fishing right ever be disputed? Obviously, the formulation of traditional fishing rights under Submission 10 was a temporary litigation strategy devoid of any legal meaning and moral credibility. China will have every reason to refrain from observing such a ruling.

For China, the water adjacent to Scarborough Shoal is Chinese territorial water, where fishing vessels with Philippine nationality only enjoy innocent passage without the right to fish. For the Philippines, the real legal basis for its fishing vessels to harvest there is its territorial claims. How could the Tribunal that has explored Sino-Philippine disputes in WPS for the past three and half years be blind to such a territorial dispute? Before settling such territorial dispute over Scarborough Shoal, to ask China to tolerate harvesting activities of Philippine fishing vessels in that water and to admit that Chinese fishermen enjoy the same degree of traditional fishing rights there[88] is, as a matter of international law, to ask China to give up its territorial claim over Scarborough Shoal and its adjacent water. How could we expect China to accept such kind of ruling impliedly denying its territorial sovereignty which is not supposed to be denied by the very award?

Territorial disputes underlying Submission 13 renders the award unenforceable

Philippine Submission 13 requested the Tribunal to declare that China has breached its UNCLOS obligations by operating its law enforcement vessels dangerously, causing risks of collision to Philippine vessels navigating in the water adjacent to Scarborough Shoal. The Merits Award was given in Philippine favor in this regard.[89] However, it seems impossible for China to implement this ruling, for the following reasons: as stated above, China gained upper hand since April 2012 in the territorial dispute over Scarborough Shoal. The Philippines still holds fast to its aspirations to regain control over this feature. This explains why from time to time Philippine coast guard and surveillance vessels attempted to enter the water adjacent to Scarborough Shoal, perhaps to see and to test how China would react. It was also in the context of such a territorial dispute that China found such Philippine creeping activities intolerable and hostile. Against this background China's actions to obstruct navigation of

Philippine vessels on 28 April and 26 May of 2012 become comprehensible. The aim was to prevent Philippine law enforcement vessels from getting closer to Scarborough Shoal and from enforcing Philippine domestic laws in the water adjacent to this feature.[90]

In the future when Philippine government vessels approach Scarborough Shoal again, the inherent right of self-defense which pertains to China as codified by Article 51 of the United Nations Charter may well be invoked by China to deter *in moderation* such activities of the Philippine law enforcement vessels as complained by the Philippines in this arbitration. Such actions of China will not be considered as a violation of the Merits Award of this Arbitration. This is because the scope of legally binding force of this Award, if any, does not cover military activities as defined by Article 298(1)(b) of UNCLOS[91] that have been excluded by China's 2006 Declaration[92] from the jurisdiction of, *inter alia*, Annex VII Tribunal which entertained this case. Prior to Philippine abandonment of its territorial claim over Scarborough Shoal and the territorial water thereof, to ask China to tolerate free navigation of Philippine law enforcement vessels in that water aiming at enforcing Philippine domestic law and seeking opportunities to enhance Philippine territorial claim there, is to loosen up its muscle guarding its territorial integrity. This perhaps explains why it is impossible for China to comply with the ruling concerning Submission 13.

Concluding remarks

Why does China refuse to comply with the Merits Award of the SCS Arbitration? People may have an exaggerated idea that China's historic rights in the *entire* region within the USL have been negated. Such an idea is groundless, as there is a geographic limit upon the jurisdiction that the Tribunal may possess when entertaining Submissions 1–2. As the Philippines is the only applicant in this arbitration case, the only possible geographic area for the Tribunal to exercise its jurisdiction, if any, is confined to the WPS. In other words, only three dashes of the USL *within the WPS* may be affected by the Merits Award.[93]

Moreover, the Philippine Final Submissions failed to include the legal ground China really invokes to claim EEZ and continental shelf in the southern WPS, i.e. the Spratly Islands Group *as a whole*. Thus, the *Non Ultra Petita* Principle would dictate that the Merits Award is without prejudice to the legality of China's position of this nature.[94] Meanwhile, the Philippines, Malaysia, and Vietnam all impliedly admit that "fully entitled islands" exist in the Spratly Islands Group.[95] China may either use the Spratly Islands Group as a whole, or alternatively, those "islands" thereof, to claim EEZ and continental shelf in the southern WPS. The issue of China's claims based on historic rights in the southern WPS becomes moot.

As for the northern part of the WPS, it seems baseless for the Tribunal to rule that China's claim under historic rights there violated UNCLOS. This is because Philippine Submission 3 (i.e. the legal status of Scarborough Shoal) suffers from mootness as this submission together with Submissions 4, 6, and 7 cannot reflect Sino-Philippine disputes.[96] The issue whether Scarborough Shoal is a rock or an island becomes unanswerable for the Tribunal. Hence, the Tribunal is powerless to deny China's EEZ and continental shelf in the northern WPS surrounding Scarborough Shoal.

As China does not need to rely on historic rights to justify its maritime jurisdiction over the southern WPS, while the Tribunal cannot declare that China does not have the right to claim EEZ and continental shelf in the northern WPS, the whole issue of China's claim of historic rights in the entire WPS becomes hypothetical and inadmissible. Thus, the Tribunal lacks the power to negate such historic rights of China anywhere in the WPS and in the SCS within USL. This perhaps can explain why China refuses to abandon its historic rights in the SCS after the Merits Award was released.

Philippine Submissions 3, 4, 6, and 7 concern the legal status of nine particular maritime features occupied or controlled by the Beijing Government in the WPS. The Merits Award was given in Philippine favor that (i) none of these features qualify as "fully entitled island"; and (ii) China may not claim EEZ and continental shelf based on any of these maritime features. Such rulings in the Merits Award are unenforceable for China, as it does not use any individual maritime features to claim EEZ and continental shelf in the WPS in the first place.

People may argue that the real ground for China to claim EEZ and continental shelf in the southern WPS, i.e. the Spratly Islands Group as a whole, is also overruled by the Merits Award.[97] However, such rulings have critical legal problems as follows.

First, the reason for the Tribunal to come out with such rulings is because the Tribunal *characterized* Philippine Submission 5 which claimed that Mischief Reef and Second Thomas Shoal, as LTEs, are part of Philippine EEZ and continental shelf. Paragraph 172 of the Jurisdictional Award considered such a Submission "in fact" required the Tribunal to look at each and every China-claimed maritime features within 200 nm of these two features to see if *any* of China-claimed features qualify as a fully entitled island.[98] To be submitted, such a characterization is in fact an illegitimate creation of a *new* set of disputes violating the *Non Ultra Petita* Principle, as the Philippines did not present such kind of *massive* claims with an opposite direction in its Final Submissions.

Second, the reason for the Tribunal to characterize Submission 5 is, as understood by the author, due to the inherent defect of that Submission suffering from mootness. China never disputed with such a claim that Mischief Reef and Second Thomas Shoal form part of Philippine EEZ and continental shelf. Reflecting no dispute is an inherent problem with Philippine Submission 5. What is really disputed is *whether these two features also are part of China's EEZ and continental shelf!* Such a real dispute, however, was not submitted by the Philippines throughout this arbitration.

Third, the new Submission as created by the Tribunal under Submission 5 in the name of characterization still suffers from mootness and is incapable of reflecting any real disputes. This is because China does not use *any* individual maritime feature in the Spratly Islands Group to claim EEZ and continental shelf. Interestingly, China's position is well-known to the Tribunal, which invoked China's 2011 Note Verbale[99] as evidence in its Jurisdictional Award.[100]

It is also hard for China to implement the rulings upholding Philippine Submissions 10 and 13 concerning Sino-Philippine confrontations in the waters adjacent to Scarborough Shoal. This is due to (i) the inherent limitation for the Annex VII Tribunal to be unable to settle territorial disputes; and (ii) the real cause behind these confrontations was the Sino-Philippine unsettled territorial disputes over Scarborough Shoal and its adjacent waters. As long as such territorial dispute remain unresolved, the actions of China complained of by Philippine Submissions 10 and 13 will repeat themselves.

Finally, this preliminary assessment of the Merits Award considers it very hard for China to comply with the rulings vindicating Philippine Submissions 8–9 premised on the lack of China's maritime entitlements of EEZ and continental shelf in the WPS, which is ruled as Philippine EEZ and continental shelf. The reason is simple: China has its unaffected maritime entitlements of EEZ and continental shelf in the WPS.

There are reasons to believe that even the Philippines, Malaysia, and Vietnam admit that fully entitled islands exist in the Spratly Islands Group.[101] The Philippines advanced the theory of the undetermined legal status of the Paracel and Spratly Islands Groups during the November Hearing,[102] negating China's territorial claims over both Paracel and Spratly Islands Groups. Such kind of arguments were not supposed to be raised in the Annex VII Tribunal powerless to settle territorial disputes. No matter how the relevant part of the rulings of the Merits Award[103] is interpreted in the future, China has every right to oppose the Tribunal's illegitimate endorsement, if any, of such Philippine theory.

Besides, the real foundation for China to claim EEZ and continental shelf in the WPS is not those nine particular maritime features, as indicated by Philippine Submissions 3, 4, 6, and 7. It is not any of those China-claimed maritime features inside of the Spratly Islands Group, either. The real legal basis is the Spratly Islands Group as a whole, embracing all the big and small maritime features within this island group. As the Philippines failed to include in its Final Submissions this real legal foundation of China to claim EEZ and continental shelf in the WPS, the Tribunal's rulings shall be without prejudice to such position of China.

Notes

* Director of the Research Institute for International Justice and Arbitration of Hainan University; Professor of International Law at Law School, Hainan University, Haikou, Hainan Province, China. The opinions here do not represent any government agencies or other people. Email: mikegau97@msn.com

1 United Nations Convention on the Law of the Sea, December 10, 1982, 1833 U.N.T.S. 3 (1982) [hereinafter UNCLOS].

2 See "Statement by the Secretary of DFA on the UNCLOS Arbitral Proceedings against China" available at: www.imoa.ph/press-releases/statement-by-secretary-of-foreign-affairs-albert-del-rosario-on-the-unclos-arbitral-proceedings-against-china-to-achieve-a-peaceful-and-durable-solution-to-the-dispute-in-the-wps/ (last visited August 31, 2016).

3 See Notification and Statement of Claims, issued by Department of Foreign Affairs of the Philippines to the Chinese Embassy in Manila, at 1, para. 1, Serial No. 13–0211, January 22, 2013, www.philippineembassy-usa.org/uploads/pdfs/embassy/2013/2013-0122-Notification%20and%20Statement%20of%20Claim%20on%20West%20Philippine%20Sea.pdf (last visited August 31, 2016).

4 Oral statement by Solicitor General Hilbay on July 7, 2015, Final Transcription Day 1-Jurisdiction Hearing, p. 8, in https://pcacases.com/web/view/7 (last visited October 11, 2016). This website contains all information about this arbitration.

5 For comment, *see* Michael Sheng-ti Gau, "The Sino-Philippine Arbitration on South China Sea (Nine-Dash-Line) Dispute: Applying the Rule of Default of Appearance," in 28 *Ocean Yearbook*, 81–133 (2014).

6 *Supra* note 3, paras. 31, 41.

7 See Statement by the Spokesperson of the Foreign Ministry of China, February 9, 2013, www.fmprc.gov.cn/eng/xwfw/s2510/2511/t1015317.shtml (last visited March 10, 2015).

8 Had China decided to join the arbitration, it would have put its territorial disputes with the Philippines into the Submissions for the Tribunal to entertain, as the Philippines since 1970s occupied several islands in the Spratly Islands Group claimed by China. China has been strongly opposed to such Philippine invasions ever since. Had such Submissions been joined, the Tribunal would have ruled them *inadmissible* as such submissions would not have been concerning the interpretation or application of UNCLOS. See Paragraphs 6–7 of China's Position Paper, *infra* note 17.

9 Made on August 25, 2006, China's declaration reads: "The Government of the People's Republic of China does not accept any of the procedures provided for in Section 2 of Part XV of the Convention with respect to all the categories of disputes referred to in paragraph 1 (a) (b) and (c) of Article 298 of the Convention." It is available in: www.un.org/Depts/los/convention_agreements/convention_declarations.htm#China upon ratification (last visited August 31, 2016).

10 *Supra* note 1, Annex VII, art. 3(e).

11 PCA First Press Release on 27 August 2013, *supra* note 4.

12 *Ibid.* It seems then that the Tribunal *did not* intend to bifurcate the proceedings.

13 For the text and Annexes of the Memorial, *supra* note 4. For comment, *see* Michael Sheng-ti Gau, The Sino-Philippine Arbitration on South China Sea Disputes: Admissibility and Jurisdiction Issues, 21 *China Oceans Law Review* (Vol. 2015, No. 1) 64–293.

14 *Id.* Volume One of the Memorial, pp. 271–72.

15 See Third Press Release, December 17, 2014, *supra* note 4.

16 Merits Award, *infra* note 26, para. 36.

17 The text is available in: www.fmprc.gov.cn/mfa_eng/zxxx_662805/t1217147.shtml (last visited October 17, 2016). For comment, *see* Natalie Klein, "The Limitations of UNCLOS Part XV in Resolving South China Sea Disputes," pp. 8–15 (2016) IJMCL (forthcoming) available at: http://papers.ssrn.com/sol3/papers.cfm?abstract_id=2730411 (last visited August 22, 2016).

18 *Supra* note 15.

19 Article 25(2) of the ROP, https://pcacases.com/web/sendAttach/233 (last visited August 31, 2016).

20 *Supra* note 15. For the whole Philippine documents, supra note 4.

21 For Transcripts of the July Hearing, *supra* note 4. For comment on the Transcripts, *see* Michael Sheng-ti Gau, "The Sino-Philippine Arbitration on the South China Sea Disputes: Ineffectiveness of the Award, Inadmissibility of the Claims, and Lack of Jurisdiction, With Special Reference to the Legal Arguments Made by the Philippines in the Hearing on 7–13 July 2015," *China Oceans Law Review*, 1–207 (Vol. 2015, No. 2).

22 The Award on Jurisdiction and admissibility, supra note 4. For comments, *see* Chris Whomersley, "The South China Sea: The Award of the Tribunal in the Case Brought by the Philippines against China – A Critique," *Chinese J. Int'l L.*, 239–64 (Vol. 15, no. 2, 2016); Michael Sheng-ti Gau, "The Agreements and Disputes Crystalized by the 2009–2011 Sino-Philippine Exchange of Notes Verbales and their Relevance to the Jurisdiction and Admissibility Phase of the South China Sea Arbitration," *Chinese J. Int'l L.*, 417–30 (Vol. 15, no. 2, 2016); Stefan Talmon, "The South China Sea Arbitration: Observations on the Award on Jurisdiction and Admissibility," *Chinese J. Int'l L.*, 309–91 (Vol. 15, no. 2, 2016); Sienho Yee, "Special Issue on Jurisdiction and Admissibility in the South China Sea Arbitration," *Chinese J. Int'l L.*, 219–37 (Vol. 15, no. 2, 2016).

23 Jurisdictional Award, *ibid.* paras 397–413.

24 For Transcripts on Merits Hearing, *supra* note 4.

25 Ninth Press Release on November 30, 2015, *ibid.*

26 The Merits Award, *ibid.*

27 *Ibid.* para. 1203. Compare with *supra* note 14.

28 The Merits Award, *supra* note 26, p. 474.

29 *Id.* paras. 573–75.

30 See 1st-2nd Claims under para 31 and 1st-3rd Reliefs under para 41 of the Notification, *supra* note 3.

31 The Philippines did not bring this arbitration on behalf any other SCS littoral States. This case is not a class action. Malaysia even drew the attention of the Tribunal not to prejudice its maritime entitlements while entertaining Philippine Submissions. *See* the Merits Award, *supra* note 26, paras. 36, 105, 634–35.

32 See its official statement on January 22, 2013: "This afternoon, the Philippines has taken the step of bringing China before an Arbitral Tribunal under Article 287 and Annex VII of the 1982 United Nations Convention on the Law of the Sea (UNCLOS) in order to achieve a peaceful and durable solution to the dispute over the West Philippine Sea (WPS)." *See* "Statement by the Secretary of DFA on the UNCLOS Arbitral Proceedings against China" available in: www.imoa.ph/press-releases/statement-by-secretary-of-foreign-affairs-albert-del-rosario-on-the-unclos-arbitral-proceedings-against-china-to-achieve-a-peaceful-and-durable-solution-to-the-dispute-in-the-wps/ (last visited August 31, 2016).

33 For example, China interfered with Philippine government vessels (i) approaching Second Thomas Shoal for rotation of personnel, (ii) navigating in the territorial waters of Scarborough Shoal. Also China conducted land-reclamation activities on the maritime features in the Spratly Islands Group. These activities all have the purpose of defending its territorial integrity with the nature of military activities. See Philippine Final Submissions 10–14, *supra* note 25, pp. 6–7.

34 Michael Sheng-ti Gau, *supra* note 5, pp. 100–3.

35 See Notification, *supra* note 3, p. 3, para. 7.

36 *Supra* note 4, Final Transcript Day 1 – Merits Hearing (Loewenstein), pp. 92–93, 98. Final Transcript Day 2 – Merits Hearing (Loewenstein), pp. 1–2, 13–17.

37 See Merits Award, paras. 197–98, 267. *Supra* note 26. Interestingly, para. 267 reads: "Because the Tribunal is not addressing questions of sovereignty, evidence concerning either Party's historical use of the islands of the South China Sea is of no interest with respect to the formation of historic rights (although, as will be discussed below (see paragraphs 549 to 551), it may bear upon the status of features pursuant to Article 121(3)). The Tribunal does find it relevant, however, to consider what would be required for it to find that China did have historic *maritime* rights to the living and non-living resources within the 'nine-dash line'."

38 Michael Sheng-ti Gau, *supra* note 5, pp. 104–6.

39 Jurisdictional Award, *supra* note 4, para. 153, p. 60.

40 When initiating this arbitration, the Philippines stated that China claimed sovereignty in the waters within USL. See Notification, *supra* note 3, paras. 2, 11, pp. 1, 4.
41 Michael Sheng-ti Gau, *supra* note 21, pp. 36–39, 135–39.
42 Merits Award, *supra* note 26, para. 200.
43 Jurisdictional Award, *supra* note 22, para. 157, p. 61.
44 See Memorial, *supra* note 13, Figure 3.4.
45 Merits Award, *supra* note 26, para. 208.
46 Michael Sheng-ti Gau, *supra* note 22, 422. Also, on August 4, 2009 the executive branch of the Philippine government forwarded a NV to the UN to protest a Vietnamese unilateral submission of outer limits of the CS beyond 200 M in the SCS dated May 6, 2009. This Philippine NV said that "[the] Submission for Extended CS by … Vietnam lays claim on areas that are disputed because they overlap with those of the Philippines'." As shown by Figure 1 of this paper, the Vietnamese unilateral submission provided a triangle-shaped area in orange far beyond the limits of 200 M from the archipelagic baselines of the Philippines facing the WPS. This triangle area is less than 200 M but beyond 12 M from KIG maritime features. Most probably, the Philippines said this because some KIG maritime features are considered as "islands," unless the Philippines used its archipelagic baselines to claim *extended* CS that might overlap with the Vietnamese triangle area. Seven years have passed without seeing the Philippine submission to the CLCS concerning its extended CS in the SCS. It means that in 2009 the Philippines admitted the existence of certain "islands" in KIG. Until October 12, 2016 this protesting Philippine NV remains on the CLCS website. Clearly, the Philippines continues to believe that "islands" exist in KIG even after the MA was granted. Dated on 4 August 2009, with the serial no. 000818, the file of this Philippine NV is available online: www.un.org/depts/los/clcs_new/submissions_files/vnm37_09/clcs_37_2009_los_phl.pdf.
47 On June 23, 2016, Malaysia sent an official communication to the Tribunal, where Malaysia recalls that it claims sovereignty over a number of features in the South China Sea and "may also have overlapping maritime entitlements (including an extended continental shelf) in the areas of some of the features that the Arbitral Tribunal has been asked to classify." It implied that fully entitled island may exist in the Spratly Islands Group. See Merits Award, *supra* note 26, paras. 634–35.
48 On May 8, 2009, Vietnam sent a NV to the United Nations (No. 86/HC-2009) stating that the Hoang Sa (Paracels) and Truong Sa (Spratlys) archipelagoes are parts of Viet Nam's territory, implying Vietnam's recognition of the existence of islands within these two groups of islands. www.un.org/depts/los/clcs_new/submissions_files/mysvnm33_09/vnm_chn_2009re_mys_vnm_e.pdf (last visited March 2, 2017).
49 Therefore, the rulings in the paras. 571–76 of the Merits Award are *ultra vires.* Merits Award, *supra* note 26, paras. 571–76. For *Non Ultra Petita* Principle, *see infra* note 64.
50 Merits Award, *supra* note 26, paras. 210–11.
51 Michael Sheng-ti Gau, *supra* note 22, pp. 424–26.
52 Michael Sheng-ti Gau, *supra* note 13, pp. 234–44.
53 Merits Award, *supra* note 26, para. 1203, pp. 471–77.
54 Jurisdictional Award, *supra* note 22, para. 169.
55 See China's NV dated on April 14, 2011, addressed to the UN, serial no. CML/8/2011. www.un.org/depts/los/clcs_new/submissions_files/mysvnm33_09/chn_2011_re_phl_e.pdf (last visited March 2, 2017).
56 It was declared by the Tribunal in the Merits Award that, as low-tide elevations, Subi Reef, Gaven Reef (South), and Hughes Reef do not generate entitlements to a territorial sea, EEZ, or continental shelf and are not features that are capable of appropriation. See Merits Award, *supra* note 26, p. 474.
57 Michael Sheng-ti Gau, *supra* note 13, pp. 212–13, 216–17.

58 *Supra* note 49.
59 Michael Sheng-ti Gau, *supra* note 13, pp. 226–27.
60 See Transcripts of the Hearing on July 7, 2015, pp. 8, 23 (Statement of Solicitor General Hilbay), 99 (Statement of Professor Sands). Also see Transcripts of the Hearing on July 8, 2015, pp. 30 (Statement of Mr. Martin), 86–87 (Statement of Professor Oxman). Also see Transcripts of the Hearing on July 13, 2015, pp. 15 (Statement of Mr. Reichler). Supra note 4.
61 *See supra* notes 50–52 and the corresponding text.
62 Michael Sheng-ti Gau, *supra* note 22, pp. 424–26.
63 This is evidenced by Malaysia's communication to the Tribunal on June 2016, *supra* note 47. Also see Merits Award, *supra* note 26, paras. 635–41.
64 ICJ: Asylum Case (Interpretation) (1950), ICJ Reports, 1950, p. 395, at p. 402. The Court said: "One must bear in mind the principle that it is the duty of the Court ... to abstain from deciding points not included in [the final] submissions [of the parties]." Also, ICJ: Corfu Channel Case (Compensation)(1949), ICJ Reports, 1949, p. 244, at p. 249.
65 See First-round submissions by Professor Sands, Final Transcript Day 1-Jurisdiction Hearing (on 7 July 2015), *supra* note 4, pp. 86–88.
66 See Robert C. Beckman and Clive H. Schofield, "Defining EEZ Claims from Islands: A Potential South China Sea Change," 29 *The International Journal of Marine and Coastal Law* (2014), pp. 210–11.
67 See Final Transcript Day 3 – Merits Hearing (Schofield), *supra* note 4, p. 6.
68 Merits Award, supra note 26, p. 474.
69 Ibid. paras. 573–75.
70 China did not provide Counter-Memorial as requested by the Tribunal in this case. Nor did China offer any formal Submissions to the Tribunal to actively complain about the actions of the Philippines in the SCS. Therefore, the Tribunal may only entertain Philippine Final Submissions made in the November Hearing. According to Final Submissions 3–4 and 6–7 of the Philippines, the Tribunal was requested to examine the legal status of nine particular maritime features occupied by China in WPS.
71 Supra note 47.
72 Merits Award, *supra* note 26, para. 1203-B-(8–10), pp. 474–75.
73 *Supra* notes 46–49.
74 Final Transcript Day 3 – Merits Hearing (Schofield), supra note 4, p. 6. Interestingly, Philippine Final Submissions did not request the Tribunal to examine the legal status of all maritime features of Spratly Islands Group.
75 *Supra* note 4, Final Transcript Day 1 – Merits Hearing (Loewenstein), pp. 92–93, 98. Also see Final Transcript Day 2 – Merits Hearing (Loewenstein), pp. 1–2.
76 *Supra* notes 46–48. *Also see* Michael Sheng-ti Gau, *supra* note 22, pp. 424–26.
77 See Notification, *supra* note 3, paras. 7, 40.
78 *Supra* note 75.
79 *Supra* note 37.
80 Merits Award, supra note 26, para. 1203-B-(7), p. 474.
81 *Supra* note 64.
82 Jurisdictional Award, *supra* note 22, para. 172.
83 Supra note 64.
84 *Supra* note 55.
85 Jurisdictional Award, *supra* note 22, para. 153, p. 59. "The Tribunal might consider that the Philippine Submissions could be understood to relate to sovereignty if it were convinced that either (a) the resolution of the Philippines' claims would require the Tribunal to first render a decision on sovereignty, either expressly or implicitly; or (b) the actual objective of the Philippines' claims was to advance its position in the Parties' dispute over sovereignty."
86 Merits Award, *supra* note 26, para. 1203-B-(11), p. 475.

87 *Supra* note 4, Final Transcript Day 2: Merits Hearing (Martin), pp. 166–67, 171, 172.
88 Merits Award, *supra* note 26, para. 793.
89 *Ibid.* para. 1203-B-(15), p. 476.
90 *Ibid.* pp. 417–20.
91 Supra note 1, Article 298(1)(b) of UNCLOS.
92 Supra note 9.
93 See para. 1203-B-(2) of the Merits Award, which can prove that even the Tribunal knows that its jurisdiction has geographic limits. *See* Merits Award, *supra* note 26, p. 473.
94 Para. 1203-B-(7)-(a), (b), and (c) of the Merits Award is therefore problematic. *Ibid*, p. 474.
95 *Supra* notes 46–48.
96 *Supra* notes 51, 54–55 and corresponding text.
97 *Supra* note 94.
98 *Supra* note 82 and corresponding text.
99 *Supra* note 55 and corresponding text.
100 *Supra* note 54 and corresponding text.
101 *Supra* notes 46–48.
102 *Supra* note 36.
103 *Supra* note 37.

12 Archipelagos and archipelagic regimes in the law of the sea

Sophia Kopela

Introduction

Dealing with archipelagos has been a challenge for the law of the sea due to the variety of their geographical characteristics. Indeed, archipelagos take various forms, being composed of small, large, few or many islands of different origin, i.e., volcanic, coral, rocky, arranged in different patterns, and located close to the mainland coast or further away in the sea.[1] Their main characteristic is the close association and interdependence between the land and the sea. This interdependence and their natural geographical unity have been considered to warrant a special protective regime in the law of the sea. Various non-geographical reasons have also been invoked: economic considerations reflecting the dependence of the archipelagic population on the marine resources, political and security concerns, and environmental threats.[2] These concerns and considerations gave birth to the archipelagic concept which advocates the consideration of the archipelago as a unit for the delimitation of its maritime zones.

Suggestions reflecting the archipelagic concept were made by various legal societies and scholars, and discussed in the 1930 Hague Conference on the codification of international law and the First and Second Conferences on the law of the sea.[3] The first approval of the archipelagic concept was given by the International Court of Justice (ICJ) in its judgment in the *Fisheries case* which validated the straight baseline system applied by Norway in its *skaergaard* archipelago.[4] This approach was endorsed by UNCLOS I in article 4 of the 1958 Geneva Convention on the Territorial Sea and Contiguous Zone (transferred almost verbatim to article 7 of the Law of the Sea Convention (LOSC)) which provided for the application of straight baselines in coasts where 'there is a fringe of islands along the coast in its immediate vicinity'. This has been thought to provide a reasonable solution for coastal archipelagos.[5]

It was, however, at the Third Conference on the Law of the Sea (UNCLOS III) when the issue of outlying or midocean archipelagos was given sufficient attention.[6] A number of archipelagic states, especially Fiji, Indonesia, Mauritius and the Philippines (with Bahamas cooperating closely), actively promoted the archipelagic concept. Apart from their special geographic circumstances, these states stressed the economic dependence of their people on the resources of the archipelago, political concerns related to their national security and territorial integrity, and environmental considerations linked to the vulnerability of their seas to marine pollution.[7] Most of these arguments were linked to the preservation and protection of their newly achieved independence and the right of these states to exploit their resources following years of colonisation. These arguments were bound to find a positive reception during UNCLOS III especially considering that, in contrast to previous conferences, the majority of the participants were developing states.[8] The content and the particularities of the regime adopted at UNCLOS III were the outcome of a compromise between the advocates of the archipelagic regime, mainly archipelagic states, and maritime powers keen to preserve their interests in the waters of archipelagos.

Part IV of the LOSC provides for the right of archipelagic states to draw archipelagic straight baselines joining the outermost points of their archipelagos and the consideration of the enclosed waters as archipelagic waters over which the state exercises sovereignty. Specific requirements were stipulated for the application of archipelagic baselines related to their length and the water-to-land ratio of the enclosure (article 47). Part IV also provides for the recognition of certain rights in favour of third states within the archipelagic waters (articles 51–54 LOSC). Despite suggestions for the application of the archipelagic regime to archipelagos that form part of a continental state, Part IV applies solely to archipelagic states (a notion unknown before the Third Conference on the Law of the Sea), which are defined in article 46 (a) LOSC as states 'constituted wholly by one or more archipelagos and may include other islands'.

Nowadays, 22 states have claimed archipelagic status and have designated archipelagic baselines encircling their archipelagos or parts of them.[9] What is more, despite the failure of UNCLOS to adopt a regime for dependent archipelagos, a number of states, such as Denmark, Ecuador, Australia, France and others, have applied straight baseline system to their archipelagos or parts of them for the delimitation of their maritime zones. This chapter will assess the application of Part IV of the LOSC and the practice of archipelagic states with respect to the drawing of archipelagic baselines and the status of archipelagic waters. It will further examine the practice of continental states in their outlying archipelagos in order to identify potential developments with respect to the endorsement of the archipelagic concept in the law of the sea. The objective of this chapter is to determine whether the LOSC has been able to effectively balance and accommodate the interests of archipelagos vis-à-vis those of third states.

The archipelagic regime of the LOSC and archipelagic state practice

Definition of archipelagos, archipelagic states and archipelagic baselines

Archipelagos cannot be easily classified into distinct geographic types due to the great variety they present. The definition included in article 46 (b) of the LOSC reflects this diversity and variety and focuses on two characteristics, namely the interconnectedness of the elements of an archipelago and its unity: 'archipelago means a group of islands, including parts of islands, interconnecting waters and other natural features which are so closely inter-related that such islands, waters and other natural features form an intrinsic geographical, economic and political entity or which historically have been regarded as such'. A few general comments can be made with respect to this definition. It does not provide any concrete requirements concerning the number of islands (and therefore two islands may be validly regarded as an archipelago), nor is there any specific reference to the distance between the islands or the area of the sea that they cover.[10] The main criterion in this respect is the adjacency or compactness of the islands, and the interconnectedness of the various features and the sea on an equal basis. This definition further recognises that an archipelago is more than a geographical concept; it is also a political and economic entity or has been historically perceived as such. The key notion of an archipelago is unity. The economic unity of the archipelago is indicated by the close interrelationship between the islands and the resources of the interconnecting waters,[11] but it can be subjective, as all states may invoke economic considerations reflecting its unity.[12] Political unity presupposes primarily that the islands of the archipelago belong to the same state.[13] Lastly, the historical criterion for the identification of the legal archipelago is provided as an alternative in case an archipelago cannot meet the other requirements. Though it is unclear what this might entail, some historical evidence that the archipelago has been consistently treated as a whole, for example, for administrative or political purposes, for a long period of time would satisfy this criterion.

The only archipelagic claim which has been contested on the basis of the definition of an archipelago and archipelagic state is that of the Dominican Republic. The Dominican Republic enacted legislation declaring itself an archipelagic state and defining the coordinates for the designation of archipelagic baselines in 2007.[14] According to this legislation, the archipelago is composed of the main island of Santo Domingo and various minor islands, reefs, low-tide elevations (LTEs) and a number of banks in the north of the main island.[15] The State Department in the *Limits in the Seas* has argued that the main island does not form 'an intrinsic geographical, economic and political entity' with the Banks in the north of the archipelago especially related to the Mouchoir Bank.[16] According to this publication, the bilateral boundary agreement concluded between the Dominican Republic and the UK (on behalf of the Turks and Caicos Islands) in 1996[17] (which never came into force) attributed the Mouchoir Bank to the Turks and Caicos and therefore the Dominican Republic did not consider it to be a part of the archipelago. The UK and the USA protested and disputed the status of the Dominican Republic as an archipelagic state, but did not clarify the reasons for this in their protests.[18] They protested against the infringement of the EEZ of the Turks and Caicos and Puerto Rico by the outer limit of the EEZ as established in the Dominican legislation, but not against the infringement of the waters of the Turks and Caicos by the actual archipelagic system, while the main issue in the protest, and for which they asked for further clarification, was the drawing of archipelagic baselines from basepoints considered to be LTEs not in compliance with article 47 (4).[19] Whether the Banks form part of the archipelago is further complicated by the issue of acquisition of sovereignty over LTEs and drying reefs especially since the ICJ has found that maritime delimitation will determine the sovereignty status of natural features falling short of islands in disputed areas.[20] This does not however provide an answer to the question of the political association and unity of LTEs and drying reefs within the framework of an archipelago. It is important to note that the boundary agreement with the Turks and Caicos was never approved by the Dominican Republic and in 2004 this state included the Mouchoir Bank and the surrounding area to the Sanctuary for Marine Mammals.[21] There is also evidence that the Dominican Republic has generally regarded the Banks in the north of the main island as an important part of the archipelago, and the inclusion of the Mouchoir Bank in the Sanctuary for Marine Mammals and the archipelagic system may demonstrate that this state considers it as part of the archipelago.[22]

For an archipelagic state to be able to apply archipelagic straight baselines around its archipelagos, a number of conditions have to be met: the length of the archipelagic baselines should be no more than 100 n.m. with an exception of up to 3 per cent of the total number of baselines which should not however exceed 25 n.m., and the water-to-land ratio should be between 1:1 and 9:1. This is the outcome of a compromise between archipelagic states, which were reluctant to accept quantitative requirements regarding the length of the baselines or the water-to-land ratio,[23] and maritime powers, determined to establish clear criteria for the application of the baselines in order to ensure that the regime would be applied in clearly determined cases without the possibility for excessive application by states (as was the case with article 7). The adoption of the minimum water-to-land ratio of 1:1 was suggested to exclude cases of a large island surrounded by smaller ones.[24] This has been criticised as unnecessary[25] but it can be argued that article 7 of the LOSC and the application of straight baseline may be more appropriate in these cases, especially since the enclosed waters will only be subjected to the right of innocent passage;[26] this might require a liberal interpretation of article 7 conditions (which has been observed in state practice), but article 7 might not always be able to justify the encirclement of the archipelago by straight baselines. The maximum water-to-land ratio requirement would preclude the application of the archipelagic regime to archipelagos with small islands spread out in a large maritime area. The adopted criteria are more generous than those initially suggested by maritime powers during UNCLOS III,[27] and mainly reflect the geographic particularities of the main archipelagic states which were active during UNCLOS III.[28] It is, however, inevitable that not all archipelagic states would be able to benefit (or benefit entirely) from this regime. Kiribati's declaration upon accession to the LOSC is indicative in this respect: it noted that the requirements would not allow it to join all elements of its archipelagos, and suggested that 'that the formula used for drawing archipelagic baselines be revisited in the future to take into consideration the above-mentioned concerns of Kiribati.'[29]

All 22 states which have proclaimed archipelagic status have designated archipelagic straight baselines and have submitted the relevant information to the UN Secretary General.[30] The great majority of archipelagic states have complied with the requirements of article 47 regarding the length of archipelagic baselines and the water-to-land ratio; some (rather minor) inconsistencies have been identified (and protested by some states, mainly the USA), which may also reflect some difficulties in the application of the conditions of article 47. Elements of the archipelagic baselines system of the Maldives have been protested by the US as exceeding the maximum allowed length.[31] One of the archipelagic lines of Papua New Guinea has also been found to exceed the allowed length (174.78 nm) and cannot be justified by the exception of article 47 (2).[32] How the exception regarding 'up to 3 per cent of the total number of baselines'[33] can be applied may be problematic as demonstrated by concerns raised with respect to the Indonesian baselines which have five baseline segments exceeding 100 nm; their validity would depend on whether the total number of baselines includes, apart from archipelagic baselines, also baselines following the low-water mark.[34] This is in line with a textual interpretation of the provision which refers to 'the total number of baselines' whereas in other parts of article 47 reference is made to 'such baselines' for archipelagic baselines. Baumert and Melchior also argue that excluding low-water baselines 'would seem to have the perverse effect of penalising an archipelagic state for using the normal baseline and encouraging the expansive use of straight archipelagic baselines in areas where they may not be appropriate'.[35]

Due to the diversity of archipelagic formations and in order to conform to the conditions regarding the length of archipelagic baselines and water-to-land ratio, archipelagic states have applied archipelagic baselines in parts of their archipelagos leaving out specific islands whose inclusion would not meet these requirements,[36] while some other archipelagic states have applied more than one sets of archipelagic baselines in different archipelagos.[37] This practice is in line with articles 47 and 48 of the LOSC.[38] Article 47 (1) provides that an archipelagic state may be constituted 'wholly by one or more archipelagos and may include other islands', while the only condition prescribed in article 47 (1) with respect to the drawing of archipelagic baselines is that the main islands of the archipelago are included within the archipelagic straight baselines. It is not clear what is meant by the main islands. The UN study suggests that this may include 'the largest islands, the most populous islands, the most economically productive islands, or the islands which are pre-eminent in an historical or cultural sense'.[39] This will depend on the specific circumstances of the islands and the archipelagic state, but it is clear that this refers to the archipelago and not the archipelagic state as the latter may be composed of more than one archipelagos.[40] The existing systems of archipelagic baselines conform to this condition.[41] An interesting case is the recently designated archipelagic baselines by Kiribati.[42] This archipelagic state has applied two separate sets of archipelagic baselines in the Gilbert archipelago (one in the North Islands, another in the South). The Gilbert Islands is Kiribati's main archipelago, whereas the subgroups of North and South Gilberts can be regarded as falling within the definition of a legal archipelago and therefore the applied archipelagic baselines include the main islands of each group.

With respect to the other conditions stipulated in article 47, the US State Department in its publications *Limits in the Seas* has identified some minor inconsistencies of some archipelagic systems with these conditions, which do not increase or only marginally increase the area of the archipelago. Concerns have been raised with respect to the basepoints: Comoros with respect to the use of Banc Vailheu which is, according to Limits in the Seas, a submerged feature;[43] Papua New Guinea with respect to the start and finish of the archipelagic baseline system which does not join basepoints on the main island of Papua New Guinea;[44] Seychelles regarding the use of basepoints in the sea where there are no features.[45] With respect to the Dominican Republic, concerns have been raised with respect to the use of LTEs in the north of the archipelago which do not meet the requirements of article 47 (4).[46] It can however be argued that as these basepoints are drying coral reefs, they do not have to meet the conditions for LTEs in article 47 (4) as the archipelagic state has the right to join the outermost points of its islands and drying reefs according to article 47 (1).[47]

The assessment of the water-to-land ratio is complicated by the calculation of the land area especially concerning the 'steep-sided oceanic plateau which is enclosed or nearly enclosed by a chain of limestone islands and drying reefs lying on the perimeter of the plateau' (article 47 (7) LOSC). Difficulties have arisen with respect to which formations may fit this description.[48] This calculation has allowed archipelagic states such as the Bahamas and the Seychelles to apply archipelagic baselines, however, not without problems in the latter case.[49]

It is also unclear how the rise of the sea level would affect the archipelagic baselines. This is a general problem for the law of the sea but the rise of the sea level will significantly affect low-lying archipelagic states.[50] For example, basepoints currently used for the drawing of archipelagic baselines may not qualify under article 47 anymore (i.e. LTEs, drying reefs and even islands might become permanently submerged),[51] or the water-to-land ratio may change due to the disappearance or changes in the land territory within the archipelagic formation.[52] Article 47 (4) does not include the exception mentioned in article 7 (4) concerning the use of LTEs as basepoints for the drawing of baselines in instances where the features 'has received general international recognition' which would arguably allow the state to continue using the LTEs even after their submersion.[53] Suggestions have been made for stability in jurisdictional claims and maritime boundaries despite changes which affect the baselines.[54] This is even more important for archipelagic states which will be able to retain their archipelagic regime and status despite such changes, and it clearly reflects the archipelagic concept which poses equal weight to the land and the waters of the archipelago. The archipelagic territory is composed of both the islands and the archipelagic waters as reflected in the unity of the archipelago not only in geographical terms but also socio-economic, political and historical. The archipelagic concept should also be taken into account in any future agreement or treaty dealing with issues related to the rise of the sea level and maritime boundaries and climate-displaced persons.

Archipelagic waters: Balancing exclusive and inclusive interests

The regime applicable to the waters enclosed by archipelagic baselines and the rights exercised by third states therein was the most controversial issue in the discussions concerning the archipelagic problem during UNCLOS III. Compromises were made in order to balance the sovereignty of archipelagic states with the interests of mainly maritime powers related to navigation and overflight.[55] The archipelagic regime of the LOSC has been criticised as being to such a degree concessionary to the interests of maritime powers that the main aspirations of archipelagic states were not ultimately attained.[56] However, despite these concessions, archipelagic states achieved the main objective of the archipelagic concept which is the unification of the waters of their archipelagos and the exercise of sovereignty over the archipelagic waters.

Archipelagic waters are neither internal waters nor part of the territorial sea but have a *sui generis* legal status[57] where the archipelagic state exercises sovereignty subject to certain rights recognised in favour of third states. The first category of such rights refers to those traditionally enjoyed by third states within the archipelagic waters: 'traditional fishing rights and other legitimate activities of the immediately adjacent neighbouring States in certain areas falling within archipelagic waters'[58] and the respect for 'existing submarine cables laid by other states and passing through its waters'.[59] Malaysia and Indonesia have signed, according to article 51, a bilateral agreement covering a wide spectrum of interests and rights.[60]

The main concessions to the initial aspirations of archipelagic states concern navigational rights. The LOSC provides for two types of such rights: innocent passage[61] and archipelagic sea-lanes (ASL) passage.[62] The former is to be exercised according to Section III of the LOSC concerning innocent passage in the territorial sea. The ASL passage, a new concept introduced by the LOSC, resembles the concept of transit passage through straits used for international navigation, and consists of a right of continuous and expeditious passage of foreign ships and aircrafts via sea lanes and air routes specially designated by the archipelagic state in consultation with the 'competent international organisation', namely the IMO.[63] ASL passage also applies to the adjacent territorial sea of archipelagic states. What normal mode would entail may be unclear but the position of maritime powers seems to be that this includes passage of submerged submarines,[64] overflight in formation, formation steaming, launching and recovery of aircraft.[65]

The majority of archipelagic states have recognised both innocent passage and archipelagic sea lane passage in their archipelagic legislation. What is more, some states have also recognised the right of innocent passage both for vessels and aircrafts[66] going thus beyond the provisions of the LOSC which recognise the right of overflight solely in designated ASL. However, there is some inconsistency in the legislation of a few states. For example, Maldives's legislation provides for archipelagic sea lane passage but not for innocent passage;[67] it also provides that archipelagic sea lane passage is to be exercised in international navigation channels and that it allows navigation but not overflight.[68] Some other states' legislation provides only for innocent passage and not for the designation of archipelagic sea lanes or archipelagic sea lane passage.[69]

The status of waters enclosed by archipelagic baselines by the Philippines is not very clear. In 2009 the Philippines enacted legislation redefining their archipelagic baselines to render them compliant with Part IV of the LOSC on the designation of archipelagic baselines.[70] This Act did not refer to the status of the enclosed waters, and it is not clear how it relates to the Constitution which declares the waters of the archipelago as internal waters of the state.[71] The constitutionality of this Act was challenged in *Magallona et al. v Executive Secretary et al.*,[72] but the Supreme Court rejected this challenge and found that any navigational rights in favour of third vessels in these waters (such as innocent passage, archipelagic sea lane passage) do not negate the sovereignty of the Philippines over these waters. Legislative proposals have been made for the definition of the maritime zones of the Republic but they have not been enacted as laws; these bills do not specifically refer to navigational rights, but define the waters enclosed by baselines as archipelagic waters.[73] It is not clear whether the right of innocent passage is recognised in all archipelagic waters, but it seems that the intention of the Philippines is to comply with the LOSC,[74] and it may be presumed that the Philippines have recognised the right of innocent passage in archipelagic waters. The US has operationally challenged the Philippines' consideration of the enclosed waters as internal almost continuously since 1978.[75] In their Freedom of Navigation Reports they note that the Philippines claims archipelagic waters as internal waters.[76]

Some archipelagic states have enacted restrictions upon the navigational rights of certain type of vessels. Some states require the prior authorisation for vessels carrying nuclear or other hazardous substances in archipelagic waters.[77] The right of states to restrict the innocent passage of vessels with special characteristics was controversial during UNCLOS III, but no such right was (at least explicitly) recognised in the LOSC.[78] A number of states have however enacted legislation requiring notification or authorisation for the passage of such vessels from their territorial sea (and even their EEZs) noting the increased danger to the environment and health from the passage of these vessels.[79] Some states have protested such attempts to restrict navigation rights.[80] There is however support for the validity of this practice, especially in the light of new developments in international environmental law related to the precautionary principle.[81] Some archipelagic states have also subjected the passage of warships through their archipelagic waters to prior authorisation.[82] Again, this reflects conflicting state practice concerning the innocent passage of warships in the territorial sea.[83]

With respect to the designation of archipelagic sea lanes, most archipelagic states have provided for this potential in their legislation and have recognised that in the interim phase this right is to be exercised in routes normally used for international navigation. The actual designation of archipelagic sea lanes has not been without problems, as can be demonstrated by the Indonesian experience and the debate concerning the potential designation of archipelagic sea lanes by the Philippines. Indonesia is the only archipelagic states which has enacted legislation providing for three archipelagic sea lanes within its archipelagic waters following a resolution of the IMO Maritime Safety Committee.[84] This has been regarded as a partial designation, and the USA has conducted operational assertions to assert the archipelagic sea lane passage in routes normally used for navigation not included in the designation.[85] The Philippines has not as yet established archipelagic sea lanes but recent bills before the Senate have provided for the designation of specific sea lanes and for the rights of third states during passage.[86] Baumert and Melchior consider this incompatible with the LOSC which requires the approval of the IMO in the designation of sea lanes.[87] Concerns about the role of the IMO in ASL designation had also been raised before and during the Indonesian designation.[88] Paragraph 9 of article 53 is not very clear with respect to the process of sea lanes designation. It requires (in mandatory terms) that the archipelagic state submit a proposal to the IMO, while reference to 'with the view to their adoption' denotes that the IMO input is required. The second part of this paragraph seems to indicate a chronological order ('the organisation may adopt ... *after which* (emphasis added) the archipelagic state may designate'); however, the non-obligatory wording in this part ('may') may cast doubts on whether the prior approval of the IMO is required. This seems to be the view of the Philippines which has stressed the urgent nature of the designation of sea lanes to protect its fragile marine environment.[89]

Dependent archipelagos: The archipelagic concept and straight baselines

Despite proposals during UNCLOS III for the application of the archipoelagic regime to all archipelagos regardless of their political status, archipelagos belonging to a continental state were not included in the archipelagic regime of Part IV of the LOSC. The Arbitral Tribunal in the *South China Sea arbitration* between the Philippines and China examined the potential application of straight baselines to dependent archipelagos in the framework of China's statements concerning the consideration of the Spratly Islands 'as a whole'.[90] The Tribunal argued that Part IV of the Law of the Sea Convention is only applicable to archipelagic states which are defined as states 'composed entirely by one or more archipelagos' and that a combination of article 7 (straight baselines) and articles 46–7 (archipelagic states) would exclude 'the possibility of employing straight baselines in other circumstances, in particular with respect to offshore archipelagos not meeting the criteria for archipelagic baselines'.[91] It noted that 'any other interpretation would effectively render the conditions in articles 7 and 47 meaningless'.[92] It thus rejected the application of straight or archipelagic baselines around dependent outlying archipelagos. It acknowledged that there is some practice by continental states which have applied straight baselines in their outlying archipelagos but found that this practice has not 'amounted to the formation of a new rule of customary international law'.[93]

However, the *travaux préparatoires* of UNCLOS III can shed some light on the absence of a provision on dependent archipelagos in the LOSC and on the approach of states concerning their outlying archipelagos. It is true that the group of archipelagic states, which was working methodically and effectively as an interest group in contrast to states possessing outlying archipelagos, sought to differentiate their claims from previous proposals (in order to enhance their legitimacy and therefore acceptability by the Conference) and stressed elements that related to their newly adopted independence related to sovereignty over resources and political integrity and security.[94] Nonetheless, initial proposals did not differentiate between archipelagos on the basis of their political status[95] and some archipelagic states were not against this extension.[96] While the archipelagic states' proposals were accepted by most states due to the support of developing states,[97] maritime powers were reluctant to accept any expansion of exclusive rights over areas of the sea which would impair freedom of navigation, including international trade and mobility of navies.[98] However, few states raised objections,[99] but most states did not take a stand on this issue as their main interest was the guarantee of innocent passage within archipelagic waters. States possessing archipelagos such as Ecuador, Spain, Greece, India, China, Argentina, Portugal, France, Canada, Australia, Honduras, sponsored and supported proposals for the extension of the archipelagic regime to archipelagos forming part of a continental state.[100] During the last stages of the Conference, some states expressed their opposition to the exclusion of dependent archipelagos from the archipelagic regime stressing its unfairness[101] and pointed out that the legal status of these archipelagos has remained unsettled.[102]

Despite the failure of UNCLOS III to address comprehensively the archipelagic problem, states have adopted systems of straight baselines encircling their archipelagos or parts of them. These states have not proclaimed these systems to be an analogical application of the archipelagic regime of the LOSC. They have applied straight baselines to join the outermost limits of the archipelagos or parts of them, but the legal basis for such application is not very clear. Taking into account the geographic circumstances of the archipelagos, this state practice can be classified in two categories which are based on a classification of the various types of archipelagos suggested by Dubner:[103] archipelagos dominated by one or two large islands and archipelagos with similarly sized islands or islands located in a random way.

In the first category, the straight baselines systems may be perceived to be in line with article 7 on straight baselines in coasts fringed by islands, as the main island or islands are fringed by the smaller islands of the group. Contrary to the comments of the South China Sea Arbitral Tribunal that 'these conditions [of article 7] do not include the situation of an offshore archipelago',[104] article 7 may be applied in the case of a relatively large island fringed by other smaller islands situated in its immediate vicinity as long as its conditions are met. The possibility of applying article 7 to outlying archipelagos has been acknowledged in principle by the ICJ in the

Qatar-Bahrain case. After rejecting Bahrain's argument for its consideration as a *de facto* archipelagic state (multi-island state),[105] since no such status had been formally declared,[106] the ICJ examined the potential application of straight baselines based on article 7 LOSC in the eastern side of the archipelago.[107] This may demonstrate the close relationship between the archipelagic concept and the system of straight baselines. The following archipelagos and the systems of straight baselines may be considered to fit this classification: Kerguelen Islands (France), Svalbard archipelago (Norway), Sjaelland and Laeso Islands (Denmark), Furneaux Group (Australia), Falkland Islands/Malvinas Islands (UK/Argentina – straight baselines have been applied by both states but in a different way), Guadeloupe (France).[108] These states have joined the outermost points of their archipelagos and consider the enclosed waters as internal waters of the state. In most instances, the conditions of article 7 are met – though in some instances a rather liberal interpretation of a fringe may be required (for example in the case of Guadeloupe).[109] In some other instances, the application of straight baselines seems to go beyond the geographic circumstances of a fringe, for example, the baselines joining the two main islands in the Falkland Islands together.[110] However, in all such instances the features are located at close distances and the enclosure of maritime space is limited and closely related to the main island(s).

States have also applied straight baselines in archipelagos with similarly sized islands or islands located in a random way. Due to the geographical realities of these archipelagos, the requirements for the application of article 7 cannot be met. The following states have applied such systems: Ecuador (Galapagos Islands), Faeroe Islands (Denmark), Houtman Abrolhos Islands (Australia), Canary islands (Spain), Balearic Islands (Spain), Azores and Madeira Islands (Portugal), Turcs and Caicos Islands (UK), Loyalty Islands (New Caledonia, France), Kong Karls Land (Svalbard, Norway), Co Co Islands and Preparis Islands (Myanmar), Andaman and Nicobar Islands – Lakshadweep Islands (India), Paracel Islands (China), Diaoyu Islands (China).[111] Most of these straight baseline systems have been applied in cases of 'closely knit' archipelagos where the islands are located close to each other in most instances in distances not exceeding double the breadth of the territorial sea. These states consider the enclosed waters as internal waters of the state, and they seem to be motivated by a broader concept of straight baselines and by general principles regarding the application of straight baselines (influenced by the dictum of the ICJ in the Fisheries case) and not the formalistic context of article 7. Few states have protested against these straight baselines systems as incompatible with the LOSC.[112] Taking into account this considerable state practice, the belief of these states in the compatibility of their systems with international law and some evidence that this practice has been tolerated by most states of the international community[113] it could be argued that there is an emerging rule of customary law complementary to the provisions of the LOSC which expands the content and scope of application of straight baselines.[114] The content of the rule as established in state practice seems to reflect and endorse the principles invoked by the ICJ in the *Fisheries case.*[115] Contrary views exist, however, especially since some states have protested against this practice.[116]

This emerging customary rule relates to the application of straight baseline to closely knit archipelagos, as there is limited practice related to the application of straight baseline in broadly scattered archipelagos.[117] However, these archipelagos should be able to benefit from an analogical application of the LOSC archipelagic regime. The restriction of the archipelagic regime to archipelagic states was indeed a compromise during UNCLOS III for the reasons explained above, but the element of statehood cannot be considered to justify the preferential legal treatment of archipelagic states.[118] Dependent outlying archipelagos do not just represent a geographical or topographical concept but also a political, economic and historical one with the same interests and needs as archipelagic states.[119] This is particularly the case for self-governing and non-self-governing archipelagic territories which can be considered as quasi archipelagic states.[120] Cogliati-Bantz, relying on a combination of articles 1 (2) (2) and 305 of the LOSC, argues that self-governing territories can be regarded to be archipelagic states as long as the parent states have delegated LOSC-related competences to them (he refers to the Cook Islands), and it is thus not necessary to be a sovereign state.[121] While this is an interesting argument, it is not very clearly based on the LOSC especially since article 47 refers to a 'state' consisted entirely by archipelagos (and not a state party) which implies sovereign statehood. Finally, the suggested analogical application of the archipelagic regime (under the conditions stipulated in Part IV of the LOSC) would not undermine the compromise between exclusive and inclusive rights and interests, as the archipelagic regime of the LOSC, as analysed above, sufficiently safeguards and guarantees the rights and interests of third states. With this analogical application, the law of the sea would provide a more comprehensive solution to the archipelagic problem.

States have also acknowledged the special circumstances of archipelagos particularly related to the protection of the marine environment and have established Marine Protected Areas in their archipelagos.[122] As mentioned above, one of the main rationales of the archipelagic concept is the protection of the sensitive and fragile marine environment of an archipelago. The establishment of a Marine Protected Area can thus be considered to be a manifestation of the archipelagic concept as it acknowledges the interaction and the interdependence between the islands, reefs, LTEs and waters as part of a geographical and ecological whole and marine ecosystem.

Conclusion

The archipelagic regime of the LOSC has been an innovative approach to the regulation of maritime space and jurisdiction as it allows archipelagic states to unify their waters into a single regime where the state exercises sovereignty. It recognises thus that the land and the water are of equal importance and provides a protective regime for archipelagos and safeguards their geographical, political and economic unity.

The archipelagic practice, as examined above, demonstrates the willingness of archipelagic states to comply with the conditions of article 47 LOSC regarding the drawing of archipelagic straight baselines despite the fact that they might be restrictive in some instances. Archipelagic states have tried to apply the requirements in such a way so as to benefit from the protective regime and the unification of the waters even in certain parts of their archipelagos. This demonstrates that the archipelagic regime is not a way of extending the jurisdiction of the state but a means of protecting vulnerable maritime areas due to their geographical, political and economic considerations. It is also a recognition of the dependence of the archipelagic population on the waters which they regard as part of their territory. This is particularly important for Small Island Developing States, whose need for protection has been recognised by the international community. The archipelagic concept has a role to play concerning the current threats facing low-lying archipelagic states such as the rise of the sea level, and should be taken into account as a means to preserve the stability of maritime jurisdiction.

The practice of archipelagic states has also demonstrated that third states' interests have been accommodated, and the regime has been applied by archipelagic states without major problems. Some concerns continue to exist with respect to the archipelagic waters of the Philippines and Indonesia, which reflect their strategically important geographic location. Restrictions related to navigational rights of vessels with special characteristics in the archipelagic waters, especially those related to vessels carrying radioactive cargos, should be seen within the general framework of potential developments regarding navigational rights and protection of the marine environment.

If the adoption of the archipelagic regime in the LOSC can be regarded as a victory (within the framework of the negotiations) of archipelagic states, and a reasonable compromise, the omission of any specific regime for archipelagos which form part of a continental state can be criticised as an unnecessary restriction. State practice has, to an extent, filled the gap and, as argued above, a customary rule may be regarded as emerging. This rule concerns closely knit archipelagos and can be regarded as an extended application of straight baselines and not an analogical application of the archipelagic regime of Part IV of the LOSC. On the other hand, there seems to be a lacuna in the law of the sea with respect to broadly scattered dependent archipelagos. It has been suggested that taking into account that there is no legitimate reason for their exclusion from a protective regime and that the inclusive interests of the international community would be sufficiently acknowledged, an analogical application of the archipelagic regime of the LOSC would contribute to a more comprehensive solution to the archipelagic problem in the law of the sea.

Notes

1 M. Munavvar, *Ocean States: Archipelagic Regimes in the Law of the Sea* (Martinus Nijhoff Publ., 1995), p. 5; D.W. Bowett, *The Legal Regime of Islands* (Oceana Publications Inc, 1979), pp. 90–97.

2 See H.W. Jayawardene, *The regime of islands in international law* (M.Nijhoff, 1990), pp. 106–10.

3 For proposals and suggestions before UNCLOS III see D.P. O'Connell, 'Midocean archipelagos in international law' 45 *BYIL* (1971), pp. 4–22. P. Rodgers,

Midocean Archipelagos and international law (Vantage Press, 1981), Part I and II. H.W. Jayawardene, *supra* note 2, pp. 114–20.

4 *Fisheries case* (United Kingdom v Norway) Judgment of 18 December 1951, ICJ Reports, pp. 127–29.

5 See analysis in S. Kopela, *Dependent archipelagos in the law of the sea* (M.Nijhoff, 2013), Chapter 2.

6 It is interesting to note that for the first time archipelagos were a separate item in the discussions, in contrast to previous negotiations where they formed part of the territorial sea issue. GA Official Records, Twenty-seventh session, Supplement No. 21 (A/8721), Chapter I, para. 23, p. 8. See P.E.J. Rodgers, *supra* note 3, p. 138.

7 See *infra* note 90. See also S.Kopela, *supra note* 5, pp. 28–29.

8 See H.W. Jayawardene, *supra* note 2, pp. 11–112. S.Kopela, *supra* note 5, pp. 25–27.

9 The following states have proclaimed archipelagic status and applied archipelagic straight baselines to their archipelagos: Antigua & Barbuda, Bahamas, Cape Verde, Comoros, Dominican Republic, Fiji, Grenada, Indonesia, Jamaica, Kiribati, Maldives, Marshall Islands, Mauritius, Papua New Guinea, Philippines, St Vincent & Grenadines, Sao Tome & Principe, Seychelles, Solomon Islands, Trinidad and Tobago, Tuvalu and Vanuatu.

10 M.Munavvar, *supra* note 1, pp. 110–11.

11 C.F. Amerasinghe, 'The problem of archipelagos in the international law of the sea', 23 *ICLQ* (1974), p. 565.

12 H.W. Jayawardene, *supra* note 2, p. 139.

13 See C.F. Amerasinghe, *supra* note 11, p. 557.

14 Act No. 66/07of 22 May 2007, 65 *Law of the Sea Bulletin* (2007), p. 18.

15 *Ibid* article 2.

16 See *Limits in the Sea No. 130 Dominican Republic: Archipelagic and other Maritime Claims and Boundaries* (US State Department, 2014), fnt 4 and accompanying text.

17 D.H. Anderson, 'Dominican Republic – UK (Turks and Caicos)' Report Number 2–22 in J.J. Charney and C.M. Alexander (eds) *International Maritime Boundaries*, Vol. III (M. Nijhoff, 1998), p. 2238.

18 Joint demarche undertaken by the UK and the USA in relation to the law of the Dominican Republic No 66-07 of 22 May 2007, done on 18 October 2007; 66 *Law of Sea Bulletin* (2008), p. 98. For the protests in 2010 and 2012 see Digest of US practice in international law for year 2010 (pp. 522–24) and 2012 (pp. 421–22) found at www.state.gov/s/l/c8183.htm. A further demarche filed by the UK, USA and Japan is mentioned in the 2010 demarche. The 2012 demarche also refers to similar demarches filed by the British Embassy and the chiefs of mission of several European Union member states in January 2012.

19 *Ibid.*

20 See *Sovereignty over Pedra Branca/Pulau Batu Puteh, Middle Rocks and South Ledge* (Malaysia v Singapore) Judgment of 23 May 2008, ICJ Reports paras. 295–99 (LTEs in overlapping territorial seas). *Case concerning territorial and maritime dispute between Nicaragua and Honduras in the Caribbean Sea* (Nicaragua v Honduras) Judgment of 8 October 2007, ICJ Reports para. 141 (LTEs beyond territorial seas).

21 Ley Sectorial de Areas Protegidas No 202–4 available at www.unesco.org/culture/natlaws/media/pdf/ dominicanrepublic/repdom_areasprotegidas_spaorof.pdf.

22 S. Kopela, '2007 Archipelagic Legislation of the Dominican Republic: An assessment', 24 *IJMCL* (2009), p. 509.

23 See M. Munavvar, *supra* note 1 pp. 130–31. Archipelagic states argued that limits in the length of baselines may contradict the archipelagic concept as it would not allow the state to unify the archipelago into a unity. UNCLOS III Official Records Vol I, pp. 113, 124–25, 132, 187–88 and Vol II p. 265.

24 Examples of this would be the UK, New Zealand, Iceland, Madagascar; H.W. Jayawardene, *supra* note 2, p. 146.

25 See R.R. Churchill and A.V. Lowe, *The Law of the Sea* (3rd edn) (Manchester University Press, 1999), p. 123.

26 UN Office for Ocean Affairs and the Law of the Sea, *Baselines: an examination of the relevant provisions of the UN Convention on the Law of the Sea* (UN Publ., 1989), p. 36. Similarly, R.D. Hodgson and R.W. Smith, 'The informal single negotiating text (Committee II): a geographical perspective', 3 *Ocean Development and International Law* (1976), p. 243. D.P. O'Connell, *supra* note 3, p. 25.
27 See suggestion by the UK for 1:5 for water-to-land ratio and 48 nm UN Doc A/AC.138/SC.II/L.44.
28 M. Munavvar, *supra* note 1, p. 130.
29 Declaration upon accession, 24 February 2003, available at www.un.org/depts/los/convention_agreements /convention_declarations.htm.
30 All legislation referred to in the following notes can be found at www.un.org/Depts/los/ LEGISLATIONANDTREATIES/regionslist.htm.
31 *Digest of United States Practice in International Law 2001*, pp. 711–14 available at www.state.gov/s/l/c8184.htm. See also *Maritime Claims Reference Manual* (2005) available at www.jag.navy.mil/organization/documents/mcrm/Maldives2017.pdf; see *Limits in the Seas* No 126 (US State Department, 2005), p. 3 for an analysis of this system. The US noted in its protest that 'these segments could be revised so as to meet the length requirements while remaining within the land to water ratios specified in article 47 (1) of the LOSC'.
32 *Limits in the Seas, No. 138, Papua New Guinea: Archipelagic and other Maritime Claims and Boundaries* (US State Department, 2014), p. 3.
33 As there is no restriction regarding the number of baselines, this provision provides flexibility to the archipelagic state to adjust its baselines so as to ensure that it meets this condition; see UN Study on baselines, *supra* note 26, p. 35.
34 See discussion in K. Baumert and B. Mechior, 'The practice of archipelagic states: a study of studies' 46 (1) *ODIL* (2015), p. 65; they note that the five baselines exceeding 100 nm are in line with the exception in article 47 (2) as the archipelagic baseline system entails 192 segments (which include 32 normal baselines segments).
35 *Ibid.*, p. 65.
36 See Tuvalu: Maritime Zones Act 2012; Vanuatu: Maritime Zones Act No. 6 of 2010. Fiji: Marine Spaces (Territorial Seas) (Rotuma and its Dependencies (Amendment) order 2012) and Marine Spaces (Archipelagic baselines and EEZ) (Amendment) Order 2012.
37 See Papua New Guinea: National Seas Act 1977 Act No. 7 of 7 February 1977 and Instrument Declaration of the baselines by method of coordinates of base points for purposes of the location of archipelagic baselines 25 July 2002(1). Seychelles: Maritime Zones (Baselines) Order, 2008 S.I. 88 of 2008. Solomon Islands: Legal Notice No. 41 of 1979: Declaration of Archipelagic Baselines (The Delimitation of Marine Waters Act (No. 32 of 1978). Mauritius: Maritime Zones (Baselines and Delineating Lines) Regulations 2005. Kiribati: Republic of Kiribati Marine Zones (Declaration) Act No. 4 of 2011. Marshall Islands: Republic of the Marshall Islands Maritime Zones Declaration Act 2016.
38 See UN Office for Ocean Affairs and the Law of the Sea, *supra* note 26, p. 37. See also M. Munavvar, *supra* note 1, pp. 135–36.
39 *Ibid*, p. 35.
40 K.Baumert and B.Melchior, *supra* note 34, p. 65.
41 *Ibid.*
42 Kiribati: Republic of Kiribati Marine Zones (Declaration) Act No. 4 of 2011.
43 *Limits in the Seas No. 134 Comoros: Archipelagic and other Maritime Claims and Boundaries* (US State Department, 2014), p. 2. K. Baumert and B. Melchior, *supra* note 34, p. 62.
44 K.Baumert and B.Melchior, *supra* note 34, p. 63.
45 *Ibid*, p. 66. Interestingly, these basepoints are not necessary, as a continuous straight baseline can be drawn and conform to the required criteria.

46 See Joint Demarches, *supra* note 18. See also *Limits in the Seas No. 130, supra* note 16, p. 3.
47 For an analysis of this system see S.Kopela, *supra* note 22, pp. 510–15.
48 UN Study on baselines, *supra* note 26, p. 36 and footnote 22.
49 *Limits in the Seas, No. No. 132 Seychelles: Archipelagic and other Maritime Claims and Boundaries* (US State Department, 2014), p. 2. See also K.Baumert and B.Melchior, *supra* note 34, p. 69.
50 A.Powers, 'Sea-level rise and its impact on vulnerable states: four examples', 73 *La.L.Rev.* (2012), p. 151.
51 Generally on the impact of sea level rise on islands see C. Schofield and D. Freeman, 'Options to protect coastlines and secure maritime jurisdictional claims in the face of global sea level rise' in M.B. Gerrard and G.E. Wannier (ed), *Threatened Island Nations legal implications of rising seas and a changing climate* (CUP, 2013), pp. 145–50.
52 M.Munavvar, *supra* note 1, p. 131.
53 See C.Schofield and D.Freeman, *supra* note 51, p. 158.
54 D.D.Caron, 'Climate change, sea level rise and the coming uncertainty in oceanic boundaries: a proposal to avoid conflict', pp. 14–17, available at SSRN: http://ssrn.com/abstract=2506092. He argues that 'the fixing of maritime boundaries ... does not affect the allocation agreed to at the Third Conference because it merely freezes the present division of authority over the oceans'. A.H.A. Soons, 'The Effects of a Rising Sea Level on Maritime Limits and Boundaries', 37 (2) *Netherlands International Law Review* (1990), p. 225; C. Schofield and D. Freeman, *supra* note 51, p. 162. R. Rayfuse, 'Sea level rise and maritime zones: preserving the maritime entitlements of "disappearing" states' in M.B. Gerrard and G.E. Wannier (eds), *supra* note 51, pp. 167–92.
55 See C.F. Amerasinghe, *supra* note 11, p. 544. J.A. Roach and R.W. Smith, *US Responses to excessive maritime claims* (3rd edn) (M.Nijhoff, 2012), p. 203; J.P. Bernhardt, 'The right of archipelagic sea lanes passage: a primer', 35 *VJIL* (1994–5), p. 721.
56 A. Dale, 'Archipelagos and the law of the sea: island straits states or island-studded sea space', 2 *Marine Policy* (1978), p. 63; R. Lattion, *L'archipel en droit international* (Editions Payot, 1984), pp. 199–200.
57 See M.Munavvar, *supra* note 1, p. 155. Munavvar points out that this new term was preferred in order 'to avoid the difficulties in applying traditional concepts to archipelagic situations'. See also E.D. Brown, The *International Law of the Sea Introductory Manual* Vol. I (Dartmouth Publ, 1994), p. 114.
58 Article 51 (1) of the LOSC. See also article 47 (6).
59 Article 51 (2) of the LOSC.
60 Jakarta Treaty, 25 February 1982; available at UN Office for Ocean Affairs and the Law of the Sea, *The Law of the Sea: Practice of Archipelagic States* (N. York: UN Publ., 1992), pp. 144–55.
61 Article 52 LOSC. Archipelagic states retained the right to suspend temporarily and after due publication the innocent passage of foreign ships in specified areas of the archipelagic waters if such suspension was found essential for the protection of their security. A number of archipelagic states specifically refer to this possibility in their archipelagic legislation.
62 Article 53–54 LOSC.
63 Article 53 LOSC. Article 53 (12) provides that that if the archipelagic state does not designate sea lanes or air routes, the right of archipelagic sea lanes passage may be exercised through the routes normally used for international navigation. However, there is uncertainty what constitutes 'routes normally used for international navigation'; see B. Kwiatkowska and E.R. Agoes, *Archipelagic Waters Regime in the light of the 1982 UNCLOS and State Practice* (Bandung: ICLOS, UNPAD, 1991), p. 48.
64 See B. Kwiatkowska and E.R.Agoes, *supra* note 63, p. 43. M.Munavvar, *supra* note 1, 168. Churchill and Lowe point out that at least this is the interpretation adopted by

maritime powers, which is consistent with the *travaux preparatoires* of UNCLOS III; R.R. Churchill and A.V. Lowe, *supra* note 25, p. 109.

65 J.A. Roach and R.W. Smith, *supra* note 55, p. 367; with specific reference to the position of the USA.

66 Dominican Republic and Solomon Islands. Kiribati, Tuvalu and Marshall Islands refer to free passage for vessels and aircrafts through the archipelagic waters.

67 Maritime Zones of Maldives Act No. 6/96.

68 This has been protested by the USA; see *Maritime Claims Reference Manual, supra* note 31. J.A. Roach and R.W. Smith, *supra* note 55, p. 374.

69 Vanuatu: Maritime Zone Act No. 6, 2010. Dominican Republic: Act No. 66/07 of 22 May 2007. Comoros, Papua New Guinea and Sao Tome and Principe do not have a provision in their enacting archipelagic legislation on navigational rights in archipelagic waters.

70 Republic Act No. 9522: An Act to Amend Certain Provisions of Republic Act No. 3046, as Amended by Republic Act No. 5446, to define the Archipelagic Baselines of the Philippines, and for Other Purposes.

71 Article 1 of the Constitution of the Republic of 17 January 1973; see also Understanding made upon signature (10 December 1982) and confirmed upon ratification (8 May 1984). This declaration was protested by Australia, Belarus, Bulgaria, former Czechoslovakia, Ukraine, former USSR and the USA. See J.A.Roach and R.W.Smith (3rd edition, 2012), pp. 214, 372. In a subsequent declaration filed by the Philippines on 26 October 1988, it was stated that: "The necessary steps are being undertaken to enact legislation dealing with archipelagic sea lanes passage and the exercise of Philippine sovereign rights over archipelagic waters in accordance with the Convention"; United Nations, *The law of the sea. Current Developments in state practice II* (N. York: UN, 1989), p. 96.

72 G.R. No. 187167, 16 August 2011.

73 See SBN-39: Philippine Maritime Zones Act: An Act to Define the Maritime Zones of the Republic of the Philippines Filed on July 1, 2013 available at www.senate.gov.ph/lis/bill_res.aspx?congress=16&q=SBN-39.

74 See H.S. Bensurto, 'Archipelagic Philippines: a question of policy and law' in M.H. Nordiquist and J.N. Moore (eds), *Maritime border diplomacy* (M.Nijohoff, 2012), p. 327; he points out that RA 9522 'clearly indicates a shift towards complete adherence to UNCLOS as regards the definition and limits of the territorial sea and archipelagic waters'.

75 See *Maritime Claims Reference Manual, supra* note 31, p. 463; see Freedom of Navigation reports http://policy.defense.gov/OUSDPOffices/FON.aspx.

76 *Ibid.*

77 Vanuatu, Dominican Republic, Mauritius and Seychelles. Maldives has a relevant provision concerning its territorial sea.

78 See M.H. Nordquist, *UN Convention on the Law of the Sea, 1982: A Commentary* (M. Nijhoff, 1985), pp. 218–20.

79 For a list of states requiring prior authorisation or notification for the exercise of innocent passage see S.Kopela, supra note 22, p. 520. In 1995, some states, including some archipelagic states (Antigua and Barbuda, Colombia, the Federal States of Micronesia, Fiji, Indonesia, the Philippines, Puerto Rico, Uruguay and the member states of CARICOM) refused entry to their territorial sea and archipelagic waters to the *Pacific Pintail* which was transporting plutonium from France to Japan. The ship changed its route to avoid the waters of protesting states; see J.M. Van Dyke, 'Applying the Precautionary Principle to Ocean Shipments of Radioactive Materials', 27 *Ocean Development and International Law* (1996), p. 387.

80 The USA has protested against most of these claims and has in many instances reiterated its view concerning the innocent passage of such vessels; see protests mentioned by J.A. Roach and R.W. Smith, *supra* note 55, at 271–75 (nuclear-powered vessels), 278–80 (vessels carrying hazardous waste); see also the objections by Germany (27 *Law of*

the Sea Bulletin (1995) at 6–7), UK (*Joint demarche, supra* note 18); Netherlands (32 *Law of the Sea Bulletin* (1996) at 8).

81 See J.M. Van Dyke, *supra* note 79, p. 379 *et seq.* M.Roscini, 'The navigational rights of nuclear ships', 15 *Leiden Journal of International Law* (2002), p. 25; L. Marin, 'Oceanic Transportation of Radioactive Materials: the Conflict between the Law of the Seas' right of innocent passage and duty to the marine environment', 13 *Florida Journal of International Law* (2000–2001), pp. 374–75.

82 Antigua and Barbuda, St Vincent and the Grenadines, Seychelles and Vanuatu. Maldives refers to this restriction with respect to its territorial sea.

83 For states imposing restrictions on the innocent passage of warships see R.R. Churchill, 'The impact of state practice on the jurisdictional framework contained in the LOS Convention' in A.G. Oude Elferink, *Stability and change in the law of the sea: the role of the LOS Convention (M.*Nijhoff, 2005), pp. 112–23.

84 See resolution MSC.72 (69) of the Maritime Safety Committee of the IMO regarding a partial system of archipelagic sea lanes for Indonesia. And Regulation No. 37 dated 28 June 2002 on the Rights and Obligations of Foreign Ships and Aircraft Exercising the Right of Archipelagic Sea Lanes Passage, which came into force on 28 December 2002. A further problem which arose and is still unclear concerns the axis line and the width of the sea lanes with respect to the 10% rule (article 53 (5) LOSC); for an overview of this issue see T. Davenport, 'The archipelagic regime' in D.R. Rothwell et al. (eds), *Oxford Handbook of the law of the sea* (OUP, 2015), pp. 151–52.

85 See Freedom of Navigation Programme at http://policy.defense.gov/OUSDPOffices/FON.aspx. Australia has also continued to use East-West routes normally used for navigation. See D.M.Sodik, 'The Indonesian Legal Framework on baselines, archipelagic passage, and innocent passage' 43 (4) *ODIL* (2012), p. 335. See also H. Djalal 'Indonesia's archipelagic sea lanes' in R. Cribb and M. Ford, *Indonesia beyond the water's edge: managing an archipelagic state* (ISEAS Publishing Singapore, 2009), p. 68.

86 See Senate Bill No. 159 The Philippine Archipelagic Sea Lanes Act, 1/7/2013 available at www.senate.gov.ph/lis/bill_res.aspx?congress=16&q=SBN-159) More recent bills delegated the designation of archipelagic sea lanes to the President of the Republic see Senate Bill SBN-2838, 6/9/2015 available at http://www.senate.gov.ph/lis/bill_res.aspx?congress=16&q= SBN-2838.

87 K. Baumert and B. Melchior, *supra* note 34, p. 73. See also J.A. Roach and R.W. Smith, *supra* note 55, pp. 365–66; they argue that 'only after adoption by the IMO may the archipelagic state implement archipelagic sea lanes'.

88 See C. Forward, 'Archipelagic sea-lanes in Indonesia – Their legality in international law', 23 *Australia and New Zealand Maritime Law Journal* (2009), pp. 152–53.

89 For a discussion on this issue see H. Bensurto, *supra* note 74, pp. 345–49.

90 *The Republic of the Philippines v the People's Republic of China, PCA Case N° 2013–19 in the matter of the South China Arbitration*, Award of 12 July 2016 (Merits), para. 571, 573. The Tribunal noted that China's statements 'could also be understood as an assertion that the Spratly Islands should be enclosed within a system of archipelagic or straight baselines, surrounding the high-tide features of the group, and accorded an entitlement to maritime zones as a single unit'.

91 *Ibid*, para. 575.

92 *Ibid.*

93 *Ibid*, para. 576.

94 See for example the comments by Indonesia UNCLOS III Official Records, Vol I, 31st Meeting, paras. 47–53. and Fiji UNCLOS III Official Records Vol. I 29th Meeting paras. 44–50.

95 See S. Kopela, *supra* note 5, p. 30 note 104.

96 See the working paper co-sponsored, among other states, by Indonesia and Mauritius *infra* note 100.

97 S. Kopela, *supra* note 5, p. 27.

98 C.F. Amerasinghe, *supra* note 11, p. 544. J.A. Roach and R.R. Smith, *supra* note 55, p. 203.

99 See UNCLOS III Official Records, 39th Meeting, paras. 29 and 42, pp. 169–70 (Turkey); 37th Meeting para. 70, p. 265 (Thailand); 37th Meeting para. 7, p. 266 (Myanmar), 37th Meeting para. 51 (Pakistan); 37th Meeting para. 21 (Bulgaria).

100 See main debate on archipelagos during UNCLOS III Official Records, Vol. II, 36th and 37th Meetings pp. 260–73. And working paper co-sponsored by Canada, Chile, Iceland, India, Indonesia, Mauritius, Mexico, New Zealand and Norway, Vol. III Doc A/CONF.62/L.4, pp. 82–83.

101 UNCLOS III Official Records Vol XVII, 187th Meeting para. 8 (India), 190th Meeting, para. 100 (Spain), para. 196 (Ecuador).

102 *Ibid* and Vol, IX Summary Records of Meetings Plenary Meetings 103th Meeting para. 48 (Greece) See similar comments by commentators, R.P. Anand, 'Midocean archipealgos in international law: theory and practice', 19 *Indian Journal of International Law* (1979), p. 255; V.S. Mani, 'National jurisdiction: islands and archipealgos' in R.P. Anand (ed.), *Law of the Sea: Caracas and beyond* (M. Nijhoff, 1980), p. 103; H.W. Jayawardene, supra note 2, p. 142.

103 B.H. Dubner, *The law of territorial waters of midocean archipelagos and archipelagic states* (M.Nijohoff Publ., 1976), pp. 67–68; he refers to the following types of archipelagos: '(1) The islands are scattered, at random, over a radius of more than twice the breadth of the territorial sea and are not grouped together in any particular pattern. In this situation, there occur wide areas of high seas between the islands, (2) the islands are not scattered over a large distance. Instead, they are grouped together, at random, with smaller areas of high seas flowing between the islands; (3) There is one large mainland-type island with a few islands located within a close proximity both to the large island and to the other fringe islands'.

104 *South China Sea arbitration* (Merits), *supra* note 90, para. 575.

105 *Case concerning maritime delimitation and territorial questions between Qatar and Bahrain* (Qatar *v.* Bahrain, Judgment of 16 March 2001, Merits), *ICJ Reports* 2001, para. 32–34, 180–83.

106 *Ibid*, para. 183.

107 *Ibid*, para. 214.

108 For an analysis of these systems and their compatibility with article 7 LOSC, see S.Kopela, *supra* note 5, pp. 113–24.

109 *Ibid*, p. 124.

110 *Ibid*, pp. 122–24.

111 For an analysis of these systems see S.Kopela, *supra* note 5, pp. 125–39.

112 *Ibid*, pp. 173–77.

113 *Ibid*, pp. 167–72.

114 The South China Sea Tribunal did not examine this practice, its details and the constituent elements of customary international law. It did imply though that the emergence of customary rules could potentially 'permit a departure' from the LOSC; South China Sea arbitration (merits), *supra* note 90, para. 576; see also para. 274.

115 See *Fisheries case*, *supra* note 4, p. 133.

116 See J.A. Roach and R.W. Smith, *supra* note 55, p. 108 et seq. and 208; E. Franckx and M. Benatar, 'Straight baselines around insular formations not constituting an archipelagic state', p. 13 available at http://nghiencuubiendong.vn/en/conferences-and-seminars-/the-third-international-workshop-on-south-china-sea/656-straight-baselines-around-insular-formations-not-constituting-an-archipelagic-state-by-erik-franckx-a-marco-benatar.

117 In some instances of broadly scattered archipelagos such as the Paracel Islands and Diaoyu Islands, it has been found that the requirements of article 47 are not met due to the water-to-land ratio; see J.A. Roach, 'China's straight baseline claim: Senakku

(Diaoyu) Islands' 17 (7) *AJIL Insights* (2013). Limits in the Seas, No 117, China: Straight baseline claim (1996), p. 8.

118 See similar arguments in N. Hong, J. Li and P. Chen, 'The concept of archipelagic state and the South China Sea: UNCLOS, state practice and implication' *China Oceans Law Review* (2013), p. 220–22; H.P. Rajan, 'The legal regime of archipelagos', 29 *German Yearbook of International Law* (1986), p. 147; M.A. Saenz de Santa Maria, 'Spain and the law of the sea: selected problems' 32 *Archiv des Volkerrechts* (1994), p. 209.

119 The arbitrariness of this differentiation was stressed by some states during UNCLOS III which argued that this would 'penalise' the states and impact on their sovereignty; see UNCLOS III Official Records, Vol 11, 36th Meeting, p. 263, para. 45 (France), 37th Meeting, p. 267, para. 17 (Ecuador), p. 270, para. 42 (Spain), p. 266, para. 5 (Portugal).

120 S.Kopela, *supra* note 5, pp. 234–36.

121 V.P. Cogliati-Bantz, 'Archipelagic states and the new law of the sea' in L. del Castillo-Laborde (ed.), *The Law of the Sea From Grotius to the United Nations Convention on the Law of the Sea: Liber Amicorum Judge Hugo Caminos* (Brill, 2015), pp. 304–5.

122 See, for example, Ecuador, Galapagos: Special Regime Law for the Preservation and Sustainable Development of the Province of Galapagos available at http://whc.unesco.org/en/list/1/documents/; UK, British Indian Ocean Territory: 2010 Proclamation No 1 of 2010 (Marine Protected Area) and Schedule; UK, Georgia and Sandwich Islands: Wildlife and Protected Areas Ordinance 2011; Australia, Heard Island and McDonald Island Marine Reserve: Section 344 Environment Protection and Biodiversity Conservation Act 1999.

13 Low-tide elevations

A contemporary analysis

Yinan Bao

Introduction

According to Professor Dipla of the University of Athens, low-tide elevations in modern law of the sea was once regarded as a subcategory of islands. To be specific, during the nineteenth century Great Britain and the Scandinavian countries treated low-tide elevations as islands, provided that such features were 'located in the immediate vicinity of the coasts'.[1] As late as the 1930 Hague Conference of Codification of International Law, there were still a number of States following the practice of the nineteenth century. Notably, it was also during the 1930 Hague Conference that the remarkable distinction between elevations which emerged only at low tide and islands which emerged at high tide, began to be widely accepted by States.[2] Nevertheless, it is recognisable that there was no strict definition of low-tide elevations in the vocabulary of international law before the mid-twentieth century, though there were sporadic use of the term 'elevations'. As Churchill and Lowe commented, 'Low-tide elevations are often referred to in older books and treaties as "dry rocks" or "banks".'[3] In the Anglo-Norwegian Fisheries Case of 1951, the British did mention the term 'low-tide elevations'.[4] However, as late as in 1956, in the commentary to Article 10 'Islands' in the 'Commentary to the Articles concerning the Law of the Sea' prepared by the International Law Commission, there was no mention of the term 'low-tide elevations'. It merely provided that 'Elevations which are above water at low tide only ... are not considered islands and have no territorial sea'.[5] Similarly, Article 11 of the Draft Articles was titled as 'Drying Rocks and Drying Shoals' instead of using the term 'Low-tide Elevations'.[6] Later, at the First United Nations Conference on the Law of the Sea in 1958, when commenting on the 1956 Draft Articles, the delegates from the United States criticised the use of the term 'Drying Rocks and Dry Shoals' as vague, irrelevant and unqualified. They proposed the use of the term 'Low-Tide Elevations' to amend the heading of Article 11.[7] The proposal was accepted by the First Committee of the Conference[8] and so, 'low-tide elevations' as a formal term in the international law of the sea appeared for the first time in Article 11 of the Convention on Territorial Sea and Contiguous Zone 1958.[9] During the Third United Nations Conference on the Law of the Sea, the entire draft concerning low-tide elevations was based on Article 11 of the 1958 Convention, 'only drafting changes were incorporated'.[10] Thus, in the United Nations Convention on the Law of the Sea 1982,[11] the text of the provision concerning low-tide elevations (Article 13) is repeated verbatim, which provides:

1. A low-tide elevation is a naturally formed area of land which is surrounded by and above water at low tide but submerged at high tide. Where a low-tide elevation is situated wholly or partly at a distance not exceeding the breadth of the territorial sea from the mainland or an island, the low water line on that elevation may be used as the baseline for measuring the breadth of the territorial sea.
2. Where a low-tide elevation is wholly situated at a distance exceeding the breadth of the territorial sea from the mainland or an island, it has no territorial sea of its own.

In addition to Article 13, the Convention contains another provision (Article 7.4) which stipulates the criteria for selecting low-tide elevations as base points to draw straight baselines:

> Straight baselines shall not be drawn to and from low-tide elevations, unless lighthouses or similar installations which are permanently above sea level have been built on them or except in instances where the drawing of baselines to and from such elevations has received general international recognition.

Indeed, the above two provisions form the essential legal regime governing low-tide elevations under the Convention. Inevitably, the limited number of provisions and the lack of elaboration of the legal status of low-tide elevation in the Convention leave lacuna in both theory and practice of the international law of the sea. Notably, at least three crucial issues related to low-tide elevations are not addressed in the Convention. First of all, the Convention has no provision elaborating the criteria for the determination of the natural status of low-tide elevations. Secondly, the issue of territoriality of low-tide elevations is not mentioned anywhere in the Convention. Thirdly, the impact of expected global sea level rise on the status of low-tide elevations is not expressly regulated by the Convention. In the following sections, the aforementioned three issues will be examined in turn.

The criteria for determining the natural status of low-tide elevations

Under the contemporary regime of international law of the sea, maritime features may be divided into three distinct categories: islands (including rocks), low-tide elevations and submerged features. Islands are regulated under Article 121 of the Convention, which stipulates that '[a]n island is a naturally formed area of land, surrounded by water, which is above water at high tide'. Low-tide elevations are regulated under Article 13 of the Convention as mentioned above. Although the legal status of submerged features remains to be regulated by customary international law, it is not difficult to recognise that submerged features should be naturally formed land areas which are submerged at low tide.[12] Based on these definitions, it can be identified that the decisive factor to distinguish one category of maritime features from another is the relative position of maritime features to low tide and high tide. Unfortunately, there is no definition of low tide and high tide in the Convention. State practice reveals that the relative position of a maritime feature to tidal levels is determined based on the choice of a specific tidal datum.[13] Thus, the criteria to determine a maritime feature as a low-tide elevation rest on the choice of both the low water datum and the high water datum. According to the information provided by the International Hydrographic Organization (IHO), there are at least 17 tidal datum that are most commonly used by States, including Lowest Low Water (LLW), Lowest Astronomical Tide (LAT), Mean Low Water Spring (MLWS), Mean High Water (MHW), Highest Astronomical Tide (HAT), Highest High Water (HHW), Mean Sea Level (MSL), etc.[14] In 1997, the IHO recommended to its member states that the LAT and HAT should be adopted as the national low tide datum and high tide datum respectively.[15] However, as a consultative organization, the resolution adopted by the IHO has no binding force on its member states. Thus, such a recommendation provides no real significance in forming an internationally accepted rule on the choice of low tide and high tide datum.

There are two main reasons that can serve to explain such a great variety in the choice of tidal datum in State practice. First, natural and geographical factors greatly influence the choice of different tidal datum by States. Previous research reveals that tidal ranges[16] varies greatly in different parts of the world. In some places, the range is between 5 and 10 metres.[17] As a result, States tend to adopt different tidal datum to avoid navigation hazard and facilitate navigation safety. Second, present technological limitations make it extremely difficult to obtain precise statistics of tidal information. As O'Connell pointed out, 'Although there has been much scientific study of tides, a complete understanding of all the factors which influence them has not been reached, and it is not possible to predict a tidal level within plus or minus 2 centimetres.'[18] It is summarised by Kapoor and Kerr that 'the fact that the tidal phenomenon varies in different localities of the world, with the result that no single formula will satisfy all tidal regimes'.[19] Similarly, Symmons and Tanaka both concluded that no customary international rules can be identified with regard to the choice of tidal datum.[20] Thus, the choices of specific low tide and high tide datum are inevitably left to the 'free appreciation' of every State.[21]

The fact that there is no customary international law in the choice of tidal datum inevitably gives rise to controversy and uncertainty in maritime and territorial disputes. For instance, in the 1977 Anglo-French Continental Shelf Arbitration, in the determination of whether Eddystone Rock can be classified as an island or a low-tide elevation, the United Kingdom claimed that its choice of tidal datum, Mean High Water Springs, appeared in the 'practice of many other States', and it is the 'only precise one'.[22] On the contrary, the opposite party of the dispute, France, claimed that the Highest Annual Tide Mark should be used to determine the insularity of Eddystone Rock. In the 2012 Territorial and Maritime Dispute Case between Nicaragua and Columbia, the two parties have different opinions on the status of several maritime features in the Quitasueno area. The tidal model used by the two disputed parties, Global Grenoble Tide Model and Admiralty Total Tide Model, produced different results for the determination of insular status for maritime features in the Quitasueno area.[23] In these two cases, different tidal datum were proposed by disputed parties and they led to contradictory results. Consequently, it is not surprised that the international arbitral and judicial body face a dilemma: it is not easy to decide which tidal datum should be adopted to determine the status of maritime features. As has been pointed out above, there is no internationally accepted standard choice of tidal datum, and State practice varies greatly in this matter. Thus, the international arbitral and judicial body cannot simply adopt any party's proposed tidal datum without considering the other party's choice. Clearly, it will be extremely difficult to convince one party that the other party's choice of tidal datum should be regarded as the suitable one to determine the status of the maritime feature. In fact, in the aforementioned Anglo-French Continental Shelf Arbitration, the Tribunal used the principle of estoppel to solve the dilemma, for France had previously regarded Eddystone Rock as an island.[24] In the aforementioned Territorial and Maritime Dispute Case, the ICJ decided that the maritime feature of QS 32 should be regarded as an island, for the status of this maritime feature can be determined as an island by the different tidal models proposed by both parties.[25] Obviously, in the above two cases, the international arbitral and judicial body adopted a pragmatic approach to solve the dilemma, instead of confining itself to the thorny issue of the choice of tidal datum. Nevertheless, in theory the difficulty in the determination of the status of maritime features by the choice of tidal datum remains. It can be asserted that each State is entitled to adopt its own choice of tidal datum in its own maritime zones. When a maritime boundary dispute arises, wherever there is an overlapping maritime area in the dispute, the international arbitral and judicial body will have to decide which party's choice of tidal datum should be adopted so as to determine the status of maritime features as low-tide elevations or islands. Unfortunately, there is few international legal principle available for use except for the principle of estoppel, which is helpful but obviously, estoppel may not be occurred in every dispute. It is therefore well summarised by Tanaka that 'international courts and tribunals may face the risk of non liquet when a dispute arises with respect to the identification of low or high tides'.[26]

In the South China Sea Arbitration initiated by the Republic of Philippines against People's Republic of China, a novel issue concerning the possible effect of the choice of different tidal datum emerged as the Arbitral Tribunal delivered its Award on 12 July 2016. In the Award, the Arbitral Tribunal asserted that the tidal range in the disputed South China Sea is 'comparatively small', based on its assessment of related evidences submitted by the Philippines. Consequently, the Arbitral Tribunal asserted that 'the selection of a vertical datum will, in most instances, make no difference regarding the status of a feature'.[27] Notwithstanding this assertion, uncertainty remains unsolved. As pointed out above, tidal range varies greatly in different part of the world. In fact, this is also true in the South China Sea, where 'tidal range also varies from close to nil to a predicted 2 m during spring tides in the northern part of the Spratlys'.[28] In addition, according to the IHO regulations, tidal range will not be appreciable if the tidal range is less than 0.3 m,[29] which means any tidal range more than 0.3 m should be taken into consideration when analysing the possible impact arising from the choice of difference tidal datum. Obviously, a close examination of statistics of the tidal ranges cited in the award reveals that in most parts of the South China Sea, tidal ranges are more than 0.3 m and so, the selection of different tidal datum should by no means be ignored.[30] Whether the jurisprudence concerning the impact of the choice of different tidal datum on the determination of the natural status of low-tide elevations in the South China Sea Arbitration will be accepted or rejected by international courts and tribunals in the foreseeable future remains a mystery. In this author's view, the issue of determining the natural status of low-tide elevations and the choice of different high tide datum has not been fully solved.

The territoriality of low-tide elevations

The second issue which has not been addressed in the Convention is the question of territoriality of low-tide elevations. Since 'low-tide elevations' appeared as a formal term in the international law of the sea in the 1958 Convention on the Territorial Sea and Contiguous Zone, the issue of whether low-tide elevations can be appropriated as territory like islands and other land territory has seldom been fully discussed by international law academics.[31] Neither do international courts and tribunals frequently elaborate this issue in their jurisprudence.[32] One commentator pointed out that it was not until the 2001 Qatar/Bahrain Case that for the first time the ICJ paid enough attention to the discussion of this crucial issue.[33]

The origin: The Qatar/Bahrain case

In the Qatar/Bahrain case, Qatar claimed that Fasht ad Dibal, a low-tide elevation recognised by both disputed parties, cannot be appropriated as territory, whereas the opponent party, Bahrain, claimed that Fasht ad Dibal can be appropriated.[34] According to Qatar's legal counsel, Professor Quenendec, at least two reasons can be put forward to support the assertion that low-tide elevations cannot be appropriated as territory. First, 'from a strictly physical, practical point of view, a low-tide elevation is hardly something that can be appropriated, in the sense that an actual taking of possession is difficult to imagine.'[35] Second, 'a low-tide elevation cannot in principle be subject to sovereignty unless it is located wholly or partly within the territorial waters of a territory which is itself capable of appropriation.'[36] The legal counsel of Bahrain, Professor Weil, disagreed with Quenendec's arguments and elaborated his assertion that 'low-tide elevations can be appropriated' in four points. First, Quenendec's second argument indicates that 'sea dominates the land', which is opposite to the well-established principle of 'land dominates the sea'.[37] Second, according to Article 7 (4) of the Convention, straight baselines can be drawn from low-tide elevations if lighthouses or similar installation which are permanently above sea level are built on them. Practically, these 'appropriate points' for drawing straight baselines cannot be 'aquatic points, out at sea'. Thus, it is implied from this provision that low-tide elevations are land and not sea. And so, they form part of State territory and can be appropriated like other land territory.[38] Thirdly, based on Article 13 of the Convention, low-tide elevations can generate territorial sea if they are situated wholly or partly within the breadth of territorial sea of mainland or an island. Thus, even though low-tide elevations are physically 'part-time' land territory due to their nature, they are nonetheless 'legally full-time State territory'. Otherwise, low-tide elevations would never generate territorial sea.[39] Fourthly, it was only until 1958 that low-tide elevations were finally broken away from islands. The fundamental and original unity between low-tide elevations and islands reveals that low-tide elevations should be always regarded as State territory, whether they are now classified as islands or not.[40]

Thanks to the minor nature of the dispute on Fasht ad Dibal in the whole case, the ICJ did not spend many paragraphs commenting on the issue. In this judgment, the Court agreed with Quenendec's arguments and pointed out that 'a coastal state has sovereignty over low-tide elevations which are situated within its territorial sea, since it has sovereignty over the territorial sea itself, including its sea-bed and subsoil.'[41] The Court went on to comment that '[i]nternational treaty law is silent on the question whether low-tide elevations can be considered to be "territory".'[42] The Court also asserted that no customary international law can be found with regard to whether low-tide elevations can be appropriated, since no uniform and widespread State practice can be identified on this issue.[43]

The Court's judgment called for further comments. In fact, the Court failed to provide a direct answer to the question 'whether low-tide elevations can be appropriated'. What is clear from the Court's judgment is that the status of low-tide elevations in modern international law of the sea is distinct from islands, and such difference is in fact, 'considerable'.[44] However, the Court's assertion only focuses on the viewpoint of the acquisition of sovereignty, which does not help to solve the issue of the territoriality of low-tide elevations, for the reason that low-tide elevations can become State territory and under the sovereignty of a State if they are situated within the breadth of the territorial sea of that State. Moreover, it seems that the Court does not expressly rule out the possibility that low-tide elevations can be appropriated. In this regard, it seems that low-tide elevations can indeed be acquired in a different way which is not 'fully assimilated' with islands. Last but not least, the judgment only deals with low-tide elevations located within the territorial sea of a State. As a matter of fact, low-tide elevations may well exist in EEZ or the high seas. The judgment fails to provide further insight on the very issue of the territoriality of low-tide elevations situated in the EEZ of a State or the high seas. To conclude, it can be asserted that the judgment regarding the territoriality of low-tide elevations in the Qatar/Bahrain is indecisive, and in the word of the dissenting Judge Oda, 'the questions of whether sovereignty over... a low-tide elevation may be acquired through appropriation by a State... remain open matters'.[45]

The development: From Nicaragua/Honduras to the South China Sea arbitration

The issue on the territoriality of low-tide elevations has become a new theoretical interest in the ICJ since the Qatar/Bahrain Case. From then on, the same issue has received notable comments in the judgment of the Court in three contentious cases in the ICJ and the recent South China Sea Arbitration. In its judgment of 2007 in the Nicaragua/Honduras Case, the Court cites its previous comment in the Qatar/Bahrain Case and asserted that it is 'not in a position to make a determinative finding on the maritime features in the area in dispute other than the four islands'.[46] Then, in the judgment of 2008 in the Pedra Branca Case between Malaysia and Singapore, in the determination of the territorial sovereignty of South Ledge, a maritime feature located within the overlapping zone of the territorial sea between Malaysia and Singapore, the Court once again followed its logic in the Qatar/Bahrain Case, and decided that the sovereignty over South Ledge should be determined based on whether South Ledge will be situated within the territorial sea of Malaysia or Singapore, a fact that can only be determined after the delimitation of the overlapping territorial sea between the two States.[47] It is worth noting that in the above cases, the low-tide elevations in question are all situated within the territorial sea of relevant States. So the territoriality of low-tide elevations is more or less covered by the delimitation of territorial sea. Eventually, in the judgment of the 2012 Nicaragua/Columbia Case, the Court delivered its most profound assertion on the issue of territoriality of low-tide elevations:

> It is well established in international law that islands, however small, are capable of appropriation. By contrast, low-tide elevations cannot be appropriated, although 'a costal State has sovereignty over low-tide elevations which are situated within its territorial sea, since it has sovereignty over the territorial sea itself.[48]

It is worth noting that the assertion used the phrase 'well established' to suggest the customary international law nature. Nevertheless, it must be cautious to read the wording and its context. In fact, there is no further elaboration on the issue of territoriality of low-tide elevations other than the mere reiteration of those already asserted in the Qatar/Bahrain Case. So how the Court come to the conclusion that low-tide elevations cannot be appropriated? In addition, how can the indecisive conclusion in the Qatar/Bahrain Case suddenly become 'well-established', considering that the previous cases (Nicaragua/Honduras, Malaysia/Singapore) all followed the judgment in the Qatar/Bahrain without adding new insights and comments?

In the 2016 South China Sea Arbitration, the territoriality of low-tide elevations is once again discussed. The Arbitral Tribunal expressly asserted that low-tide elevations cannot be appropriated, which echoed the similar judgment in the Nicaragua/Columbia. The Arbitral Tribunal briefly explained that low-tide elevations 'do not form part of the land territory of a State in the legal sense', despite the reference to the word 'land' in Article 13 of the Convention.[49] The Arbitral Tribunal concluded its analysis by citing the well-known lines in the Qatar/Bahrain that 'low-tide elevations cannot be appropriated'.[50] In the present author's point of view, the assertion that 'low-tide elevations cannot be appropriated' in the judgment of Nicaragua/Columbia and the Award of the South China Sea Arbitration can both be regarded as reasonable assertions that consummate the inchoate conclusion in the judgement of Qatar/Bahrain, for the reason that in the Qatar/Bahrain Case, the very same issue was well elaborated by counsels of both disputed parties. The issue can be well explained by recalling and analysing the arguments presented in that case in the next section.

The arguments in the Qatar/Bahrain Case revisited

Recalling the Qatar/Bahrain Case, it is essential to analyse arguments of both parties. In the view of the present author, the two points argued by Professor Quenendec, the legal counsel of Qatar, deserve to be praised. Above all, Quenendec incisively pointed out the very nature of low-tide elevations: above water at low tide but submerged at high tide. The susceptibility to tidal levels makes low-tide elevations terra infirma ('unstable land') instead of terra firma ('solid land').[51] As Clive Schofield and Richard Schofield pointed out, 'The submerged state of LTEs during part of the tidal cycle has given rise to uncertainty as to whether such features are truly land territory which can be subject to appropriation, that is, to claim to sovereignty over it.'[52] It is inconceivable that low-tide elevations can be physically appropriated as far as it is fully submerged during the high tide. As has been pointed out by the Court in the judgment of Qatar/Bahrain, it is never doubted that terra firma like islands can be appropriated.[53] More importantly, as pointed out by three dissenting judges in the Qatar/Bahrain Case, even maritime features remain above water at high tide, such as cays, may not be deemed as assimilated to islands for the reason that they lack the characteristics of terra firma.[54] Moreover, the three judges further pointed out that: 'Sovereignty, in international law, implies a minimal stable terrestrial base, which is not to be found in maritime features above the waterline which are not islands.'[55]

Thus, the unstable characteristics of low-tide elevations make them terra infirma, and they are not subjected to appropriation. Secondly, Article 2 of the Convention does stipulate that the sovereignty of a coastal state extends to territorial sea as well as to its bed and subsoil. Naturally, all maritime features including low-tide elevations that are situated within the breadth of the territorial sea, are subjected to the sovereignty of the coastal state, just as Professor Quenendec had pointed out. To conclude, the two reasons why low-tide elevations cannot be appropriated, argued by Professor Quenendec on behalf of Qatar, deserved to be praised.

On the contrary, in the view of the present author, the legal counsel of Bahrain, Professor Weil's four reasons, though appearing plausible, are not well-grounded. Firstly, Weil argued that Quenendec's reasoning indicates that 'sea dominates the land', which is opposite to the well-established principle of 'land dominates the sea'. However, such an accusation can be refuted based on a close examination of what Quenedec actually asserted. As has been pointed out above, a coastal state enjoys sovereignty over all maritime features that are situated within its territorial sea. This is indeed a logic corollary from the text of Article 2 of the Convention. By admitting that low-tide elevations that situated within the territorial sea of the coastal state naturally fall into the sovereignty of that State does not necessarily suggest that 'sea dominates the land', for the sovereignty over territorial sea itself comes from the sovereignty of land. Therefore, the corollary that low-tide elevations situated within the territorial sea of a coastal state naturally fall into the sovereignty of that State can be traced back to the sovereignty over relevant land territory of that State, a fact that faithfully reflects the principle of 'land dominates the sea'. In this regard, Weil's first point of argument cannot be justified. Secondly, Weil argued that Article 7 (4) of the Convention suggests that low-tide elevation should be deemed as land territory, for 'aquatic points' can never be used for the drawing of straight baselines. However, such an argument can also be refuted. In fact, the text of Article 7(4) expressly exposes a special condition for drawing straight baseline on points based on low-tide elevations: lighthouses or similar installation which are permanently above sea level should be built on these low-tide elevations. Otherwise, normal low-tide elevations which do not have these buildings or structures can never be chosen as base points for drawing straight baselines. This conclusion is also reflected in the judgment of the Qatar/Bahrain Case in which the Court pointed out that 'low-tide elevations cannot be equated with islands, which under all circumstances qualify as basepoints for straight baselines'.[56] Thirdly, Weil pointed out that according to Article 13 of the Convention, low-tide elevations can generate territorial sea if they are situated wholly or partly within the breadth of territorial sea of mainland or an island. He argued that if low-tide elevations are not territory, they can never generate territorial sea. This argument actually can be refuted by the rejection of the so-called 'leap-frogging method'.[57] In the judgment of the Qatar/Bahrain Case, it states that:

> [W]hereas a low-tide elevation which is situated within the limits of the territorial sea may be used for the determination of its breadth, this does not hold for a low-tide elevation which is situated less than 12 nautical miles from that low-tide elevation but is beyond the limits of the territorial sea. ... In this respect, [a low-tide elevation] does not generate a territorial sea.[58]

Thus, it can be concluded that low-tide elevations cannot generate territorial sea on their own.[59] Fourthly, Weil argued that it was only in 1958 that low-tide elevations were finally broken away from islands. It is true that from a historic perspective, low-tide elevations were considered as a subcategory of islands, especially before the 1930 Hague Conference of Codification of International Law as mentioned at the very beginning of this chapter. However, it is worth emphasising that in the contemporary international law of the sea, low-tide elevations can no longer be treated as similar to islands. Low-tide elevations and islands are stipulated in two distinct legal regimes in the Convention, and their similarities do not survive to the present date.[60] One more evidence contained in the Convention to explain the sheer difference between low-tide elevations and islands is that in Article 121, islands are referred to as 'area of land' and the maritime entitlement of islands can be determined in accordance with the provisions in the Convention applicable to 'other land territory'. In contrast, there is no mention of any similar rules concerning the maritime entitlement of low-tide elevations in Article 13. Therefore, it is not correct to over-emphasise the similarities between low-tide elevations and islands before the formation of the modern legal regime of the law of the sea, and ignore that great differences lies between them in the Convention.

By revisiting the arguments from both disputed parties in the Qatar/Bahrain Case, it can be concluded that the arguments that low-tide elevations can be appropriated as territory are not well-grounded, whereas the arguments that low-tide elevations cannot be appropriated are well-founded both in fact and in law, which are also evidenced by the judgments of the Qatar/Bahrain Case.

The territoriality of low-tide elevations situated in other maritime zones

The above sections mainly focus on low-tide elevations situated within the territorial sea of a coastal state. Nevertheless, it is normal that low-tide elevations exist well beyond the territorial sea of any State. Indeed, as mentioned in the above footnote, Article 13 (2) of the Convention stipulates that low-tide elevations situated outside the territorial sea of a State do not have territorial sea of their own. Low-tide elevations situated outside territorial sea of a State can be further divided into three categories: those situated within the EEZ of a State, those situated within archipelago waters of an archipelago State, and those situated on the High Seas.

Concerning the low-tide elevations situated in the EEZ of a coastal state, Article 56 provides that the coastal state has jurisdiction over the establishment and use of artificial islands, installations and structures. Furthermore, Article 60 provides that the coastal state 'shall have the exclusive right to construct and to authorize and regulate the construction, operation and use of artificial islands, installations and structures' within its EEZ. Accordingly, it can be admitted that the coastal state can exercise exclusive jurisdiction over the establishment and use of artificial islands, installations and structures on low-tide elevations situated within its EEZ, as well as enjoying the exclusive rights to construct and to authorise and regulate the construction, operation and use of artificial islands, installations and structures on low-tide elevations situated within its EEZ. If low-tide elevations could be appropriated by another State as territory, that State would enjoy these rights and exercise exclusive jurisdiction, for it would have

State sovereignty over low-tide elevations after it appropriates them. If this scenario happens, inevitably, there will be a clash of jurisdiction and rights between the coastal state and the appropriation State[61] over that low-tide elevation. On one hand, the jurisdiction and exclusive right enjoyed by the coastal state are well stipulated in the Convention. On the other hand, the jurisdiction and exclusive right enjoyed by the appropriation State are derived from its territorial sovereignty over the low-tide elevation once it appropriates it. Obviously, such a clash will give rise to the legal conflict between treaty law and customary international law, and potentially undermine the legal regime of EEZ and the integrity of the Convention. Moreover, Article 13 clearly indicates that low-tide elevations cannot generate territorial sea of their own. If a State other than the coastal state does appropriate low-tide elevations situated within the EEZ of that coastal state, what the appropriation State occupied becomes merely enclaves located within the EEZ of that coastal state. These kind of enclaves even cannot claim 500 metres' safety zones.[62] To sum up, it can be concluded that low-tide elevations situated within the EEZ of a coastal state cannot be appropriated.[63]

With respect to low-tide elevations situated within archipelagic waters of an archipelagic State, it is clear from Article 46 (a) of the Convention that low-tide elevations can be considered as 'other natural features' that constitute archipelago. Thus, the legal status of low-tide elevations form part of the archipelago can be determined by the legal status of archipelagic waters in which the low-tide elevations are situated. In this regard, the territoriality of low-tide elevations is subsumed into the legal regime of archipelagic waters. As Article 49 of the Convention stipulates, the sovereignty of an archipelagic State extends to its archipelagic waters within its archipelagic baselines.[64] Accordingly, the territorial sovereignty of low-tide elevations situated within the archipelagic waters of an archipelagic State naturally belongs to that archipelagic State. Similar to the territoriality of low-tide elevations situated within the territorial sea of a coastal state, the issue of appropriation is not relevant in this context.

Finally, concerning low-tide elevations situated on the high seas, it can be directly determined by Article 89 of the Convention that no territorial sovereignty can be claimed upon features on the high seas.[65] Therefore, low-tide elevations situated on the high seas cannot be appropriated by any State, and no territorial sovereignty can be claimed by appropriation.[66]

Based on the above analysis of low-tide elevations situated within the territorial sea of a coastal state, the EEZ of a coastal state, the archipelagic waters of an archipelagic State as well as low-tide elevations situated on the high seas, the territoriality of low-tide elevations can be fully revealed. It can be asserted that low-tide elevations, no matter where they situate, cannot be appropriated as territory.

Low-tide elevations and the rise of sea levels

The third and final issue which has not been addressed in the Convention is the impact of the rise of sea levels on the status of low-tide elevations. In recent decades, the phenomenon of continuous sea level rising attracts scientists and scholars alike.

In a recent report published by the Intergovernmental Panel on Climate Change in 2013, it was predicted that the rate of global sea level rising during the twenty-first century 'will exceed the rate during 1971–2010' due to 'increases in ocean warming and loss of mass from glacier and ice sheets'.[67] Notably, this natural phenomenon may have a great impact on the status of low-tide elevations. To be specific, for those islands which are only several centimetres above water at high tide, and for those low-tide elevations only several centimetres above water at low tide, the continuous rise of sea level may make those islands downgraded to low-tide elevations and those low-tide elevations downgraded to submerged features. Thus, in addition to the legal status of low-tide elevations analysed in the above sections, it is necessary to examine the impact of sea level rise on the status of low-tide elevations. Two issues are particularly important and worth discussing.

First, whether an island as defined in Article 121 of the Convention will lose its island status once it becomes fully submerged at high tide due to the rise of sea level, or in a similar circumstance, a low-tide elevation will lose its status and becomes a submerged feature? It seems that the answer is 'yes', based on international case law and opinion of scholars. With regard to the first circumstance, in the 2007 Nicaragua/Honduras Case, the final judgment citing a 'question and answer' in the oral proceeding reveals that the Media Luna Cay, a maritime feature considered by both parties as an island before the initiation of the case, was considered as a low-tide elevation by both parties at the time of the oral proceeding.[68] With regard to the second circumstance, in the Anglo-Belgian Agreement concerning the Delimitation of Continental Shelf, the two parties agreed that the maritime feature of Shipwash Sand downgraded from a low-tide elevation to a submerged feature.[69] Concerning the opinion of scholars, Professor Tim Stephens points out that '[A]lthough Article 121 is ambiguous, it does suggest that States with islands, or island States, may lose an entitlement to EEZ or continental shelf areas following significant sea level rise.'[70] This assertion can further enhance the conclusion that the continuous rise of sea level could well endanger the status of islands and low-tide elevations.

The second issue concerning the impact of continuous rise of sea level on the status of low-tide elevations is when a maritime dispute arises, whether the disputed parties and third-party dispute settlement body should take into account the original status of a maritime feature, or consider the present status of that maritime feature instead, regardless of the impact of the rise of sea level and the consequence of the change of status of a maritime feature? One case can be served to illustrate this issue. In the 2012 Territorial and Maritime Dispute Case between Nicaragua and Columbia, the Court pointed out that:

> [The Court] does not consider that surveys conducted many years (in some cases many decades) before the present proceedings are relevant in resolving that issue. ... The Court considers that what is relevant to the issue before it is the contemporary evidence.[71]

The above judgment of the Court suggests that the principle of 'inter-temporal law' might not be applicable when an issue of the change of status of a maritime feature arises. What the third-party dispute settlement body really concerns is the present status. Thus, when a dispute concerning the status of a low-tide elevations arises, it is essential that both disputed parties submit updated survey reports and relevant natural-geographic statistics of that low-tide elevation, so as to prove the claimed status of that low-tide elevation, for the reason that any previous survey report and natural-geographic statistics may be deemed by the third-party dispute settlement body as obsolete and of little use.

Conclusions

Based on the above analysis, this chapter comes to three conclusions to answer the three unaddressed issues concerning the status low-tide elevations. First, in the determination of the natural status of low-tide elevations, State practice as well as international case law reveals that there is no uniform rule on the choice of tidal datum, the key criteria for the determination of the status of low-tide elevations. This legal impasse may well give rise to the uncertainty of determining whether a maritime feature is an island, a low-tide elevation or a submerged feature. For international courts and tribunals, they may also face the risk of non liquet when a dispute arises with respect to the determination of the status of a low-tide elevation. Second, concerning the crucial issue of the territoriality of low-tide elevations, from both international case law and theoretical point of view, it can be concluded that low-tide elevations, no matter where they situate, cannot be subjected to appropriation as territory. So far there has been no case that supports that low-tide elevations can be appropriated. In addition, the unstable nature (terra infirma) of low-tide elevations make them unable to be appropriated. Third, concerning the impact of the rise of sea level on the status of low-tide elevations, it can be summarised from the judgment of the ICJ and scholar's opinion that low-tide elevations could be downgraded to submerged features if they are no longer above water at low tide due to the significant rise of sea level. An island could also be downgraded to a low-tide elevation due to the rise of sea level. Thus, the impact of the rise of sea level on the status of low-tide elevations is enormous.

The above three conclusions explain the contemporary issues arising from the lack of elaboration of the legal status of low-tide elevations in the Convention. It can be predicted that the uncertainty in the determination of the status of low-tide elevations, the issue of the territoriality of low-tide elevations, as well as the impact of the rise of sea level on the status of low-tide elevations will continue to be hotly debated in international maritime and boundary disputes, and among scholars, until a more integral legal regime of low-tide elevations is incorporated in the contemporary international law of the sea.

Notes

1 Haritini Dipla, *Le Regime Juridique Des Iles Dans Le Droit International De La Mer* (Paris: Presses Universitaires de France, 1984), 23, 43, in Hugo Ignacio Llanos, 'Low-tide Elevations: Reassessing Their Impact on Maritime Delimitation', *Pace International Law Review* 14 (2002): 258–59.

2 See ibid, 43–44, in Llanos, 'Low-tide Elevations: Reassessing Their Impact on Maritime Delimitation', 259.
3 Robin Churchill and Vaughan Lowe, *The Law of the Sea* (Manchester: Manchester University Press, 3rd edition, 1999), 48.
4 See *Anglo-Norwegian Fisheries Case* (United Kingdom v. Norway), Judgement [1951] *ICJ Reports*, 120.
5 'Commentary to the Articles concerning the Law of the Sea', *Yearbook of International Law Commission*, vol.II, (1965): 270.
6 See ibid.
7 See UN Document A/CONF.13/C.1/L.115, *First United Nations Conference on the Law of the Sea, Official Records*, vol. III (A/CONF.13/39), 243.
8 See ibid, 256.
9 516 UNTS 206; adopted 29 April 1958, entered into force 10 September 1964. Hereafter referred to as 'the 1958 Convention'. As of September 2016, the Convention on the Territorial Sea and Contiguous Zone has 52 State parties. See 'Convention on the Territorial Sea and the Contiguous Zone, current status' (*United Nations Treaty Collection*) https://treaties.un.org/doc/Publication/MTDSG/Volume%20II/Chapter%20XXI/XXI-1.en.pdf (last visited on 2 September 2016).
10 See Satya N. Nandan, Shatai Rosenne and Neal R. Grany (eds.), *United Nations Convention on the Law of the Sea 1982: A Commentary*, vol. II (Dordrecht: Martinus Nijhoff, 1993), 128, para. 13.4.
11 1833 UNTS 3; adopted 10 December 1982, entered into force 16 November 1994. Hereafter referred to as the 'LOSC' or 'the Convention'. The Republic of Azerbaijan has recently acceded to the Convention on 16 June 2016. As of September 2016, the LOSC has 168 parties. See 'United Nations Convention on the Law of the Sea, current status' (*United Nations Treaty Collection*) https://treaties.un.org/doc/Publication/MTDSG/Volume%20II/Chapter%20XXI/XXI-6.en.pdf (last visited on 2 September 2016).
12 See Clive R. Symmons, 'Some Problems Relating to the Delimitation of Insular Formations in International Law: Islands and Low-Tide Elevations' in Clive Schofield and Peter Hocknell (eds.), *Maritime Briefing*, vol. 1, No. 5 (Durham: International Boundaries Research Unit, 1995): 9–10. See also P. B. Beazley, 'Reefs and the 1982 Convention on the Law of the Sea', *International Journal of Estuarine and Costal Law* 6 (1991): 298.
13 Tidal datum can be defined as 'the reference plane (or surface) to which the height of the predicted tide is referred'. See Nuno Sergio Marques Antunes, 'The Importance of the Tidal Datum in the Definition of Maritime Limits and Boundaries' in Rachael Bradley and Clive Schofield (eds.), *Maritime Briefing*, vol. 2, No. 7 (Durham: International Boundaries Research Unit, 2000), 5.
14 See ibid, 5.
15 See ibid, 7, 13.
16 Tidal range, or the range of tide, can be defined as 'the difference in height between consecutive high and low waters at one place'. See, ibid, 4.
17 See Victor Prescott and Clive Schofield, *The Maritime Political Boundaries of the World* (Leiden: Martinus Nijhoff Publishers, 2nd edn, 2005), 94–95.
18 D. P. O'Connell, I. Shearer (ed.), *The International Law of the Sea* (Oxford: Clarendon Press, 1982), vol.1, 176.
19 D. C. Kooper and Adam J. Kerr, *A Guide to Maritime Boundary Delimitation* (Toronto: Carswell, 1986), 17, in Antunes, 'The Importance of the Tidal Datum in the Definition of Maritime Limits and Boundaries', 6.
20 See Clive R. Symmons, 'Maritime Zones from Islands and Rocks' in S. Jayakumar, Tommy Koh and Robert Beckman (eds.), *The South China Sea Disputes and Law of the Sea* (Cheltenham: Edward Elgar, 2014), 80–81; Yoshifumi Tanaka, 'Low-Tide Elevation in International Law of the Sea', *Ocean Yearbook* 20 (2006): 193.

21 Symmons, 'Some Problems Relating to the Delimitation of Insular Formations in International Law: Islands and Low-Tide Elevations', 28.

22 See *Anglo-French Continental Shelf Case* (*United Kingdom v. France*), 1977, 18 *RIAA* 3: 68, para. 127. Antunes, 'The Importance of the Tidal Datum in the Definition of Maritime Limits and Boundaries', 21; Symmons, 'Some Problems Relating to the Delimitation of Insular Formations in International Law: Islands and Low-Tide Elevations', 23.

23 See *Territorial and Maritime Dispute Case* (*Nicaragua v. Columbia*), Judgement, *ICJ Reports*, 2012, 624: 642–43, paras. 30–31.

24 See *Anglo-French Continental Shelf Case*, 72–74, paras. 139–44.

25 See *Territorial and Maritime Dispute Case*, 645, para. 37.

26 Tanaka, 'Low-Tide Elevation in International Law of the Sea', 196–97.

27 See *The Republic of the Philippines v. The People's Republic of China*, Award, 12 July 2016, para. 313.

28 See Youna Lyons, 'Prospects for Satellite Imagery of Insular Features and Surrounding Marine Habitats in the South China Sea', *Marine Polocy* 45 (2014): 146–55.

29 See International Hydrographic Organization, *Regulations of the IHO for International (INT) Charts and Chart Specifications of the IHO* (Monaco: International Hydrographic Bureau, Edition 4.6.0, April 2016), Section B-400: 5.

30 The detailed statistics of tidal ranges summarised from various nautical charts can be found in paragraphs 314, 315 and 316 of the Award. In fact, the Award expressly concludes that the average tidal range is about 0.85 to 1.2 m in the Spratlys. See *The Republic of the Philippines v. The People's Republic of China*, Award, 12 July 2016, para. 316. See Yinan Bao, 'Critiques on the Determination of Natural Status of Low-Tide Elevations in the Award of the South China Sea Arbitration', Contemporary Law Review 31(2) (2017): 144–45.

31 The term 'appropriate' does appear in the Convention, in Article 137 (1), concerning the legal status of 'the Area'. 'Appropriate' in that context means 'taking any action through national judicial proceedings, self-help measures or other action by a State, a natural person or a juridical person, that takes, or attempts to take, title or possession, exercise of sovereignty or exercise of sovereign rights, or exercise of jurisdiction.' See George K, Walk (ed.), *Definitions for the Law of the Sea: Terms Not Defined by the 1982 Convention* (Leiden: Martinus Nijhoff Publishers, 2012), 97.

32 Robert Beckman and Leonardo Bernard comment that 'The ICJ considered this issue in several cases, but its decisions were not entirely clear.' See Robert Beckman and Leonardo Bernard, 'The Significance of Offshore Geographic Features to Maritime Claims' in Shicun Wu and Keyuan Zou (eds), *Arbitration Concerning the South China Sea: Philippines versus China* (London: Routledge, 2016), 246.

33 Llanos, 'Low-tide Elevations: Reassessing Their Impact on Maritime Delimitation', 269.

34 See *Case Concerning Maritime Delimitation and Territorial Questions Between Qatar and Bahrain (Qatar v. Bahrain)*, Merits, *ICJ Reports*, 2001, 100, para. 200.

35 *Case Concerning Maritime Delimitation and Territorial Questions Between Qatar and Bahrain*, Oral Proceedings, CR2000/9 (Translations), 46, para. 43.

36 Ibid.

37 See *Case Concerning Maritime Delimitation and Territorial Questions Between Qatar and Bahrain*, Oral Proceedings, CR2000/15 (Translations), 36–37, paras. 52–54.

38 See ibid, 47–48, para. 76.

39 See *Case Concerning Maritime Delimitation and Territorial Questions Between Qatar and Bahrain*, Oral Proceedings, CR2000/25 (Translations), 16, para. 9.

40 See ibid., 18, para. 16.

41 See *Case Concerning Maritime Delimitation and Territorial Questions Between Qatar and Bahrain*, Merits, 101, para. 204.

42 Ibid., para. 205.

43 See ibid., 102, para. 205.
44 See ibid., 102, para. 206.
45 See *Case Concerning Maritime Delimitation and Territorial Questions Between Qatar and Bahrain*, Separate opinion of Judge Oda, *ICJ Reports*, 2001, 124, para. 7.
46 *Case Concerning Territorial and Maritime Dispute Between Nicaragua and Honduras in the Caribbean Sea* (*Nicaragua v. Honduras*), Judgement, *ICJ Reports*, 2007, 702–804, paras. 138–44.
47 See *Case Concerning Sovereignty over Pedra Branca/ Pulau Batu Puteh, Middle Rocks and South Ledge* (*Malaysia v. Singapore*), Judgement, *ICJ Reports*, 2008, 101, para. 299.
48 *Territorial and Maritime Dispute Case* (*Nicaragua v. Columbia*), Judgement, *ICJ Reports*, 2012, 641, para. 26.
49 See *The Republic of the Philippines v. The People's Republic of China*, Award, 12 July 2016, para. 309.
50 See ibid.
51 See 'Terra Firma' in Aaron X. Fellmeth and Maurice Horwitz (eds), *Guide to Latin in International Law* (New York: Oxford University Press, 2009), 276.
52 Clive Schofield and Richard Schofield, 'Testing the Waters: Charting the Evolution of Claims to and from Low-Tide Elevations and Artificial Islands under the Law of the Sea', *Asia-Pacific Journal of Ocean Law and Policy* 1 (2016): 60.
53 See *Case Concerning Maritime Delimitation and Territorial Questions Between Qatar and Bahrain*, Merits, 102, para. 206.
54 See *Case Concerning Maritime Delimitation and Territorial Questions Between Qatar and Bahrain*, Joint dissenting opinion of Judges Bedjaoui, Ranjeva and Koroma (translation), *ICJ Reports*, 2001, 209, paras. 199–200.
55 Ibid, para. 200.
56 See *Case Concerning Maritime Delimitation and Territorial Questions Between Qatar and Bahrain*, Merits, 102, para. 208.
57 This method makes use of a low-tide elevation situated near the 12nm limit of the territorial sea to extend the territorial sea to a further 12nm, and then extend even larger scope of the territorial sea by making use of a second low-tide elevation situated near the new 12nm limit which the first low-tide elevation generates. By using this method, the coastal State can greatly extend its territorial sea by making use of a series of low-tide elevations situated near the 12nm limit of its territorial sea. See Hugo Ignacio Llanos, 'Low-tide Elevations: Reassessing Their Impact on Maritime Delimitation', 271.
58 See *Case Concerning Maritime Delimitation and Territorial Questions Between Qatar and Bahrain*, Merits, 102, para. 207.
59 Notably, Article 13 (2) of the Convention stipulates that '[w]here a low-tide elevation is wholly situated at a distance exceeding the breadth of the territorial sea from the mainland or an island, it has no territorial sea of its own'.
60 See Yoshifumi Tanaka, 'Low-Tide Elevation in International Law of the Sea', 207.
61 In this chapter, the 'appropriation State' denotes the State other than the coastal State that appropriates low-tide elevations within the EEZ of a coastal State.
62 Article 60 (4) of the Convention stipulates that the coastal State can establish safety zones around artificial islands, installations and structures, and Article 60 (5) of the Convention provides that the breadth of the safety zones shall be determined by the coastal State.
63 See Beckman and Bernard, 'The Significance of Offshore Geographic Features to Maritime Claims', 250.
64 Article 49 (1) provides: 'The sovereignty of an archipelagic State extends to the waters enclosed by the archipelagic baselines drawn in accordance with article 47, described as archipelagic waters, regardless of their depth or distance from the coast.'
65 Article 89 provides: 'No State may validly purport to subject any part of the high seas to its sovereignty.'

66 See Roberto Lavalle, 'The Rights of States over Low-tide Elevations: A Legal Analysis', *The Journal of Marine and Coastal Law*, 29 (2014): 477.

67 Intergovernmental Panel on Climate Change Working Group I, *Climate Change 2013: The Physical Science Basis* (Cambridge: Cambridge University Press, 2013), p.1140. Electronic version available at http://ipcc.ch/pdf/assessment-report/ar5/wg1/WG1AR5_Chapter13_FINAL.pdf, last visited on 8 June 2016. See also Tim Stephens, 'Warming Waters and Souring Seas: Climate Change and Ocean Acidification' in Donald R. Rothwell et al. (eds.), *The Oxford Handbook of the Law of the Sea* (Oxford: Oxford University Press, 2015), 779.

68 The parties have stated that 'Media Luna Cay is now submerged and thus that it is no longer an island.' See *Case Concerning Territorial and Maritime Dispute Between Nicaragua and Honduras in the Caribbean Sea* (*Nicaragua v. Honduras*), Judgment, [2007] *ICJ Reports* 659:703–4, paras. 143.

69 See Antunes, 'The Importance of the Tidal Datum in the Definition of Maritime Limits and Boundaries', 19.

70 Stephens, 'Warming Waters and Souring Seas: Climate Change and Ocean Acidification', 791.

71 *Territorial and Maritime Dispute Case* (*Nicaragua v. Columbia*), Judgement, *ICJ Reports*, 2012, 644, paras. 35–36.

14 Resolving disputes under UNCLOS when the coastal and user states are disputed

*Natalie Klein**

Introduction

The dispute settlement procedures available under Part XV of the UN Convention on the Law of the Sea (UNCLOS) provide an essential means to resolve conflicting views as to the interpretation and application of that Convention.[1] The importance of providing State parties with a process to resolve these disputes is manifest in the inclusion of compulsory jurisdiction: a State party consents to the possibility of arbitration or adjudication at the time it consents to be bound by the Convention. There are options built in for State parties in relation to the forum to hear the dispute,[2] utilizing dispute settlement procedures other than those in UNCLOS,[3] as well as the possibility of excluding particular subjects from the scope of compulsory procedures entailing binding decisions.[4]

The scope of jurisdiction that may be exercised in relation to maritime UNCLOS disputes has been an increasingly contested issue,[5] and this tension was especially evident in the recent *South China Sea* arbitration.[6] One of the particularly difficult issues in this case was that coastal and user state actions were challenged in maritime areas adjacent to land features over which sovereignty was disputed. In instituting proceedings against China, the Philippines did not seek to resolve the territorial sovereignty issues through the arbitration under UNCLOS. Instead, the case was configured on the basis that specific questions relating to maritime entitlements could be resolved irrespective of any uncertainty as to which State those entitlements would accrue. I have questioned the logic of this position elsewhere,[7] and in this chapter will focus on some distinct consequences for States where there is a land feature generating maritime zones over which sovereignty is disputed.

The questions I address in this chapter concern the international legal consequences that emerge where there is a State in occupation of an island ("the occupying State") but another State contests sovereignty ("the disputing State"). For example, is it legally permissible for the occupying State to construct facilities on the island or in the waters surrounding that island? The constructions in the adjacent waters might include ports, or other docking facilities or other structures or installations outside the territorial sea for the purposes of research or resource exploration and exploitation. If the occupying State proceeds with the exercise of its sovereignty over the disputed land, are there steps or limits that should be taken into account to reduce the likelihood of legal challenges in the event of a dispute emerging under the UNCLOS dispute settlement procedure? A key lesson from the *South China Sea* arbitration is that the occupying State faces significant legal consequences if it is eventually determined not to be the coastal state with rights over the adjacent maritime area. The occupying State could expect that some of its actions in relation to a disputed island may be challenged within the framework of the UNCLOS dispute settlement regime, even in the possible absence of a determination as to which State is the "coastal state" or "user state" under UNCLOS.

Challenging existing constructions on disputed islands and in their immediately adjacent waters

Where a State is in occupation of an island and considers it has sovereignty over that island, an ordinary consequence of that situation would be the development of infrastructure and other constructions to facilitate the utilization of the land and its surrounding waters as well as supporting the communities living on that island. The legal basis for doing so would rest on the purported sovereignty over the island, which would then also include sovereignty over internal waters and the territorial sea of that island.

The questions that emerge are whether the occupying State is prohibited from undertaking building activities when sovereignty is contested and what legal consequences exist when a State undertakes construction in a disputed territory. In the absence of armed conflict and hence the inapplicability of the body of law relating to occupation, there does not appear to be any general legal principle that requires a State in occupation of contested territory not to alter the territory in question. This section considers a disputing State's claims against construction, first, on a disputed island and, second, in the water immediately adjacent to that island.

Construction on disputed islands

A State's conduct within its own territory is protected by its sovereignty over that territory and a requirement on other States not to interfere in the domestic affairs of a State. The State's conduct should not, however, infringe on the environment of other States pursuant to a long-standing principle of *sic utere tuo ut alienum non laedas*, which requires States not to use their territory in such a way as to cause unreasonable harm to other States.[8]

Where ownership of an island is disputed, activities on the island may become relevant for a determination of which state has sovereignty. Under the laws relating to the acquisition of territorial sovereignty, the actions of a State that demonstrate its intention to act as sovereign, as well as the actions themselves, amount to *effectivités*. These are acts undertaken in the exercise of State authority through which a State manifests its intention to act as the sovereign over a territory.[9]

From the law relating to territorial acquisition, an assessment of the competing claims may identify a "critical date" as to when the dispute between the States concerned crystallized. After the critical date, actions taken by either party following that time are no longer *effectivités*.[10] Any construction or other manifestation of sovereignty would thus no longer be relevant to an assessment of territorial sovereignty over the disputed island. The question that emerges would be whether constructions undertaken by a State subsequent to the critical date would be viewed as a violation of international law if that State did not hold sovereignty over the land at issue. Such a question could only emerge at the point that sovereignty is determined, presumably by an international court or tribunal. Whether territorial sovereignty disputes may be resolved under UNCLOS remains a question of some controversy among commentators.[11]

As to what violations of international law might be argued, the most likely submissions from the disputing State would be (1) a simple violation of territorial sovereignty and (2) a violation of an obligation not to aggravate the dispute between them. In relation to a violation of territorial sovereignty, an argument would have to be presented that a violation arises when a State that is not sovereign over land prevents the sovereign State from accessing that land and/or undertakes construction on that land. That position is relatively straightforward when the sovereignty over the land is always known.

Yet it would need to be argued in response that such a violation does not arise when sovereignty was contested as between the States in question. In *Cameroon v Nigeria*, Cameroon presented arguments alleging Nigeria was responsible for acts undertaken during its occupation of territory determined to belong to Cameroon by the International Court of Justice (ICJ). The Court opted not to address these claims in any detail but considered the very fact of the judgment and Nigeria's evacuation from the contested area would constitute sufficient redress for any injuries.[12] In the 2007 case between Guyana and Suriname, Suriname asserted that "there has been no case in the context of a territorial dispute where a State found not to have title to territory has been held responsible for its actions in an area which had been the subject of dispute."[13]

Subsequently, a different conclusion was reached in the 2013 decision of the ICJ in *Certain Activities carried out by Nicaragua in the Border Area (Costa Rica v Nicaragua)*. In that case, the ICJ considered the legality of dredging and other activities carried out by Nicaragua in territory claimed by both Nicaragua and Costa Rica. The Court held that the disputed territory fell under the sovereignty of Costa Rica and that the activities carried out by Nicaragua were thus in breach of Costa Rica's territorial sovereignty. The ICJ did not find it necessary to examine whether the acts were unlawful in themselves, finding it sufficient to note that the unlawful character of the activities stemmed from the fact that they had been carried out on the territory of another State, without that State's consent. Nicaragua was held to be responsible for these breaches and was obliged to make reparation for the damage caused by its unlawful activities.[14]

This finding raises the legal stakes for occupying States that seek to continue their activities on disputed islands. If a court or tribunal has jurisdiction to resolve the territorial sovereignty question, a finding of international responsibility in relation to the activities undertaken on the island may result. Further, a court or tribunal may determine that reparations are necessary.

Construction in waters immediately surrounding a disputed island

For construction work within the internal waters or territorial sea of a disputed island, such work would normally be permissible by virtue of the exercise of the coastal state's sovereignty over that body of water.[15] A risk associated with any such construction would be that if the occupying State undertook such work, and the island was subsequently determined to belong to the disputing State, the occupying State would also potentially be responsible for violating the disputing State's rights of sovereignty over the territorial sea. Challenges to the exercise of sovereignty recognized in Article 2 of UNCLOS may be more likely to be resolved through UNCLOS dispute settlement (subject to the need to resolve the outstanding territorial sovereignty question).

The question of construction also arose in the *South China Sea* arbitration in the context of an infringement of the Philippines' sovereign rights in its Exclusive Economic Zone (EEZ) because of the construction on the low-tide elevation of Mischief Reef. The configuration of the case was complicated inasmuch as both the Philippines and China believed prior to the case that they had sovereign rights in the area around Mischief Reef. The Tribunal acknowledged as much in its Award, observing "[the] root of the disputes […] lies not in any intention on the part of China or the Philippines to infringe on the legal rights of the other, but rather […] in fundamentally different understandings of their respective rights under the Convention in the waters of the South China Sea."[16]

The difficulty for China in this configuration was that at the point that the Tribunal determined that China did not have sovereign rights around Mischief Reef (because of the Tribunal's earlier determinations that the nine-dash line was invalid and that Mischief Reef was a low-tide elevation), China's conduct *prior to that determination* was then assessed on the basis that it lacked sovereign rights. That is, China's genuine belief (or incorrect assertion) that it had sovereign rights could not serve as a defense for its actions.

This configuration indicates that where a State asserts it has rights in a particular maritime area and conducts itself in accordance with those asserted rights, it may be found internationally responsible for its conduct at that time if it is later determined to lack the rights asserted. The situation at sea thus would be similar to such claims on land.

There is no circumstance precluding wrongfulness based on mistake of fact or mistake of law in the law of State responsibility, but this defense is limited to the field of international criminal law.[17] Rather, States will be held responsible for the actions of their officials even when those officials have acted outside their authority on the basis of a genuine belief in the legality of their conduct.[18] In relation to Mischief Reef, the *South China Sea* Tribunal therefore considered that the reef fell within the EEZ and continental shelf of the Philippines and so China's conduct had to be assessed against the Philippines' sovereign rights within that maritime area.[19] Although the decision in this case concerned sovereign rights, it would seem equally applicable in relation to the exercise of sovereignty over maritime areas.

A possible argument in response to a claimed sovereignty violation, which was not discussed in the *South China Sea* arbitration, might be based on the principle of non-retroactivity. Article 13 of the International Law Commission's Articles on State Responsibility provides: "An act of a State does not constitute a breach of an international obligation unless the State is bound by the obligation in question at the time the act occurs."[20] There is consistent international law authority supporting the view that the wrongfulness of an act must be established based on obligations in force at the time the act was performed.[21] This principle does not sit entirely easily with the situation in *South China Sea* inasmuch as the principle of respect for the inviolability of territorial sovereignty has long existed under international law. Arguably, the principle that a State can only be held responsible for breach of an obligation which was in force for that State at the time of its conduct means that respect for the disputing State's sovereignty in and immediately around the island was not in force at the time of the occupying State's conduct because of the contested sovereignty.

This issue was subsequently addressed in the context of a maritime boundary delimitation dispute between Ghana and Côte d'Ivoire.[22] Côte d'Ivoire alleged that Ghana should be found internationally responsible for violating its sovereign rights "by conducting or licensing hydrocarbon activities in an area over which Côte d'Ivoire claims to have sovereign rights."[23] The Special Chamber considered that when there were overlapping claims and the parties exercise rights therein in good faith, both parties have an entitlement to the relevant maritime area.[24] A decision on the maritime boundary was to be viewed as constitutive in determining the priority of the claims to the maritime areas.[25] In this setting, no finding of international responsibility would be made.[26] Arguably the decision in *Ghana/ Côte d'Ivoire* could be distinguished from the *South China Sea* arbitration, which was not referenced at all, as the former was a maritime boundary delimitation case whereas the latter was ostensibly a different scenario. It remains to be seen which approach will be preferred by other courts or tribunals in the future.

Legality of activities in the EEZ of a disputed island

Assuming the disputed island was considered a fully entitled island and a continental shelf and EEZ could therefore be claimed, the coastal State has sovereign rights over the natural resources and jurisdiction to protect and preserve the marine environment within those extended maritime zones. In addition, the coastal state has exclusive jurisdiction to construct and regulate artificial islands, installations and structures in this maritime area.[27] I assess the legality of activities in the EEZ of a disputed island in this section. My first question concerns the rights of an occupying State in the EEZ, especially in relation to construction or other building activities. Second, I look to the requirements that arise in relation to showing due regard under Articles 56 and 58 of UNCLOS, which are applicable to both coastal States and user States in the EEZ. Finally, I examine the obligations relating to provisional arrangements that may be relevant if overlapping maritime entitlements are at issue.

Coastal state's exclusive rights in the EEZ

Article 56 of UNCLOS provides:

1. In the exclusive economic zone, the coastal state has:
   (a) sovereign rights for the purpose of exploring and exploiting, conserving and managing the natural resources, whether living or non-living, of the waters superjacent to the seabed and of the seabed and its subsoil, and with regard to other activities for the economic exploitation and exploration of the zone, such as the production of energy from the water, currents and winds;
   (b) jurisdiction as provided for in the relevant provisions of this Convention with regard to:
      (i) the establishment and use of artificial islands, installations and structures;
      (ii) marine scientific research;
      (iii) the protection and preservation of the marine environment;
   (c) other rights and duties provided for in this Convention.
2. In exercising its rights and performing its duties under this Convention in the exclusive economic zone, the coastal state shall have due regard to the rights and duties of other States and shall act in a manner compatible with the provisions of this Convention.
3. The rights set out in this article with respect to the seabed and subsoil shall be exercised in accordance with Part VI.

For construction activities within the EEZ, the relevant provisions of UNCLOS are Articles 56(1)(b) and 60. Article 56(1)(b) grants the coastal State exclusive jurisdiction with regard to "the establishment and use of artificial islands, installations and structures." Under Article 60, this jurisdiction is described as "an exclusive right" of the coastal State in relation to the construction as well as authorization and regulation of the construction, operation and use of structures for "the purposes provided for in Article 56 and other economic purposes."[28] The exclusive jurisdiction of the coastal State over these structures also extends to "jurisdiction with regard to customs, fiscal health, safety and immigration laws and regulations." The latter is important to note depending on how any structure, installation or other construction work is to be put to use.

The obligations of a coastal State over artificial islands, installations and structures within its EEZ under Article 60 (or on its continental shelf under Article 80) relate to providing notice of such construction, following procedures in establishing safety zones around such installations or structures, and having to remove any abandoned or disused installations and structures. For an occupying State to contemplate undertaking any such building within the claimed EEZ around a disputed island, it would be important to ensure that the notice requirements and safety zone procedures were followed.

The occupying State could be subject to dispute settlement proceedings under UNCLOS for violating these provisions, provided the occupying State could be established as the "coastal state" for the purposes of applying Articles 60 and 80. Otherwise, if the occupying State proceeded with construction or other development in an area that was ultimately determined to be the disputing State's EEZ by a court or tribunal, then it could also potentially be found responsible for violating the disputing State's rights as a coastal State for artificial structures in its EEZ. Such a finding was established in relation to China's conduct in the *South China Sea* arbitration with regard to its construction of installations and artificial islands at Mischief Reef. Alternatively, obligations of due regard would be at issue.

Obligations of due regard

It would also be expected that in the exercise of the exclusive rights of the coastal State that adherence to Article 56(2) would still be respected by the occupying State; notably, that due regard would be shown to the rights of other States. Equally, if the disputing State was determined in the course of an arbitration or adjudication to be the relevant coastal State, the occupying State is still bound by an obligation of due regard under Article 58(3) of UNCLOS. Following the approach of the *South China Sea* Tribunal, a court or tribunal might opt to discuss an obligation of due regard applying generally in the absence of a determination as to which State is the "coastal state." A State could not go so far as suggesting that Article 56(2) reflected a "universal rule of conduct," as this argument was not accepted in the *Chagos Archipelago* arbitration.[29]

The disputing State could potentially assert that the occupying State was failing to show due regard to its rights in proceeding to assert exclusive rights associated with installations or structures. These rights could be infringed in this situation when the disputing State had a potential claim to exclusive rights itself in that maritime area (i.e. prior to the determination of the maritime boundary and prior to a resolution of the territorial sovereignty dispute). A finding of an UNCLOS violation of the due regard would require a relative assessment, as indicated in the *Chagos Archipelago* arbitration. In this regard, the Tribunal stated:

> Rather, the extent of the regard required by the Convention will depend on the nature of the rights held by Mauritius, their importance, the extent of the anticipated impairment, the nature and importance of the activities contemplated by the United Kingdom, and the availability of alternative approaches. In the majority of cases, this assessment will necessarily involve some consultation with the rights-holding State.[30]

Much therefore depends on what activities are undertaken by the disputing State or occupying State and how the other State's rights are violated in any particular scenario.

Obligations relating to provisional arrangements in maritime boundary disputes

If the maritime area surrounding the disputed island constitutes an overlapping entitlement between the occupying State and the disputing State, and is subject to a maritime boundary delimitation, Articles 74(3) and 83(3) of UNCLOS must also be considered as regulating State conduct in the area. Violations of these provisions could be alleged in the context of proceedings under Part XV of UNCLOS, unless a State has opted to exclude sea boundary delimitation disputes under Articles 74 and 83 by virtue of Article 298(1)(a) of UNCLOS.

For the delimitation of the EEZ between States with opposite or adjacent coasts and overlapping entitlements, Article 74(3) of UNCLOS provides:

> Pending agreement as provided for in paragraph 1, the States concerned, in a spirit of understanding and cooperation, shall make every effort to enter into provisional arrangements of a practical nature and, during this transitional period, not to jeopardize or hamper the reaching of the final agreement. Such arrangements shall be without prejudice to the final delimitation.

An identical provision is included in Article 83(3) of UNCLOS in relation to the delimitation of the continental shelf.[31] There are two core obligations emerging from this provision: first, the obligation to endeavor to reach agreement, and second, the obligation not to jeopardize or hamper the final agreement. These are discussed immediately below.[32]

Obligation to endeavor to reach agreement

For a State to claim that this obligation was violated, it must show that it sought to enter into provisional arrangements of a practical nature with the other State concerned.[33] The UNCLOS text makes clear that States are under no obligation to devise provisional arrangements but must only endeavor to reach agreement on these arrangements.[34] The importance of this requirement should not be completely dismissed, however. The obligation to negotiate in good faith "is not merely a nonbinding recommendation or encouragement, but a mandatory rule whose breach would represent a violation of international law."[35] The Tribunal in *Guyana v Suriname* held that there was a duty to negotiate in good faith in pursuit of provisional arrangements of a practical nature.[36]

In relation to what might constitute an obligation to negotiate in good faith, the ICJ assessed this duty in the *North Sea Continental Shelf* cases. The Court considered that this duty entailed more than merely going through a formal process, but that the negotiations had to be meaningful.[37] To be meaningful, it was not enough for either of the parties "to insist upon its own position without contemplating any modification of it."[38] Failure to reach agreement does not nullify the other obligation contained in Articles 74(3) and 83(3), namely not to jeopardize or hamper the reaching of the final agreement.[39]

Obligation not to jeopardize or hamper the final agreement

The *Guyana v Suriname* Tribunal further considered that the UNCLOS provision entailed a negative obligation not to jeopardize or hamper the reaching of the final agreement, although the time period for this obligation was unclear.[40] The Tribunal's interpretation of this obligation admitted the possibility of some activity in the disputed area, so long as those activities would not prejudice the final agreement.[41]

While the *Guyana v Suriname* Tribunal emphasized activities that could "lead to a permanent physical change" as a violation of this obligation,[42] it was still acknowledged that Articles 74(3) and 83(3) were "not intended to preclude all activities in a disputed maritime area."[43] To this end, the Tribunal stated:

> [U]nilateral acts that cause a physical damage to the marine environment will generally be comprised in a class of activities that can be undertaken only jointly or by agreement between the parties. This is due to the fact that these activities may jeopardize or hamper the reaching of a final delimitation agreement as a result of the perceived change to the status quo that they would engender. Indeed, such activities could be perceived to, or may genuinely, prejudice the position of the other party in the delimitation dispute, thereby both hampering or jeopardizing the reaching of a final agreement.[44]

Moreover, "[i]t should not be permissible for a party to a dispute to undertake any unilateral activity that might affect *the other party's rights* in a permanent manner."[45] The Tribunal thus appears to recognize that the duty not to jeopardize or hamper might be breached because of a permanent physical change and also because of a permanent change to the rights of the other party. What precisely might fall into these categories may ultimately depend on the particular factual circumstances existing between the parties concerned and even potentially their subjective views as to how their rights are implicated.[46]

It should not be anticipated that a State is restrained from undertaking activities that strengthen its claim to sovereignty over a disputed island because of the obligations in Articles 74(3) and 83(3). These provisions relate to the final determination of the maritime boundary, and do not relate to the territorial sovereignty dispute.[47]

A study by the British Institute of International and Comparative Law on Articles 74(3) and 83(3) has suggested that at sea enforcement activities could well be seen as provocative in disputed maritime areas. As a result, depending on the precise circumstances, at sea enforcement may run the risk of breaching the obligation not to jeopardize or hamper.[48] Yet arguably, such activities do not meet the thresholds discussed in *Guyana v Suriname*, which were more focused on permanent changes of status of rights.

In light of the obligations in Articles 62 and 63 of UNCLOS and the renewable nature of fish stocks, it may well be permissible under Articles 74(3) and 83(3) for States to continue their fishing activities in an undelimited area so long as their combined efforts did not lead to the over-exploitation of the stocks in question.[49]

Articles 74(3) and 83(3) do not require that consent be obtained for any activities relating to non-renewable resources, although obviously such consent would negate any subsequent claims of wrong-doing. The relevant test would again relate to the permanency of the activities. In *Guyana v Suriname*, the Tribunal noted that "acts that do cause physical change would have to be undertaken pursuant to an agreement between the parties to be permissible, as they may hamper or jeopardize the reaching of a final agreement on delimitation."[50] Instead, the Tribunal sought to balance the rights of the parties to pursue economic development in a disputed area against the obligation to make every effort not to hamper or jeopardize the final agreement.[51]

What exactly will be acceptable economic development may depend on whether the other party can be compensated because of that activity. There may also be consideration as to whether the activity is of such a nature that it would not be possible to provide reparations (in terms of putting any injured party back in the position it would have been in if the wrongdoing had not occurred).

Conclusion on legal risks for EEZ activities

In sum, this section demonstrates a number of legal rights and duties that may be at issue when an occupying State seeks to exercise sovereign rights or exclusive jurisdiction in its claimed EEZ. These actions may well be challenged by a disputing State because of the contested sovereignty, but also because of claimed UNCLOS violations. These violations include potential breaches of the due regard obligation and the provisional arrangements obligations as discussed. UNCLOS dispute settlement may therefore play an important role in resolving these disputes even when the coastal or user State status is unresolved.

Environmental obligations associated with construction activities

Environmental obligations must also be considered as giving rise to possible claims under UNCLOS as between an occupying and a disputing State. These environmental obligations apply in all maritime zones. Requirements associated with the protection and preservation of the marine environment under UNCLOS could be said to apply *erga omnes* and so will be at issue even when the coastal and user States are not known or sovereignty is contested in a particular maritime area.

In assessing China's land reclamation activities on seven reefs in the Spratly Islands, the *South China Sea* Tribunal noted that small, minor works by different

States had been undertaken but large-scale construction by China began in 2013.[52] A 2016 study found up to 60% of the shallow reef habitat at the seven reefs had been directly destroyed.[53] The *South China Sea* Tribunal assessed this massive land reclamation activity for its consistency with UNCLOS provisions relating to the protection and preservation of the marine environment.

The *South China Sea* Tribunal noted that Chinese scientists had claimed that a range of steps had been taken to protect and preserve the marine environment, such as avoiding spawning seasons, not using fine sands, and building on dead coral.[54] However, independent experts employed by the Tribunal and the Philippines refuted all of these claims. As a result of these findings, the Tribunal concluded that:

> through its construction activities, China has breached its obligation under Article 192 to protect and preserve the marine environment, has conducted dredging in such a way as to pollute the marine environment with sediment in breach of Article 194(1), and has violated its duty under Article 194(5) to take measures necessary to protect and preserve rare or fragile ecosystems as well as the habitat of depleted, threatened or endangered species and other forms of marine life.[55]

As noted above, the obligations to protect and preserve the marine environment apply in all maritime zones, including the territorial sea.[56] Consequently, the *South China Sea* Tribunal did not distinguish as to whether the construction activities on the reefs were occurring in the territorial sea of a particular State or within the EEZ. The reality is that the Tribunal could not do so, because sovereignty over those reefs classified as "rocks" (namely, Cuarteron Reef, Fiery Cross Reef and Gaven Reef (North)) is contested and it could not be stated as to whether the owner of the rock would be permitted to undertake those activities within its own territorial sea.

Further obligations under UNCLOS that were implicated by China's mass reconstruction activities were:

- Article 197, requiring cooperation on a regional basis to formulate standards and practices for the protection and preservation of the marine environment;[57]
- Article 123, concerning efforts to coordinate in addressing protection and preservation of the marine environment of semi-enclosed seas;[58]
- Article 206, obliging States to assess the potential effects of activities that may cause significant and harmful changes to the marine environment, and communicate reports of those assessment results.[59]

In the context of Article 206, the Tribunal noted in particular the need "as far as practicable" for an environmental impact assessment to be prepared and to communicate that assessment.[60] The Tribunal's requirements in relation to the preparation and communication of an environmental impact assessment were supported by a previous decision of the ICJ, the *Construction of a Road (Nicaragua v Costa Rica)*. In that case, the Court noted that it was not enough for Costa Rica just to assert that such an assessment had occurred.[61]

In the *South China Sea* arbitration, the Tribunal noted that it had not received information as to any environmental impact assessment occurring, despite legislation in China requiring such an assessment to be done. Moreover, China had not provided any information to the Tribunal when requested, nor was evidence available to suggest China had communicated the assessment to any relevant international organization as expected under Article 205 of UNCLOS. On this basis, irrespective of the existence or quality of any environmental impact assessment, what the Tribunal could determine definitively was the failure to communicate the assessment as required under Article 206.[62]

The *South China Sea* decision thus puts in sharp relief the importance for States to undertake the required procedural steps of an environmental impact assessment, to communicate the results of that assessment, seek to cooperate or coordinate where necessary, as well as to adhere to general obligations of protecting and preserving the marine environment. Any activities undertaken either on a disputed island or in its surrounding waters would need to involve fulfilment of international environmental law obligations as required under UNCLOS, including clear communication of those efforts to relevant parties and organizations.

Consequences for the occupying State

If an occupying State is found to have violated obligations under UNCLOS, rules of State responsibility under international law become relevant for assessing the legal consequences of those findings of unlawful conduct. This section first assesses possible reparations. Second, as emerged from the *South China Sea* arbitration, an occupying State that persists in activities on or around a disputed island further risks a determination that those actions unlawfully aggravated the dispute between the parties. This claim may also be asserted in UNCLOS dispute settlement, as seen in the *South China Sea* arbitration.

Reparations for any international law violations

In terms of consequences for unlawful construction activities, it is remarkable that there was no remedial action required by the *South China Sea* Tribunal in light of its findings that China was in violation of various UNCLOS provisions. The Tribunal issued no declaration that China undertake restorative activity in relation to the environmental damage caused by any of its construction activities, nor any order that China vacate the artificial island created on Mischief Reef.

The Tribunal did not even go so far as to make a prospective declaration, requiring that China comply with its international environmental obligations in the future. One rationale for this decision was that it would not add to the Award's findings that had already served the purpose of clarifying the parties' rights and obligations.[63] A similar conclusion was reached in *Guyana v Suriname* and *Cameroon v Nigeria*.

The declaratory nature of the *South China Sea* Award leaves it squarely within the discretion of the Philippines to determine how, or if, it wishes to enforce any of the rulings of the Tribunal against China. It would be within the Philippines' rights to demand China's departure from Mischief Reef but whether it makes such a demand is a political decision of the Philippines. Commentators have noted that States are more concerned with stopping China from expanding its construction activities further rather than forcing it to vacate any of the seven reefs.[64]

Guyana did seek reparations from Suriname for the monetary loss it alleged to sustain as a result of oil companies discontinuing work in the disputed area, but the Tribunal denied this relief. It would be open to the disputing State to seek such reparations, even though the Philippines did not do so in relation to China. It could therefore be anticipated that if a disputing State did judicially challenge the occupying State's activities on or around the island, the likely outcome would be a declaration of illegality at most, rather than a requirement for restitution or other form of reparations.

Preventing aggravation of the dispute

The *South China Sea* Tribunal noted that China greatly intensified its program of building artificial islands and installations at Mischief Reef, Cuarteron Reef, Fiery Cross Reef, Gaven Reef (North), Johnson Reef, Hughes Reef, and Subi Reef. In particular, the Tribunal recalled that these activities started, intensified and were brought to the Tribunal's attention in the period following the commencement of the arbitration.[65]

The Tribunal considered the relevant jurisprudence on provisional measures, and concluded that the proper understanding is that there exists a duty on parties engaged in a dispute settlement procedure to refrain from aggravating or extending the dispute during the pendency of the settlement process.[66] The recognition of a duty to refrain from aggravating or extending a dispute during settlement proceedings is apparent in the widespread inclusion of express provisions to such effect in multilateral conventions,[67] inherent in the central role of good faith in the international legal relations between States,[68] and expressly within the text of UNCLOS.[69]

The Tribunal found that China's dredging, artificial-island building and construction activities in the relevant areas bore on a number of disputes submitted by the Philippines for resolution, specifically: the dispute concerning the status and entitlements of a number of features in the South China Sea; the dispute concerning respective entitlements to maritime zones and corresponding rights under the Convention; and the dispute concerning the protection and preservation of the marine environment.[70]

The Tribunal found that the intensified construction of artificial islands on the relevant seven features in the Spratly Islands unequivocally aggravated the disputes between the parties. First, Mischief Reef could not be returned to its original state before the construction work began. Second, China had caused irreparable harm to the coral reef habitat. Third, China had undermined the integrity of the proceedings, and permanently destroyed evidence of the natural status of the relevant features.[71]

What is notable about this finding is that it concerned the pendency of the arbitration; that is, it focused on the activities that had occurred after the Philippines had instituted arbitral proceedings. The Tribunal was clear that there is no duty on a State to refrain from aggravating generally their relations with one another.[72]

On this basis, it could be envisaged that no claim of aggravating or extending the dispute would be successful against an occupying State if no further activities on or around, or changes to the disputed island occurred at the point that legal proceedings begin. Prior to the institution of proceedings, the occupying State's construction could not be considered as a violation of any international law obligation not to aggravate relations with the disputing State as no such duty exists. Such a broad obligation would not allow for any meaningful reparations and is unlikely to be accepted by a court or tribunal.

Also curious about this holding in *South China Sea* is the litigation posture pursued by the Philippines on this point. Normally, as the Tribunal noted, a court or tribunal would issue an order not to aggravate a dispute as a result of a provisional measures application. No such order was sought in this case, which may have been because of the difficult arguments that would have been needed to meet the criteria for provisional measures. It was also perhaps a political decision so as not to have an initial order that might have been flouted by China and would not have been easily enforceable. It could potentially arise, however, in other UNCLOS dispute settlement proceedings in the future.

Conclusion

In assessing the legality of construction activities on and around a disputed island, regard must be had to those works on the territory of the island, as well as constructions in the internal waters and territorial sea and activities in the EEZ or on the continental shelf as aspects of the relevant legal regime change depending on the location. Construction activity is permissible in territory or maritime areas over which a State exercises sovereignty. The complication for the occupying State is if there is any subsequent determination that the disputing State has sovereignty over the island instead. In that case, an argument may be raised that the occupying State's constructions have violated the disputing State's sovereignty or its sovereign rights.

Such an argument was successfully pursued by the Philippines in the *South China Sea* arbitration in relation to China's violation of its sovereign rights. Even though China considered it was the coastal State with sovereign rights in the relevant area at the time it undertook its construction work, it was held to be internationally responsible for violating the Philippines' rights when the Tribunal subsequently held that the Philippines instead was the coastal State with sovereign rights. The reasoning for this approach was not fully articulated by the Tribunal in the *South China Sea* arbitration and a different result has now been achieved in *Ghana / Côte d'Ivoire* in the context of a maritime boundary delimitation.

Where a coastal State has sovereign rights and undertakes construction activities pursuant to its rights under Articles 60 and 80 of UNCLOS, there are different procedural obligations that must be followed and due regard must be accorded to the rights of third States consistent with the EEZ and continental shelf legal regimes.

In relation to activity in any overlapping entitlements to EEZ or continental shelf areas, regard must be had to the obligations in Articles 74(3) and 83(3). In particular, the obligation to make every effort not to jeopardize or hamper the final maritime boundary agreement will limit the range of activities that may be lawfully undertaken in an un-delimited area. Those activities that produce permanent physical changes or permanently impair the rights of one of the States will most likely violate this obligation.

For any construction activities in any maritime zones, international law obligations associated with the protection and preservation of the marine environment must be observed, particularly the obligation to undertake and communicate an environmental impact assessment. The duty to cooperate and a duty to take measures to prevent, reduce and control pollution would moderate the activities that an occupying State would be allowed to take around the disputed island. The fulfilment of these obligations would require some level of interaction with the disputing State, as outlined above. Alternatively, construction activity could be prevented on the basis that it may violate obligations to protect and preserve the marine environment, including obligations to protect marine biodiversity and fragile ecosystems.

If the occupying State undertook activities in or around the disputed island once arbitration or adjudication had commenced, a court or tribunal might find that it has violated an obligation not to aggravate or extend the dispute between the parties. However, there is no general duty not to aggravate relations that exists under international law outside the confines of a dispute settlement process and this particular duty would not therefore hinder the occupying State in its activities in or around the island prior to any final determination of sovereignty over the islands.

Overall, there is much potential to resolve disputes through UNCLOS dispute settlement even if the relevant coastal and user states are not known because of a territorial dispute. The facts of any particular case and the precise claims will ultimately be decisive and so the discussion in this chapter can only be indicative of potential results depending on the final configuration of the arguments presented. The prospects for UNCLOS dispute settlement remain notable, even if territorial sovereignty disputes remain outside the scope of this dispute settlement regime. Most particularly, the opportunity for State parties to UNCLOS to resort to compulsory arbitration or adjudication may help with the peaceful resolution of international disputes and limit unilateral actions at sea.

Notes

* Professor, UNSW Faculty of Law. This chapter was written while Professor, Macquarie University and MacCormick Fellow, University of Edinburgh. The author gratefully acknowledges both institutions for their support as well as the research and editorial assistance provided by Danielle Kroon in preparing material for this chapter. Any remaining errors are of course my own.

1 *United Nations Convention on the Law of the Sea*, opened for signature 10 December 1982, 1833 UNTS 3 (entered into force 16 November 1994) ("UNCLOS").

2 UNCLOS, Article 287.

3 As seen in Articles 280, 281 and 282 of UNCLOS.

4 UNCLOS, Article 298.

5 See Natalie Klein, "Vicissitudes of the UNCLOS Dispute Settlement Regime" (2017) 32 *International Journal of Marine and Coastal Law*, 332.

6 *South China Sea Arbitration (Philippines v China) (Award)* (UNCLOS Arbitral Tribunal, July 12, 2016) [2] (*"South China Sea (Award)"*).

7 See Natalie Klein, "The limitations of UNCLOS Part XV dispute settlement in resolving South China Sea disputes: The South China Sea – An international law perspective conference" (March 9, 2015) SSRN, available at http://ssrn.com/abstract=2730411. After the decisions on jurisdiction and the merits in the *South China Sea* Arbitration were released, an updated version of the paper was prepared and presented at the Public International Law Colloquium on Maritime Disputes Settlement, July 15–16, 2016, hosted by the Hong Kong International Arbitration Centre and the Chinese Society of International Law: Natalie Klein, "Expansions and restrictions in the UNCLOS dispute settlement regime: Lessons from recent decisions" (2016) 15(2) *Chinese Journal of International Law*, 403–15.

8 The ICJ has held that under customary international law States are obliged to "ensure that activities within their jurisdiction and control respect the environment of other States." *Legality of the Threat or Use of Nuclear Weapons*, Advisory Opinion [1996] ICJ Rep 226, [29]; *Case Concerning Pulp Mills on the River Uruguay (Argentina v Uruguay) (Judgment)*, [2010] ICJ Rep 14 [101].

9 See, eg, Marcelo G Kohen, Mamadou Hébié, "Territory, Acquisition" in *Max Planck Encyclopedia of Public International Law* (Oxford: Oxford University Press, 2016) [25].

10 In *Sovereignty over Pedra Branca/Pulau Batu Puteh*, the International Court of Justice considered that the critical date "distinguish[es] ... between those acts which should be taken into consideration for the purpose of establishing or ascertaining sovereignty and those acts occurring after such date." *Sovereignty over Pedra Branca/Pulau Batu Puteh, Middle Rocks and South Ledge (Malaysia v Singapore) (Judgment)* [2008] ICJ Rep 12, para. 32.

11 For a survey of these views, see Irina Buga, "Territorial Sovereignty Issues in Maritime Disputes: A Jurisdictional Dilemma for Law of the Sea Tribunals" (2012) 27 *International Journal of Marine and Coastal Law* 65.

12 *Land and Maritime Boundary between Cameroon and Nigeria* (Cameroon v. Nigeria; Equatorial Guinea Intervening), Merits, (2002) ICJ Rep. 303, para. 308-para. 324.

13 *Guyana v Suriname*, Award, 17 September 2007, para. 271.

14 *Certain Activities carried out by Nicaragua in the Border Area* (Costa Rica v. Nicaragua) (2013) ICJ Rep. para. 93.

15 UNCLOS, Article 2(1).

16 *South China Sea (Award)*, para. 1198.

17 See the discussion of these principles in Elies van Sliedregt, *Individual Criminal Responsibility in International Law* (Oxford: Oxford University Press, 2012) 269–86.

18 Professor Ian Brownlie refers to this position as an objective basis of State responsibility. See James Crawford, *Brownlie's Principles of International Law* (Oxford: Oxford University Press, 8th ed. 2012) 556.

19 *South China Sea (Award)* para. 1030.

20 International Law Commission, *Draft Articles on Responsibility of States for Internationally Wrongful Acts*, UNGAOR, 56th Sess, Supp No 10, UN Doc A/56/10 (2001), Article 13 ("*ILC Articles on State Responsibility*").

21 See Commentary to the *ILC Articles on State Responsibility*, Article 13, para. 1-para. 4.

22 *Dispute Concerning Delimitation of the Maritime Boundary between Ghana and Côte d'Ivoire in the Atlantic Ocean* (Ghana / Côte d'Ivoire), Judgment, September 23, 2017, available at www.itlos.org/fileadmin/itlos/documents/cases/case_no.23_merits/C23_Judgment_23.09.2017_corr.pdf ("*Ghana / Côte d'Ivoire*").

23 *Ghana / Côte d'Ivoire* para. 544.

24 *Ghana / Côte d'Ivoire* paras 591–592.

25 *Ghana / Côte d'Ivoire* para. 591.

26 The Special Chamber noted that its position was convergent with the 2012 decision of the ICJ, *Territorial and Maritime Dispute* (Nicaragua v. Colombia), Judgment, (2012) ICJ Rep. 624, para. 250. See *Ghana / Côte d'Ivoire* para. 593.

27 UNCLOS, Article 60 and Article 80 (which applies Article 60 to the continental shelf *mutatis mutandis*).

28 UNCLOS, Article 60(1)(b).

29 *Chagos Marine Protected Area (Mauritius v United Kingdom) (Award)* (UNCLOS Arbitral Tribunal, 18 March 2015) (*"Chagos Archipelago"*), para. 519.

30 Chagos Archipelago, para. 519.

31 UNCLOS, Article 83(3).

32 This discussion is partially drawn from Natalie Klein, "Provisional Measures and Provisional Arrangements" in Alex Oude Elferink et al. (eds), *Maritime Boundary Delimitation: The Case Law* (Cambridge: Cambridge University Press, in press).

33 *Ghana / Côte d'Ivoire* para. 628.

34 "This would seem to be an obligation of conduct, not of result." British Institute of International and Comparative Law, *Report on the Obligations of States under Articles 74(3) and 83(3) of UNCLOS in respect of Undelimited Maritime Areas* (2016), para. 47. See also *Ghana / Côte d'Ivoire* para. 627.

35 R Lagoni, "Interim Measures Pending Maritime Delimitation Agreements" (1984) 78 *American Journal of International Law* 345, 354. See also D M Ong, "Joint Development of Common Offshore Oil and Gas Deposits: "Mere" State Practice or Customary International Law?" (1999) 93 *American Journal of International Law* 771, 784 (noting that the duty to negotiate in good faith is "widely recognized as a general principle well-founded in international law").

36 *Delimitation of the maritime boundary between Guyana and Suriname (Guyana v Suriname) (Award)* (UNCLOS Tribunal, 17 September 2007), para. 461.

37 *North Sea Continental Shelf (Federal Republic of Germany/Denmark; Federal Republic of Germany/Netherlands) (Judgment)* [1969] ICJ Rep 3, para. 85.

38 *North Sea Continental Shelf (Federal Republic of Germany/Denmark; Federal Republic of Germany/Netherlands) (Judgment)* [1969] ICJ Rep 3, para. 85. See also British Institute of International and Comparative Law, *Report on the Obligations of States under Articles 74(3) and 83(3) of UNCLOS in respect of Undelimited Maritime Areas* (2016), para. 35-para. 37.

39 British Institute of International and Comparative Law, *Report on the Obligations of States under Articles 74(3) and 83(3) of UNCLOS in respect of Undelimited Maritime Areas* (2016), para. 41.

40 See discussion in Y Tanaka, "Unilateral Exploration and Exploitation of Natural Resources in Disputed Areas: A Note on the Ghana/Côte d'Ivoire Order of 25 April 2015 before the Special Chamber of ITLOS" (2015) 46 *Ocean Development and International Law* 315, 316.

41 *Guyana v Suriname* para. 460 and para. 465.

42 *Guyana v Suriname* para. 467.
43 *Guyana v Suriname* para. 467.
44 *Guyana v Suriname* para. 480.
45 *Guyana v Suriname* para. 470 (emphasis added).
46 Y van Logchem, "The Scope for Unilateralism in Disputed Maritime Areas" in C Schofield, S Lee and M-S Kwon (eds), *The Limits of Maritime Jurisdiction* (Leiden: Martinus Nijhoff 2014), 186. See also British Institute of International and Comparative Law, *Report on the Obligations of States under Articles 74(3) and 83(3) of UNCLOS in respect of Undelimited Maritime Areas* (2016), para. 83-para. 84.
47 D Anderson and Y van Logchem, "Rights and Obligations in Areas of Overlapping Maritime Claims" in S. Jayakumar, T. Koh and R. Beckman (eds), *The South China Sea Disputes and the Law of the Sea* (Edward Elgar, 2014), 222.
48 British Institute of International and Comparative Law, *Report on the Obligations of States under Articles 74(3) and 83(3) of UNCLOS in respect of Undelimited Maritime Areas* (2016), para. 99.
49 British Institute of International and Comparative Law, *Report on the Obligations of States under Articles 74(3) and 83(3) of UNCLOS in respect of Undelimited Maritime Areas* (2016), para. 95.
50 *Guyana v Suriname*, para. 467.
51 *Guyana v Suriname*, para. 470.
52 *South China Sea (Award)* para. 977.
53 *South China Sea (Award)* para. 978.
54 *South China Sea (Award)* para. 982.
55 *South China Sea (Award)* para. 983.
56 *South China Sea (Award)* para. 940.
57 *South China Sea (Award)* para. 984.
58 *South China Sea (Award)* para. 984.
59 *South China Sea (Award)* para. 987.
60 *South China Sea (Award)* para. 988.
61 *Construction of a Road in Costa Rica along the San Juan River (Nicaragua v Costa Rica) (Judgment)* (International Court of Justice, 16 December 2015) para. 154.
62 *South China Sea (Award)* para. 991.
63 *South China Sea (Award)* para. 1182-para. 1201. See also Joshua Paine, "Environmental Aspects of the South China Sea Award" (July 21, 2016) *EJIL Talk* www.ejiltalk.org/environmentalaspectsofthesouthchinaseaaward/.
64 See, e.g., Brahma Chellaney, "China's challenge to the Law of the Sea" (July 15, 2016) *The Strategist* www.aspistrategist.org.au/chinas-challenge-law-sea/printni/27692/.
65 *South China Sea (Award)* para. 1128-para. 1129.
66 *South China Sea (Award)* para. 1169.
67 *South China Sea (Award)* para. 1170.
68 *South China Sea (Award)* para. 1171.
69 *South China Sea (Award)* para. 1172- para. 1173.
70 *South China Sea (Award)* para. 1175.
71 *South China Sea (Award)* para. 1177-para.1179.
72 *South China Sea (Award)* para. 1174: "Neither the Convention, nor international law, go so far as to impose a legal duty on a State to refrain from aggravating generally their relations with one another, however desirable it might be for States to do so."

Index